Curiosities of Literature

Curiosities of Literature

BY ISAAC D'ISRAELI, 1766 - 1848.

Selected, edited and introduced by
EVERETT BLEILER

Dover Publications, Inc., New York

This Dover edition is a new selection of essays from the four-volume collection published by W. J. Widdleton, New York, in 1871; the Widdleton edition was derived from the fourteenth corrected London edition. All the essays in the present volume are unabridged and unaltered (or very slightly corrected), except for two which have been abridged: "Literary Composition" and "Expression of Suppressed Opinion." The biographical introduction by Benjamin Disraeli, later Lord Beaconsfield, has been adapted from the text of the Widdleton edition.

The present selection was made by Everett Bleiler, who wrote the Preface to this Dover edition.

Library of Congress Catalog Card Number 64-16331

Manufactured in the United States of America

Dover Publications, Inc.
180 Varick Street
New York 14, N.Y.

Preface

For more than 150 years the *Curiosities of Literature* by Isaac D'Israeli has been an entertainer and mentor to readers of scholarly taste. Among the finest browsing books in English, the *Curiosities* has long been esteemed an inexhaustible mine of amusement and delight, full of nuggets of curious information. Scores of literary men have raided it for source material, and the greatest writers have spoken of it with pleasure. To quote only a single opinion of its value: "A most entertaining and searching writer, D'Israeli, whose works in general I have read oftener perhaps than those of any other English writer," Lord Byron.

The secret of the greatness of the *Curiosities* is the zest and gusto which its author brought into the libraries of Europe. Certainly, other men before him had read the classical authors, the scholars of the Renaissance, and the diplomatic archives of the eighteenth century. But no one writing in English, not even the learned Selden whom D'Israeli admired so much, possessed D'Israeli's remarkable ability as a gemmologist: he alone could uncover the curious fact that had lain buried and unappreciated for generations, polish it, and place it in a structure which would delight the bookishly inclined reader.

The *Curiosities* leaps nimbly among the great works and the minor works, the books and the unpublished manuscripts of D'Israeli's day. It reveals small unsuspected incidents in the lives of important men, and it corrects many old misunderstandings. In lighter moments it quotes the secret memoirs of statesmen, and often reveals facets and motives that official history does not show—that Chamillart, Louis XIV's minister of finance, owed his position to the fact that he was the only man in France who could beat Louis at billiards; that when a quarrel over precedence between the French and Spanish ambassadors to England almost led to a diplomatic rupture, the problem was solved by importing a papal nuncio who took precedence over both; that a Greek gourmand nicknamed "The Furnace" used to gargle with boiling water so that he could attack a hot feast earlier and get more than his fellow banqueters. The *Curiosities* is a florilegium of piquant moments that otherwise might have remained unpicked.

On the serious side is the remarkable picture that it projects of the great scholarship of the past. We do not often think of scholarship as occurring in historical divisions, but a reading of D'Israeli makes it obvious that there are periods of scholarship, just as there are periods of music, literature and art; and that within each period scholars have problems, techniques and data in common. The analogy with the arts is not perfect, however, for while we can try to use and understand the arts of earlier periods, previous periods of scholarship seem to remain isolated behind barriers which cannot be penetrated. Perhaps this is because there is no real reason for absorbing the scholarship of the past, for who really cares about the details of the work of Valla or Bentley or Isaac Casaubon or the other great virtuosi of classical scholarship? We are content to accept their results as they have been passed down to us.

Such a moat between the older and the newer scholarship came into being in the middle and late eighteenth century. Before this time the works of the giants of classical scholarship were still studied; the memoirs and treatises on statecraft were still read; and Latin was still the most important language for advanced knowledge. Samuel Johnson reached into this earlier world; Voltaire, Lessing and Gibbon looked into it, but beyond them it became a sealed province. By the early nineteenth century it had vanished; the names that used to overwhelm argument had lost their power and a new group of authorities had emerged. In English letters, in all probability only Isaac D'Israeli and to a lesser extent William Godwin were at home within it, and only D'Israeli was so saturated with its lore that he was able to drag it slightly into his own time.

This was the great world of baroque scholarship, which is now almost completely lost to us. It was a phenomenon bursting with strength and vigor, crude at times, cruel at times, yet always large; it cared more for the gigantic result than the tiny detail. In most areas it worked with inadequate data, yet it was incredibly rich in imagination, and since it was close to the ancient world and worked directly and unhampered, it was often surprisingly apt in its conclusions. Let anyone who doubts this look, for example, at the history of some of our understandings of the classical world: the spread of Oriental ideas, the nature of the Mysteries, the interrelation of myth and symbol, or the status of doubtful works like the letters of Plato. We have gradually come back to the basic positions that were generally held by scholarship in the Renaissance.

Isaac D'Israeli is now our only surviving entry to this world, beyond the actual books themselves, and they are in an unfamiliar language and in any case inaccessible. D'Israeli tells us of the great virtuosi of scholarship, and their ambitious programs of reading thousands of books in planned sequence over many years; of their shifts to see publication; of their lost and won battles with religious and political censorship; of their own reference libraries, now totally forgotten; of their encyclopedic ranging over all knowledge. It was an age when every scholar had the chance to be a Columbus: the monasteries still concealed material beside which the Dead Sea finds seem pallid. Poggio found Quintilian in the jakes of St. Gall, and bribed a monk to steal Livy and Ammianus Marcellinus from the convent library of Hersfeld. Petronius emerged as a soldier's booty in Yugoslavia; Epicurus emerged from the ashes of buried Herculaneum; and Dioscorides was redeemed from a pawnshop in Istanbul.

This age of baroque scholarship was an age of great champions —of heroes and villains who jousted and duelled with one another in a fashion that is now dead. Scholarship was held in high emotion, and with a sense that it was the most important thing in life. Milton and Salmasius could involve most of scholarly Europe in their feud over Charles I; Newton and Leibnitz could accuse each other of the lowest theft; Poggio and Valla could assail one another with impossible scurrilities; Julius Caesar Scaliger could abuse both Erasmus and Cardan, and be himself attacked as an illegitimate impostor. Very often the champions were right; very often they were wrong. But theirs was a living world with a vigor that has since been lost. It is one of Isaac D'Israeli's remarkable achievements that he makes us once again aware of this forgotten arena of study.

D'Israeli has been called one of the founders of modern history, since he stressed the use of primary sources (as opposed to the rewriting of earlier compilations) and was one of the few scholars of his day to study the public document collections. Certainly, his own essays tell of many earlier historians who went astray in matters of fact or interpretation because they did not bother to check primary sources, or unwittingly used bowdlerized and censored editions of earlier works. There is some truth to this claim for D'Israeli. If his interest in the ephemera of the past (which he called "secret history") had been followed in the history of English literature, British scholarship would have escaped major reproaches: that the basic material about Marlowe and Malory in the Public Records Office, for example, had been ignored by generations of writers and had to await the coming of American doctoral candidates.

Yet although D'Israeli was one of the great students of history, with a clear idea of methodology and a factual apparatus that would have been enviable in any age, he cannot be called either a great scholar or a great historian. He founded no school, he made no great discoveries, he wrote no great historical works. His books that he considered important—the histories of James I and Charles I—are now no longer read. The reason for this seems to be that as a historian D'Israeli was a dilettante, an absorber and a classifier rather than a creator or an interpreter.

Today D'Israeli is primarily an entertainer rather than a historian. His mature prose is fresh and clear, precise and graceful, probably because he followed the prose writers of the eighteenth century rather than the modernists. He is certainly a much better writer than his better-known son, the prime minister and novelist, who learned little from him. Isaac D'Israeli, who is still unexcelled as a historical colorist, can convey an enthusiasm that is contagious, and can make the reader wish he had ten or fifteen years to reexamine the library of D'Israeli's operations.

The essays in this selection, which amount to about one-fifth of the final edition of the *Curiosities of Literature,* have been picked upon the frankly irrational basis of personal preference. I have selected those that are outstanding either for content or for felicitous expression. It is a difficult choice, for as many again might have been included. I have omitted the many apologetic essays about James I and Charles I, since the modern American (or even British) reader will care nothing about reestablishing the reputations of the Stuarts. I have also omitted most of the earliest essays, which are often just compilations of reading notes. The later D'Israeli would have written them better.

New York, 1963.   EVERETT BLEILER

Contents

Curiosities of Literature

On the Life and Writings of Mr. Isaac D'Israeli by His Son, Benjamin Disraeli

MY ANCESTORS were one of those Hebrew families whom the Inquisition forced to emigrate from the Spanish Peninsula at the end of the fifteenth century. Undisturbed and unmolested, they flourished as merchants [in Ferrara] for more than two centuries, but towards the middle of the eighteenth century, the altered circumstances of England, now favourable to commerce and religious liberty, attracted the attention of my great-grandfather, and he resolved that the youngest of his two sons, Benjamin, the "son of his right hand," should settle there.

My grandfather, Benjamin D'Israeli, became an English denizen in 1748. He was only eighteen when he commenced his career [in this place], and when a great responsibility devolved upon him. He was not unequal to it. He was a man of ardent character; sanguine, courageous, speculative, and fortunate; with a temper which no disappointment could disturb, and a brain, amid reverses, full of resource. He made his fortune in the midway of life, and settled near Enfield, where he formed an Italian garden, entertained his friends, played whist with Sir Horace Mann, sang canzonettas, and notwithstanding a wife [Sarah Syprut de Gabay] who never pardoned him for his name, and a son who disappointed all his plans, and who to the last hour of his life was an enigma to him, lived till he was nearly ninety, and then died in 1817, in the full enjoyment of prolonged existence.

My grandfather had only one child [Isaac D'Israeli, my father, born 1766], and nature had disqualified [this child] from his cradle for the busy pursuits of men. A pale, pensive child, with large dark brown eyes, and flowing hair, he had grown up beneath this roof of worldly energy and enjoyment, indicating even in his infancy, by the whole carriage of his life, that he was of a different order from those among whom he lived. Timid, susceptible, lost in reverie, fond of solitude, or seeking no better company than a book, he eventually arrived at that mournful period of boyhood when eccentricities excite attention and command no sympathy. His mother, who lived until eighty without indulg-

ing in a tender expression, did not recognize in her only offspring a being qualified to control or vanquish his impending
fate. His existence only served to swell the aggregate of many
humiliating particulars. The tart remark and the contemptuous
comment on her part, elicited, on the other, all the irritability
of the poetic idiosyncrasy. After frantic ebullitions for which,
when the circumstances were analyzed by an ordinary mind,
there seemed no sufficient cause, my grandfather always interfered to soothe with good-tempered commonplaces, and promote
peace. He was a man who thought that the only way to make
people happy was to make them a present.

A crisis arrived when, after months of unusual abstraction and
irritability, my father produced a poem. For the first time, my
grandfather was seriously alarmed. The loss of one of his argo-
sies, uninsured, could not have filled him with more blank dis-
may. His idea of a poet was formed from one of the prints of
Hogarth hanging in his room, where an unfortunate wight in a
garret was inditing an ode to riches, while dunned for his milk-
score. Decisive measures were required to eradicate this evil, and
to prevent future disgrace—so it was resolved that my father
should be sent abroad, where a new scene and a new language
might divert his mind from the ignominious pursuit which so
fatally attracted him. The unhappy poet was consigned, like a
bale of goods, to my grandfather's correspondent at Amsterdam,
who had instructions to place him at some collegium of repute.
Here were passed some years not without profit, though his
tutor, who was a great impostor, taught his charge little; but he
gave him free warren in his library, and before his pupil was
fifteen, he had read the works of Voltaire and had dipped into
Bayle.

When he was eighteen, my father returned to England a
disciple of Rousseau. He had exercised his imagination during
the voyage in idealizing the interview with his mother, which
was to be conducted on both sides with sublime pathos. He was
prepared to throw himself on his mother's bosom, to bedew her
hand with his tears, and to stop her own with his lips; but, when
he entered, his strange appearance, his gaunt figure, his excited
manners, his long hair, and his unfashionable costume only filled
her with a sentiment of tender aversion; she broke into derisive
laughter. Whereupon Emile, of course, went into heroics, wept,
sobbed, and finally shut up in his chamber, composed an impassioned epistle. My grandfather, to soothe him, dwelt on the
united solicitude of his parents for his welfare, and broke to him

their intention, if it were agreeable to him, to place him in the establishment of a great merchant of Bordeaux. My father replied that he had written a poem of considerable length, which he wished to have published, against Commerce, which was the corruptor of man. For forty-eight hours confusion reigned.

My father, who had lost the timidity of his childhood, was no longer to be controlled. He sent his poem to Dr. Johnson, with an impassioned statement of his case, complaining, which he always did, that he had never found a counsellor or literary friend. He left his packet himself at Bolt Court, where he was received by Mr. Francis Barber, the doctor's well-known Negro servant, and told to call again in a week. Be sure that he was very punctual; but the packet was returned to him unopened, with the message that the illustrious doctor was too ill to read anything. A few weeks later the great soul of Johnson quitted earth.

My grandparents looked upon my father as moonstruck, and in these perplexities the usual alternative was again had recourse to—absence; he was sent abroad, to travel in France, which the peace then permitted, visit some friends, see Paris, and then proceed to Bordeaux if he felt inclined. My father travelled in France and then proceeded to Paris, where he remained till the eve of great events [the Revolution] in that capital. This was a visit recollected with satisfaction. He lived with learned men and moved in vast libraries, and returned in the earlier part of 1788, with some little knowledge of life, and with a considerable quantity of books.

At this time Peter Pindar flourished in all the wantonness of literary riot. He was at the height of his flagrant notoriety. The most exalted station was not exempt from his audacious criticism, and learned institutions trembled at the sallies whose ribaldry often cloaked taste, intelligence, and good sense. The powerful and the learned quailed beneath his lash. There now appeared a satire "On the Abuse of Satire." The verses were polished and pointed, and offered a contrast to the irregular effusions of the popular assailant, Pindar, whom they in turn assailed. The poem was anonymous, and was addressed to Dr. Warton. Its publication was opportune. There are moments when every one is inclined to praise, especially when the praise of a new pen may at the same time revenge the insults of an old one. My father, who came up to town to read the newspapers at the St. James Coffee-house, found their columns filled with extracts from the fortunate effusion of the hour, conjectures as to its writer, and much gossip respecting Pindar. He returned to Enfield laden with the journals, and presenting them to his parents, broke to them the intelligence that at length he was not only an author, but a successful one.

About two years later my father, being then in his twenty-fifth year, influenced by the circle in which he then lived, gave an anonymous volume to the press, the fate of which he could little have foreseen. My father had maintained to his friends that the most interesting of miscellanies might be drawn up by a well-read man from the library in which he lived. It was objected, on the other hand, that such a work would be a mere compilation, and could not succeed in interesting the public. To test the truth of his claim my father occupied himself in the preparation of an octavo volume, the principal materials of which were found in the diversified collections of the French Ana; but he enriched his subjects with as much of our own literature as his reading afforded, and he conveyed the result in that lively and entertaining style which he from the first commanded. This collection he invested with the happy baptism of *Curiosities of Literature.*

He sought by this publication neither reputation nor a coarser reward, for he published his work anonymously, and avowedly as a compilation; and he not only published the work at his own expense, but in his heedlessness made a present of the copyright to the bookseller, which three or four years afterwards, he was fortunate enough to purchase at a public sale. The success of the volume was so decided that its projector was tempted to add a second volume two years afterwards. For twenty years the brother volumes remained favourites of the public; when after that long interval their writer, taking advantage of a popular title, poured forth all the riches of his matured intellect, his refined taste, and accumulated knowledge into their pages, and produced what may be fairly described as the most celebrated Miscellany of Modern Literature.

It so happened, that about the year 1795, when he was in his 29th year, there came over my father that mysterious illness to which the youth of men of sensibility, and especially literary men, is frequently subject—a failing of nervous energy, occasioned by study and too sedentary habits, early and habitual reverie, restless and indefinite purpose. The symptoms, physical and moral, are most distressing: lassitude and despondency. And it usually happens, as in the present instance, that the cause of suffering is not recognized; and that medical men, misled by the superficial symptoms, and not seeking to acquaint themselves with the psychology of their patients, arrive at erroneous, often fatal, conclusions. In this case, the most eminent of the faculty gave it as their opinion, that the disease was consumption. Dr. Turton, if I recollect right, was then the most considered physician of the day. An immediate visit to a warmer climate was his specific; and as the Continent was then disturbed and foreign residence out of the question, Dr. Turton recommended that his patient should establish himself without delay in Devonshire.

Wolcot [Peter Pindar], who had by now become my father's close friend, gave my father several letters of introduction to persons of consideration at Exeter. A combination of circumstances had made Exeter at this time a literary metropolis. A number of distinguished men flourished there at the same moment: some of their names are even now remembered. Jackson of Exeter still survives as a native composer of original genius. The heroic poems of Hole are forgotten, but his essay on the Arabian Nights is still a cherished volume of elegant and learned criticism. Hayter was the classic antiquary who first discovered the art of unrolling the MSS. of Herculaneum. There were many others, noisier and more bustling, who are now forgotten.

With such companions, by whom he was received with a kindness and hospitality which to the last he often dwelt on, it may easily be supposed that the banishment of my father from the delights of literary London was not a source of gloom, and the illness of my father was relieved, if not removed, by this change of life.

Dr. Downman was his physician, and this wise physician recognized the temperament of his patient, and perceived that his physical derangement was an effect rather than a cause. My father instead of being in a consumption, was endowed with a frame of almost superhuman strength, and which was destined for half a century of continuous labour and sedentary life. The vital principle in him, indeed, was so strong that when he left us at eighty-two, it was only as the victim of a violent epidemic, against whose virulence he struggled with so much power, that it was clear, but for this casualty, he might have been spared to this world even for several years.

I should think that this illness of his youth, and which, though of a fitful character, was of many years' duration, arose from his inability to direct to a satisfactory end the intellectual power which he was conscious of possessing. He would mention the ten years of his life, from twenty-five to thirty-five years of age, as a period very deficient in self-contentedness. The fact is, with a

poetic temperament, he had been born in an age when the poetic
faith of which he was a votary had fallen into decrepitude. He
was a pupil of Pope and Boileau, yet both from his native impulse and from the glowing influence of Rousseau, he felt the
necessity and desire of infusing into the verse of the day more
passion than might resound from the frigid lyre of Mr. Hayley.
My father had fancy, sensibility, and an exquisite taste, but he
had not that rare creative power, which the blended and simul-
taneous influence of the individual organization and the spirit
of the age, reciprocally acting upon each other, can alone, perhaps, perfectly develop.

How much there was of freshness, and fancy, and natural
pathos in his mind, may be discerned in his Persian romance
of "The Loves of Mejnoon and Leila." We who have been
accustomed to the great poets of the nineteenth century seeking their best inspiration in the climate and manners of the East,
who are familiar with the land of the Sun from the isles of
Ionia to the vales of Cashmere, can scarcely appreciate the literary originality of a writer who, fifty years ago, dared to devise a
real Eastern story, and seeking inspiration in the pages of
Oriental literature, compose it with reference to the Eastern
mind, and customs, and landscape. One must have been familiar
with the *Almoran and Hamets*, the visions of Mirza and the kings
of Ethiopia, and the other dull and monstrous masquerades of
Orientalism then prevalent, to estimate such an enterprise. The
reception of this work by the public, and of other works of fiction
which its author gave to them anonymously, was in every respect
encouraging, and their success may impartially be registered as
fairly proportionate to their merits; but it was not a success or
a proof of power, which, in my father's opinion, compensated
for that life of literary research and study which their composition disturbed and enfeebled. It was at the ripe age of five-and-
thirty that he renounced his dreams of being an author, and
resolved to devote himself for the rest of his life to the acquisition of knowledge.

It was during the ten years that now occurred, that he mainly
acquired that store of facts which were the foundation of his
future speculations. His pen was never idle, but it was to note
and to register, not to compose. His researches were prosecuted
among the MSS. of the British Museum, while his own ample collections permitted him to pursue his investigations in his own
library into the night. The materials which he accumulated
during this period are only partially exhausted. At the end of

ten years, during which, with the exception of one anonymous work, he never indulged in composition, the irresistible desire of communicating his conclusions to the world came over him, and after all his almost childish aspirations, his youth of reverie and hesitating and imperfect effort, he arrived at the mature age of forty-five before his career as a great author, influencing opinion, really commenced.

The next ten years passed entirely in production; from 1812 to 1822 the press abounded with his works. His *Calamities of Authors*, his *Memoirs of Literary Controversy* in the manner of Bayle, his *Essay on the Literary Character*, were all chapters in a history of English literature which he then commenced to meditate, and which it was fated should never be completed. It was during this period, also, that he published his *Inquiry into the Literary and Political Character of James the First.*

But what retarded his project of a history of our literature at this time was the almost embarrassing success of his juvenile production, *The Curiosities of Literature.* These two volumes had already reached five editions, and their author found himself, by the public demand, again called upon to sanction their reappearance. Resolving to make the work more worthy of the favour which it enjoyed, he revised and enriched these first two volumes without attempting materially to alter them, while at the same time he added a third volume. The success of this publication was so great, that its author, after much hesitation, resolved, as he was wont to say, to take advantage of a popular title, and pour forth the treasures of his mind in three additional volumes. These six volumes, after many editions, are now condensed into the form given to the public.

I have ventured to enter into some details as to the earlier and obscurer years of my father's life, because I thought that they threw light upon human character, and that without them, indeed, a just appreciation of his career could hardly be formed. I am mistaken, if we do not recognize in his instance two very interesting qualities of life: predisposition and self-formation. There was a third, which I think is to be honoured, and that was his sympathy with his order. No one has written so much about authors, and so well. Indeed, before his time the Literary Character had never been fairly placed before the world. He comprehended its idiosyncrasy: all its strength and all its weakness. He could soften, because he could explain, its infirmities. Though he shared none of the calamities, and scarcely any of the controversies, of literature, no one has sympathized so in-

timately with the sorrows, or so zealously and impartially registered the instructive disputes, of literary men. He loved to
celebrate the exploits of great writers, and to show that, in these
ages, the pen is a weapon as puissant as the sword. Above all
writers, he has maintained the greatness of intellect, and the
immortality of thought.

He was himself a complete literary character, a man who really
passed his life in his library. Even marriage [in 1802 to Maria
Basevi, who bore him five children] produced no change in these
habits; he rose to enter the chamber where he lived alone with
his books, and at night his lamp was ever lit within the same
walls. Nothing, indeed, was more remarkable than the isolation
of this prolonged existence, and it could only be accounted for
by the united influence of three causes: his birth, which brought
him no relations or family acquaintance, the bent of his disposition, and the circumstance of his inheriting an independent
fortune, which rendered unnecessary those exertions that would
have broken up his self-reliance. He disliked business, and he
never required relaxation; he was absorbed in his pursuits. In
London his only amusement was to ramble among booksellers;
if he entered a club, it was only to go into the library. In the
country, he scarcely ever left his room but to saunter in abstraction upon a terrace, muse over a chapter, or coin a sentence. He
had not a single passion or prejudice: all his convictions were
the result of his own studies, and were often opposed to the impressions which he had early imbibed. He not only never entered
into the politics of the day, but he could never understand them.
He never was connected with any particular body or set of men,
comrades of school or college, or confederates in that public life
which in England is, perhaps, the only foundation of real friendship.

Although in private life he was of a timid nature, his moral
courage as a writer was unimpeachable. Most certainly, throughout his long career, he never wrote a sentence which he did not
believe was true. He will generally be found to be the advocate
of the discomfited and the oppressed. So his conclusions are often
opposed to popular impressions. This was from no love of paradox, to which he was quite superior; but because in the conduct
of his researches, he too often found that the unfortunate are
calumniated. His vindication of King James I, he has himself
described as "an affair of literary conscience;" his greater work
on the life and times of the son of the first Stuart arose from the
same impulse.

He was five years in the composition of his work on the *Life and Reign of Charles the First,* and the five volumes appeared at intervals between 1828 and 1831. It was feared by his publisher, that the distracted epoch at which this work was issued, and the tendency of the times, apparently so adverse to his own views, might prove very injurious to its reception. But the effect of these circumstances was the reverse. The success of this work was eminent; and its author appeared, for the first and only time of his life, in public, when amidst the cheers of under-graduates, and the applause of graver men, the solitary student received an honorary degree from the University of Oxford, a fitting homage, in the language of the great University, "OPTIMI REGIS OPTIMO VINDICI."

Notwithstanding he was now approaching his seventieth year, his health being unbroken and his constitution very robust, my father resolved vigorously to devote himself to the composition of the history of our vernacular literature. Hitherto, in his publications, he had always felt an extreme reluctance to travel over ground which others had previously visited. He liked to give new matter, and devote himself to detached points, on which he entertained different opinions from those prevalent. Thus his works are generally of a supplementary character, and assume in their readers a certain degree of preliminary knowledge. In the present instance, he was induced to frame his undertaking on a different scale, and to prepare a history which should be complete in itself, and supply the reader with a perfect view of the gradual formation of our language and literature. He proposed to effect this in six volumes; though, I apprehend, he would not have succeeded in fulfilling his intentions within that limit.

But all these great plans were destined to a terrible defeat. Towards the end of the year 1839, still in the full vigour of his health and intellect, he suffered a paralysis of the optic nerve; and that eye, which for so long a term had kindled with critical interest over the volumes of so many literatures and so many languages, was doomed to pursue its animated course no more. Considering the bitterness of such a calamity to one whose powers were otherwise not in the least impaired, he bore on the whole his fate with magnanimity, even with cheerfulness. Unhappily, his previous habits of study and composition rendered the habit of dictation intolerable, even impossible to him. But with the assistance of his daughter, whose intelligent solicitude he has commemorated in more than one grateful passage, he selected from his manuscripts three volumes, which were eventually given to the public under the title of *Amenities of Literature*.

In this notice of the career of my father, I have ventured to draw attention to three circumstances which, I thought, would be esteemed interesting; namely, predisposition, self-formation, and sympathy with his order. There is yet another which completes and crowns the character,—constancy of purpose; and it is only in considering his course as a whole, that we see how harmonious and consistent have been that life and its labours, which, in a partial and brief view, might be supposed to have been somewhat desultory and fragmentary.

On his moral character I shall scarcely presume to dwell. The philosophic sweetness of his disposition, the serenity of his lot, and the elevating nature of his pursuits, combined to enable him to pass through life without an evil act, almost without an evil thought. As the world has always been fond of personal details respecting men who have been celebrated, I will mention that he was fair, with a Bourbon nose, and brown eyes of extraordinary beauty and lustre. He wore a small black velvet cap, but his white hair latterly touched his shoulders in curls almost as flowing as in his boyhood. His extremities were delicate and well-formed, and his leg, at his last hour, as shapely as in his youth, which showed the vigour of his frame. Latterly he had become corpulent. He did not excel in conversation, though in his domestic circle he was garrulous. Everything interested him; and blind, and eighty-two, he was still as susceptible as a child. One of his last acts [before his death in 1848] was to compose some verses of gay gratitude to his daughter-in-law, who was his London correspondent, and to whose lively pen his last years were indebted for constant amusement. He had by nature a singular volatility which never deserted him. His feelings, though always amiable, were not painfully deep, and amid joy or sorrow, the philosophic vein was ever evident. He more resembled Goldsmith than any man that I can compare him to: in his conversation, his apparent confusion of ideas ending with some felicitous phrase of genius, his *naïveté*, his simplicity not untouched with a dash of sarcasm affecting innocence. There was, however, one trait in which my father did not resemble Goldsmith: he had no vanity. Indeed, one of his few infirmities was rather a deficiency of self-esteem.

On the whole, I hope—nay I believe—that taking all into consideration—the integrity and completeness of his existence, the fact that, for sixty years, he largely contributed to form the taste, charm the leisure, and direct the studious dispositions, of the great body of the public, and that his works have extensively and curiously illustrated the literary and political history of our country—it will be conceded, that in his life and labours, he repaid England for the protection and the hospitality which this country accorded to his father a century ago.

D.

Hughenden Manor
Christmas, 1848

A Glance into the French Academy

IN THE republic of letters the establishment of an academy has been a favourite project; yet perhaps it is little more than an Utopian scheme. The united efforts of men of letters in Academies have produced little. It would seem that no man likes to bestow his great labours on a small community, for whose members he himself does not feel, probably, the most flattering partiality. The French Academy made a splendid appearance in Europe; yet when this society published their *Dictionary,* that of Furetière's became a formidable rival; and Johnson did as much as the *forty* themselves. Voltaire confesses that the great characters of the literary republic were formed without the aid of academies.—"For what then," he asks, "are they necessary?—To preserve and nourish the fire which great geniuses have kindled." By observing the *Junto* at their meetings we may form some opinion of the indolent manner in which they trifled away their time. We are fortunately enabled to do this, by a letter in which Patru describes, in a very amusing manner, the visit which Christina of Sweden took a sudden fancy to pay to the academy.

The Queen of Sweden suddenly resolved to visit the French Academy, and gave so short a notice of her design, that it was impossible to inform the majority of the members of her intention. About four o'clock fifteen or sixteen academicians were assembled. M. Gombaut, who had never forgiven her majesty, because she did not relish his verses, thought proper to show his resentment by quitting the assembly.

She was received in a spacious hall. In the middle was a table covered with rich blue velvet, ornamented with a broad border of gold and silver. At its head was placed an armchair of black velvet embroidered with gold, and round the table were placed chairs with tapestry backs. The chancellor had forgotten to hang in the hall the portrait of the queen, which she had presented to the Academy, and which was considered as a great omission. About five, a footman belonging to the queen inquired if the company were assembled. Soon after, a servant of the king informed the chancellor that the queen was at the end of the street; and immediately her carriage drew up in the court-yard. The chancellor, followed by the rest of the members, went to receive her as she stepped out of her chariot; but the crowd was so great, that few of them could reach her majesty. Accompanied by the chancellor, she passed through the first hall, followed by one of her ladies, the captain of her guards, and one or two of her suite.

When she entered the Academy she approached the fire, and spoke in a low voice to the chancellor. She then asked why M. Menage was not there? and when she was told that he did not belong to the Academy, she asked why he did not? She was answered, that, however he might merit the honour, he had rendered himself unworthy of it by several disputes he had had with its members. She then inquired aside of the chancellor whether the academicians were to sit or stand before her? On this the chancellor consulted with a member, who observed that in the time of Ronsard, there was held an assembly of men of letters before Charles IX. several times, and that they were always seated. The queen conversed with M. Bourdelot; and suddenly turning to Madame de Bregis, told her that she believed she must not be present at the assembly; but it was agreed that this lady deserved the honour. As the queen was talking with a member she abruptly quitted him, as was her custom, and in her quick way sat down in the arm-chair; and at the same time the members seated themselves. The queen observing that they did not, out of respect to her, approach the table, desired them to come near; and they accordingly approached it.

During these ceremonious preparations several officers of state had entered the hall, and stood behind the academicians. The chancellor sat at the queen's left hand by the fire-side; and at the right was placed M. de la Chambre, the director; then Boisrobert, Patru, Pelisson, Cotin, the Abbé Tallemant, and others. M. de Mezeray sat at the bottom of the table facing the queen, with an inkstand, paper, and the portfolio of the company lying before him: he occupied the place of the secretary. When they were all seated the director rose, and the academicians followed him, all but the chancellor, who remained in his seat. The director made his complimentary address in a low voice, his body was quite bent, and no person but the queen and the chancellor could hear him. She received his address with great satisfaction.

All compliments concluded, they returned to their seats. The director then told the queen that he had composed a treatise on Pain, to add to his character of the Passions, and if it was agreeable to her majesty, he would read the first chapter.—"Very willingly," she answered. Having read it, he said to her majesty, that he would read no more lest he should fatigue her. "Not at all," she replied, "for I suppose what follows is like what I have heard."

M. de Mezeray observed that M. Cotin had some verses, which her majesty would doubtless find beautiful, and if it was agreeable they should be read. M. Cotin read them: they were versions of two passages from Lucretius: the one in which he attacks a Providence, and the other, where he gives the origin of the world according to the Epicurean system: to these he added twenty lines of his own, in which he maintained the existence of a Providence. This done, an abbé rose, and, without being desired or ordered, read two sonnets, which by courtesy were allowed to be tolerable. It is remarkable that both the *poets* read their verses standing, while the rest read their compositions seated.

After these readings, the director informed the queen that the ordinary exercise of the company was to labour on the dictionary; and that if her majesty should not find it disagreeable, they would read a *cahier.* "Very willingly," she answered. M. de Mezeray then read what related to the word *Jeu; Game.* Amongst other proverbial expressions was this: *Game of Princes, which only pleases the player,* to express a malicious violence committed by one in power. At this the queen laughed heartily; and they continued reading all that was fairly written. This lasted about an hour, when the queen observing that nothing more remained, arose, made a bow to the company, and returned in the manner she entered.

Furetière, who was himself an academican, has described the miserable manner in which time was consumed at their assemblies. I confess he was a satirist, and had quarrelled with the academy; there must have been, notwithstanding, sufficient resemblance for the following picture, however it may be overcharged. He has been blamed for thus exposing the Eleusinian mysteries of literature to the uninitiated.

"He who is most clamorous, is he whom they suppose has most reason. They all have the art of making long orations upon a trifle. The second repeats like an echo what the first said; but generally three or four speak together. When there is a bench of five or six members, one reads, another decides, two converse, one sleeps, and another amuses himself with reading some dictionary which happens to lie before him. When a second member is to deliver his opinion, they are obliged to read again the article, which at the first perusal he had been too much engaged to hear. This is a happy manner of finishing their work. They can hardly get over two lines without long digressions; without some one telling a pleasant story, or the news of the day; or talking of affairs of state, and reforming the government."

That the French Academy was generally frivolously employed appears also from an epistle to Balzac, by Boisrobert, the amusing companion of Cardinal Richelieu. "Every one separately," says he, "promises great things; when they meet they do nothing. They have been *six years* employed on the letter F; and I should be happy if I were certain of living till they got through G."

The following anecdote concerns the *forty arm-chairs* of the academicians. Those cardinals who were academicians for a long time had not attended the meetings of the academy, because they thought that *arm-chairs* were indispensable to their dignity, and the academy had then only common chairs. These cardinals were desirous of being present at the election of M. Monnoie, that they might give him a distinguished mark of their esteem. "The king," says D'Alembert, "to satisfy at once the delicacy of their friendship, and that of their cardinalship, and to preserve at the same time that academical equality, of which this enlightened monarch (Louis XIV.) well knew the advantage, sent to the academy forty arm-chairs for the forty academicians, the same chairs which we now occupy; and the motive to which we owe them is sufficient to render the memory of Louis XIV. precious to the republic of letters, to whom it owes so many more important obligations!"

Poetical and Grammatical Deaths

IT WILL appear by the following anecdotes, that some men may be said to have died *poetically* and even *grammatically*.

There must be some attraction existing in poetry which is not merely fictitious, for often have its genuine votaries felt all its powers on the most trying occasions. They have displayed the energy of their mind by composing or repeating verses, even with death on their lips.

The Emperor Hadrian, dying, made that celebrated address to his soul, which is so happily translated by Pope. Lucan, when he had his veins opened by order of Nero, expired reciting a passage from his *Pharsalia,* in which he had described the wound of a dying soldier. Petronius did the same thing on the same occasion.

Patris, a poet of Caen, perceiving himself expiring composed some verses which are justly admired. In this little poem he relates a dream, in which he appeared to be placed next to a beggar, when, having addressed him in the haughty strain he would probably have employed on this side of the grave, he receives the following reprimand:—

> Ici tous sont égaux; je ne te dois plus rien;
> Je suis sur mon fumier comme toi sur le tien.

> Here all are equal! now thy lot is mine!
> I on my dunghill, as thou art on thine.

Des Barreaux, it is said, wrote on his death-bed that well-known sonnet which is translated in the *Spectator.*

Margaret of Austria, when she was nearly perishing in a storm at sea, composed her epitaph in verse. Had she perished, what would have become of the epitaph? And if she escaped, of what use was it? She should rather have said her prayers. The verses however have all the *naïveté* of the times. They are—

> Cy gist Margot, la gente demoiselle,
> Qu'eut deux maris, et si mourut pucelle.

> Beneath this tomb is high-born Margaret laid,
> Who had two husbands, and yet died a maid.

She was betrothed to Charles VIII. of France, who forsook her; and being next intended for the Spanish infant, in her voyage to Spain, she wrote these lines in a storm.

Mademoiselle de Serment was surnamed the philosopher. She was celebrated for her knowledge and taste in polite literature. She died of a cancer in her breast, and suffered her misfortune with exemplary patience. She expired in finishing these verses, which she addressed to Death:—

> Nectare clausa suo,
> Dignum tantorum pretium tulit illa laborum.

It was after Cervantes had received extreme unction that he wrote the dedication of his *Persiles.*

Roscommon, at the moment he expired, with an energy of voice that expressed the most fervent devotion, uttered two lines of his own version of "Dies Iræ!" Waller, in his last moments, repeated some lines from Virgil; and Chaucer seems to have taken his farewell of all human vanities by a moral ode, entitled,

"A balade made by Geffrey Chaucyer upon his dethe-bedde lying in his grete anguysse."

Cornelius de Witt fell an innocent victim to popular prejudice. His death is thus noticed by Hume: "This man, who had bravely served his country in war, and who had been invested with the highest dignities, was delivered into the hands of the executioner, and torn in pieces by the most inhuman torments. Amidst the severe agonies which he endured he frequently repeated an ode of Horace, which contained sentiments suited to his deplorable condition." It was the third ode of the third book which this illustrious philosopher and statesman then repeated.

Metastasio, after receiving the sacrament, a very short time before his last moments, broke out with all the enthusiasm of poetry and religion in these stanzas:—

> T'offro il tuo proprio Figlio,
> Che già d'amore in pegno,
> Racchiuso in picciol segno
> Si volle a noi donar.

> A lui rivolgi il ciglio.
> Guarda chi t' offro, e poi
> Lascia, Signor, se vuoi,
> Lascia di perdonar.

I offer to thee, O Lord, thine own Son, who already has given the pledge of love, enclosed in this thin emblem. Turn on him thine eyes: ah! behold whom I offer to thee, and then desist, O Lord! If thou canst desist from mercy.

"The muse that has attended my course," says the dying Gleim in a letter to Klopstock, "still hovers round my steps to the very verge of the grave." A collection of lyrical poems, entitled *Last Hours,* composed by old Gleim on his death-bed, was intended to be published. The death of Klopstock was one of the most poetical: in this poet's "Messiah," he had made the death of Mary, the sister of Martha and Lazarus, a picture of the death of the Just; and on his own death-bed he was heard repeating, with an expiring voice, his own verses on Mary; he was exhorting himself to die by the accents of his own harp, the sublimities of his own muse! The same song of Mary was read at the public funeral of Klopstock.

Chatelar, a French gentleman, beheaded in Scotland for having loved the queen, and even for having attempted her honour, Brantome says, would not have any other viaticum than a poem of Ronsard. When he ascended the scaffold he took the hymns of this poet, and for his consolation read that on death, which our old critic says is well adapted to conquer its fear.

When the Marquis of Montrose was condemned by his judges to have his limbs nailed to the gates of four cities, the brave soldier said that "he was sorry he had not limbs sufficient to be nailed to all the gates of the cities in Europe, as monuments of his loyalty." As he proceeded to his execution, he put this thought into verse.

Philip Strozzi, imprisoned by Cosmo the First, Great Duke of Tuscany, was apprehensive of the danger to which he might expose his friends who had joined in his conspiracy against the duke, from the confessions which the rack might extort from him. Having attempted every exertion for the liberty of his country, he considered it as no crime therefore to die. He resolved on suicide. With the point of the sword, with which he killed himself, he cut out on the mantel-piece of the chimney this verse of Virgil:—

> Exoriare aliquis nostris ex ossibus ultor.
>
> Rise some avenger from our blood!

I can never repeat without a strong emotion the following stanzas, begun by André Chenier, in the dreadful period of the French revolution. He was waiting for his turn to be dragged to the guillotine, when he commenced this poem:—

> Comme un dernier rayon, comme un dernier zéphyre
> Anime la fin d'un beau jour;
> Au pied de l'échafaud j'essaie encore ma lyre,
> Peut-être est-ce bientôt mon tour;
>
> Peut-être avant que l'heure en cercle promenée
> Ait posé sur l'émail brillant,
> Dans les soixante pas où sa route est bornée
> Son pied sonore et vigilant,
>
> Le sommeil du tombeau pressera ma paupière——

Here, at this pathetic line, was André Chenier summoned to the guillotine! Never was a more beautiful effusion of grief interrupted by a more affecting incident!

Several men of science have died in a scientific manner. Haller, the poet, philosopher, and physician, beheld his end approach with the utmost composure. He kept feeling his pulse to the last moment, and when he found that life was almost gone, he turned to his brother physician, observing, "My friend, the artery ceases to beat," and almost instantly expired. The same remarkable circumstance had occurred to the great Harvey: he kept making observations on the state of his pulse, when life was drawing to its close, "as if," says Dr. Wilson, in the oration spoken a few days after the event, "that he who had taught us the beginnings of life might himself, at his departing from it, become acquainted with those of death."

De Lagny, who was intended by his friends for the study of the law, having fallen on an Euclid, found it so congenial to his dispositions, that he devoted himself to mathematics. In his last moments, when he retained no further recollection of the friends who surrounded his bed, one of them, perhaps to make a philosophical experiment, thought proper to ask him the square of twelve: our dying mathematician instantly, and perhaps without knowing that he answered, replied, "One hundred and forty-four."

The following anecdotes are of a different complexion, and may excite a smile.

Père Bohours was a French grammarian, who had been justly accused of paying too scrupulous an attention to the minutiæ of letters. He was more solicitous of his *words* than his *thoughts*. It is said, that when he was dying, he called out to his friends (a correct grammarian to the last), "*Je* VAS, *ou je* VAIS *mourir; l'un ou l'autre se dit!*"

When Malherbe was dying, he reprimanded his nurse for making use of a solecism in her language; and when his confessor represented to him the felicities of a future state in low and trite expressions, the dying critic interrupted him:— "Hold your tongue," he said, "your wretched style only makes me out of conceit with them!"

The favourite studies and amusements of the learned La Mothe le Vayer consisted in accounts of the most distant countries. He gave a striking proof of the influence of this master-passion, when death hung upon his lips. Bernier, the celebrated traveller, entering and drawing the curtains of his bed to take his eternal farewell, the dying man turning to him, with a faint voice inquired, "Well, my friend, what news from the Great Mogul?"

Royal Promotions

IF THE golden gate of preferment is not usually opened to men of real merit, persons of no worth have entered it in a most extraordinary manner.

Chevreau informs us that the Sultan Osman having observed a gardener planting a cabbage with some peculiar dexterity, the manner so attracted his imperial eye that he raised him to an office near his person, and shortly afterwards he rewarded the planter of cabbages by creating him *beglerbeg* or viceroy of the Isle of Cyprus.

Marc Antony gave the house of a Roman citizen to a cook, who had prepared for him a good supper! Many have been raised to extraordinary preferment by capricious monarchs for the sake of a jest. Lewis XI. promoted a poor priest whom he found sleeping in the porch of a church, that the proverb might be verified, that to lucky men good fortune will come even when they are asleep! Our Henry VII. made a viceroy of Ireland if not for the sake of, at least with a clench.* When the king was told that all Ireland could not rule the Earl of Kildare, he said, then shall this earl rule all Ireland.

It is recorded of Henry VIII. that he raised a servant to considerable dignity because he had taken care to have a roasted boar prepared for him, when his majesty happened to be in the humour of feasting on one! and the title of *Sugar-loaf-court,* in Leadenhall-street, was probably derived from another piece of munificence of this monarch: the widow of a Mr. Cornwallis was rewarded by the gift of a dissolved priory there situated, for some *fine puddings* with which she had presented his majesty!

When Cardinal de Monte was elected pope, before he left the conclave he bestowed a cardinal's hat upon a servant, whose chief merit consisted in the daily attentions he paid to his holiness's monkey!

Louis Barbier owed all his good fortune to the familiar knowledge he had of Rabelais. He knew his Rabelais by heart. This served to introduce him to the Duke of Orleans, who took great pleasure in reading that author. It was for this he gave him an abbey, and he was gradually promoted till he became a cardinal.

---

*[Play on words.—ED.]

George Villiers was suddenly raised from a private station, and loaded with wealth and honours by James the First, merely for his personal beauty. Almost all the favourites of James became so from their handsomeness.

M. de Chamillart, minister of France, owed his promotion merely to his being the only man who could beat Louis XIV. at billiards. He retired with a pension, after ruining the finances of his country.

The Duke of Luynes was originally a country lad, who insinuated himself into the favour of Louis XIII., then young, by making bird-traps (*pies-grièches*) to catch sparrows. It was little expected (says Voltaire,) that these puerile amusements were to be terminated by a most sanguinary revolution. De Luynes, after causing his patron, the Marshal D'Ancre, to be assassinated, and the queen mother to be imprisoned, raised himself to a title and the most tyrannical power.

Sir Walter Raleigh owed his promotion to an act of gallantry to Queen Elizabeth, and Sir Christopher Hatton owed his preferment to his dancing: Queen Elizabeth, observes Granger, with all her sagacity, could not see the future lord chancellor in the fine dancer. The same writer says, "Nothing could form a more curious collection of memoirs than *anecdotes of preferment.*" Could the secret history of great men be traced, it would appear that merit is rarely the first step to advancement. It would much oftener be found to be owing to superficial qualifications, and even vices.

Influence of a Name

What's in a NAME? That which we call a rose,
By any other name would smell as sweet.

NAMES, by an involuntary suggestion, produce an extraordinary illusion. Favour or disappointment has been often conceded as the *name* of the claimant has affected us; and the accidental affinity or coincidence of a *name*, connected with ridicule or hatred, with pleasure or disgust, has operated like magic. But the facts connected with this subject will show how this prejudice has branched out.

Sterne has touched on this unreasonable propensity of judging by *names*, in his humorous account of the elder Mr.

Shandy's system of Christian names. And Wilkes has expressed, in Boswell's life of Johnson, all the influence of baptismal *names*, even in matters of poetry! He said, "The last city poet was *Elkanah* Settle. There is *something* in *names* which one cannot help feeling. Now *Elkanah* Settle sounds so queer, who can expect much from *that name?* We should have no hesitation to give it for *John Dryden* in preference to *Elkanah Settle,* from the *names only,* without knowing their different merits."

A lively critic noticing some American poets says, "There is or was a Mr. Dwight who wrote a poem in the shape of an epic; and his baptismal name was *Timothy;*" and involuntarily we infer the sort of epic that a *Timothy* must write. Sterne humorously exhorts all godfathers not "to Nicodemus a man into nothing."

There is more truth in this observation than some may be inclined to allow; and that it affects mankind strongly, all ages and all climates may be called on to testify. Even in the barbarous age of Louis XI., they felt a delicacy respecting *names,* which produced an ordinance from his majesty. The king's barber was named *Olivier le Diable.* At first the king allowed him to get rid of the offensive part by changing it to *Le Malin;* but the improvement was not happy, and for a third time he was called *Le Mauvais.* Even this did not answer his purpose; and as he was a great racer, he finally had his majesty's ordinance to be called *Le Dain,* under penalty of law if any one should call him *Le Diable, Le Malin,* or *Le Mauvais.* According to Platina, Sergius the Second was the first pope who changed his name in ascending the papal throne; because his proper name was *Hog's-mouth,* very unsuitable with the pomp of the tiara. The ancients felt the same fastidousness; and among the Romans, those who were called to the equestrian order, having low and vulgar *names,* were new named on the occasion, lest the former one should disgrace the dignity.

When *Barbier,* a French wit, was chosen for the preceptor of Colbert's son, he felt his *name* was so uncongenial to his new profession, that he assumed the more splendid one of *D'Acuour,* by which he is now known. Madame *Gomez* had married a person named *Bonhomme,* but she would never exchange her nobler Spanish name to prefix her married one to her romances, which indicated too much of meek humility. *Guez* (a beggar) is a French writer of great pomp of style;

but he felt such extreme delicacy at so low a name, that to give some authority to the splendour of his diction, he assumed the name of his estate; and is well known as *Balzac*. A French poet of the name of Theophile *Viaut,* finding that his surname pronounced like *veau* (calf), exposed him to the infinite jests of the minor wits, silently dropped it, by retaining the more poetical appellation of *Theophile.* Various literary artifices have been employed by some who, still preserving a natural attachment to the names of their fathers, yet blushing at the same time for their meanness, have in their Latin works attempted to obviate the ridicule which they provoked. One *Gaucher* (left-handed) borrowed the name of *Scevola,* because Scevola, having burnt his right arm, became consequently left-handed. Thus also one *De la Borgne* (one-eyed) called himself *Strabo; De Charpentier* took that of *Fabricius; De Valet* translated his *Servilius*; and an unlucky gentleman, who bore the name of *Du bout d'Homme,* boldly assumed that of *Virulus.* Dorat, a French poet, had for his real name *Disnemandi*, which, in the dialect of the Limousins, signifies one who dines in the morning; that is, who has no other dinner than his breakfast. This degrading name he changed to *Dorat,* or gilded, a nickname which one of his ancestors had borne for his fair tresses. But by changing his *name,* his feelings were not entirely quieted, for unfortunately his daughter cherished an invincible passion for a learned man, who unluckily was named *Goulu,* that is, a shark, or gluttonous as a shark. Miss *Disnemandi* felt naturally a strong attraction for a *goulu*; and in spite of her father's remonstrances, she once more renewed his sorrows in this alliance!

There are unfortunate names, which are very injurious to the cause in which they are engaged; for instance, the long parliament in Cromwell's time, called by derision the *Rump,* was headed by one *Barebones,* a leather-seller. It was afterwards called by his unlucky name, which served to heighten the ridicule cast over it by the nation.

Formerly a custom prevailed with learned men to change their names. They showed at once their contempt for vulgar denominations and their ingenious erudition. They christened themselves with Latin and Greek. This disguising of names came, at length, to be considered to have a political tendency, and so much alarmed Pope Paul the Second, that he imprisoned several persons for their using certain affected names, and some, indeed, which they could not give a reason why they

assumed. *Desiderius Erasmus* was a name formed out of his
family name *Gerard*, which in Dutch signifies amiable; or Gᴀᴿ
all, ᴀᴇʀᴅ *nature*. He first changed it to a Latin word of much
the same signification, *desiderius*, which afterwards he refined
into the Greek *Erasmus*, by which name he is now known.
The celebrated *Reuchlin*, which in German signifies *smoke*,
considered it more dignified to smoke in Greek by the name
of *Capnio*. An Italian physician of the name of *Senza Malizia*
prided himself as much on his translating it into the Greek
Akakia, as on the works which he published under that name.
One of the most amiable of the reformers was originally named
Hertz Schwarts (black earth), which he elegantly turned into
the Greek name *Melanchthon*. The vulgar name of a great
Italian poet was *Trapasso*; but when the learned Gravina
resolved to devote the youth to the muses, he gave him a
mellifluous name, which they have long known and cherished—
Metastasio.

Harsh names will have, in spite of all our philosophy, a
painful and ludicrous effect on our ears and our associations:
it is vexatious that the softness of delicious vowels, or the
ruggedness of inexorable consonants, should at all be connected
with a man's happiness, or even have an influence on his
fortune.

The actor *Macklin* was softened down by taking in the first
and last syllables of the name of *Macklaughlin*, as *Malloch*
was polished to *Mallet*; and even our sublime Milton, in
a moment of humour and hatred to the Scots, condescends to
insinuate that their barbarous names are symbolical of their
natures,—and from a man of the name of *Mac Collkittok*, he
expects no mercy. Virgil, when young, formed a design of
a national poem, but was soon discouraged from proceeding,
merely by the roughness and asperity of the old Roman names,
such as *Decius Mus; Lucumo; Vibius Caudex*. The same thing
has happened to a friend who began an Epic on the subject
of *Drake's* discoveries; the name of the hero often will produce
a ludicrous effect, but one of the most unlucky of his chief
heroes must be *Thomas Doughty*! One of Blackmore's chief
heroes in his *Alfred* is named *Gunter*; a printer's erratum
might have been fatal to all his heroism; as it is, he makes
a sorry appearance. Metastasio found himself in the same situation. In one of his letters he writes, "The title of my new
opera is *Il Re Pastor*. The chief incident is the restitution of
the kingdom of Sidon to the lawful heir: a prince with such

a *hypochondriac name,* that he would have disgraced the title-page of any piece; who would have been able to bear an opera entitled *L'Abdolonimo*? I have contrived to name him as seldom as possible." So true is it, as the caustic Boileau exclaims of an epic poet of his days, who had shown some dexterity in cacophony, when he chose his hero—

> O le plaisant projet d'un poète ignorant,
> Qui de tant de héros va choisir *Childebrand!*
> D'un seul nom quelquefois le son dur et bizarre
> Rend un poème entier, ou burlesque ou barbare.
> *Art Poétique,* c. iii v. 241

> In such a crowd the Poet were to blame
> To choose *King Chilperic* for his hero's name.
> SIR W. SOAMES

This epic poet perceiving the town joined in the severe raillery of the poet, published a long defence of his hero's name; but the town was inexorable, and the epic poet afterwards changed *Childebrand's* name to *Charles Martel,* which probably was discovered to have something more humane. Corneille's *Pertharite* was an unsuccessful tragedy, and Voltaire deduces its ill fortune partly from its barbarous *names,* such as *Garibald* and *Edvidge.* Voltaire, in giving the *names* of the founders of Helvetic freedom, says, the difficulty of pronouncing these respectable names is injurious to their celebrity; they are *Melchthal, Stauffarcher,* and *Valtherfurst.*

We almost hesitate to credit what we know to be true, that the *length* or the *shortness* of a *name* can seriously influence the mind. But history records many facts of this nature. Some nations have long cherished a feeling that there is a certain elevation or abasement in proper names. Montaigne on this subject says, "A gentleman, one of my neighbours, in over-valuing the excellences of old times, never omitted noticing the pride and magnificence of the *names* of the nobility of those days! Don *Grumedan, Quadragan, Argesilan,* when fully sounded, were evidently men of another stamp than *Peter, Giles,* and *Michel.*" What could be hoped for from the names of Ebenezer, Malachi, and Methusalem? The Spaniards have long been known for cherishing a passion for dignified names, and are marvellously affected by long and voluminous ones; to enlarge them they often add the places of their residence. We ourselves seem affected by triple names; and the authors of certain periodical publications always assume for their *nom de guerre* a triple name, which doubtless raises them much higher in their readers' esteem than a mere Christian and surname. Many Spaniards have given themselves *names* from some remarkable incident in their lives. One took the name of the Royal Transport, for having conducted the Infanta in Italy. Orendayes added de la Paz, for having signed the peace in 1725. Navarro, after a naval battle off Toulon, added la Vittoria, though he had remained in safety at Cadiz while the French admiral Le Court had fought the battle, which was entirely in favour of the English. A favourite of the King of Spain, a great genius, and the friend of Farinelli, who had sprung from a very obscure origin, to express his contempt of these empty and haughty *names,* assumed, when called to the administration, that of the Marquis of *La Ensenada* (nothing in himself).

But the influence of *long names* is of very ancient standing. Lucian notices one *Simon,* who coming to a great fortune, aggrandized his name to *Simonides. Diocletian* had once been plain *Diocles* before he was emperor. When *Bruna* became Queen of France, it was thought proper to convey some of the regal pomp in her name by calling her *Brunehault.*

The Spaniards then must feel a most singular contempt for a *very short name,* and on this subject Fuller has recorded a pleasant fact. An opulent citizen of the name of *John Cuts* (what name can be more unluckily short?) was ordered by Elizabeth to receive the Spanish ambassador; but the latter complained grievously, and thought he was disparaged by the *shortness* of his *name.* He imagined that a man bearing a monosyllabic name could never, in the great alphabet of civil life, have performed anything great or honourable; but when he found that honest *John Cuts* displayed a hospitality which had nothing monosyllabic in it, he groaned only at the utterance of the *name* of his host.

There are *names* indeed, which in the social circle will in spite of all due gravity awaken a harmless smile, and Shenstone solemnly thanked God that his name was not liable to a pun. There are some names which excite horror, such as Mr. Stabback; others contempt, as Mr. Twopenny; and others of vulgar or absurd signification, subject too often to the insolence of domestic witlings, which occasions irritation even in the minds of worthy, but suffering, men.

There is an association of pleasing ideas with certain *names,—* and in the literary world they produce a fine effect. *Bloomfield*

is a name apt and fortunate for a rustic bard; as *Florian* seems
to describe his sweet and flowery style. Dr. Parr derived his first
acquaintance with the late Mr. *Homer* from the aptness of his
name, associating with his pursuits. Our writers of romances and
novels are initiated into all the arcana of *names*, which cost them
many painful inventions. It is recorded of one of the old Spanish
writers of romance, that he was for many days at a loss to coin a
fit name for one of his giants; he wished to hammer out one
equal in magnitude to the person he conceived in imagination;
and in the haughty and lofty name of *Traquitantos*, he thought
he had succeeded. Richardson, the great father of our novelists,
appears to have considered the *name* of Sir *Charles Grandison*
as *perfect* as his character, for his heroine writes, "You know his
noble name, my Lucy." He felt the same for his *Clementina*, for
Miss Byron writes, "Ah, Lucy, what a *pretty name* is *Clementina!*" We experience a certain tenderness for *names*, and persons of refined imaginations are fond to give affectionate or
lively epithets to things and persons they love. Petrarch would
call one friend *Lelius*, and another *Socrates*, as descriptive of
their character.

In our own country, formerly, the ladies appear to have been
equally sensible to poetical or elegant *names*, such as *Alicia,
Celicia, Diana, Helena,* &c. Spenser, the poet, gave to his two sons
two *names* of this kind; he called one *Silvanus*, from the woody
Kilcolman, his estate; and the other *Peregrine*, from his having
been born in a strange place, and his mother then travelling.
The fair Eloisa gave the whimsical name of *Astrolabus* to her
boy; it bore some reference to the stars, as her own to the sun.

Whether this name of *Astrolabus* had any scientific influence
over the son, I know not; but I have no doubt that whimsical
names may have a great influence over our characters. The practice of romantic names among persons, even of the lowest orders
of society, has become a very general evil: and doubtless many
unfortunate beauties, of the names of *Clarissa* and *Eloisa*, might
have escaped under the less dangerous appellatives of *Elizabeth*
or *Deborah*. I know a person who has not passed his life without
some inconvenience from his *name*, mean talents and violent
passions not according with *Antoninus*; and a certain writer of
verses might have been no versifier, and less a lover of the true
Falernian, had it not been for his namesake *Horace*. The Ameri-
cans, by assuming *Roman* names, produce ludicrous associations;
Romulus Riggs, and *Junius Brutus* Booth. There was more
sense, when the Foundling Hospital was first instituted, in bap-

tizing the most robust boys, designed for the sea-service, by the
names of Drake, Norris, or Blake, after our famous admirals.

It is no trifling misfortune in life to bear an illustrious name;
and in an author it is peculiarly severe. A history now by a Mr.
Hume, or a poem by a Mr. Pope, would be examined with different eyes than had they borne any other name. The relative of
a great author should endeavour not to be an author. Thomas
Corneille had the unfortunate honour of being brother to a great
poet, and his own merits have been considerably injured by the
involuntary comparison. The son of Racine has written with an
amenity not unworthy of his celebrated father; amiable and
candid, he had his portrait painted, with the works of his father
in his hand, and his eye fixed on this verse from Phædra,

> Et moi, fils inconnu d'un si glorieux père!

But even his modesty only served to whet the dart of epigram.
It was once bitterly said of the son of an eminent literary
character,

> He tries to write because his father writ,
> And shows himself a bastard by his wit.

Amongst some of the disagreeable consequences attending
some *names*, is, when they are unluckily adapted to an uncommon rhyme; how can any man defend himself from this malicious
ingenuity of wit? *Freret,* one of those unfortunate victims to
Boileau's verse, is said not to have been deficient in the decorum
of his manners, and he complained that he was represented as a
drunkard, merely because his *name rhymed* to *Cabaret.* Murphy,
no doubt, felicitated himself in his literary quarrel with Dr.
Franklin, the poet and critical reviewer, by adopting the singular
rhyme of "envy rankling" to his rival's and critic's name.

Superstition has interfered even in the *choice of names*, and
this solemn folly has received the name of a science, called
Onomantia; of which the superstitious ancients discovered a
hundred foolish mysteries. They cast up the numeral letters of
names, and Achilles was therefore fated to vanquish Hector,
from the numeral letters in his name amounting to a higher
number than his rival's. They made many whimsical divisions
and subdivisions of names, to prove them lucky or unlucky. But
these follies are not those that I am now treating on. Some names
have been considered as more auspicious than others. Cicero informs us that when the Romans raised troops, they were anxious
that the *name* of the first soldier who enlisted should be one of

good augury. When the censors numbered the citizens, they always began by a fortunate name, such as *Salvius Valereus*. A person of the name of *Regillianus* was chosen emperor, merely from the royal sound of his name, and *Jovian* was elected because his name approached nearest to the beloved one of the philosophic *Julian*. This fanciful superstition was even carried so far that some were considered as auspicious, and others as unfortunate. The superstitious belief in *auspicious names* was so strong, that Cæsar, in his African expedition, gave a command to an obscure and distant relative of the Scipios, to please the popular prejudice that the Scipios were invincible in Africa. Suetonius observes that all those of the family of Cæsar who bore the surname of Caius perished by the sword.

The Emperor Severus consoled himself for the licentious life of his empress Julia, from the fatality attending those of her *name*. This strange prejudice of lucky and unlucky names prevailed in modern Europe. The successor of Adrian VI. (as Guicciardini tells us) wished to preserve his own name on the papal throne; but he gave up the wish when the conclave of cardinals used the powerful argument that all the popes who had preserved their own names had died in the first year of their pontificates. Cardinal Marcel Cervin, who preserved his name when elected pope, died on the twentieth day of his pontificate, and this confirmed this superstitious opinion. La Motte le Vayer gravely asserts that all the queens of Naples of the name of *Joan*, and the kings of Scotland of the names of *James*, have been unfortunate; and we have formal treatises of the fatality of Christian names. It is a vulgar notion that every female of the name of *Agnes* is fated to become mad. Every nation has some names labouring with this popular prejudice.

Herrera, the Spanish historian, records an anecdote in which the choice of a queen entirely arose from her *name*. When two French ambassadors negotiated a marriage between one of the Spanish princesses and Louis VIII., the names of the royal females were *Urraca* and *Blanche*. The former was the elder and the more beautiful, and intended by the Spanish court for the French monarch; but they resolutely preferred *Blanche*, observing that the *name* of *Urraca* would never do! and for the sake of a more mellifluous sound, they carried off, exulting in their own discerning ears, the happier named, but less beautiful princess.

There are *names* indeed which are painful to the feelings, from the associations of our passions. I have seen the Christian *name* of a gentleman, the victim of the caprice of his godfather, who is called *Blast us Godly*,—which, were he designed for a bishop, must irritate religious feelings. I am not surprised that one of the Spanish monarchs refused to employ a sound Catholic for his secretary, because his name (*Martin Lutero*) had an affinity to the *name* of the reformer. Mr. Rose has recently informed us that an architect called *Malacarne*, who, I believe, had nothing against him but his *name*, was lately deprived of his place as principal architect by the Austrian government,—let us hope not for his unlucky *name*; though that government, according to Mr. Rose, acts on capricious principles! The fondness which some have felt to perpetuate their *names*, when their race has fallen extinct, is well known; and a fortune has then been bestowed for a change of name. But the affection for names has gone even farther. A *similitude of names*, Camden observes, "dothe kindle sparkes of love and liking among meere strangers." I have observed the great pleasure of persons with uncommon names meeting with another of the same name; an instant relationship appears to take place; and I have known that fortunes have been bequeathed for *namesakes*. An ornamental manufacturer, who bears a name which he supposes to be very uncommon, having executed an order for a gentleman of the *same name*, refused to send his bill, never having met with the like, preferring to payment the honour of serving him for *namesake*.

Among the Greeks and the Romans, beautiful and significant names were studied. The sublime Plato himself has noticed the present topic; his visionary ear was sensible to the delicacy of a name; and his exalted fancy was delighted with *beautiful names*, as well as every other species of beauty. In his *Cratylus* he is solicitous that persons should have happy, harmonious, and attractive *names*. According to Aulus Gellius, the Athenians enacted by a public decree, that no slave should ever bear the consecrated names of their two youthful patriots, Harmodius and Aristogiton,—names which had been devoted to the liberties of their country, they considered would be contaminated by servitude. The ancient Romans decreed that the surnames of infamous patricians should not be borne by any other patrician of that family, that their very names might be degraded and expire with them. Eutropius gives a pleasing proof of national friendships being cemented by a *name*; by a treaty of peace between the Romans and the Sabines, they agreed to melt the two nations into one mass, that they should bear their *names* conjointly; the Roman should add his to the Sabine, and the Sabine take a Roman name.

The ancients *named* both persons and things from some event or other circumstance connected with the object they were to name. Chance, fancy, superstition, fondness, and piety, have invented *names*. It was a common and whimsical custom among the ancients, (observes Larcher) to give as *nicknames* the *letters* of the alphabet. Thus a lame girl was called *Lambda,* on account of the resemblance which her lameness made her bear to the letter λ, or *lambda!* Æsop was called *Theta* by his master, from his superior acuteness. Another was called *Beta,* from his love of beet. It was thus Scarron, with infinite good temper, alluded to his zig-zag body, by comparing himself to the letter s or z.

The learned Calmet also notices among the Hebrews *nicknames* and names of raillery taken from defects of body or mind, &c. One is called Nabal, or *fool*; another Hamor, the *Ass*; Hagab, the *Grasshopper*, &c. Women had frequently the names of animals; as Deborah, the *Bee*; Rachel, the *Sheep*. Others from their nature or other qualifications; as Tamar, the *Palm-tree;* Hadassa, the *Myrtle;* Sarah, the *Princess;* Hannah, the *Gracious.* The Indians of North America employ sublime and picturesque *names*; such are the great Eagle—the Partridge—Dawn of the Day!—Great swift Arrow!—Path-opener!—Sun-bright!

Literary Composition

To LITERARY composition we may apply the saying of an ancient philosopher: "A little thing gives perfection, although perfection is not a little thing."

The great legislator of the Hebrews orders us to pull off the fruit for the first three years, and not to taste them. He was not ignorant how it weakens a young tree to bring to maturity its first fruits. Thus, on literary compositions, our green essays ought to be picked away. The word *Zamar*, by a beautiful metaphor from *pruning trees*, means in Hebrew to *compose verses*. Blotting and correcting was so much Churchill's abhorrence, that I have heard from his publisher he once energetically expressed himself, that *it was like cutting away one's own flesh*. This strong figure sufficiently shows his repugnance to an author's duty. Churchill now lies neglected, for posterity will only respect those who

File off the mortal part
Of glowing thought with Attic art.
YOUNG

I have heard that this careless bard, after a successful work, usually precipitated the publication of another, relying on its crudeness being passed over by the public curiosity excited by its better brother. He called this getting double pay, for thus he secured the sale of a hurried work. But Churchill was a spendthrift of fame, and enjoyed all his revenue while he lived; posterity owes him little, and pays him nothing!

Bayle, an experienced observer in literary matters, tells us that *correction* is by no means practicable by some authors, as in the case of Ovid. In exile, his compositions were nothing more than spiritless repetitions of what he had formerly written. He confesses both negligence and idleness in the corrections of his works. The vivacity which animated his first productions failing him when he revised his poems, he found correction too laborious, and he abandoned it. This, however, was only an excuse. "It is certain that *some authors cannot correct*. They compose with pleasure, and with ardour; but they exhaust all their force. They fly with but one wing when they review their works; the first fire does not return; there is in their imagination a certain calm which hinders their pen from making any progress. Their mind is like a boat, which only advances by the strength of oars."

Dr. More, the Platonist, had such an exuberance of fancy, that *correction* was a much greater labour than *composition*. He used to say, that in writing his works, he was forced to cut his way through a crowd of thoughts as through a wood, and that he threw off in his compositions as much as would make an ordinary philosopher. More was a great enthusiast, and, of course, an egotist, so that *criticism* ruffled his temper, notwithstanding all his Platonism. When accused of obscurities and extravagancies, he said that, like the ostrich, he laid his eggs in the sands, which would prove vital and prolific in time; however, these ostrich eggs have proved to be addled.

A habit of correctness in the lesser parts of composition will assist the higher. It is worth recording that the great Milton was anxious for correct punctuation, and that Addison was solicitous after the minutiæ of the press. Savage, Armstrong, and others, felt tortures on similar objects. It is said of Julius Scaliger, that he had this peculiarity in his manner of composition: he wrote with such accuracy that his MSS. and the printed copy corresponded page for page, and line for line.

Malherbe, the father of French poetry, tormented himself by a prodigious slowness; and was employed rather in perfecting than in forming works. His muse is compared to a fine woman in the pangs of delivery. He exulted in his tardiness, and, after finishing a poem of one hundred verses, or a discourse of ten pages, he used to say he ought to repose for ten years. Balzac, the first writer in French prose who gave majesty and harmony to a period, did not grudge to expend a week on a page, never satisfied with his first thoughts. Our "costive" Gray entertained the same notion: and it is hard to say if it arose from the sterility of their genius, or their sensibility of taste.

The MSS. of Tasso, still preserved, are illegible from the vast number of their corrections. I have given a fac-simile, as correct as it is possible to conceive, of one page of Pope's MS. Homer, as a specimen of his continual corrections and critical erasures. The celebrated Madame Dacier never could satisfy herself in translating Homer: continually retouching the version, even in its happiest passages. There were several parts which she translated in six or seven manners; and she frequently noted in the margin—*I have not yet done it.*

When Pascal became warm in his celebrated controversy, he applied himself with incredible labour to the composition of his *Provincial Letters.* He was frequently twenty days occupied on a single letter. He recommenced some above seven and eight times, and by this means obtained that perfection which has made his work, as Voltaire says, "one of the best books ever published in France."

The *Quintus Curtius* of Vaugelas occupied him thirty years: generally every period was translated in the margin five or six several ways. Chapelain and Conrart, who took the pains to review this work critically, were many times perplexed in their choice of passages; they generally liked best that which had been first composed. Hume had never done with corrections; every edition varies from the preceding ones. But there are more fortunate and fluid minds than these. Voltaire tells us of Fenelon's *Telemachus,* that the amiable author composed it in his retirement, in the short period of three months. Fenelon had, before this, formed his style, and his mind overflowed with all the spirit of the ancients. He opened a copious fountain, and there were not ten erasures in the original MS. The same facility accompanied Gibbon after the experience of his first volume; and the same copious readiness attended Adam Smith, who dictated to his amanuensis, while he walked about his study.

The publication of Gibbon's *Memoirs* conveyed to the world a faithful picture of the most fervid industry; it is in *youth*, the foundations of such a sublime edifice as his history must be laid. The world can now trace how this Colossus of erudition, day by day, and year by year, prepared himself for some vast work.

Gibbon has furnished a new idea in the art of reading! We ought, says he, not to attend to the *order of our books, so much as of our thoughts*. "The perusal of a particular work gives birth perhaps to ideas unconnected with the subject it treats; I pursue these ideas, and quit my proposed plan of reading." Thus in the midst of Homer he read Longinus; a chapter of Longinus led to an epistle of Pliny; and having finished Longinus, he followed the train of his ideas of the sublime and beautiful, in the *Inquiry* of Burke, and concluded with comparing the ancient with the modern Longinus. Of all our popular writers the most experienced reader was Gibbon, and he offers an important advice to an author engaged on a particular subject: "I suspended my perusal of any new book on the subject till I had reviewed all that I knew, or believed, or had thought on it, that I might be qualified to discern how much the authors added to my original stock."

These are valuable hints to students, and such have been practised by others. Ancillon was a very ingenious student; he seldom read a book throughout without reading in his progress many others; his library-table was always covered with a number of books, for the most part open: this variety of authors bred no confusion; they all assisted to throw light on the same topic; he was not disgusted by frequently seeing the same thing in different writers; their opinions were so many new strokes, which completed the ideas which he had conceived. The celebrated Father Paul studied in the same manner. He never passed over an interesting subject till he had confronted a variety of authors. In historical researches he never would advance, till he had fixed, once for all, the places, time, and opinions—a mode of study which appears very dilatory, but in the end will make a great saving of time, and labour of mind: those who have not pursued this method are all their lives at a loss to settle their opinions and their belief, from the want of having once brought them to such a test.

I shall now offer a plan of Historical Study, and a calculation of the necessary time it will occupy, without specifying the authors; as I only propose to animate a young student, who feels he has not to number the days of a patriarch, that he should not be alarmed at the vast labyrinth historical researches present to his eye. If we look into public libraries, more than thirty thousand volumes of history may be found.

Lenglet du Fresnoy, one of the greatest readers, calculated that he could not read, with satisfaction, more than ten hours a day, and ten pages in folio an hour; which makes one hundred pages every day. Supposing each volume to contain one thousand pages, every month would amount to three volumes, which make thirty-six volumes in folio in the year. In fifty years a student could only read eighteen hundred volumes in folio. All this, too, supposing uninterrupted health, and an intelligence as rapid as the eyes of the laborious researcher. A man can hardly study to advantage till past twenty, and at fifty his eyes will be dimmed, and his head stuffed with much reading that should never be read. His fifty years for eighteen hundred volumes are reduced to thirty years, and one thousand volumes! And, after all, the universal historian must resolutely face thirty thousand volumes!

But to cheer the historiographer, he shows, that a public library is only necessary to be consulted; it is in our private closet where should be found those few writers who direct us to their rivals, without jealousy, and mark, in the vast career of time, those who are worthy to instruct posterity. His calculation proceeds on this plan, that *six hours* a day, and the term of *ten years*, are sufficient to pass over, with utility, the immense field of history.

He calculates an alarming extent of historical ground.

For a knowledge of Sacred History he gives . . . 3 months.
Ancient Egypt, Babylon, and Assyria, modern Assyria
    or Persia . . . . 1 do.
Greek History . . . . 6 do.
Roman History by the moderns . . . . . . 7 do.
Roman History by the original writers . . . 6 do.
Ecclesiastical History, general and particular . . . 30 do.
Modern History . . . . 24 do.
To this may be added for recurrences and re-perusals 48 do.

The total will amount to 10½ years.

Thus, in *ten years and a half*, a student in history has obtained an universal knowledge, and this on a plan which permits as much leisure as every student would choose to indulge.

As a specimen of Du Fresnoy's calculations, take that of Sacred History.

For reading Père Calmet's learned dissertations in
the order he points out . . . . . . } 12 days.
For Père Calmet's History, in 2 vols. 4to. (now in 4) . . 12
For Prideaux's History 10
For Josephus 12
For Basnage's History of the Jews 20

In all 66 days.

He allows, however, ninety days for obtaining a sufficient knowledge of Sacred History.

In reading this sketch, we are scarcely surprised at the erudition of a Gibbon; but having admired that erudition, we perceive the necessity of such a plan, if we would not learn what we have afterwards to unlearn.

A plan, like the present, even in a mind which should feel itself incapable of the exertion, will not be regarded without that reverence we feel for genius animating such industry. This scheme of study, though it may never be rigidly pursued, will be found excellent. Ten years' labour of happy diligence may render a student capable of consigning to posterity a history as universal in its topics, as that of the historian who led to this investigation.

Introducers of Exotic Flowers, Fruits, etc.

THERE HAS been a class of men whose patriotic affection, or whose general benevolence, have been usually defrauded of the gratitude their country owes them: these have been the introducers of new flowers, new plants, and new roots into Europe; the greater part which we now enjoy was drawn from the luxuriant climates of Asia, and the profusion which now covers our land originated in the most anxious nursing, and were the gifts of individuals. Monuments are reared, and medals struck, to commemorate events and names, which are less deserving our regard than those who have transplanted into the colder gardens of the North the rich fruits, the beautiful flowers, and the succulent pulse and roots of more favoured spots; and carrying into their own country, as it were, another Nature, they have, as old Gerard well expresses it, "laboured with the soil to make it fit for the plants, and with the plants to make them delight in the soil."

There is no part of the characters of PEIRESC and EVELYN,

accomplished as they are in so many, which seems more delightful to me, than their enthusiasm for the garden, the orchard, and
the forest.

Peiresc, whose literary occupations admitted of no interrup-
tion, and whose universal correspondence throughout the habita-
ble globe was more than sufficient to absorb his studious life, yet
was the first man, as Gassendus relates in his interesting manner,
whose incessant inquiries procured a great variety of jessamines;
those from China, whose leaves, always green, bear a clay-
coloured flower, and a delicate perfume; the American, with a
crimson-coloured, and the Persian, with a violet-coloured flower;
and the Arabian, whose tendrils he delighted to train over "the
banqueting-house in his garden"; and of fruits, the orange-trees
with a red and parti-coloured flower; the medlar; the rough
cherry without stone; the rare and luxurious vines of Smyrna
and Damascus; and the fig-tree called Adam's, whose fruit by its
size was conjectured to be that with which the spies returned
from the land of Canaan. Gassendus describes the transports of
Peiresc, when the sage beheld the Indian ginger growing green
in his garden, and his delight in grafting the myrtle on the musk
vine, that the experiment might show us the myrtle wine of
the ancients. But transplanters, like other inventors, are sometimes baffled in their delightful enterprises; and we are told of
Peiresc's deep regret when he found that the Indian cocoa nut
would only bud, and then perish in the cold air of France, while
the leaves of the Egyptian papyrus refused to yield him their
vegetable paper. But it was his garden which propagated the
exotic fruits and flowers, which he transplanted into the French
king's, and into Cardinal Barberini's, and the curious in Europe;
and these occasioned a work on the manuring of flowers by
Ferrarius, a botanical Jesuit, who there described these novelties
to Europe.

Had Evelyn only composed the great work of his *Sylva, or a
Discourse of Forest Trees,* his name would have excited the
gratitude of posterity. The voice of the patriot exults in the
dedication to Charles II. prefixed to one of the later editions. "I
need not acquaint your majesty, how many millions of timber-
trees, besides infinite others, have been propagated and planted
throughout your vast dominions, at the instigation and by the
sole direction of this work, because your majesty has been pleased
to own it publicly for my encouragement." And surely while
Britain retains her awful situation among the nations of Europe,
the *Sylva* of Evelyn will endure with her triumphant oaks. It was

a retired philosopher who aroused the genius of the nation, and who, casting a prophetic eye towards the age in which we live, contributed to secure our sovereignty of the seas. The present navy of Great Britain has been constructed with the oaks which the genius of Evelyn planted!

Animated by a zeal truly patriotic, De Serres in France, 1599, composed a work on the art of raising silk-worms, and dedicated it to the municipal body of Paris, to excite the inhabitants to cultivate mulberry-trees. The work at first produced a strong sensation, and many planted mulberry-trees in the vicinity of Paris; but as they were not yet used to raise and manage the silk-worm, they reaped nothing but their trouble for their pains. They tore up the mulberry-trees they had planted, and, in spite of De Serres, asserted that the northern climate was not adapted for the rearing of that tender insect. The great Sully, from his hatred of all objects of luxury, countenanced the popular clamour, and crushed the rising enterprise of De Serres. The monarch was wiser than the minister. The book had made sufficient noise to reach the ear of Henry IV.; who desired the author to draw up a memoir on the subject, from which the king was induced to plant mulberry-trees in all the royal gardens; and having imported the eggs of silk-worms from Spain, this patriotic monarch gave up his orangeries, which he considered but as his private gratification, for that leaf which, converted into silk, became a part of the national wealth. It is to De Serres, who introduced the plantations of mulberry-trees, that the commerce of France owes one of her staple commodities; and although the patriot encountered the hostility of the prime minister, and the hasty prejudices of the populace in his own day, yet his name at this moment is fresh in the hearts of his fellow-citizens; for I have just received a medal, the gift of a literary friend from Paris, which bears his portrait, with the reverse, *"Société de l'Agriculture du Département de la Seine."* It was struck in 1807. The same honour is the right of Evelyn from the British nation.

There was a period when the spirit of plantation was prevalent in this kingdom; it probably originated from the ravages of the soldiery during the civil wars. A man, whose retired modesty has perhaps obscured his claims on our regard, the intimate friend of the great spirits of that age, by birth a Pole, but whose mother had probably been an Englishwoman, Samuel Hartlib, to whom Milton addressed his tract on education, published every manuscript he collected on the subjects of horticulture and agriculture. The public good he effected attracted the notice of Cromwell, who rewarded him with a pension, which after the restoration of Charles II. was suffered to lapse, and Hartlib died in utter neglect and poverty. One of his tracts is *A design for plenty by an universal planting of fruit-trees.* The project consisted in inclosing the waste lands and commons, and appointing officers, whom he calls fruiterers, or wood-wards, to see the plantations were duly attended to. The writer of this project observes on fruit, that it is a sort of provisions so natural to the taste, that the poor man and even the child will prefer it before better food, "as the story goeth," which he has preserved in these ancient and simple lines:—

> The poor man's child invited was to dine,
> With flesh of oxen, sheep, and fatted swine,
> (Far better cheer than he at home could find,)
> And yet this child to stay had little minde.
> You have, quoth he, no apple, froise, nor pie,
> Stewed pears, with bread and milk, and walnuts by.

The enthusiasm of these transplanters inspired their labours. They have watched the tender infant of their planting, till the leaf and the flowers and the fruit expanded under their hand; often indeed they have ameliorated the quality, increased the size, and even created a new species. The apricot, drawn from America, was first known in Europe in the sixteenth century: an old French writer has remarked, that it was originally not larger than a damson; our gardeners, he says, have improved it to the perfection of its present size and richness. One of these enthusiasts is noticed by Evelyn, who for forty years had in vain tried by a graft to bequeathe his name to a new fruit; but persisting on wrong principles this votary of Pomona has died without a name. We sympathize with Sir William Temple when he exultingly acquaints us with the size of his orange-trees, and with the flavour of his peaches and grapes, confessed by Frenchmen to have equalled those of Fontainebleau and Gascony, while the Italians agreed that his white figs were as good as any of that sort in Italy; and of his "having had the honour" to naturalize in this country four kinds of grapes, with his liberal distributions of cuttings from them, because "he ever thought all things of this kind the commoner they are the better."

The greater number of our exotic flowers and fruits were carefully transported into this country by many of our travelled nobility and gentry; some names have been casually preserved. The learned Linacre first brought, on his return from Italy, the damask rose; and Thomas Lord Cromwell, in the reign of Henry

VIII., enriched our fruit gardens with three different plums. In the reign of Elizabeth, Edward Grindal, afterwards Archbishop of Canterbury, returning from exile, transported here the medicinal plant of the tamarisk: the first oranges appear to have been brought into England by one of the Carew family; for a century after, they still flourished at the family seat at Beddington, in Surrey. The cherry orchards of Kent were first planted about Sittingbourne, by a gardener of Henry VIII.; and the currant-bush was transplanted when our commerce with the island of Zante was first opened in the same reign. The elder Tradescant, in 1620, entered himself on board of a privateer, armed against Morocco, solely with a view of finding an opportunity of stealing apricots into Britain: and it appears that he succeeded in his design. To Sir Walter Raleigh we have not been indebted solely for the luxury of the tobacco-plant, but for that infinitely useful root, which forms a part of our daily meal, and often the entire meal of the poor man—the potato, which deserved to have been called a *Raleigh*. Sir Anthony Ashley, of Winburne St. Giles, Dorsetshire, first planted cabbages in this country, and a cabbage at his feet appears on his monument: before his time we had them from Holland. Sir Richard Weston first brought clover grass into England from Flanders, in 1645; and the figs planted by Cardinal Pole at Lambeth, so far back as the reign of Henry VIII., are said to be still remaining there: nor is this surprising, for Spilman, who set up the first paper-mill in England, at Dartford, in 1590, is said to have brought over in his portmanteau the first two lime-trees, which he planted here, and which are still growing. The Lombardy poplar was introduced into England by the Earl of Rochford, in 1758. The first mulberry-trees in this country are now standing at Sion-house. By an Harleian MS. 6,884, we find that the first general planting of mulberries and making of silk in England was by William Stallenge, comptroller of the custom-house, and Monsieur Verton, in 1608. It is probable that Monsieur Verton transplanted this novelty from his own country, where we have seen De Serres's great attempt. Here the mulberries have succeeded better than the silk-worms.

The very names of many of our vegetable kingdom indicate their locality, from the majestic cedar of Lebanon, to the small Cos-lettuce, which came from the isle of Cos; the cherries from Cerasuntis, a city of Pontus; the peach, or *persicum,* or *mala Persica*, Persian apples, from Persia; the pistachio, or *psittacia*, is the Syrian word for that nut; the chestnut, or *châtaigne*, in French, and *castagna* in Italian, from Castagna, a town of Magnesia. Our plums coming chiefly from Syria and Damascus, the damson, or damascene plum, reminds us of its distant origin.

It is somewhat curious to observe on this subject, that there exists an unsuspected intercourse between nations, in the propagation of exotic plants. Lucullus, after the war with Mithridates, introduced cherries from Pontus into Italy; and the newly-imported fruit was found so pleasing that it was rapidly propagated, and six-and-twenty years afterwards Pliny testifies the cherry-tree passed over into Britain. Thus a victory obtained by a Roman consul over a king of Pontus, with which it would seem that Britain could not have the remotest interest, was the real occasion of our countrymen possessing cherry-orchards. Yet to our shame must it be told, that these cherries from the king of Pontus's city of Cerasuntis are not the cherries we are now eating; for the whole race of cherry-trees was lost in the Saxon period, and was only restored by the gardener of Henry VIII., who brought them from Flanders—without a word to enhance his own merits, concerning the *bellum Mithridaticum*!

A calculating political economist will little sympathize with the peaceful triumphs of those active and generous spirits, who have thus propagated the truest wealth, and the most innocent luxuries of the people. The project of a new tax, or an additional consumption of ardent spirits, or an act of parliament to put a convenient stop to population by forbidding the banns of some happy couple, would be more congenial to their researches; and they would leave without regret the names of those, whom we have held out to the grateful recollections of their country. The Romans, who, with all their errors, were at least patriots, entertained very different notions of these introducers into their country of exotic fruits and flowers. Sir William Temple has elegantly noticed the fact. "The great captains, and even consular men, who first brought them over, took pride in giving them their own names, by which they ran a great while in Rome, as in memory of some great service or pleasure they had done their country; so that not only laws and battles, but several sorts of apples and pears, were called Manlian, and Claudian, Pompeyan and Tiberian, and by several other such noble names." Pliny has paid his tribute of applause to Lucullus, for bringing cherry and nut-trees from Pontus into Italy. And we have several modern instances, where the name of the transplanter, or rearer, has been preserved in this sort of creation. Peter Collinson, the botanist, to "whom the English gardens are indebted for many new and curious species which he acquired by means of an extensive correspondence in America," was highly gratified when Linnæus baptized a plant with his name; and with great spirit asserts his honourable claim: "Something, I think, was due to me for the great number of plants and seeds I have annually procured from abroad, and you have been so good as to pay it, by giving me a species of eternity, botanically speaking; that is, a name as long as men and books endure." Such is the true animating language of these patriotic enthusiasts!

Some lines at the close of Peacham's *Emblems* give an idea of an English fruit-garden in 1612. He mentions that cherries were not long known, and gives an origin to the name of filbert.

> The Persian Peach, and fruitful Quince;*
> And there the forward Almond grew,
>> With Cherries knowne no longer time since;
> The Winter Warden, orchard's pride;
>> The *Philibert* † that loves the vale,
> And red queen apple,‡ so envide
>> Of school-boies, passing by the pale.

The Diary of a Master of the Ceremonies

OF COURT-ETIQUETTE few are acquainted with the mysteries, and still fewer have lost themselves in its labyrinth of forms. Whence its origin? Perhaps from those grave and courtly Italians, who, in their petty pompous courts, made the whole business of their effeminate days consist in *punctilios*; and, wanting realities to keep themselves alive, affected the mere shadows of life and action, in a world of these mockeries of state. It suited well the genius of a people who boasted of elementary works to teach how

---

* The *quince* comes from Sydon, a town of Crete, we are told by Le Grand, in his *Vie privée des François*, vol. i. p. 143; where may be found a list of the origin of most of our fruits.

† Peacham has here given a note. "The *filbert*, so named of *Philibert*, a king of France, who caused by arte sundry kinds to be brought forth: as did a gardener of Otranto in Italie by cloue-gilliflowers, and carnations of such colours as we now see them."

‡ The queen-apple was probably thus distinguished in compliment to Elizabeth. In Moffet's *Health's Improvement*, I find an acount of apples which are said to have been "graffed upon a mulberry-stock, and then wax thorough red as our queen apples, called by Ruellius, *Rubelliana*, and *Claudiana* by Pliny." I am told the race is not extinct; but though an apple of this description may yet be found, it seems to have sadly degenerated.

affronts were to be given, and how to be taken; and who had some reason to pride themselves in producing the *Cortegiano* of Castiglione, and the *Galateo* of Della Casa. They carried this refining temper into the most trivial circumstances, when a court was to be the theatre, and monarchs and their representatives, the actors. Precedence, and other honorary discriminations, establish the useful distinctions of ranks, and of individuals; but their minuter court forms, subtilized by Italian conceits, with an erudition of precedents, and a logic of nice distinctions, imparted a mock dignity of science to the solemn fopperies of a master of the ceremonies, who exhausted all the faculties of his soul on the equiponderance of the first place of inferior degree with the last of a superior; who turned into a political contest the placing of a chair and a stool; made a reception at the stairs'-head, or at the door, raise a clash between two rival nations; a visit out of time require a negotiation of three months; or an awkward invitation produce a sudden fit of sickness; while many rising antagonists, in the formidable shapes of ambassadors, were ready to dispatch a courier to their courts, for the omission or neglect of a single *punctilio.* The pride of nations, in pacific times, has only these means to maintain their jealousy of power: yet should not the people be grateful to the sovereign who confines his campaigns to his drawing-room: whose field-marshal is a tripping master of the ceremonies; whose stratagems are only to save the inviolability of court-etiquette; and whose battles of peace are only for precedence?

When the Earls of Holland and Carlisle, our ambassadors extraordinary to the court of France, in 1624, were at Paris, to treat of the marriage of Charles with Henrietta, and to join in a league against Spain, before they showed their propositions, they were desirous of ascertaining in what manner Cardinal Richelieu would receive them. The Marquis of Ville-aux-Clers was employed in this negotiation, which appeared at least as important as the marriage and the league. He brought for answer, that the cardinal would receive them as he did the ambassadors of the Emperor and the King of Spain; that he could not give them the right hand in his own house, because he never honoured in this way those ambassadors; but that, in reconducting them out of his room, he would go farther than he was accustomed to do, provided that they would permit him to cover this unusual proceeding with a pretext, that the others might not draw any consequences from it in their favour. Our ambassadors did not disapprove of this expedient, but they begged time to receive

the instructions of his majesty. As this would create a considerable delay, they proposed another, which would set at rest, for
the moment, the *punctilio*. They observed, that if the cardinal
would feign himself sick, they would go to see him: on which the
cardinal immediately went to bed, and an interview, so important to both nations, took place, and articles of great difficulty
were discussed, by the cardinal's bedside! When the Nuncio
Spada would have made the cardinal jealous of the pretensions
of the English ambassadors, and reproached him with yielding
his precedence to them, the cardinal denied this. "I never go
before them, it is true, but likewise I never accompany them; I
wait for them only in the chamber of audience, either seated in
the most honourable place, or standing till the table is ready: I
am always the first to speak, and the first to be seated; and besides, I have never chosen to return their visit, which has made
the Earl of Carlisle so outrageous."*

Such was the ludicrous gravity of those court etiquettes, or
punctilios, combined with political consequences, of which I
am now to exhibit a picture.

When James the First ascended the throne of his united kingdoms, and promised himself and the world long halcyon days of
peace, foreign princes, and a long train of ambassadors from
every European power, resorted to the English court. The pacific
monarch, in emulation of an office which already existed in the
courts of Europe, created that of MASTER OF THE CEREMONIES,
after the mode of France, observes Roger Coke.† This was now
found necessary to preserve the state, and allay the perpetual
jealousies of the representatives of their sovereigns. The first
officer was Sir Lewis Lewknor,‡ with an assistant, Sir John
Finett, who at length succeeded him, under Charles the First,
and seems to have been more amply blest with the genius of the
place; his soul doted on the honour of the office; and in that age
of peace and of ceremony, we may be astonished at the subtilty
of his inventive shifts and contrivances, in quieting that school
of angry and rigid boys whom he had under his care—the ambassadors of Europe!

Sir John Finett, like a man of genius, in office, and living
too in an age of diaries, has not resisted the pleasant labour

---

* *La Vie de Card. Richelieu*, anonymous, but written by J. Le Clerc,
1695, vol. i. pp. 116-125.
† *A Detection of the Court and State of England*, vol. i. p. 13.
‡ *Stowe's Annals*, p. 824.

of perpetuating his own narrative.* He has told every circumstance, with a chronological exactitude, which passed in
his province as master of the ceremonies; and when we consider that he was a busy actor amidst the whole diplomatic
corps, we shall not be surprised by discovering, in this small
volume of great curiosity, a vein of secret and authentic history; it throws a new light on many important events, in
which the historians of the times are deficient, who had not
the knowledge of this assiduous observer. But my present
purpose is not to treat Sir John with all the ceremonious
punctilios, of which he was himself the arbiter; nor to quote
him on grave subjects, which future historians may well do.

This volume contains the ruptures of a morning, and the
peace-makings of an evening; sometimes, it tells of "a
clash between the Savoy and Florence ambassadors for precedence";—now of "*questions* betwixt the Imperial and Venetian ambassadors, concerning *titles* and *visits*," how they were
to address one another, and who was to pay the first visit!—
then "the Frenchman takes *exceptions* about *placing*." This
historian of the levee now records, "that the French ambassador gets ground of the Spanish"; but soon after, so
eventful were these drawing-room politics, that a day of festival has passed away in suspense, while a privy council has
been hastily summoned, to inquire *why* the French ambassador had "a defluction of rheum in his teeth, besides a fit of
the ague," although he hoped to be present at the same festival next year! or being invited to a mask, declared "his
stomach would not agree with cold meats": "thereby pointing" (shrewdly observes Sir John) "at the invitation and
presence of the Spanish ambassador, who, at the mask *the
Christmas before,* had appeared in the first place."

Sometimes we discover our master of the ceremonies dis-
entangling himself and the lord chamberlain from the most

---

*I give the title of this rare volume, *Finetti Philoxensis: Some choice
observations of Sir John Finett, Knight, and master of the ceremonies to
the last two kings; touching the reception and precedence, the treatment
and audience, the punctilios and contests of forren ambassadors in England. Legati ligant Mundum. 1656.*" This very curious diary was published after the author's death by his friend James Howell, the well-known
writer; and Oldys, whose literary curiosity scarcely any thing in our
domestic literature has escaped, has analyzed the volume with his accustomed care. He mentions that there was a manuscript in being, more full
than the one published, of which I have not been able to learn farther.—
British Librarian, p. 163.

provoking perplexities by a clever and civil lie. Thus it happened, when the Muscovite ambassador would not yield precedence to the French nor Spaniard. On this occasion, Sir John, at his wits' end, contrived an obscure situation, in which the Russ imagined he was highly honoured, as there he enjoyed a full sight of the king's face, though he could see nothing of the entertainment itself; while the other ambassadors were so kind as "not to take exception," not caring about the Russian, from the remoteness of his country, and the little interest the court then had in Europe! But Sir John displayed even a bolder invention when the Muscovite, at his reception at Whitehall, complained that only one lord was in waiting at the stairs-head, while no one had met him in the court-yard. Sir John assured him that in England it was considered a greater honour to be received by one lord than by two!

Sir John discovered all his acumen in the solemn investigation of "Which was the upper end of the table?" Arguments and inferences were deduced from precedents quoted; but as precedents sometimes look contrary ways, this affair might still have remained *sub judice*, had not Sir John oracularly pronounced that "in spite of the chimneys in England, where the best man sits, is that end of the table." Sir John, indeed, would often take the most enlarged view of things; as when the Spanish ambassador, after hunting with the king at Theobalds, dined with his majesty in the privy-chamber, his son Don Antonio dined in the council-chamber with some of the king's attendants. Don Antonio seated himself on a stool at the end of the table. "One of the gentlemen-ushers took exception at this, being, he said, irregular and unusual, that place being ever wont to be reserved *empty for state!*" In a word, no person in the world was ever to sit on that stool; but Sir John, holding a conference before he chose to disturb the Spanish grandee, finally determined that "this was the *superstition* of a gentleman-usher, and it was therefore neglected." Thus Sir John could, at a critical moment, exert a more liberal spirit, and risk an empty stool against a little ease and quiet; which were no common occurrences with that martyr of state, a master of ceremonies!

But Sir John,—to me he is so entertaining a personage that I do not care to get rid of him,—had to overcome difficulties which stretched his fine genius on tenter-hooks. Once,

—rarely did the like unlucky accident happen to the wary master of the ceremonies,—did Sir John exceed the civility of his instructions, or rather his half-instructions. Being sent to invite the Dutch ambassador, and the States' commissioners, then a young and new government, to the ceremonies of St. George's day, they inquired whether they should have the same respect paid to them as other ambassadors? The bland Sir John, out of the milkiness of his blood, said he doubted it not. As soon, however, as he returned to the lord chamberlain, he discovered that he had been sought for up and down, to stop the invitation. The lord chamberlain said, Sir John had exceeded his commission, if he had invited the Dutchmen "to stand in the closet of the queen's side; because the Spanish ambassador would never endure them *so near him, where there was but a thin wainscot board between, and a window which might be opened*"! Sir John said gently, he had done no otherwise than he had been desired; which however the lord chamberlain, *in part*, denied, (cautious and civil!) "and I was not so unmannerly as to contest against," (supple, but uneasy!) This affair ended miserably for the poor Dutchmen. Those new republicans were then regarded with the most jealous contempt by all the ambassadors, and were just venturing on their first dancing-steps, to move among crowned heads. The Dutch now resolved not to be present; declaring they had just received an *urgent invitation*, from the Earl of Exeter, to dine at Wimbledon. A piece of *supercherie* to save appearances; probably the happy contrivance of the combined geniuses of the lord chamberlain and the master of the ceremonies!

I will now exhibit some curious details from these archives of fantastical state, and paint a courtly world, where politics and civility seem to have been at perpetual variance.

When the Palatine arrived in England to marry Elizabeth, the only daughter of James the First, "the feasting and jollity" of the court were interrupted by the discontent of the archduke's ambassador, of which these were the material points:—

Sir John waited on him, to honour with his presence the solemnity on the second or third days, either to dinner or supper, or both.

The archduke's ambassador paused: with a troubled countenance inquiring whether the Spanish ambassador was invited. "I answered, answerable to my instructions in case of such demand, that he was sick, and could not be there. He was yesterday, quoth he, so well, as that the offer might have very well been made him, and perhaps accepted."

To this, Sir John replied, that the French and Venetian ambassadors holding between them one course of correspondence, and the Spanish and the archduke's another, their invitations had been usually joint.

This the archduke's ambassador denied; and affirmed that they had been separately invited to Masques, &c. but he had never;—that France had always yielded precedence to the archduke's predecessors, when they were. but Dukes of Burgundy, of which he was ready to produce "ancient proofs"; and that Venice was a mean republic, a sort of burghers, and a handful of territory, compared to his monarchical sovereign: —and to all this he added, that the Venetian bragged of the frequent favours he had received.

Sir John returns in great distress to the lord chamberlain and his majesty. A solemn declaration is drawn up, in which James I. most gravely laments that the archduke's ambassador has taken this offence; but his majesty offers these most cogent arguments in his own favour: that the Venetian had announced to his majesty, that his republic had ordered his men new liveries on the occasion, an honour, he adds, not usual with princes—the Spanish ambassador, not finding himself well for the first day (because, by the way, he did not care to dispute precedence with the Frenchman), his majesty conceiving that the solemnity of the marriage being one continued act through divers days, it admitted neither *prius* nor *posterius*: and then James proves too much, by bolding asserting, that the *last day* should be taken for the *greatest day*!—as in other cases, for instance, in that of Christmas, where Twelfth-day, the last day is held as the greatest.

But the French and Venetian ambassadors, so envied by the Spanish and the archduke's, were themselves not less chary, and crustily fastidious. The insolent Frenchman first attempted to take precedence of the Prince of Wales; and the Venetian stood upon this point, that they should sit on chairs, though the prince had but a stool; and, particularly, that the carver should not stand before him! "But," adds Sir John, "neither of them prevailed in their reasonless pretences."

Nor was it peaceable even at the nuptial dinner, which closed with the following catastrophe of etiquette:—

Sir John having ushered among the countesses the lady of
the French ambassador, he left her to the ranging of the lord
chamberlain, who ordered she should be placed at the table
next beneath the countesses, and above the baronesses. But
lo! "The Viscountess of Effingham standing to her *woman's
right,* and possessed already of her proper place (as she called
it) would not remove lower, so *held the hand* of the ambas-
sadrice, till after dinner, when the French ambassador, informed of the difference and opposition, called out for his
wife's coach!" With great trouble, the French lady was persuaded to stay, the Countess of Kildare and the Viscountess
of Haddington making no scruple of yielding their places.
Sir John, unbending his gravity, facetiously adds, "The Lady
of Effingham, in the interim, forbearing (with rather too much
than little stomach) both her supper and her company."
This spoilt child of quality, tugging at the French ambassa-
dress to keep her down, mortified to be seated at the side of
the Frenchwoman that day, frowning and frowned on, and
going supperless to bed, passed the wedding-day of the Palatine and Princess Elizabeth, like a cross girl on a form.

One of the most subtle of these men of *punctilio,* and the
most troublesome, was the Venetian ambassador; for it was
his particular aptitude to find fault, and pick out jealousies
among all the others of his body.

On the marriage of the Earl of Somerset, the Venetian
was invited to the masque, but not the dinner, as last year
the reverse had occurred. The Frenchman, who drew always
with the Venetian, at this moment chose to act by himself
on the watch of precedence, jealous of the Spaniard newly
arrived. When invited, he inquired if the Spanish ambassador
was to be there? and humbly beseeched his majesty to be
excused, from indisposition. We shall now see Sir John put
into the most lively action by the subtle Venetian.

"I was scarcely back at court with the French ambassador's
answer, when I was told that a gentleman from the Venetian
ambassador had been to seek me; who, having at last found
me, said that his lord desired me, that if ever I would
do him favour, I would take the pains to come to him
instantly. I, winding the cause to be some new buzz gotten
into his brain, from some intelligence he had from the French
of that morning's proceeding, excused my present coming,
that I might take further instructions from the lord chamber-

lain; wherewith, as soon as I was sufficiently armed, I went to the Venetian."

But the Venetian would not confer with Sir John, though he sent for him in such a hurry, except in presence of his own secretary. Then the Venetian desired Sir John to repeat the *words* of his *invitation,* and *those* also of his own *answer!* which poor Sir John actually did! For he adds, "I yielded, but not without discovering my insatisfaction to be so peremptorily pressed on, as if he had meant to trip me."

The Venetian having thus compelled Sir John to con over both invitation and answer, gravely complimented him on his correctness to a tittle! Yet still was the Venetian not in less trouble: and now he confessed that the king had given a formal invitation to the French ambassador,—and not to him!

This was a new stage in this important negotiation: it tried all the diplomatic sagacity of Sir John to extract a discovery; and which was, that the Frenchman had, indeed, conveyed the intelligence secretly to the Venetian.

Sir John now acknowledged that he had suspected as much when he received the message; and not to be taken by surprise, he had come prepared with a long apology, ending, for peace's sake, with the same formal invitation for the Venetian. Now the Venetian insisted again that Sir John should deliver the invitation in the *same precise words* as it had been given to the Frenchman. Sir John, with his never-failing courtly docility, performed it to a syllable. Whether both parties during all these proceedings could avoid moving a risible muscle at one another, our grave authority records not.

The Venetian's final answer seemed now perfectly satisfactory, declaring he would not excuse his absence as the Frenchman had, on the most frivolous pretence; and farther, he expressed his high satisfaction with last year's substantial testimony of the royal favour, in the public honours conferred on him, and regretted that the quiet of his majesty should be so frequently disturbed by these *punctilios* about invitations, which so often "over-thronged his guests at the feast."

Sir John now imagined that all was happily concluded, and was retiring with the sweetness of a dove, and the quietness of a mouse, to fly to the lord chamberlain, when behold the Venetian would not relinquish his hold, but turned on him "with the reading of another scruple, *et hinc illæ lachrymæ!* asking whether the archduke's ambassador was also invited?"

Poor Sir John, to keep himself clear "from categorical as-
severations," declared "he could not resolve him." Then the
Venetian observed, "Sir John was dissembling! and he hoped
and imagined that Sir John had in his instructions, that he
was first to have gone to him (the Venetian), and on his return to the archduke's ambassador." Matters now threatened
to be as irreconcilable as ever, for it seems the Venetian was
standing on the point of precedency with the archduke's ambassador. The political Sir John, wishing to gratify the Venetian
at no expense, adds, "he thought it ill manners to mar a belief
of an ambassador's making," and so allowed him to think that
he had been invited before the archduke's ambassador!

This Venetian proved himself to be, to the great torment
of Sir John, a stupendous genius in his own way; ever on
the watch to be treated *al paro di teste coronate*—equal with
crowned heads; and, when at a tilt, refused being placed
among the ambassadors of Savoy and the States-general, &c.,
while the Spanish and French ambassadors were seated alone
on the opposite side. The Venetian declared that this would
be a diminution of his quality; *the first place of an inferior
degree being ever held worse than the last of a superior.* This
refined observation delighted Sir John, who dignifies it as an
axiom, yet afterwards came to doubt it with a *sed de hoc
quære*—query this! If it be true in politics, it is not so in
common sense, according to the proverbs of both nations; for
the honest English declares, that "Better be the *head* of the
yeomanry than the *tail* of the gentry"; while the subtle
Italian has it, "*È meglio esser testa di Luccio, che coda di
Storione*"; "better be the head of a pike than the tail of a
sturgeon." But before we quit Sir John, let us hear him in
his own words, reasoning with fine critical tact, which he
undoubtedly possessed, on right and left hands, but reasoning
with infinite modesty as well as genius. Hear this sage of
punctilios, this philosopher of courtesies.

"The Axiom before delivered by the Venetian ambassador
was *judged* upon *discourse* I had with *some of understanding,*
to be of value in a *distinct company, but might be otherwise
in a joint assembly!*" And then Sir John, like a philosophical
historian, explores some great public event—"As at the conclusion of the peace at Vervins (the only part of the peace
he cared about,) the French and Spanish meeting, contended
for precedence—who should sit at the right hand of the pope's

legate: an expedient was found, of sending into France for
the pope's *nuncio* residing there, who, seated at the right hand
of the said *legate,* (the legate himself sitting at the table's
end,) the French ambassador being offered the choice of the
next place, he took that at the legate's left hand, leaving the
second at the right hand to the Spanish, who, taking it, persuaded himself to have the better of it; *sed de hoc quære*." How
modestly, yet how shrewdly insinuated!

So much, if not too much, of the Diary of a Master of the
Ceremonies; where the important personages strangely contrast
with the frivolity and foppery of their actions.

By this work it appears that all foreign ambassadors were
entirely entertained, for their diet, lodgings, coaches, with all
their train, at the cost of the English monarch, and on their
departure received customary presents of considerable value;
from 1,000 to 5,000 ounces of gilt plate; and in more cases
than one, the meanest complaints were made by the ambassadors, about short allowances. That the foreign ambassadors
in return made presents to the masters of the ceremonies,
from thirty to fifty "pieces," or in plate or jewels; and some
so grudgingly, that Sir John Finett often vents his indignation, and commemorates the indignity. As thus,—on one of
the Spanish ambassadors-extraordinary waiting at Deal for
three days, Sir John, "expecting the wind with the patience
of an *hungry entertainment* from a *close-handed ambassador,*
as his *present to me* at his parting from Dover being but an
old gilt livery pot, that had lost his fellow, not worth above
twelve pounds, accompanied with two pair of Spanish gloves
to make it almost thirteen, to my shame and his." When he
left this scurvy ambassador-extraordinary to his fate aboard
the ship, he exults that "the cross-winds held him in the Downs
almost a seven-night before they would blow him over."

From this mode of receiving ambassadors, two inconveniences resulted; their perpetual jars of *punctilios,* and
their singular intrigues to obtain precedence, which so completely harassed the patience of the most pacific sovereign,
that James was compelled to make great alterations in his
domestic comforts, and was perpetually embroiled in the most
ridiculous contests. At length Charles I. perceived the great
charge of these embassies, ordinary and extraordinary, often
on frivolous pretences; and with an empty treasury, and
an uncomplying parliament, he grew less anxious for such

ruinous honours.* He gave notice to foreign ambassadors, that he should not any more "defray their diet, nor provide coaches for them," &c. "This frugal purpose" cost Sir John many altercations, who seems to view it as the glory of the British monarch being on the wane. The unsettled state of Charles was appearing in 1636, by the querulous narrative of the master of the ceremonies; the etiquettes of the court were disturbed by the erratic course of its great star; and the master of the ceremonies was reduced to keep blank letters to superscribe, and address to any nobleman who was to be found, from the absence of the great officers of state. On this occasion the ambassador of the Duke of Mantua, who had long desired his parting audience, when the king objected to the unfitness of the place he was then in, replied, that, "if it were under a tree, it should be to him as a palace."

Yet although we smile at this science of etiquette and these rigid forms of ceremony, when they were altogether discarded a great statesman lamented them, and found the inconvenience and mischief in the political consequences which followed their neglect. Charles II., who was no admirer of these regulated formalities of court etiquette, seems to have broken up the pomp and pride of the former master of the ceremonies; and the grave and great chancellor of human nature, as Warburton calls Clarendon, censured and felt all the inconveniences of this open intercourse of an ambassador with the king. Thus he observed in the case of the Spanish ambassador, who, he writes, "took the advantage of the license of the court, where no rules or formalities were yet

---

* Charles I. had, however, adopted them, and long preserved the stateliness of his court with foreign powers, as appears by these extracts from manuscript letters of the time:

Mr. Mead writes to Sir M. Stuteville, July 25, 1629.

"His majesty was wont to answer the French ambassador in his own language; now he speaks in English, and by an *interpreter*. And so doth Sir Thomas Edmondes to the French king; contrary to the ancient custom: so that altho' of late we have not equalled them in arms, yet now we shall equal them in ceremonies."

Oct. 31, 1628.

"This day fortnight, the States' ambassador going to visit my lord treasurer about some business, whereas his lordship was wont always to bring them but to the stairs' head, he then, after a great deal of courteous resistance on the ambassador's part, attended him through the hall and courtyard, even to the very boot of his coache"—*Sloane MSS.* 4,178.

established, (and to which the king himself was not enough inclined,) but all doors open to all persons; which the ambassador finding he made himself a domestic, came to the king at all hours, and spake to him when, and as long as he would, without any ceremony, or *desiring an audience according to the old custom*; but came into the bed-chamber while the king was dressing himself, and mingled in all discourses with the same freedom he would use in his own. And from this never-heard-of license, introduced by the *French* and the *Spaniard at this time, without any dislike in the king though not permitted in any court in Christendom,* many inconveniences and mischiefs broke in, which could never after be shut out."*

Ancient Cookery, and Cooks

THE MEMORABLE grand dinner given by the classical doctor in *Peregrine Pickle,* has indisposed our tastes for the cookery of the ancients; but, since it is often "the cooks who spoil the broth," we cannot be sure but that even "the black Lacedæmonian," stirred by the spear of a Spartan, might have had a poignancy for him, which did not happen at the more recent classical banquet.

The cookery of the ancients must have been superior to our humbler art, since they could find dainties in the tough membraneous parts of the matrices of a sow, and the flesh of young hawks, and a young ass. The elder Pliny records, that one man had studied the art of fattening snails with paste so successfully, that the shells of some of his snails would contain many quarts.† The same monstrous taste fed up those prodigious goose livers; a taste still prevailing in Italy. Swine were fattened with whey and figs; and even fish in their ponds were increased by such artificial means. Our prize oxen might have astonished a Roman, as much as one of their crammed peacocks would ourselves. Gluttony produces monsters, and turns away from nature to feed on unwholesome meats. The flesh of young foxes about au-

---

* *Clarendon's Life,* vol. ii. p. 160.
† *Nat. Hist.* lib. ix. 56.

tumn, when they fed on grapes, is praised by Galen; and
Hippocrates equals the flesh of puppies to that of birds.
The humorous Dr. King, who has touched on this subject,
suspects that many of the Greek dishes appear charming
from their mellifluous terminations, resounding with a *floios*
and *toios*. Dr. King's descriptions of the Virtuoso Bentivog-
lio or Bentley, with his "Bill of Fare" out of Athenæus,
probably suggested to Smollett his celebrated scene.

The numerous descriptions of ancient cookery which Athenæus has preserved indicate an unrivalled dexterity and re-
finement: and the ancients, indeed, appear to have raised the
culinary art into a science, and dignified cooks into professors.
They had writers who exhausted their erudition and ingenuity in verse and prose; while some were proud to immortalize
their names by the invention of a poignant sauce, or a popular *gâteau*. Apicius, a name immortalized, and now synonymous with a gorger, was the inventor of cakes called Apicians;
and one Aristoxenes, after many unsuccessful combinations,
at length hit on a peculiar manner of seasoning hams, thence
called Aristoxenians. The name of a late nobleman among
ourselves is thus invoked every day.

Of these *Eruditæ gulæ* Archestratus, a culinary philosopher,
composed an epic or didactic poem on good eating. His
Gastrology became the creed of the epicures, and its pathos
appears to have made what is so expressively called "their
mouths water." The idea has been recently successfully imitated
by a French poet. Archestratus thus opens his subject:—

> I write these precepts for immortal Greece,
> That round a table delicately spread,
> Or three, or four, may sit in choice repast,
> Or five at most. Who otherwise shall dine,
> Are like a troop marauding for their prey.

The elegant Romans declared that a repast should not
consist of less in number than the Graces, nor of more than the
Muses. They had, however, a quaint proverb, which Alexander
ab Alexandro has preserved, not favourable even to so large
a dinner-party as nine; it turns on a play of words:—

> Septem convivium, novem convicium facere.*

An elegant Roman, meeting a friend, regretted he could
not invite him to dinner, "because my *number* is complete."

---

* *Genial. Dierum*, II. 283, Lug. 1673. The writer has collected in this
chapter a variety of curious particulars on this subject.

When Archestratus acknowledges that some things are for the winter, and some for the summer, he consoles himself, that though we cannot have them at the same time, yet, at least, we may talk about them at all times.

This great genius seems to have travelled over land and seas that he might critically examine the things themselves, and improve, with new discoveries, the table-luxuries. He indicates the places for peculiar edibles and exquisite potables; and promulgates his precepts with the zeal of a sublime legislator, who is dictating a code designed to ameliorate the imperfect state of society.

A philosopher worthy to bear the title of cook, or a cook worthy to be a philosopher, according to the numerous curious passages scattered in Athenæus, was an extraordinary genius, endowed not merely with a natural aptitude, but with all acquired accomplishments. The philosophy, or the metaphysics, of cookery appears in the following passage:—

> "Know then, the COOK, a dinner that's bespoke,
> Aspiring to prepare, with prescient zeal
> Should know the tastes and humours of the guests;
> For if he drudges through the common work,
> Thoughtless of manner, careless what the place
> And seasons claim, and what the favouring hour
> Auspicious to his genius may present,
> Why, standing 'midst the multitude of men,
> Call we this plodding *fricasseer* a Cook?
> Oh differing far! and one is not the other!
> We call indeed the *general* of an army
> Him who is charged to lead it to the war;
> But the true general is the man whose mind,
> Mastering events, anticipates, combines;
> Else is he but a *leader* to his men!
> With our profession thus: the first who comes
> May with a humble toil, or slice, or chop,
> Prepare the ingredients, and around the fire
> Obsequious, him I call a fricasseer!
> But ah! the cook a brighter glory crowns!
> Well skill'd is he to know the place, the hour,
> Him who invites, and him who is invited,
> What fish in season makes the market rich,
> A choice delicious rarity! I know
> That all, we always find; but always all,
> Charms not the palate, critically fine.
> Archestratus, in culinary lore
> Deep for his time, in this more learned age
> Is wanting; and full oft he surely talks
> Of what he never ate. Suspect his page,

Nor load thy genius with a barren precept.
Look not in books for what some idle sage
So idly raved; for cookery is an art
Comporting ill with rhetoric; 'tis an art
Still changing, and of momentary triumph!
Know on thyself thy genius must depend.
All books of cookery, all helps of art,
All critic learning, all commenting notes,
Are vain, if, void of genius, thou wouldst cook!"
  The culinary sage thus spoke; his friend
Demands, "Where is the ideal cook thou paint'st?"
"Lo, I the man!" the savouring sage replied.
"Now be thine eyes the witness of my art!
This tunny drest, so odorous shall steam,
The spicy sweetness so shall steal thy sense,
That thou in a delicious reverie
Shalt slumber heavenly o'er the Attic dish!"

In another passage a Master-Cook conceives himself to be
a pupil of Epicurus, whose favourite but ambiguous axiom,
that "Voluptuousness is the sovereign good," was interpreted
by the *bon-vivans* of antiquity in the plain sense.

MASTER COOK
Behold in me a pupil of the school
Of the sage Epicurus.

FRIEND
  Thou a sage!

MASTER COOK
Ay! Epicurus too was sure a cook,
And knew the sovereign good. Nature his study,
While practice perfected his theory.
Divine philosophy alone can teach
The difference which the fish *Glociscus** shows
In winter and in summer: how to learn

---

* The commentators have not been able always to assign known names
to the great variety of fish, particularly sea-fish, the ancients used, many
of which we should revolt at. One of their dainties was a shell-fish, prickly
like a hedge-hog, called *Echinus*. They ate the dog-fish, the star-fish, por-
poises or sea-hogs, and even seals. In Dr. Moffet's "regiment of diet,"
an exceeding curious writer of the reign of Elizabeth, republished by Oldys,
may be found an ample account of the "sea-fish" used by the ancients.—
Whatever the *Glociscus* was, it seems to have been of great size, and a
shell-fish, as we may infer from the following curious passage in Athenæus.
A father, informed that his son is leading a dissolute life, enraged, remon-
strates with his pedagogue:—"Knave! thou art the fault! hast thou ever
known a philosopher yield himself so entirely to the pleasures thou tellest
me of?" The pedagogue replies by a Yes! and that the sages of the
portico are great drunkards, and none know better than they *how to attack
a Glociscus*.

Which fish to choose, when set the Pleiades,
And at the solstice. 'Tis change of seasons
Which threats mankind, and shakes their changeful frame.
This dost thou comprehend? Know, what we use
In season, is most seasonably good!

FRIEND

Most learned cook, who can observe these canons?

MASTER COOK

And therefore phlegm and colics make a man
A most indecent guest. The aliment
Dress'd in my kitchen is true aliment;
Light of digestion easily it passes;
The chyle soft-blending from the juicy food
Repairs the solids.

FRIEND

                    Ah! the chyle! the solids!
Thou new Democritus! thou sage of medicine!
Versed in the mysteries of the Iatric art!

MASTER COOK

Now mark the blunders of our vulgar cooks!
See them prepare a dish of various fish,
Showering profuse the pounded Indian grain,
An overpowering vapour, gallimaufry
A multitude confused of pothering odours!
But, know, the genius of the art consists
To make the nostrils feel each scent distinct;
And not in washing plates to free from smoke.
I never enter in my kitchen, I!
But sit apart, and in the cool direct,
Observant of what passes, scullions' toil.

FRIEND

          What dost thou there?

MASTER COOK

                    I guide the mighty whole;
Explore the causes, prophesy the dish.
'Tis thus I speak: "Leave, leave that ponderous ham;
Keep up the fire, and lively play the flame
Beneath those lobster patties; patient here,
Fix'd as a statue, skim, incessant skim.
Steep well this small Glociscus in its sauce,
And boil that sea-dog in a cullender;
This eel requires more salt and marjoram;
Roast well that piece of kid on either side
Equal; that sweetbread boil not over much."
'Tis thus, my friend, I make the concert play.

FRIEND

O man of science! 'tis thy babble kills!

MASTER COOK

And then no useless dish my table crowds;
Harmonious ranged, and consonantly just.

FRIEND

Ha! what means this?

MASTER COOK

               Divinest music all!
As in a concert instruments resound,
My ordered dishes in their courses chime.
So Epicurus dictated the art
Of sweet voluptuousness, and ate in order,
Musing delighted o'er the sovereign good!
Let raving Stoics in a labyrinth
Run after virtue; they shall find no end.
Thou, what is foreign to mankind, abjure.

FRIEND

Right honest Cook! thou wak'st me from their dreams!

Another cook informs us that he adapts his repasts to his personages.

I like to see the faces of my guests,
To feed them as their age and station claim.
My kitchen changes, as my guests inspire
The various spectacle; for lovers now,
Philosophers, and now for financiers.
If my young royster be a mettled spark,
Who melts an acre in a savoury dish
To charm his mistress, scuttle-fish and crabs,
And all the shelly race, with mixture due
Of cordials filtered, exquisitely rich.
For such a host, my friend! expends much more
In oil than cotton; solely studying love!
To a philosopher, that animal,
Voracious, solid ham and bulky feet;
But to the financier, with costly niceness,
Glociscus rare, or rarity more rare.
Insensible the palate of old age,
More difficult than the soft lips of youth
To move, I put much mustard in their dish;
With quickening sauces make their stupor keen,
And lash the lazy blood that creeps within.

Another genius, in tracing the art of cookery, derives from it nothing less than the origin of society; and I think that some philosopher has defined man to be "a cooking animal."

COOK

The art of cookery drew us gently forth
From that ferocious life, when void of faith

The Anthropophaginian ate his brother!
To cookery we owe well-ordered states,
Assembling men in dear society.
Wild was the earth, man feasting upon man,
When one of nobler sense and milder heart
First sacrificed an animal; the flesh
Was sweet; and man then ceased to feed on man!
And something of the rudeness of those times
The priest commemorates; for to this day
He roasts the victim's entrails without salt.
In those dark times, beneath the earth lay hid
The precious salt, that gold of cookery!
But when its particles the palate thrill'd,
The source of seasonings, charm of cookery! came.
They served a paunch with rich ingredients stored;
And tender kid, within two covering plates,
Warm melted in the mouth. So art improved!
At length a miracle not yet perform'd,
They minced the meat, which roll'd in herbage soft,
Nor meat nor herbage seem'd, but to the eye
And to the taste, the counterfeited dish
Mimick'd some curious fish; invention rare!
Then every dish was season'd more and more,
Salted, or sour, or sweet, and mingled oft
Oatmeal and honey. To enjoy the meal
Men congregated in the populous towns,
And cities flourish'd which we cooks adorn'd
With all the pleasures of domestic life.

An arch-cook insinuates that there remain only two "pillars of the state," besides himself, of the school of Sinon, one of the great masters of the condimenting art. Sinon, we are told, applied the elements of all the arts and sciences to this favourite one. Natural philosophy could produce a secret seasoning for a dish; and architecture the art of conducting the smoke out of a chimney: which, says he, if ungovernable, makes a great difference in the dressing. From the military science he derived a sublime idea of order; drilling the under cooks, marshalling the kitchen, hastening one, and making another a sentinel. We find, however, that a portion of this divine art, one of the professors acknowledges to be vapouring and bragging!—a seasoning in this art, as well as in others. A cook ought never to come unaccompanied by all the pomp and parade of the kitchen: with a scurvy appearance, he will be turned away at sight; for all have eyes, but few only understanding.

Another occult part of this profound mystery, besides vapouring, consisted, it seems, in filching. Such is the counsel of a

patriarch to an apprentice! a precept which contains a truth for
all ages of cookery.

> Carian! time well thy ambidextrous part,
> Nor always filch. It was but yesterday,
> Blundering, they nearly caught thee in the fact;
> None of thy balls had livers, and the guests,
> In horror, pierced their airy emptiness.
> Not even the brains were there, thou brainless hound!
> If thou art hired among the middling class,
> Who pay thee freely, be thou honourable!
> But for this day, where now we go to cook,
> E'en cut the master's throat for all I care;
> "A word to th' wise," and show thyself my scholar!
> There thou mayst filch and revel; all may yield
> Some secret profit to thy sharking hand.
> 'Tis an old miser gives a sordid dinner,
> And weeps o'er every sparing dish at table;
> Then if I do not find thou dost devour
> All thou canst touch, e'en to the very coals
> I will disown thee! Lo! old Skin-flint comes;
> In his dry eyes what parsimony stares!

These cooks of the ancients, who appear to have been hired
for a grand dinner, carried their art to the most whimsical perfection. They were so dexterous as to be able to serve up a whole
pig boiled on one side, and roasted on the other. The cook who
performed this feat defies his guests to detect the place where the
knife had separated the animal, or how it was contrived to stuff
the belly with an olio, composed of thrushes and other birds,
slices of the matrices of a sow, the yolks of eggs, the bellies of
hens with their soft eggs, flavoured with a rich juice, and minced
meats highly spiced. When this cook is entreated to explain his
secret art, he solemnly swears by the manes of those who braved
all the dangers of the plain of Marathon, and combated at sea
at Salamis, that he will not reveal the secret that year. But of an
incident, so triumphant in the annals of the gastric art, our
philosopher would not deprive posterity of the knowledge. The
animal had been bled to death by a wound under the shoulder,
whence, after a copious effusion, the master-cook extracted the
entrails, washed them with wine, and hanging the animal by
the feet, he crammed down the throat the stuffings already prepared. Then covering the half of the pig with a paste of barley,
thickened with wine and oil, he put it in a small oven, or on a
heated table of brass, where it was gently roasted with all due
care: when the skin was browned, he boiled the other side; and
then, taking away the barley paste, the pig was served up, at

once boiled and roasted. These cooks, with a vegetable, could counterfeit the shape and the taste of fish and flesh. The king of Bithynia, in some expedition against the Scythians, in the winter, and at a great distance from the sea, had a violent long-ing for a small fish called *aphy*—a pilchard, a herring, or an anchovy. His cook cut a turnip to the perfect imitation of its shape; then fried in oil, salted, and well powdered with the grains of a dozen black poppies, his majesty's taste was so ex-quisitely deceived, that he praised the root to his guests as an excellent fish. This transmutation of vegetables into meat or fish is a province of the culinary art which we appear to have lost; yet these are *cibi innocentes*, compared with the things them-selves. No people are such gorgers of mere animal food as our own; the art of preparing vegetables, pulse, and roots, is scarcely known in this country. This cheaper and healthful food should be introduced among the common people, who neglect them from not knowing how to dress them. The peasant, for want of this skill, treads under foot the best meat in the world; and sometimes the best way of dressing it is least costly.

The gastric art must have reached to its last perfection, when we find that it had its history; and that they knew how to ascer-tain the æra of a dish with a sort of chronological exactness. The philosophers of Athenæus at table dissert on every dish, and tell us of one called *maati*, that there was a treatise composed on it; that it was first introduced at Athens, at the epocha of the Macedonian empire, but that it was undoubtedly a Thessalian invention; the most sumptuous people of all the Greeks. The *maati* was a term at length applied to any dainty, of excessive delicacy, always served the last.

But as no art has ever attained perfection without numerous admirers, and as it is the public which only can make such ex-quisite cooks, our curiosity may be excited to inquire, whether the patrons of the gastric art were as great enthusiasts as its professors.

We see they had writers who exhausted their genius on these professional topics; and books of cookery were much read: for a comic poet, quoted by Athenæus, exhibits a character exulting in having procured "The new Kitchen of Philoxenus, which," says he, "I keep for myself to read in my solitude." That these devotees to the culinary art undertook journeys to remote parts of the world, in quest of these discoveries, sufficient facts authen-ticate. England had the honour to furnish them with oysters,

which they fetched from about Sandwich. Juvenal* records, that
Montanus was so well skilled in the science of good eating, that
he could tell by the first bite whether they were English or not.
The well-known Apicius poured into his stomach an immense
fortune. He usually resided at Minturna, a town in Campania,
where he ate shrimps at a high price: they were so large, that
those of Smyrna, and the prawns of Alexandria, could not be
compared with the shrimps of Minturna. However, this luckless
epicure was informed that the shrimps in Africa were more
monstrous; and he embarks without losing a day. He encounters
a great storm, and through imminent danger arrives at the shores
of Africa. The fishermen bring him the largest for size their nets
could furnish. Apicius shakes his head: "Have you never any
larger?" he inquires. The answer was not favourable to his hopes.
Apicius rejects them, and fondly remembers the shrimps of his
own Minturna. He orders his pilot to return to Italy, and leaves
Africa with a look of contempt.

A fraternal genius was Philoxenus: he whose higher wish was
to possess a crane's neck, that he might be the longer in savouring his dainties; and who appears to have invented some expedients which might answer, in some degree, the purpose. This
impudent epicure was so little attentive to the feelings of his
brother guests, that in the hot bath he avowedly habituated himself to keep his hands in the scalding water; and even used to
gargle his throat with it, that he might feel less impediment in
swallowing the hottest dishes. He bribed the cooks to serve up
the repast smoking hot, that he might gloriously devour what
he chose before any one else could venture to touch the dish. It
seemed as if he had used his fingers to handle fire. "He is an
oven, not a man!" exclaimed a grumbling fellow-guest. Once
having embarked for Ephesus, for the purpose of eating fish, his
favourite food, he arrived at the market, and found all the stalls
empty. There was a wedding in the town, and all the fish had
been bespoken. He hastens to embrace the new-married couple,
and singing an epithalamium, the dithyrambic epicure enchanted
the company. The bridegroom was delighted by the honour of
the presence of such a poet, and earnestly requested he would
come on the morrow. "I will come, young friend, if there is no
fish at the market!"—It was this Philoxenus, who, at the table of
Dionysius, the tyrant of Sicily, having near him a small barbel,

---

* *Sat.* iv. 140.

and observing a large one near the prince, took the little one, and held it to his ear. Dionysius inquired the reason. "At present," replied the ingenious epicure, "I am so occupied by my *Galatea*," (a poem in honour of the mistress of the tyrant,) "that I wished to inquire of this little fish, whether he could give me some information about Nereus; but he is silent, and I imagine they have taken him up too young: I have no doubt that old one, opposite to you, would perfectly satisfy me." Dionysius rewarded the pleasant conceit with the large barbel.

Expression of Suppressed Opinion

A PEOPLE denied the freedom of speech or of writing, have usually left some memorials of their feelings in that silent language which addresses itself to the eye. Many ingenious inventions have been contrived, to give vent to their suppressed indignation. The voluminous grievance which they could not trust to the voice or the pen, they have carved in wood, or sculptured on stone; and have sometimes even facetiously concealed their satire among the playful ornaments designed to amuse those of whom they so fruitlessly complained! Such monuments of the suppressed feelings of the multitude are not often inspected by the historian—their minuteness escapes all eyes but those of the philosophical antiquary: nor are these satirical appearances always considered as grave authorities, which unquestionably they will be found to be by a close observer of human nature. An entertaining history of the modes of thinking, or the discontents, of a people, drawn from such dispersed efforts, in every æra, would cast a new light of secret history over many dark intervals.

Did we possess a secret history of the Saturnalia, it would doubtless have afforded some materials for the present article. In those revels of venerable radicalism, when the senate was closed, and the *Pileus*, or cap of liberty, was triumphantly worn, all things assumed an appearance contrary to what they were; and human nature, as well as human laws, might be said to have been *parodied*. Among so many whimsical regulations in favour of the licentious rabble, there was one which forbad the circulation of money; if any one offered the coin of the state, it was to be condemned as an act of madness, and the man was brought to his senses by a penitential fast for that day. An ingenious French antiquary seems to have discovered a class of wretched medals, cast in lead or copper, which formed the circulating medium of these mob lords, who, to ridicule the idea of *money*, used the basest metals, stamping them with grotesque figures, or odd devices—such as a sow; a chimerical bird; an imperator in his car, with a monkey behind him; or an old woman's head, *Acca Laurentia*, either the traditional old nurse of Romulus, or an old courtesan of the same name, who bequeathed the fruits of her labours to the Roman people! As all things were done in mockery, this base metal is stamped with s. c., to ridicule the *Senatûs consulto*, which our antiquary happily explains, in the true spirit of this government of mockery, *Saturnalium consulto*, agreeing with the legend of the reverse, inscribed in the midst of four *tali*, or bones, which they used as dice, *Qui ludit arram det, quod satis sit*—"Let them who play give a pledge, which will be sufficient." This mock-money served not only as an expression of the native irony of the radical gentry of Rome during their festival, but had they spoken their mind out, meant a ridicule of money itself; for these citizens of equality have always imagined that society might proceed without this contrivance of a medium which served to represent property, in which they themselves must so little participate.

When the art of medal-engraving was revived in Europe, the spirit we are now noticing took possession of those less perishable and more circulating vehicles. Satiric medals were almost unknown to the ancient mint, notwithstanding those of the Saturnalia, and a few which bear miserable puns on the unlucky names of some consuls. Medals illustrate history, and history reflects light on medals; but we should not place such unreserved confidence on medals, as their advocates, who are warm in their favourite study. It has been asserted, that medals are more authentic memorials than history itself; but a medal is not less susceptible of the bad passions than a pamphlet or an epigram. Ambition has its vanity, and engraves a dubious victory; and Flattery will practise its art, and deceive us in gold! A calumny or a fiction on metal may be more durable than on a fugitive page; and a libel has a better chance of being preserved, when the artist is skilful, than simple truths when miserably executed. Medals of this class are numerous, and were the precursors of those political satires exhibited in caricature prints. There is a large collection of wooden cuts about the time of Calvin, where the Romish religion is represented by the most grotesque forms which the ridicule of the early Reformers could invent. More than a thousand figures attest the exuberant satire of the designers. This work is equally rare and costly.*

Satires of this species commenced in the freedom of the Reformation; for we find a medal of Luther in a monk's habit, satirically bearing for its reverse Catherine de Bora, the nun whom this monk married; the first step of his personal reformation! Nor can we be certain that Catherine was not more concerned in that great revolution than appears in the voluminous lives we have of the great reformer. However, the reformers were as great sticklers for medals as the "papelins." Of Pope John VIII., an effeminate voluptuary, we have a medal with his portrait, inscribed *Pope Joan!* and another of Innocent X., dressed as a woman holding a spindle; the reverse, his famous mistress, Donna Olympia, dressed as a Pope, with the tiara on her head, and the keys of St. Peter in her hands!

When, in the reign of Mary, England was groaning under Spanish influence, and no remonstrance could reach the throne, the queen's person and government were made ridiculous to the people's eyes, by prints or pictures, "representing her majesty naked, meagre, withered, and wrinkled, with every aggravated circumstance of deformity that could disgrace a female figure, seated in a regal chair; a crown on her head, surrounded with M. R. and A. in capitals, accompanied by small letters; *Maria Regina Angliæ!* a number of Spaniards were sucking her to skin and bone, and a specification was added of the money, rings, jewels, and other presents with which she had secretly gratified her husband Philip."† It is said that the queen suspected some of her own council of this invention, who alone were privy to these transactions. It is, however, in this manner that the voice, which is suppressed by authority, comes at length in another shape to the eye.

The age of Elizabeth, when the Roman pontiff and all his adherents were odious to the people, produced a remarkable caricature, and ingenious invention—a gorgon's head! A church bell forms the helmet; the ornaments, instead of the feathers, are a wolf's head in a mitre devouring a lamb, an ass's head with spectacles reading, a goose holding a rosary: the face is made out

---

* Mr. Douce possessed a portion of this very curious collection: for a complete one De Bure asked about twenty pounds.

† Warton's *Life of Sir Thomas Pope*, p. 58.

with a fish for the nose, a chalice and water for the eye, and other priestly ornaments for the shoulder and breast, on which rolls of parchment pardons hang.*

A famous bishop of Munster, Bernard de Galen, who, in his charitable violence for converting Protestants, got himself into such celebrity that he appears to have served as an excellent *sign-post* to the inns in Germany, was the true church militant: and his figure was exhibited according to the popular fancy. His head was half mitre and half helmet; a crosier in one hand and a sabre in the other; half a rochet and half a cuirass: he was made performing mass as a dragoon on horseback, and giving out the charge when he ought the *Ite, missa est!* He was called the *converter!* and the "Bishop of Munster" became popular as a sign-post in German towns; for the people like fighting men, though they should even fight against themselves.

It is rather curious to observe of this new species of satire, so easily distributed among the people, and so directly addressed to their understandings, that it was made the vehicle of national feeling. Ministers of state condescended to invent the devices. Lord Orford says, that *caricatures on cards* were the invention of George Townshend in the affair of Byng, which was soon followed by a pack. I am informed of an ancient pack of cards which has caricatures of all the Parliamentarian Generals, which might be not unusefully shuffled by a writer of secret history. We may be surprised to find the grave Sully practising this artifice on several occasions. In the civil wars of France the Duke of Savoy had taken by surprise Saluces, and struck a medal; on the reverse a centaur appears shooting with a bow and arrow, with the legend *Opportune!* But when Henry the Fourth had reconquered the town, he published another, on which Hercules appears killing the centaur, with the word *Opportunius.* The great minister was the author of this retort! A medal of the Dutch ambassador at the court of France, Van Beuninghen, whom the French represent as a haughty burgomaster, but who had the vivacity of a Frenchman and the haughtiness of a Spaniard, as Voltaire characterizes him, is said to have been the occasion of the Dutch war in 1672; but wars will be hardly made for an idle medal. Medals may, however, indicate a preparatory war. Louis the Fourteenth was so often compared to the sun at its meridian, that some of his creatures may have imagined that, like the sun,

---

* This ancient caricature, so descriptive of the popular feelings, is tolerably given in Malcolm's history of *Caricaturing*, plate ii. fig. I.

he could dart into any part of Europe as he willed, and be as cheerfully received. The Dutch minister, whose Christian name was *Joshua*, however, had a medal struck of Joshua stopping the sun in his course, inferring that this miracle was operated by his little republic. The medal itself is engraven in Van Loon's voluminous *Histoire Médallique du Pays Bas*, and in Marchand's *Dictionnaire Historique*, who labours to prove against twenty authors that the Dutch ambassador was not the inventor; it was not, however, unworthy of him, and it conveyed to the world the high feeling of her power which Holland had then assumed. Two years after the noise about this medal, the republic paid dear for the device; but thirty years afterwards this very burgomaster concluded a glorious peace, and France and Spain were compelled to receive the mediation of the Dutch Joshua with the French Sun.* In these vehicles of national satire, it is odd that the phlegmatic Dutch, more than any other nation, and from the earliest period of their republic, should have indulged freely, if not licentiously. It was a republican humour. Their taste was usually gross. We owe to them, even in the reign of Elizabeth, a severe medal on Leicester, who, having retired in disgust from the government of their provinces, struck a medal with his bust, reverse a dog and sheep,

Non gregem, sed ingratos invitus desero;

on which the angry juvenile states struck another, representing an ape and young ones; reverse, Leicester near a fire,

Fugiens fumum, incidit in ignem.

Another medal, with an excellent portrait of Cromwell, was struck by the Dutch. The protector, crowned with laurels, is on his knees, laying his head in the lap of the commonwealth, but loosely exhibiting himself to the French and Spanish ambassadors with gross indecency: the Frenchman, covered with *fleurs de lis*, is pushing aside the great Don, and disputes with him the precedence—*Retire-toy; l'honneur appartient au roy mon maître, Louis le Grand*. Van Loon is very right in denouncing this same medal, so grossly flattering to the English, as most detestable and indelicate! But why does Van Loon envy us this lumpish invention? why does the Dutchman quarrel with his own cheese? The honour of the medal we claim, but the invention belongs to his

---

* The history of this medal is useful in more than one respect; and may be found in Prosper Marchand.

country. The Dutch went on, commenting in this manner on
English affairs, from reign to reign. Charles the Second declared
war against them in 1672 for a malicious medal, though the
States-General offered to break the die, by purchasing it of the
workman for one thousand ducats; but it served for a pretext for
a Dutch war, which Charles cared more about than the *mala
bestia* of his exergue. Charles also complained of a scandalous
picture which the brothers De Witt had in their house, representing a naval battle with the English. Charles the Second seems to
have been more sensible to this sort of national satire than we
might have expected in a professed wit; a race, however, who are
not the most patient in having their own sauce returned to their
lips. The king employed Evelyn to write a history of the Dutch
war, and "enjoined him *to make it a little keen*, for the Hol-
landers had very unhandsomely abused him in their pictures,
books, and libels." The Dutch continued their career of conveying their national feeling on English affairs more triumphantly
when their stadtholder ascended an English throne. The birth of
the Pretender is represented by the chest which Minerva gave to
the daughters of Cecrops to keep, and which, opened, discovered
an infant with a serpent's tail: *Infantemque vident apporrectum-
que draconem*; the chest perhaps alluding to the removes of the
warming-pan; and, in another, James and a Jesuit flying in terror, the king throwing away a crown and sceptre, and the Jesuit
carrying a child, *Ite missa est*, the words applied from the mass.
But in these contests of national feeling, while the grandeur of
Louis the Fourteenth did not allow of these ludicrous and satirical exhibitions; and while the political idolatry which his forty
academicians paid to him, exhausted itself in the splendid fictions of a series of famous medals, amounting to nearly four
hundred; it appears that we were not without our reprisals: for I
find Prosper Marchand, who writes as a Hollander, censuring his
own country for having at length adulated the grand monarque
by a complimentary medal. He says, "The English cannot be reproached with a similar *debonaireté*." After the famous victories
of Marlborough, they indeed inserted in a medal the head of the
French monarch and the English queen, with this inscription,
Ludovicus Magnus, Anna Major. Long ere this one of our queens
had been exhibited by ourselves with considerable energy. On
the defeat of the Armada, Elizabeth, Pinkerton tells us, struck a
medal representing the English and Spanish fleets, *Hesperidum
regem devicit virgo*. Philip had medals dispersed in England of
the same impression, with this addition, *Negatur. Est meretrix*

vulgi. These the queen suppressed, but published another medal, with this legend:

> Hesperidum regem devicit virgo; negatur,
> Est meretrix vulgi; res eo deterior.

An age fertile in satirical prints was the eventful æra of Charles the First: they were showered from all parties, and a large collection of them would admit of a critical historical commentary, which might become a vehicle of the most curious secret history. Most of them are in a bad style, for they are allegorical; yet that these satirical exhibitions influenced the eyes and minds of the people is evident, from an extraordinary circumstance. Two grave collections of historical documents adopted them. We are surprised to find prefixed to Rushworth's and Nalson's historical collections, two such political prints! Nalson's was an act of retributive justice; but he seems to have been aware, that satire in the shape of pictures is a language very attractive to the multitude; for he has introduced a caricature print in the solemn folio of the trial of Charles the First. Of the happiest of these political prints is one by Taylor the water-poet, not included in his folio, but prefixed to his "Mad fashions, odd fashions, or the emblems of these distracted times." It is the figure of a man whose eyes have left their sockets, and whose legs have usurped the place of his arms; a horse on his hind legs is drawing a cart; a church is inverted; fish fly in the air; a candle burns with the flame downwards; and the mouse and rabbit are pursuing the cat and the fox!

The animosities of national hatred have been a fertile source of these vehicles of popular feeling—which discover themselves in severe or grotesque caricatures. The French and the Spaniards mutually exhibited one another under the most extravagant figures. The political caricatures of the French, in the seventeenth century, are numerous. The *badauds* of Paris amused themselves for their losses, by giving an emetic to a Spaniard, to make him render up all the towns his victories had obtained: seven or eight Spaniards are seen seated around a large turnip, with their frizzled mustachios, their hats *en pot-à-beurre*; their long rapiers, with their pummels down to their feet, and their points up to their shoulders; their ruffs stiffened by many rows, and pieces of garlick stuck in their girdles. The Dutch were exhibited in as great variety as the uniformity of frogs would allow. We have largely participated in the vindictive spirit, which these grotesque emblems keep up among the people; they mark the secret feelings of national pride. The Greeks despised foreigners, and considered them only as fit to be slaves;* the ancient Jews, inflated with a false idea of their small territory, would be masters of the world; the Italians placed a line of demarcation for genius and taste, and marked it by their mountains. The Spaniards once imagined that the conferences of God with Moses on Mount Sinai were in the Spanish language. If a Japanese become the friend of a foreigner, he is considered as committing treason to his emperor; and rejected as a false brother in a country which, we are told, is figuratively called *Tenka*, or the Kingdom under the Heavens. John Bullism is not peculiar to Englishmen; and patriotism is a noble virtue, when it secures our independence without depriving us of our humanity.

The civil wars of the League in France, and those in England under Charles the First, bear the most striking resemblance; and in examining the revolutionary scenes exhibited by the graver in the famous *Satire Ménippée*, we discover the foreign artist revelling in the *caricature* of his ludicrous and severe exhibition; and in that other revolutionary period of *La Fronde*, there was a mania for *political songs*; the curious have formed them into collections; and we not only have "the Rump Songs" of Charles the First's times, but have repeated this kind of evidence of the public feeling at many subsequent periods. *Caricatures* and *political songs* might with us furnish a new sort of history; and perhaps would preserve some truths, and describe some particular events, not to be found in more grave authorities.

The History of Writing-Masters

THERE IS a very apt letter from James the First to Prince Henry when very young, on the neatness and fairness of his handwriting. The royal father suspecting that the prince's tutor, Mr., afterwards Sir Adam, Newton, had helped out the young prince in the composition; and that in this specimen of calligraphy he had relied also on the pains of Mr. Peter Bales, the great writing-master, for touching up his letters; his majesty shows a laudable

---

* A passage may be found in Aristotle's *Politics,* vol. i. c. 3-7; where Aristotle advises Alexander to govern the Greeks like his *subjects,* and the barbarians like *slaves*; for that the one he was to consider as companions, and the other as creatures of an inferior race.

anxiety that the prince should be impressed with the higher importance of the one over the other. James shall himself speak. "I confess I long to receive a letter from you that may be wholly yours, as well matter as form; as well formed by your mind as drawn by your fingers; for ye may remember, that in my book to you I warn you to beware with (of) that kind of wit that may fly out at the end of your fingers; not that I commend not a fair handwriting; *sed hoc facito, illud non omittito*: and the other is *multo magis præcipuum.*" Prince Henry, indeed, wrote with that elegance which he borrowed from his own mind; and in an age when such minute elegance was not universal among the crowned heads of Europe. Henry IV., on receiving a letter from Prince Henry, immediately opened it, a custom not usual with him, and comparing the writing with the signature, to decide whether it were of one hand, Sir George Carew, observing the French king's hesitation, called Mr. Douglas to testify to the fact; on which Henry the Great, admiring an art in which he had little skill, and looking on the neat elegance of the writing before him, politely observed, "I see that in writing fair, as in other things, the elder must yield to the younger."

Had this anecdote of neat writing reached the professors of calligraphy, who in this country have put forth such painful panegyrics on the art, these royal names had unquestionably blazoned their pages. Not indeed that these penmen require any fresh inflation; for never has there been a race of professors in any art, who have exceeded in solemnity and pretensions the practitioners in this simple and mechanical craft. I must leave to more ingenious investigators of human nature, to reveal the occult cause which has operated such powerful delusions on these *"Vive la Plume!"* men, who have been generally observed to possess least intellectual ability, in proportion to the excellence they have obtained in their own art. I suspect this maniacal vanity is peculiar to the writing-masters of England; and I can only attribute the immense importance which they have conceived of their art, to the perfection to which they have carried the art of shorthand writing; an art which was always better understood, and more skilfully practised, in England, than in any other country. It will surprise some, when they learn that the artists in verse and colours, poets and painters, have not raised loftier pretensions to the admiration of mankind. Writing-masters, or calligraphers, have had their engraved "effigies," with a Fame in flourishes, a pen in one hand, and a trumpet in the

other; and fine verses inscribed, and their very lives written!
They have compared

> The nimbly-turning of their silver quill,

to the beautiful in art and the sublime in invention; nor is this
wonderful, since they discover the art of writing, like the invention of language, in a divine original; and from the tablets of
stone which the Deity himself delivered, they trace their German
broad text, or their fine running-hand. One, for "the bold striking of those words, *Vive la Plume*," was so sensible of the reputation that this last piece of command of hand would give the
book which he thus adorned, and which his biographer acknowledges was the product of about a minute,—(but then how many
years of flourishing had that single minute cost him!)—that he
claims the glory of an artist; observing,—

> We seldom find
> The *man of business* with the *artist* join'd.

Another was flattered that his *writing* could impart immortality
to the most wretched compositions!—

> And any lines prove pleasing, when you write.

Sometimes the calligrapher is a sort of hero:—

> To you, you rare commander of the quill,
> Whose wit and worth, deep learning, and high skill,
> Speak you the honour of Great Tower Hill!

The last line became traditionally adopted by those who were
so lucky as to live in the neighbourhood of this Parnassus. But
the reader must form some notion of that charm of caligraphy
which has so bewitched its professors, when,

> Soft, bold, and free, your manuscripts still please.

> How justly bold in SNELL's improving hand
> The pen at once joins freedom with command!
> With softness strong, with ornaments not vain,
> Loose with proportion, and with neatness plain;
> Not swell'd, not full, complete in every part,
> And artful most, when not affecting art.

And these describe those pencilled knots and flourishes, "the
angels, the men, the birds, and the beasts," which, as one of them
observed, he could

> Command
> Even by the *gentle motion of his hand,*

all the *speciosa miracula* of calligraphy;

Thy *tender strokes,* inimitably fine,
Crown with perfection every *flowing line;*
And to each *grand performance* add a grace,
As *curling hair* adorns a beauteous face:
In every page *new fancies* give delight,
And *sporting round the margin* charm the sight.

One Massey, a writing-master, published, in 1763, *The Origin and Progress of Letters.* The great singularity of this volume is "A new species of biography never attempted before in English." This consists of the lives of "English Penmen," otherwise writing-masters! If some have foolishly enough imagined that the sedentary lives of authors are void of interest from deficient incident and interesting catastrophe, what must they think of the barren labours of those, who, in the degree they become eminent, to use their own style, in the art of "dish, dash, long-tail fly," the less they become interesting to the public; for what can the most skilful writing-master do but wear away his life in leaning over his pupil's copy, or sometimes snatch a pen to decorate the margin, though he cannot compose the page? Montaigne has a very original notion on writing-masters: he says that some of those calligraphers who had obtained promotion by their excellence in the art, afterwards *affected to write carelessly, lest their promotion should be suspected to have been owing to such an ordinary acquisition!*

Massey is an enthusiast, fortunately for his subject. He considers that there are *schools of writing,* as well as of painting or sculpture; and expatiates with the eye of fraternal feeling on "a natural genius, a tender stroke, a grand performance, a bold striking freedom, and a liveliness in the sprigged letters, and pencilled knots and flourishes"; while this Vasari of writing-masters relates the controversies and the libels of many a rival pen-nibber. "George Shelley, one of the most celebrated worthies who have made a shining figure in the commonwealth of English calligraphy, born I suppose of obscure parents, because brought up in Christ's Hospital, yet under the humble blue-coat he laid the foundation of his calligraphic excellence and lasting fame, for he was elected writing-master to the hospital." Shelley published his *Natural Writing;* but, alas! Snell, another blue-coat, transcended the other. He was a genius who would "bear no brother near the throne."—"I have been informed that there were jealous heart-burnings, if not bickerings, between him and Col. Ayres, another of our *great reformers* in the writing commonweal, both eminent men, yet, like our most celebrated poets

Pope and Addison, or, to carry the comparison still higher, like *Cæsar and Pompey*, one could bear no superior, and the other no equal." Indeed, the great Snell practised a little stratagem against Mr. Shelley, for which, if writing-masters held courts-martial, this hero ought to have appeared before his brothers. In one of his works he procured a number of friends to write letters, in which Massey confesses "are some satyrical strokes upon Shelley," as if he had arrogated too much to himself in his book of *Natural Writing.* They find great fault with pencilled knots and sprigged letters. Shelley, who was an advocate for ornaments in fine penmanship, which Snell utterly rejected, had parodied a well-known line of Herbert's in favour of his favourite decorations:—

> A *Knot* may take him who from *letters* flies,
> And turn *delight* into an *exercise.*

These reflections created ill-blood, and even an open differ-ence amongst several of the *superior artists in writing.* The commanding genius of Snell had a more terrific contest when he published his *Standard Rules,* pretending to have *demon-strated* them as Euclid would. "This proved a bone of conten-tion, and occasioned a terrific quarrel between Mr. Snell and Mr. Clark. This quarrel about *Standard Rules* ran so high between them, that they could scarce forbear *scurrilous language* therein, and a treatment of each other unbecoming *gentlemen*! Both sides in this dispute had their abettors; and to say which had the most truth and reason, *non nostrum est tantas com-ponere lites*; perhaps *both parties might be too fond of their own schemes.* They should have left them to people to choose which they liked best." A candid politician is our Massey, and a philosophical historian too; for he winds up the whole story of this civil war by describing its results, which happened as all such great controversies have ever closed. "Who now-a-days takes those *Standard Rules,* either one or the other, for their *guide* in writing?" This is the finest lesson ever offered to the furious heads of parties, and to all their men; let them meditate on the nothingness of their "Standard Rules," by the fate of Mr. Snell.

It was to be expected, when once these writing-masters imag-ined that they were artists, that they would be infected with those plague-spots of genius—envy, detraction, and all the *jalousie du métier.* And such to this hour we find them! An extraordinary scene of this nature has long been exhibited

in my neighbourhood, where two doughty champions of the
quill have been posting up libels in their windows respecting
the inventor of *a new art of writing,* the Carstairian, or the
Lewisian? When the great German philosopher asserted that
he had discovered the method of fluxions before Sir Isaac,
and when the dispute grew so violent that even the calm
Newton sent a formal defiance in set terms, and got even
George the Second to try to arbitrate (who would rather have
undertaken a campaign), the method of fluxions was no more
cleared up than the present affair between our two heroes of
the quill.

A recent instance of one of these egregious calligraphers
may be told of the late Tomkins. This vainest of writing-
masters dreamed through life that penmanship was one of the
fine arts, and that a writing-master should be seated with his
peers in the Academy! He bequeathed to the British Museum
his *opus magnum*—a copy of Macklin's Bible, profusely embellished with the most beautiful and varied decorations of his
pen; and as he conceived that both the workman and the work
would alike be darling objects with posterity, he left something
immortal with the legacy, his fine bust, by Chantrey, unaccompanied by which they were not to receive the unparalleled gift!
When Tomkins applied to have his bust, our great sculptor
abated the usual price, and, courteously kind to the feelings
of the man, said that he considered Tomkins as an artist!
It was the proudest day of the life of our writing-master!

But an eminent artist and wit now living, once looking on
this fine bust of Tomkins, declared, that "this man had died
for want of a dinner!"—a fate, however, not so lamentable
as it appeared! Our penman had long felt that he stood
degraded in the scale of genius by not being received at the
Academy, at least among the class of *engravers*; the next
approach to academic honour he conceived would be that of
appearing as a *guest* at their annual dinner. These invitations
are as limited as they are select, and all the Academy persisted
in considering Tomkins *as a writing-master*! Many a year
passed, every intrigue was practised, every remonstrance was
urged, every stratagem of courtesy was tried; but never ceasing
to deplore the failure of his hopes, it preyed on his spirits,
and the luckless calligrapher went down to his grave—without
dining at the Academy! This authentic anecdote has been
considered as "satire improperly directed"—by some friend of

Mr. Tomkins—but the criticism is much too grave! The foible of Mr. Tomkins as a writing-master, presents a striking illustration of the class of men here delineated. I am a mere historian—and am only responsible for the veracity of this fact. That "Mr. Tomkins lived in familiar intercourse with the Royal Academicians of his day, and was a frequent guest at their private tables," and moreover was a most worthy man, I believe—but is it less true that he was ridiculously mortified by being never invited to the Academic dinner, on account of his calligraphy? He had some reason to consider that his art was of the exalted class, to which he aspired to raise it, when this friend concludes his eulogy of this writing-master thus— "Mr. Tomkins, as an artist, stood foremost in his own profession, and his name will be handed down to posterity with the *Heroes* and *Statesmen,* whose excellences his *penmanship* has contributed to illustrate and to commemorate." I always give the *Pour* and the *Contre*!

Such men about such things have produced public contests, *combats à l'outrance,* where much ink was spilled by the knights in a joust of goose-quills; these solemn trials have often occurred in the history of the writing-masters, which is enlivened by public defiances, proclamations, and judicial trials by umpires! The prize was usually a golden pen of some value. One as late as in the reign of Anne took place between Mr. German and Mr. More. German having courteously insisted that Mr. More should set the copy, he thus set it, ingeniously quaint!

> As more, and MORE, our understanding clears,
> So more and more our ignorance appears.

The result of this pen-combat was really lamentable; they displayed such an equality of excellence that the umpires refused to decide, till one of them espied that Mr. German had omitted the tittle of an i! But Mr. More was evidently a man of genius, not only by his couplet, but in his *Essay on the Invention of Writing,* where occurs this noble passage: "Art with me is of no party. A noble emulation I would cherish, while it proceeded neither from, nor to malevolence. Bales had his Johnson, Norman his Mason, Ayres his Matlock and his Shelley; yet Art the while was no sufferer. The busy-body who officiously employs himself in creating misunderstandings between artists, may be compared to a turn-stile, which stands in every man's way, yet hinders nobody; and he is the slanderer who gives ear to the slander."*

Among these knights of the *Plume volante,* whose chivalric exploits astounded the beholders, must be distinguished Peter Bales in his joust with David Johnson. In this tilting-match the guerdon of calligraphy was won by the greatest of calligraphers; its *arms* were assumed by the victor, *azure, a pen or;* while the "golden pen," carried away in triumph, was painted with a hand over the door of the calligrapher. The history of this renowned encounter was only traditionally known, till with my own eyes I pondered on this whole trial of skill in the precious manuscript of the champion himself; who, like Cæsar, not only knew how to win victories, but also to record them. Peter Bales was a hero of such transcendent eminence, that his name has entered into our history. Holingshed chronicles one of his curiosities of microscopic writing at a time when the taste prevailed for admiring writing which no eye could read! In the compass of a silver penny this calligrapher put more things than would fill several of these pages. He presented Queen Elizabeth with the manuscript set in a ring of gold covered with a crystal; he had also contrived a magnifying glass of such power, that, to her delight and wonder, her majesty read the whole volume, which she held on her thumb nail, and "commended the same to the lords of the council, and the ambassadors"; and frequently, as Peter often heard, did her majesty vouchsafe to wear this calligraphic ring.

"Some will think I labour on a cobweb"—modestly exclaimed Bales in his narrative, and his present historian much fears for himself! The reader's gratitude will not be proportioned to my pains, in condensing such copious pages into the size of a "silver penny," but without its worth!

For a whole year had David Johnson affixed a challenge "To any one who should take exceptions to this my writing and teaching." He was a young friend of Bales, daring and longing for an encounter; yet Bales was magnanimously silent, till he discovered that he was "doing much less in writing and teaching" since this public challenge was proclaimed! He then set up his counter challenge, and in one hour afterwards Johnson arrogantly accepted it, "in a most despiteful and disgraceful manner." Bales's challenge was delivered "in good

---

* I have not met with More's book, and am obliged to transcribe this from the *Biog. Brit.*

terms." "To all Englishmen and strangers." It was to write for
a gold pen of twenty pounds value in all kinds of hands, "best,
straightest, and fastest," and most kind of ways; "a full, a mean,
a small, with line, and without line; in a slow set hand, a mean
facile hand, and a fast running hand"; and further, "to write
truest and speediest, most secretary and clerk-like, from a man's
mouth reading or pronouncing, either English or Latin."

Young Johnson had the hardihood now of turning the tables
on his great antagonist, accusing the veteran Bales of arro-
gance. Such an absolute challenge, says he, was never witnessed
by man, "without exception of any in the world!" And a few
days after meeting Bales, "of set purpose to affront and disgrace
him what he could, showed Bales a piece of writing of secretary's
hand, which he had very much laboured in fine abortive parchment,"* uttering to the challenger, these words: "Mr. Bales,
give me one shilling out of your purse, and if within six months
you better, or equal this piece of writing, I will give you
forty pounds for it." This legal deposit of the shilling was made,
and the challenger, or appellant, was thereby bound by law
to the performance.

The day before the trial a printed declaration was affixed
throughout the city, taunting Bales's "proud poverty," and
his pecuniary motives, as "a thing ungentle, base, and mer-
cenary, and not answerable to the dignity of the golden pen!"
Johnson declares he would maintain his challenge for a
thousand pounds more, but for the respondent's inability to
perform a thousand groats. Bales retorts on the libel; declares
it as a sign of his rival's weakness, "yet who so bold as blind
Bayard, that hath not a word of Latin to cast at a dog, or
say Bo! to a goose!"

On Michaelmas day, 1595, the trial opened before five
judges: the appellant and the respondent appeared at the
appointed place, and an ancient gentleman was intrusted with
"the golden pen." In the first trial, for the manner of teaching
scholars, after Johnson had taught his pupil a fortnight, he
would not bring him forward! This was awarded in favour of
Bales.

The second, for secretary and clerk-like writing, dictating to
them both in English and in Latin, Bales performed best,

---

* This was written in the reign of Elizabeth. Holyoke notices "virgin-
perchment made of an *abortive skin; membrano virgo*." Peacham on
Drawing, calls parchment simply *an abortive*.

being first done; written straightest without line, with true orthography: the challenger himself confessing that he wanted the Latin tongue, and was no clerk!

The third and last trial for fair writing in sundry kinds of hands, the challenger prevailed for the beauty and most "authentic proportion," and for the superior variety of the Roman hand. In the court-hand the respondent exceeded the appellant, and likewise in the set text; and in bastard secretary was also somewhat perfecter.

At length Bales, perhaps perceiving an equilibrium in the judicial decision, to overwhelm his antagonist presented what he distinguishes as his "master-piece," composed of secretary and Roman hand four ways varied, and offering the defendant to let pass all his previous advantages if he could better this specimen of calligraphy! The challenger was silent! At this moment some of the judges perceiving that the decision must go in favour of Bales, in consideration of the youth of the challenger, lest he might be disgraced to the world, requested the other judges not to pass judgment in public. Bales assures us, that he in vain remonstrated; for by these means the winning of the golden pen might not be so famously spread as otherwise it would have been. To Bales the prize was awarded. But our history has a more interesting close; the subtle Machiavelism of the first challenger!

When the great trial had closed, and Bales, carrying off the golden pen, exultingly had it painted and set up for his sign, the baffled challenger went about reporting that *he* had *won* the golden pen, but that the defendant had obtained the same by "plots and shifts, and other base and cunning practices." Bales vindicated his claim, and offered to show the world his "master-piece" which had acquired it. Johnson issued an "Appeal to all impartial Pen-men," which he spread in great numbers through the city for ten days, a libel against the judges and the victorious defendant! He declared that there had been a subtle combination with one of the judges concerning the place of trial; which he expected to have been "before pen-men," but not before a multitude like a stage-play, and shouts and tumults, with which the challenger had hitherto been unacquainted. The judges were intended to be twelve; but of the five, four were the challenger's friends, honest gentlemen, but unskilled in judging of most hands; and he offered again forty pounds to be allowed in six months to equal Bales's master-piece. And he closes his "appeal" by declaring that Bales had lost in several parts of the trial, neither did the judges deny that Bales possessed himself of the golden pen by a trick! Before judgment was awarded, alleging the sickness of his wife to be extreme, he desired she might have a *sight of the golden pen to comfort her*! The ancient gentleman who was the holder, taking the defendant's word, allowed the golden pen to be carried to the sick wife; and Bales immediately pawned it, and afterwards, to make sure work, sold it at a great loss, so that when the judges met for their definite sentence, nor pen nor penny-worth was to be had! The judges being ashamed of their own conduct, were compelled to give a verdict as suited the occasion.

Bales rejoins; he publishes to the universe the day and the hour when the judges brought the golden pen to his house, and while he checks the insolence of this Bobadil, to show himself no recreant, assumes the golden pen for his sign.

Such is the shortest history I could contrive of this chivalry of the pen; something mysteriously clouds over the fate of the defendant; Bales's history, like Cæsar's, is but an *ex-parte* evidence. Who can tell whether he has not slurred over his defeats, and only dwelt on his victories?

There is a strange phrase connected with the art of the calligrapher, which I think may be found in most, if not in all modern languages, *to write like an angel*! Ladies have been frequently compared with angels; they are *beautiful* as angels, and *sing* and *dance* like angels; but, however intelligible these are, we do not so easily connect penmanship with the other celestial accomplishments. This fanciful phrase, however, has a very human origin. Among those learned Greeks who emigrated to Italy, and afterwards into France, in the reign of Francis I. was one *Angelo Vergecio,* whose beautiful calligraphy excited the admiration of the learned. The French monarch had a Greek fount cast, modelled by his writing. The learned Henry Stephens, who, like our Porson for correctness and delicacy, was one of the most elegant writers of Greek, had learnt the practice from our *Angelo.* His name became synonymous for beautiful writing, and gave birth to the vulgar proverb, or familiar phrase, *to write like an angel*!

Dreams at the Dawn of Philosophy

MODERN PHILOSOPHY, theoretical or experimental, only amuses while the action of discovery is suspended or advances; the interest ceases with the inquirer when the catastrophe is ascertained, as in the romance whose *dénouement* turns on a mysterious incident, which, once unfolded, all future agitation ceases. But in the true infancy of science, philosophers were as imaginative a race as poets: marvels and portents, undemonstrable and undefinable, with occult fancies, perpetually beginning and never ending, were delightful as the shifting cantos of Ariosto. Then science entranced the eye by its thaumaturgy; when they looked through an optic tube, they believed they were looking into futurity; or, starting at some shadow darkening the glassy globe, beheld the absent person; while the mechanical inventions of art were toys and tricks, with sometimes an automaton, which frightened them with life.

The earlier votaries of modern philosophy only witnessed, as Gaffarel calls his collection, *Unheard-of Curiosities*. This state of the marvellous, of which we are now for ever deprived, prevailed among the philosophers and the *virtuosi* in Europe, and with ourselves, long after the establishment of the Royal Society. Philosophy then depended mainly on authority—a single one however was sufficient: so that when this had been repeated by fifty others, they had the authority of fifty honest men—whoever the first man might have been! They were then a blissful race of children, rambling here and there in a golden age of innocence and ignorance, where at every step each gifted discoverer whispered to the few, some half-concealed secret of nature, or played with some toy of art; some invention which with great difficulty performed what, without it, might have been done with great ease. The cabinets of the lovers of mechanical arts formed enchanted apartments, where the admirers feared to stir or look about them; while the philosophers themselves half imagined they were the very thaumaturgi, for which the world gave them too much credit, at least for their quiet! Would we run after the shadows in this gleaming land of moonshine, or sport with these children in the fresh morning of science, ere Aurora had scarcely peeped on the hills, we must enter into their feelings, view with their eyes, and believe all they confide to us; and out of these bundles of dreams sometimes pick out one or two for our own dreaming. They are the fairy tales and the Arabian Nights' entertainments of science. But if the reader is stubbornly mathematical and logical, he will only be holding up a great torch against the muslin curtain, upon which the fantastic shadows playing upon it must vanish at the instant. It is an amusement which can only take place by carefully keeping himself in the dark.

What a subject, were I to enter on it, would be the narratives of magical writers! These precious volumes have been so constantly wasted by the profane, that now a book of real magic requires some to find it, as well as a great magician to use it. Albertus Magnus, or Albert the Great, as he is erroneously styled—for this sage only derived this enviable epithet from his surname *De Groot,* as did Hugo Grotius—this sage, in his *Admirable Secrets* delivers his opinion that these books of magic should be most preciously preserved; for, he prophetically added, the time is arriving when they would be understood! It seems they were not intelligible in the thirteenth century; but if Albertus has not miscalculated, in the present day they may be! Magical terms with talismanic figures may yet conceal many a secret; gunpowder came down to us in a sort of anagram, and the kaleidoscope, with all its interminable multiplications of forms, lay at hand for two centuries in Baptista Porta's *Natural Magic.* The abbot Trithemius, in a confidential letter, happened to call himself a magician, perhaps at the moment he thought himself one, and sent three or four leaves stuffed with the names of devils and with their evocations. At the death of his friend these leaves fell into the unworthy hands of the prior, who was so frightened on the first glance at the diabolical nomenclature, that he raised the country against the abbot, and Trithemius was nearly a lost man! Yet, after all, this evocation of devils has reached us in his *Steganographia,* and proves to be only one of this ingenious abbot's polygraphic attempts at *secret writing;* for he had flattered himself that he had invented a mode of concealing his thoughts from all the world, while he communicated them to a friend. Roger Bacon promised to raise thunder and lightning, and disperse clouds by dissolving them into rain. The first magical process has been obtained by Franklin; and the other, of far more use to our agriculturists, may perchance be found lurking in some corner which has been overlooked in the *Opus majus* of our *Doctor mirabilis.* Do we laugh at their magical works of art? Are we ourselves such indifferent artists? Cornelius Agrippa, before he wrote his

Vanity of the Arts and Sciences, intended to reduce into a system and method the secret of communicating with spirits and demons. On good authority, that of Porphyrius, Psellus, Plotinus, Jamblichus—and on better, were it necessary to allege it—he was well assured that the upper regions of the air swarmed with what the Greeks called *dæmones,* just as our lower atmosphere is full of birds, our waters of fish, and our earth of insects. Yet this occult philosopher, who knew perfectly eight languages, and married two wives, with whom he had never exchanged a harsh word in any of them, was everywhere avoided as having by his side, for his companion, a personage no less than a demon! This was a great black dog; whom he suffered to stretch himself out among his magical manuscripts, or lie on his bed, often kissing and patting him, and feeding him on choice morsels. Yet for this, would Paulus Jovius and all the world have had him put to the ordeal of fire and fagot! The truth was afterwards boldly asserted by Wierus, his learned domestic, who believed that his master's dog was really nothing more than what he appeared! "I believe," says he, "that he was a real natural dog; he was indeed black, but of a moderate size, and I have often led him by a string, and called him by the French name Agrippa had given him, Monsieur! and he had a female who was called Mademoiselle! I wonder how authors of such great character should write so absurdly on his vanishing at his death, nobody knows how!" But as it is probable that Monsieur and Mademoiselle must have generated some puppy demons, Wierus ought to have been more circumstantial.

Albertus Magnus, for thirty years, had never ceased working at a man of brass, and had cast together the qualities of his materials under certain constellations, which threw such a spirit into his man of brass, that it was reported his growth was visible; his feet, legs, thighs, shoulders, neck, and head, expanded, and made the city of Cologne uneasy at possessing one citizen too mighty for them all. This man of brass, when he reached his maturity, was so loquacious, that Albert's master, the great scholastic Thomas Aquinas, one day, tired of his babble, and declaring it was a devil, or devilish, with his staff knocked the head off; and, what was extraordinary, this brazen man, like any human being thus effectually silenced, "word never spake more." This incident is equally historical and authentic; though whether heads of brass can speak, and even prophesy, was indeed a subject of profound inquiry, even at a later period. Naudé, who never questioned their vocal powers, and yet was puzzled concerning the nature of this new species of animal, has no doubt most judiciously stated the question. Whether these speaking brazen heads had a sensitive and reasoning nature, or whether demons spoke in them? But brass has not the faculty of providing its own nourishment, as we see in plants, and therefore they were not sensitive; and as for the act of reasoning, these brazen heads presumed to know nothing but the future: with the past and the present they seemed totally unacquainted, so that their memory and their observation were very limited; and as for the future, that is always doubtful and obscure—even to heads of brass! This learned man then infers, that "These brazen heads could have no reasoning faculties, for nothing altered their nature; they said what they had to say, which no one could contradict; and having said their say, you might have broken the head for any thing more that you could have got out of it. Had they had any life in them, would they not have moved, as well as spoken? Life itself is but motion, but they had no lungs, no spleen; and, in fact, though they spoke, they had no tongue. Was a devil in them? I think not. Yet why should men have taken all this trouble to make, not a man, but a trumpet?"

Our profound philosopher was right not to agitate the question whether these brazen heads had ever spoken. Why should not a man of brass speak, since a doll can whisper, a statue play chess, and brass ducks have performed the whole process of digestion? Another magical invention has been ridiculed with equal reason. A magician was annoyed, as philosophers still are, by passengers in the street; and he, particularly so, by having horses led to drink under his window. He made a magical horse of wood, according to one of the books of Hermes, which perfectly answered its purpose, by frightening away the horses, or rather the grooms! the wooden horse, no doubt, gave some palpable kick. The same magical story might have been told of Dr. Franklin, who finding that under his window the passengers had discovered a spot which they made too convenient for themselves, he charged it with his newly-discovered electrical fire. After a few remarkable incidents had occurred, which at a former period would have lodged the great discoverer of electricity in the Inquisition, the modern magician succeeded just as well as the ancient, who had the advantage of conning over the books of Hermes. Instead of ridiculing these works of magic, let us rather become magicians ourselves!

The works of the ancient alchemists have afforded numberless discoveries to modern chemists: nor is even their grand operation despaired of. If they have of late not been so renowned, this has arisen from a want of what Ashmole calls "apertness"; a qualification early inculcated among these illuminated sages. We find authentic accounts of some who have lived three centuries, with tolerable complexions, possessed of nothing but a crucible and a bellows! but they were so unnecessarily mysterious, that whenever such a person was discovered, he was sure in an instant to disappear, and was never afterwards heard of.

In the *Liber Patris Sapientiæ* this selfish cautiousness is all along impressed on the student, for the accomplishment of the great mystery. In the commentary on this precious work of the alchemist Norton, who counsels,

> Be thou in a place secret, by thyself alone,
> That no man see or hear what thou shalt say or done.
> Trust not thy friend too much wheresoe'er thou go,
> For he thou trustest best, sometyme may be thy foe,

Ashmole observes, that "Norton gives exceeding good advice to the student in this science where he bids him be secret in the carrying on of his studies and operations, and not to let any one know of his undertakings but his good angel and himself": and such a close and retired breast had Norton's master, who,

> When men disputed *of colours of the rose*,
> He would not speak, but kept himself full close!

We regret, that by each leaving all his knowledge to "his good angel and himself," it has happened that "the good angels" have kept it all to themselves!

It cannot, however, be denied, that if they could not always extract gold out of lead, they sometimes succeeded in washing away the pimples on ladies' faces, notwithstanding that Sir Kenelm Digby poisoned his most beautiful lady, because, as Sancho would have said, he was one of those who would "have his bread whiter than the finest wheaten." Van Helmont, who could not succeed in discovering the true elixir of life, however hit on the spirit of hartshorn, which for a good while he considered was the wonderful elixir itself, restoring to life persons who seemed to have lost it. And though this delightful enthusiast could not raise a ghost, yet he thought he had; for he raised something aerial from spa-water, which mistaking for a ghost, he gave it that very name; a name which we still retain in *gas*, from the German, *geist*, or ghost! Paracelsus carried the tiny spirits about

him in the hilt of his great sword! Having first discovered the
qualities of laudanum, this illustrious quack made use of it as an
universal remedy, and distributed it in the form of pills, which
he carried in the basket-hilt of his sword; the operations he
performed were as rapid as they seemed magical. Doubtless we
have lost some inconceivable secrets by some unexpected occurrences, which the secret itself it would seem ought to have pre-
vented taking place. When a philosopher had discovered the art
of prolonging life to an indefinite period, it is most provoking
to find that he should have allowed himself to die at an early
age! We have a very authentic history from Sir Kenelm Digby
himself, that when he went in disguise to visit Descartes at his
retirement at Egmond, lamenting the brevity of life, which
hindered philosophers getting on in their studies, the French
philosopher assured him that "he had considered that matter; to
render a man immortal was what he could not promise, but that
he was very sure it was possible to lengthen out his life to the
period of the patriarchs." And when his death was announced
to the world, the Abbé Picot, an ardent disciple, for a long time
would not believe it possible; and at length insisted, that if it had
occurred, it must have been owing to some mistake of the philosopher's.

The late Holcroft, Loutherbourg, and Cosway, imagined that
they should escape the vulgar era of scriptural life by reorganiz-
ing their old bones, and moistening their dry marrow; their new
principles of vitality were supposed by them to be found in the
powers of the mind; this seemed more reasonable, but proved
to be as little efficacious as those other philosophers, who imagine
they have detected the hidden principle of life in the eels frisk-
ing in vinegar, and allude to "the bookbinder who creates the
book-worm!"

Paracelsus has revealed to us one of the grandest secrets of
nature. When the world began to dispute on the very existence
of the elementary folk, it was then that he boldly offered to give
birth to a fairy, and has sent down to posterity the recipe. He
describes the impurity which is to be transmuted into such
purity, the gross elements of a delicate fairy, which, fixed in a
phial, placed in fuming dung, will in due time settle into a full-
grown fairy, bursting through its vitreous prison—on the vivify-
ing principle by which the ancient Egyptians hatched their eggs
in ovens. I recollect, at Dr. Farmer's sale, the leaf which preserved
this recipe for making a fairy, forcibly folded down by the learned
commentator; from which we must infer the credit he gave to the

experiment. There was a greatness of mind in Paracelsus, who, having furnished a recipe to make a fairy, had the delicacy to refrain from its formation. Even Baptista Porta, one of the most enlightened philosophers, does not deny the possibility of engendering creatures, which, "at their full growth shall not exceed the size of a mouse"; but he adds "they are only pretty little dogs to play with." Were these akin to the fairies of Paracelsus?

They were well convinced of the existence of such elemental beings; frequent accidents in mines showed the potency of the metallic spirits; which so tormented the workmen in some of the German mines, by blindness, giddiness, and sudden sickness, that they have been obliged to abandon mines well known to be rich in silver. A metallic spirit at one sweep annihilated twelve miners, who were all found dead together. The fact was unquestionable; and the safety-lamp was undiscovered.

Never was a philosophical imagination more beautiful than that exquisite *Palingenesis,* as it has been termed from the Greek, or a regeneration: or rather, the apparitions of animals, and plants. Schott, Kircher, Gaffarel, Borelli, Digby, and the whole of that admirable school, discovered in the ashes of plants their primitive forms, which were again raised up by the force of heat. Nothing, they say, perishes in nature; all is but a continuation, or a revival. The semina of resurrection are concealed in extinct bodies, as in the blood of man; the ashes of roses will again revive into roses, though smaller and paler than if they had been planted; unsubstantial and unodoriferous, they are not roses which grow on rose-trees, but their delicate apparitions; and, like apparitions, they are seen but for a moment! The process of the *Palingenesis,* this picture of immortality, is described. These philosophers having burnt a flower, by calcination disengaged the salts from its ashes, and deposited them in a glass phial; a chemical mixture acted on it, till in the fermentation they assumed a bluish and a spectral hue. This dust, thus excited by heat, shoots upwards into its primitive forms; by sympathy the parts unite, and while each is returning to its destined place, we see distinctly the stalk, the leaves, and the flower arise; it is the pale spectre of a flower coming slowly forth from its ashes. The heat passes away, the magical scene declines, till the whole matter again precipitates itself into the chaos at the bottom. This vegetable phœnix lies thus concealed in its cold ashes, till the presence of heat produces this resurrection—in its absence it returns to its death. Thus the dead naturally revive; and a corpse may give out its shadowy reanimation, when not too deeply buried in the earth. Bodies corrupted in their graves have risen, particularly the murdered; for murderers are apt to bury their victims in a slight and hasty manner. Their salts, exhaled in vapour by means of their fermentation, have arranged themselves on the surface of the earth, and formed those phantoms, which at night have often terrified the passing spectator, as authentic history witnesses. They have opened the graves of the phantom, and discovered the bleeding corpse beneath; hence it is astonishing how many ghosts may be seen at night, after a recent battle, standing over their corpses! On the same principle, my old philosopher Gaffarel conjectures on the raining of frogs; but these frogs, we must conceive, can only be the ghosts of frogs; and Gaffarel himself has modestly opened this fact by a "peradventure." A more satisfactory origin of ghosts modern philosophy has not afforded.

And who does not believe in the existence of ghosts? for, as Dr. More forcibly says, "That there should be so universal a *fame* and *fear* of that which never was, nor is, nor can be ever in the world, is to me the greatest miracle of all. If there had not been, at some time or other, true miracles, it had not been so easy to impose on the people by false. The alchemist would never go about to sophisticate metals to pass them off for true gold and silver, unless that such a thing was acknowledged as true gold and silver in the world."

The pharmacopœia of those times combined more of morals with medicine than our own. They discovered that the agate rendered a man eloquent and even witty; a laurel leaf placed on the centre of the skull, fortified the memory; the brains of fowls, and birds of swift wing, wonderfully helped the imagination. All such specifics have now disappeared, and have greatly reduced the chances of an invalid recovering that which perhaps he never possessed. Lentils and rape-seed were a certain cure for the small-pox, and very obviously—their grains resembling the spots of this disease. They discovered that those who lived on "fair" plants became fair, those on fruitful ones were never barren; on the principle that Hercules acquired his mighty strength by feeding on the marrow of lions. But their talismans, provided they were genuine, seem to have been wonderfully operative; and had we the same confidence, and melted down the guineas we give physicians, engraving on them talismanic figures, I would answer for the good effects of the experiment. Naudé, indeed, has utterly ridiculed the occult virtues of talismans, in his defence of Virgil, accused of being a magician: the poet, it seems, cast into a well a talisman of a horse-leech, graven on a plate of gold, to drive

away the great number of horse-leeches which infested Naples.
Naudé positively denies that talismans ever possessed any such
occult virtues: Gaffarel regrets that so judicious a man as Naudé
should have gone this length, giving the lie to so many authentic
authors; and Naudé's paradox is, indeed, as strange as his denial;
he suspects the thing is not true because it is so generally told!
"It leads one to suspect," says he, "as animals are said to have
been driven away from so many places by these talismans,
whether they were ever driven from any one place." Gaffarel,
suppressing by his good temper his indignant feelings at such
reasoning, turns the paradox on its maker: "As if, because of the
great number of battles that Hannibal is reported to have fought
with the Romans, we might not, by the same reason, doubt
whether he fought any one with them." The reader must be
aware that the strength of the argument lies entirely with the
firm believer in talismans. Gaffarel, indeed, who passed his days
in collecting *Curiosités inouïes*, is a most authentic historian of
unparalleled events, even in his own times! Such as that heavy
rain in Poitou, which showered down *petites bestioles,* little
creatures like bishops with their mitres, and monks with their
capuchins over their heads; it is true, afterwards they all turned
into butterflies!

The museums, the cabinets, and the inventions of our early
virtuosi, were the baby-houses of philosophers. Baptista Porta,
Bishop Wilkins, and old Ashmole, were they now living, had
been enrolled among the quiet members of "The Society of
Arts," instead of flying in the air, collecting "a wing of the
Phœnix, as tradition goes"; or catching the disjointed syllables of
an old doting astrologer. But these early dilettanti had not derived the same pleasure from the useful inventions of the afore-
said "Society of Arts," as they received from what Cornelius
Agrippa, in a fit of spleen, calls "things vain and superfluous,
invented to no other end but for pomp and idle pleasure." Baptista Porta was more skilful in the mysteries of art and nature
than any man in his day. Having founded the Academy *degli
Oziosi,* he held an inferior association in his own house, called
di Secreti, where none was admitted but those elect who had
communicated some *secret*; for, in the early period of modern art
and science, the slightest novelty became a secret, not to be con-
fided to the uninitiated. Porta was unquestionably a fine genius,
as his works still show; but it was his misfortune that he attributed his own penetrating sagacity to his skill in the art of
divination. He considered himself a prognosticator; and, what

was more unfortunate, some eminent persons really thought he was. Predictions and secrets are harmless, provided they are not believed; but his Holiness finding Porta's were, warned him that magical sciences were great hindrances to the study of the Bible, and paid him the compliment to forbid his prophesying. Porta's genius was now limited, to astonish, and sometimes to terrify, the more ingenious part of *I Secreti*. On entering his cabinet, some phantom of an attendant was sure to be hovering in the air, moving as he who entered moved; or he observed in some mirror that his face was twisted on the wrong side of his shoulders, and did not quite think that all was right when he clapped his hand on it; or passing through a darkened apartment a magical landscape burst on him, with human beings in motion, the boughs of trees bending, and the very clouds passing over the sun; or sometimes banquets, battles, and hunting-parties, were in the same apartment. "All these spectacles my friends have witnessed!" exclaims the self-delighted Baptista Porta. When his friends drank wine out of the same cup which he had used, they were mortified with wonder; for he drank wine, and they only water! or on a summer's day, when all complained of the sirocco, he would freeze his guests with cold air in the room; or, on a sudden, let off a flying dragon to sail along with a cracker in its tail, and a cat tied on its back; shrill was the sound, and awful was the concussion; so that it required strong nerves, in an age of apparitions and devils, to meet this great philosopher when in his best humour. Albertus Magnus entertained the Earl of Holland, as that earl passed through Cologne, in a severe winter, with a warm summer scene, luxuriant in fruits and flowers. The fact is related by Trithemius—and this magical scene connected with his vocal head, and his books *De Secretis Mulierum*, and *De Mirabilibus*, confirmed the accusations they raised against the great Albert, for being a magician. His apologist, Theophilus Raynaud, is driven so hard to defend Albertus, that he at once asserts, the winter changed to summer, and the speaking head, to be two infamous flams! He will not believe these authenticated facts, although he credits a miracle which proves the sanctity of Albertus,—after three centuries, the body of Albert the Great remained as sweet as ever!

"Whether such enchauntments," as old Mandeville cautiously observeth, two centuries preceding the days of Porta, were "by craft or by nygromancye, I wot nere." But that they were not unknown to Chaucer, appears in his "Frankelein's Tale," where, minutely describing them, he communicates the same pleasure he must himself have received from the ocular illusions of "the Tregetoure," or "Jogelour." Chaucer ascribes the miracle to a "naturall magique!" in which, however, it was as unsettled, whether the "Prince of Darkness" was a party concerned.

> For I am siker that there be sciences
> By which men maken divers apparences
> Swiche as thise subtil tregetoures play.
> For oft at festes have I wel herd say
> That tregetoures, within an halle large,
> Have made come in a water and a barge,
> And in the halle rowen up and doun.
> Sometime hath semed come a grim leoun,
> And sometime floures spring as in a mede,
> Sometime a vine and grapes white and rede,
> Sometime a castel al of lime and ston,
> And whan hem liketh voideth it anon:
> Thus semeth it to every mannes sight.

Bishop Wilkins's museum was visited by Evelyn, who describes the sort of curiosities which occupied and amused the children of science. "Here, too, there was a hollow statue, which gave a voice, and uttered words by a long concealed pipe that went to its mouth, whilst one speaks through it at a good distance": a circumstance, which, perhaps, they were not then aware revealed the whole mystery of the ancient oracles, which they attributed to demons, rather than to tubes, pulleys, and wheels. The learned Charles Patin, in his scientific travels, records, among other valuable productions of art, a cherry-stone, on which were engraven about a dozen and a half of portraits! Even the greatest of human geniuses, Leonardo da Vinci, to attract the royal patronage, created a lion which ran before the French monarch, dropping *fleurs de lis* from its shaggy breast. And another philosopher who had a spinet which played and stopped at command, might have made a revolution in the arts and sciences, had the half-stifled child that was concealed in it not been forced, unluckily, to crawl into day-light, and thus it was proved that a philosopher might be an impostor!

The arts, as well as the sciences, at the first institution of the Royal Society, were of the most amusing class. The famous Sir Samuel Moreland had turned his house into an enchanted palace. Every thing was full of devices, which showed art and mechanism in perfection: his coach carried a travelling kitchen; for it had a fireplace and grate, with which he could make a soup, broil cutlets, and roast an egg; and he dressed his meat by clock-work. Another of these virtuosi, who is described as "a gentleman of

superior order, and whose house was a knick-knackatory," valued
himself on his multifarious inventions, but most in "sowing
salads in the morning, to be cut for dinner." The house of
Winstanley, who afterwards raised the first Eddystone light-
house, must have been the wonder of the age. If you kicked aside
an old slipper, purposely lying in your way, up started a ghost
before you; or if you sat down in a certain chair, a couple of
gigantic arms would immediately clasp you in. There was an
arbour in the garden, by the side of a canal; you had scarcely
seated yourself when you were sent out afloat to the middle of
the canal—from whence you could not escape till this man of art
and science wound you up to the arbour. What was passing at
the Royal Society, was also occurring at the *Académie des Sciences* at Paris. A great and gouty member of that philosophical
body, on the departure of a stranger, would point to his legs to
show the impossibility of conducting him to the door; yet the
astonished visitor never failed finding the virtuoso waiting for
him on the outside, to make his final bow! While the visitor
was going down stairs, this inventive genius was descending with
great velocity in a machine from the window: so that he proved,
that if a man of science cannot force nature to walk down stairs,
he may drive her out at the window!

If they travelled at home, they set off to note down prodigies.
Dr. Plott, in a magnificent project of journeying through England, for the advantage of "Learning and Trade," and the discovery of "Antiquities and other Curiosities," for which he
solicited the royal aid which Leland enjoyed, among other
notable designs, discriminates a class thus: "Next I shall inquire
of animals; and first of strange people."—"Strange accidents that
attend corporations or families, as that the deans of Rochester
ever since the foundation by turns have died deans and bishops;
the bird with a white breast that haunts the family of Oxenham
near Exeter just before the death of any of that family; the
bodies of trees that are seen to swim in a pool near Brereton in
Cheshire, a certain warning to the heir of that honourable family
to prepare for the next world." And such remarkables as "Number of children, such as the Lady Temple, who before she died
saw seven hundred descended from her." This fellow of the
Royal Society, who lived nearly to 1700, was requested to give
an edition of Pliny: we have lost the benefit of a most copious
commentary! Bishop Hall went to "the Spa." The wood about
that place was haunted not only by "freebooters, but by wolves
and witches; although these last are oft-times but one." They

were called *loups-garoux*; and the Greeks, it seems, knew them by the name of λυκάνθρωποι, men-wolves; witches that have put on the shapes of those cruel beasts. "We sawe a boy there, whose half-face was devoured by one of them near the village; yet so, as that the eare was rather cut than bitten off." Rumour had spread that the boy had had half his face devoured; when it was examined, it turned out that his ear had only been scratched! However, there can be no doubt of the existence of "witch-wolves"; for Hall saw at Limburgh "one of those miscreants executed, who confessed on the wheel to have devoured two-and-forty children in that form." They would probably have found it difficult to have summoned the mothers who had lost the children. But observe our philosopher's reasoning: "It would aske a large volume to scan this problem of *lycanthropy*." He had laboriously collected all the evidence, and had added his arguments: the result offers a curious instance of acute reasoning on a wrong principle.*

Men of science and art then passed their days in a bustle of the marvellous. I will furnish a specimen of philosophical correspondence in a letter to old John Aubrey. The writer betrays the versatility of his curiosity by very opposite discoveries. "My hands are so full of work that I have no time to transcribe for Dr. Henry More an account of the Barnstable apparition—Lord Keeper North would take it kindly from you—give a sight of this letter from Barnstable to Dr. Whitchcot." He had lately heard of a Scotchman who had been carried by fairies into France; but the purpose of his present letter is to communicate other sort of apparitions than the ghost of Barnstable. He had gone to Glastonbury, "to pick up a few berries from the holy thorn which flowered every Christmas day." The original thorn had been cut down by a military saint in the civil wars; but the trade of the place was not damaged, for they had contrived not to have a single holy thorn, but several, "by grafting and inoculation." He

---

* Hall's postulate is, that God's work could not admit of any substantial change, which is above the reach of all infernal powers; but "Herein the divell plays the double sophister; the sorcerer with sorcerers. Hee both deludes the witch's conceit and the beholder's eyes." In a word, Hall believes in what he cannot understand! Yet Hall will not believe one of the Catholic miracles of "the Virgin of Louvain," though Lipsius had written a book to commemorate "the goddess," as Hall sarcastically calls her. Hall was told, with great indignation, in the shop of the bookseller of Lipsius, that when James the First had just looked over this work, he flung it down, vociferating "Damnation to him that made it, and to him that believes it!"

promises to send these "berries"; but requests Aubrey to inform "that person of quality who had rather have a *bush*, that it was impossible to get one for him. I am told," he adds, "that there is a person about Glastonbury who hath a nursery of them, which he sells for a crown a piece," but they are supposed not to be "of the right kind."

The main object of this letter is the writer's "suspicion of gold in this country"; for which he offers three reasons. Tacitus says there was gold in England, and that Agrippa came to a spot where he had a prospect of Ireland—from which place he writes; secondly, that "an honest man" had in this spot found stones from which he had extracted good gold, and that he himself "had seen in the broken stones a clear appearance of gold"; and thirdly, "there is a story which goes by tradition in that part of the country, that in the hill alluded to there was a door into a hole, that when any wanted money they used to go and knock there, that a woman used to appear, and give to such as came. At a time one by greediness or otherwise gave her offence, she flung to the door, and delivered this old saying, still remembered in the country:

> When all *the Daws* be gone and dead,
> Then . . . . Hill shall shine gold red.

My fancy is, that this relates to an ancient family of this name, of which there is now but one man left, and he not likely to have any issue." These are his three reasons; and some mines have perhaps been opened with no better ones! But let us not imagine that this great naturalist was credulous; for he tells Aubrey that "he thought it was but a monkish tale, forged in the abbey, so famous in former time; but as I have learned not to despise our forefathers, I question whether this may not refer to some rich mine in the hill, formerly in use, and now lost. I shall shortly request you to discourse with my lord about it, to have advice, &c. In the mean time it will be best to *keep all private* for his majesty's service, his lordship's, and perhaps some private person's benefit." But he has also positive evidence: "A mason not long ago coming to the renter of the abbey for a freestone, and sawing it, out came divers pieces of gold of £3 10s. value apiece, of ancient *coins*. The stone belonged to some chimney-work; the gold was hidden in it, perhaps when the Dissolution was near." This last incident of finding coins in a chimney-piece, which he had accounted for very rationally, serves only to confirm his dream, that they were coined out of the gold of the mine in the hill; and he becomes more urgent for "a private search into these mines, which I have, I think, a way to." In the postscript he adds an account of a well, which by washing wrought a cure on a person deep in the king's evil. "I hope you don't forget your promise to communicate whatever thing you have, relating to your IDEA."

This promised *Idea* of Aubrey may be found in his MSS., under the title of *The Idea of Universal Education*. However whimsical, one would like to see it. Aubrey's life might furnish a volume of these Philosophical dreams; he was a person who from his incessant bustle and insatiable curiosity was called "The Carrier of Conceptions of the Royal Society." Many pleasant nights were "privately" enjoyed by Aubrey and his correspondent about the "Mine in the Hill"; Ashmole's manuscripts at Oxford contain a collection of many secrets of the Rosicrucians; one of the completest inventions is "a Recipe how to walk invisible." Such were the fancies which rocked the children of science in their cradles! and so feeble were the steps of our curious infancy! —But I start in my dreams! dreading the reader may also have fallen asleep!

"Measure is most excellent," says one of the oracles; "to which also we being in like manner persuaded, O most friendly and pious Asclepiades, here finish"—the dreams at the dawn of philosophy!

Literary Forgeries

THE PRECEDING article* has reminded me of a subject by no means incurious to the lovers of literature. A large volume might be composed on literary impostors; their modes of deception, however, were frequently repetitions; particularly those at the restoration of letters, when there prevailed a *mania* for burying spurious antiquities, that they might afterwards be brought to light to confound their contemporaries. They even perplex us at the present day. More sinister forgeries have been performed by Scotchmen, of whom Archibald Bower, Lauder, and Macpherson, are well known.

---

* ["On Puck the Commentator," not reprinted here.—ED.]

Even harmless impostures by some unexpected accident have driven an unwary inquirer out of the course. George Steevens must again make his appearance for a memorable trick played on the antiquary Gough. This was the famous tombstone on which was engraved the drinking-horn of Hardyknute, to indicate his last fatal carouse; for this royal Dane died drunk! To prevent any doubt, the name, in Saxon characters, was sufficiently legible. Steeped in pickle to hasten a precocious antiquity, it was then consigned to the corner of a broker's shop, where the antiquarian eye of Gough often pored on the venerable odds and ends; it perfectly succeeded on the "Director of the Antiquarian Society." He purchased the relic for a trifle, and dissertations of a due size were preparing for the *Archæologia*!* Gough never forgave himself nor Steevens for this flagrant act of ineptitude. On every occasion in the *Gentleman's Magazine,* when compelled to notice this illustrious imposition, he always struck out his own name, and muffled himself up under his titular office of "The Director"! Gough never knew that this "modern antique" was only a piece of retaliation. In reviewing Masters's *Life of Baker* he found two heads, one scratched down from painted glass by George Steevens, who would have passed it off for a portrait of one of our kings. Gough, on the watch to have a fling at George Steevens, attacked his graphic performance, and reprobated a portrait which had nothing human in it! Steevens vowed, that, wretched as Gough deemed his pencil to be, it should make "The Director" ashamed of his own eyes, and be fairly taken in by something scratched much worse. Such was the origin of his adoption of this fragment of a chimney-slab, which I have seen, and with a better judge wondered at the injudicious antiquary, who could have been duped by the slight and ill-formed scratches, and even with a false spelling of the name, which however succeeded in being passed off as a genuine Saxon inscription:

---

* I have since been informed that this famous invention was originally a flim-flam of a Mr. Thomas White, a noted collector and dealer in antiquities. But it was Steevens who placed it in the broker's shop, where he was certain of *catching* the antiquary. When the late Mr. Pegge, a profound brother, was preparing to write a dissertation on it, the first inventor of the flam stepped forward to save any further tragical termination; the wicked wit had already succeeded too well!

but he had counted on his man.* The trick is not so original as it seems. One De Grassis had engraved on marble the epitaph of a mule, which he buried in his vineyard: some time after, having ordered a new plantation on the spot, the diggers could not fail of disinterring what lay ready for them. The inscription imported that one Publius Grassus had raised this monument to his mule! De Grassis gave it out as an odd coincidence of names, and a prophecy about his own mule! It was a simple joke! The marble was thrown by, and no more thought of. Several years after it rose into celebrity, for with the erudite it then passed for an ancient inscription, and the antiquary Poracchi inserted the epitaph in his work on *Burials*. Thus De Grassis and his mule, equally respectable, would have come down to posterity, had not the story by some means got wind! An incident of this nature is recorded in Portuguese history, contrived with the intention to keep up the national spirit, and diffuse hopes of the new enterprise of Vasco da Gama, who had just sailed on a voyage of discovery to the Indies. Three stones were discovered near Cintra, bearing in ancient characters a Latin inscription; a sibylline oracle addressed prophetically "To the inhabitants of the West!" stating that when these three stones shall be found, the Ganges, the Indus, and the Tagus, should exchange their commodities! This was the pious fraud of a Portuguese poet, sanctioned by the approbation of the king. When the stones had lain a sufficient time in the damp earth, so as to become apparently antique, our poet invited a numerous party to a dinner at his country-house; in the midst of the entertainment a peasant rushed in, announcing the sudden discovery of this treasure! The inscription was placed among the royal collections as a sacred curiosity! The prophecy was accomplished, and the oracle was long considered genuine!

In such cases no mischief resulted; the annals of mankind were not confused by spurious dynasties and fabulous chronolo-

---

* The stone may be found in the British Museum. HARDCNVT is the reading on the *Harthacnut* stone; but the true orthography of the name is HARÐACNVT.

Sylvanus Urban, my once excellent and old friend, seems a trifle uncourteous on this grave occasion—He tells us, however, that "The history of this wanton trick, with a *fac-simile* of Schnebbelie's drawing, may be seen in his volume lx. p. 217." He says that this wicked contrivance of George Steevens was to entrap this famous draftsman! Does Sylvanus then deny that "the Director" was not also "entrapped?" and that he always struck out his own *name* in the proof-sheets of the Magazine, substituting his official designation, by which the whole society itself seemed to screen "the Director!"

gies; but when literary forgeries are published by those whose character hardly admits of a suspicion that they are themselves the impostors, the difficulty of assigning a motive only increases that of forming a decision; to adopt or reject them may be equally dangerous.

In this class we must place Annius of Viterbo, who published a pretended collection of historians of the remotest antiquity, some of whose *names* had descended to us in the works of ancient writers, while their works themselves had been lost. Afterwards he subjoined commentaries to confirm their authority by passages from known authors. These at first were eagerly accepted by the learned; the blunders of the presumed editor, one of which was his mistaking the right name of the historian he forged, were gradually detected, till at length the imposture was apparent! The pretended originals were more remarkable for their number than their volume; for the whole collection does not exceed 171 pages, which lessened the difficulty of the forgery; while the commentaries which were afterwards published, must have been manufactured at the same time as the text. In favour of Annius, the high rank he occupied at the Roman court, his irreproachable conduct, and his declaration that he had recovered some of these fragments at Mantua, and that others had come from Armenia, induced many to credit these pseudo-historians. A literary war soon kindled; Niceron has discriminated between four parties engaged in this conflict. One party decried the whole of the collection as gross forgeries; another obstinately supported their authenticity; a third decided that they were forgeries before Annius possessed them, who was only credulous; while a fourth party considered them as partly authentic, and ascribed their blunders to the interpolations of the editor, to increase their importance. Such as they were, they scattered confusion over the whole face of history. The false Berosus opens his history before the deluge, when, according to him, the Chaldeans through preceding ages had faithfully preserved their historical evidences! Annius hints, in his commentary, at the archives and public libraries of the Babylonians: the days of Noah comparatively seemed modern history with this dreaming editor. Some of the fanciful writers of Italy were duped: Sansovino, to delight the Florentine nobility, accommodated them with a new title of antiquity in their ancestor Noah, *Imperatore e monarcha delle genti, visse e morì in quelle parti*. The Spaniards complained that in forging these fabulous origins of different nations, a new series of kings from the ark of Noah had been introduced by some of their rhodomontade historians to pollute the sources of their history. Bodin's otherwise valuable works are considerably injured by Annius's supposititious discoveries. One historian died of grief, for having raised his elaborate speculations on these fabulous originals; and their credit was at length so much reduced, that Pignoria and Maffei both announced to their readers that they had not referred in their works to the pretended writers of Annius! Yet, to the present hour, these presumed forgeries are not always given up. The problem remains unsolved—and the silence of the respectable Annius, in regard to the forgery, as well as what he affirmed when alive, leave us in doubt whether he really intended to laugh at the world by these fairy tales of the giants of antiquity. Sanchoniathon, as preserved by Eusebius, may be classed among these ancient writings, or forgeries, and has been equally rejected and defended.

Another literary forgery, supposed to have been grafted on those of Annius, involved the Inghirami family. It was by digging in their grounds that they discovered a number of Etruscan antiquities, consisting of inscriptions, and also fragments of a chronicle, pretended to have been composed sixty years before the vulgar era. The characters on the marbles were the ancient Etruscan, and the historical work tended to confirm the pretended discoveries of Annius. They were collected and enshrined in a magnificent folio by Curtius Inghirami, who, a few years after, published a quarto volume exceeding one thousand pages to support their authenticity. Notwithstanding the erudition of the forger, these monuments of antiquity betrayed their modern condiment. There were uncial letters which no one knew; but these were said to be undiscovered ancient Etruscan characters; it was more difficult to defend the small italic letters, for they were not used in the age assigned to them; besides that there were dots on the letter *i*, a custom not practised till the eleventh century. The style was copied from the Latin of the Psalms and the Breviary; but Inghirami discovered that there had been an intercourse between the Etruscans and the Hebrews, and that David had imitated the writings of Noah and his descendants! Of Noah the chronicle details speeches and anecdotes!

The Romans, who have preserved so much of the Etruscans, had not, however, noticed a single fact recorded in these Etruscan antiquities. Inghirami replied, that the manuscript was the work of the secretary of the college of the Etrurian augurs, who alone was permitted to draw his materials from the archives, and who, it would seem, was the only scribe who has favoured posterity with so much secret history. It was urged in favour of the authenticity of these Etruscan monuments, that Inghirami was so young an antiquary at the time of the discovery, that he could not even explain them; and that when fresh researches were made on the spot, other similar monuments were also disinterred, where evidently they had long lain; the whole affair, however contrived, was confined to the *Inghirami family*. One of them, half a century before, had been the librarian of the Vatican, and to him is ascribed the honour of the forgeries which he buried where he was sure they would be found. This, however, is a mere conjecture! Inghirami, who published and defended their authenticity, was not concerned in their fabrication; the design was probably merely to raise the antiquity of Volaterra, the family estate of the Inghirami; and for this purpose one of its learned branches had bequeathed his posterity a collection of spurious historical monuments, which tended to overturn all received ideas on the first ages of history.*

It was probably such impostures, and those of *false decretals* of Isidore, which were forged for the maintenance of the papal supremacy, and for eight hundred years formed the fundamental basis of the canon law, the discipline of the church, and even the faith of Christianity, which led to the monstrous pyrrhonism of Father Hardouin, who, with immense erudition, had persuaded himself, that, excepting the Bible and Homer, Herodotus, Plautus, Pliny the elder, with fragments of Cicero, Virgil, and Horace, all the remains of classical literature were forgeries of the thirteenth and fourteenth centuries! In two dissertations he imagined that he had proved that the *Æneid* was not written by Virgil, nor the *Odes* of Horace by that poet. Hardouin was one of those wrong-headed men, who once having fallen into a delusion, whatever afterwards occurs to them on their favourite subject only tends to strengthen it. He died in his own faith! He seems not to have been aware, that by ascribing such prodigal inventions as Plutarch, Thucydides, Livy, Tacitus, and other historians, to the men he did, he was raising up an unparalleled age of learning and genius when monks could only write meagre chronicles, while learning and genius themselves lay in an enchanted slumber with a suspension of all their vital powers.

---

* The volume of these pretended Antiquities is entitled *Etruscarum Antiquitatum Fragmenta*. fo. Franc. 1637. That which Inghirami published to defend their authenticity is in Italian, *Discorso sopra l'Opposizioni fatte all'Antichità Toscane*, 4to. Firenze, 1645.

There are numerous instances of the forgeries of smaller documents. The Prayer-Book of Columbus, presented to him by the Pope, which the great discoverer of a new world bequeathed to the Genoese republic, has a codicil in his own writing as one of the leaves testifies, but as volumes composed against its authenticity deny. The famous description in Petrarch's Virgil, so often quoted, of his first *rencontre* with Laura in the church of St. Clair on a Good Friday, 6 April, 1327, it has been recently attempted to be shown is a forgery. By calculation, it appears that the 6 April, 1327, fell on a Monday! The Good Friday seems to have been a blunder of the manufacturer of the note. He was entrapped by reading the second sonnet, as it appears in the *printed* editions!

> Era il giorno ch'al sol *si scolorano*
> Per la pietà del suo fattore *i rai.*

"It was on the day when the rays of the sun were obscured by compassion for his Maker." The forger imagined this description alluded to Good Friday and the eclipse at the Crucifixion. But how stands the passage in the MS. in the Imperial Library of Vienna, which Abbé Costaing has found?

> Era il giorno ch'al sol *di color raro*
> Parve la pietà di suo fattore, *ai rai*
> Quand'io fu preso; e non mi guardai
> Che ben vostri occhi dentro mi legaro.

"It was on the day that I was captivated, devotion for its Maker appeared in the rays of a brilliant sun, and I did not well consider that it was your eyes that enchained me!"

The first meeting, according to the Abbé Costaing, was not in a *church*, but in a *meadow*—as appears by the ninety-first sonnet. The Laura of Sade was *not* the Laura of Petrarch; but Laura de Baux, unmarried, and who died young, residing in the vicinity of Vaucluse. Petrarch had often viewed her from his own window, and often enjoyed her society amidst her family.* If the Abbé Costaing's discovery be confirmed, the good name of Petrarch is

---

* I draw this information from a little "new year's gift," which my learned friend, the Rev. S. Weston, presented to his friends in 1822, entitled *A Visit to Vaucluse*, accompanied by a Supplement. He derives his account apparently from a curious publication of L'Abbé Costaing de Pusigner d'Avignon, which I with other inquirers have not been able to procure, but which it is absolutely necessary to examine, before we can decide on the very curious but unsatisfactory accounts we have hitherto possessed of the Laura of Petrarch.

freed from the idle romantic passion for a married woman. It would be curious if the famous story of the first meeting with Laura in the church of St. Clair originated in the blunder of the forger's misconception of a passage which was incorrectly printed, as appears by existing manuscripts!

Literary forgeries have been introduced into bibliography; dates have been altered; fictitious titles affixed; and books have been reprinted, either to leave out or to interpolate whole passages! I forbear entering minutely into this part of the history of literary forgery, for this article has already grown voluminous. When we discover, however, that one of the most magnificent of *amateurs,* and one of the most critical of bibliographers, were concerned in a forgery of this nature, it may be useful to spread an alarm among collectors. The Duke de la Vallière, and the Abbé de St. Léger, once concerted together to supply the eager purchaser of literary rarities with a copy of *De Tribus Impostoribus,* a book, by the date, pretended to have been printed in 1598, though, probably, a modern forgery of 1698. The title of such a work had long existed by rumour, but never was a copy seen by man! Works printed with this title have all been proved to be modern fabrications. A copy, however, of the *introuvable* original was sold at the Duke de la Vallière's sale! The history of this volume is curious. The Duke and the Abbé having manufactured a text, had it printed in the old Gothic character, under the title *De Tribus Impostoribus.* They proposed to put the great bibliopolist, De Bure, in good humour, whose agency would sanction the imposture. They were afterwards to dole out copies at twenty-five louis each, which would have been a reasonable price for a book which no one ever saw! They invited De Bure to dinner, flattered and cajoled him, and, as they imagined at a moment they had wound him up to their pitch, they exhibited their manufacture; the keen-eyed glance of the renowned cataloguer of the *Bibliographie Instructive* instantly shot like lightning over it, and, like lightning, destroyed the whole edition. He not only discovered the forgery, but reprobated it! He refused his sanction; and the forging Duke and Abbé, in confusion, suppressed the *livre introuvable*; but they owed a grudge to the honest bibliographer, and attempted to write down the work whence the De Bures derive their fame.

Among the extraordinary literary impostors of our age, if we except Lauder, who, detected by the Ithuriel pen of Bishop Douglas, lived to make his public recantation of his audacious forgeries, and Chatterton, who has buried his inexplicable story in his own grave; a tale, which seems but half told: we must place a man well known in the literary world under the assumed name of George Psalmanazar. He composed his autobiography as the penance of contrition, not to be published till he was no more, when all human motives have ceased which might cause his veracity to be suspected. The life is tedious; but I have curiously traced the progress of the mind in an ingenious imposture, which is worth preservation. The present literary forgery consisted of personating a converted islander of Formosa: a place then little known but by the reports of the Jesuits, and constructing a language and a history of a new people, and a new religion, entirely of his own invention! This man was evidently a native of the south of France; educated in some provincial college of the Jesuits, where he had heard much of their discoveries of Japan; he had looked over their maps, and listened to their comments. He forgot the manner in which the Japanese wrote; but supposed, like orientalists, they wrote from the right to the left, which he found difficult to manage. He set about excogitating an alphabet; but actually forgot to give names to his letters, which afterwards baffled him before literary men.

He fell into gross blunders; having inadvertently affirmed that the Formosans sacrificed eighteen thousand male infants annually, he persisted in not lessening the number. It was proved to be an impossibility in so small an island, without occasioning a depopulation. He had made it a principle in this imposture never to vary when he had once said a thing. All this was projected in haste, fearful of detection by those about him.

He was himself surprised at his facility of invention, and the progress of his forgery. He had formed an alphabet, a considerable portion of a new language, a grammar, a new division of the year into twenty months, and a new religion! He had accustomed himself to write his language; but being an inexpert writer with the unusual way of writing backwards, he found this so difficult, that he was compelled to change the complicated forms of some of his letters. He now finally quitted his home, assuming the character of a Formosan convert, who had been educated by the Jesuits. He was then in his fifteenth or sixteenth year. To support his new character, he practised some religious mummeries; he was seen worshipping the rising and setting sun. He made a prayer-book with rude drawings of the sun, moon, and stars, to which he added some gibberish prose and verse, written in his invented character, muttering or chanting it, as the humour took him. His custom of eating raw flesh seemed to assist his deception more than the sun and moon.

In a garrison at Sluys he found a Scotch regiment in the Dutch pay; the commander had the curiosity to invite our Formosan to confer with Innes, the chaplain to his regiment. This Innes was probably the chief cause of the imposture being carried to the extent it afterwards reached. Innes was a clergyman, but a disgrace to his cloth. As soon as he fixed his eye on our Formosan, he hit on a project; it was nothing less than to make Psalmanazar the ladder of his own ambition, and the stepping-place for him to climb up to a good living! Innes was a worthless character; as afterwards appeared, when by an audacious imposition Innes practised on the Bishop of London, he avowed himself to be the author of an anonymous work, entitled *A Modest Inquiry after Moral Virtue*; for this he obtained a good living in Essex: the real author, a poor Scotch clergyman, obliged him afterwards to disclaim the work in print, and to pay him the profit of the edition which Innes had made! He lost his character, and retired to the solitude of his living; if not penitent, at least mortified.

Such a character was exactly adapted to become the foster-father of imposture. Innes courted the Formosan, and easily won on the adventurer, who had hitherto in vain sought for a patron. Meanwhile no time was lost by Innes to inform the unsuspicious and generous Bishop of London of the prize he possessed—to convert the Formosan was his ostensible pretext; to procure preferment his concealed motive. It is curious enough to observe, that the ardour of conversion died away in Innes, and the most marked neglect of his convert prevailed, while the answer of the bishop was protracted or doubtful. He had at first proposed to our Formosan impostor to procure his discharge, and convey him to England; this was eagerly consented to by our pliant adventurer. A few Dutch schellings, and fair words, kept him in good humour; but no letter coming from the bishop, there were fewer words, and not a stiver! This threw a new light over the character of Innes to the inexperienced youth. Psalmanazar sagaciously now turned all his attention to some Dutch ministers; Innes grew jealous lest they should pluck the bird which he had already in his net. He resolved to baptize the impostor—which only the more convinced Psalmanazar that Innes was one himself; for before this time Innes had practised a stratagem on him, which had clearly shown what sort of a man his Formosan was.

This stratagem was this: he made him translate a passage in

Cicero, of some length, into his pretended language, and give it him in writing; this was easily done by Psalmanazar's facility of inventing characters. After Innes had made him construe it, he desired to have another version of it on another paper. The proposal, and the arch manner of making it, threw our impostor into the most visible confusion. He had had but a short time to invent the first paper, less to recollect it; so that in the second transcript not above half the words were to be found which existed in the first. Innes assumed a solemn air, and Psalmanazar was on the point of throwing himself on his mercy, but Innes did not wish to unmask the impostor; he was rather desirous of fitting the mask closer to his face. Psalmanazar, in this hard trial, had given evidence of uncommon facility, combined with a singular memory. Innes cleared his brow, smiled with a friendly look, and only hinted in a distant manner, that he ought to be careful to be better provided for the future! An advice which Psalmanazar afterwards bore in mind, and at length produced the forgery of an entire new language; and which, he remarkably observes, "by what I have tried since I came into England, I cannot say but I could have compassed it with less difficulty than can be conceived had I applied closely to it." When a version of the catechism was made into the pretended Formosan language, which was submitted to the judgment of the first scholars, it appeared to them grammatical, and was pronounced to be a real language, from the circumstance that it resembled no other! and they could not conceive that a stripling could be the inventor of a language. If the reader is curious to examine this extraordinary imposture, I refer him to that literary curiosity, *An Historical and Geographical Description of Formosa, with Accounts of the Religion, Customs and Manners of the Inhabitants, by George Psalmanazar, a Native of the said Isle*, 1704; with numerous plates, wretched inventions! of their dress! religious ceremonies! their tabernacle and altars to the sun, the moon, and the ten stars! their architecture! the viceroy's castle! a temple! a city house! a countryman's house! and the Formosan alphabet! In his conferences before the Royal Society with a Jesuit just returned from China, the Jesuit had certain strong suspicions that our hero was an impostor. The good father remained obstinate in his own conviction, but could not satisfactorily communicate it to others; and Psalmanazar, after politely asking pardon for the expression, complains of the Jesuit that "HE *lied most impudently," mentitur impudentissime!* Dr. Mead absurdly insisted Psalmanazar was a Dutchman or a German;

some thought him a Jesuit in disguise, a tool of the non-jurors; the Catholics thought him bribed by the Protestants to expose their church; the Presbyterians that he was paid to explode their doctrine, and cry up Episcopacy! This fabulous history of Formosa seems to have been projected by his artful prompter Innes, who put Varenius into Psalmanazar's hands to assist him; trumpeted forth in the domestic and foreign papers an account of this converted Formosan; maddened the booksellers to hurry the author, who was scarcely allowed two months to produce this extraordinary volume; and as the former accounts which the public possessed of this island were full of monstrous absurdities and contradictions, these assisted the present imposture. Our forger resolved not to describe new and surprising things as they had done, but rather studied to clash with them, probably that he might have an opportunity of pretending to correct them. The first edition was immediately sold; the world was more divided than ever in opinion; in a second edition he prefixed a vindication!—the unhappy forger got about twenty guineas for an imposture, whose delusion spread far and wide! Some years afterwards Psalmanazar was engaged in a minor imposture; one man had persuaded him to father a white composition called the *Formosan japan!* which was to be sold at a high price! It was curious for its whiteness, but it had its faults. The project failed, and Psalmanazar considered the miscarriage of the white *Formosan japan* as a providential warning to repent of all his impostures of Formosa!

Among these literary forgeries may be classed several ingenious ones fabricated for a *political* purpose. We had certainly numerous ones during our civil wars in the reign of Charles the First. This is not the place to continue the controversy respecting the mysterious *Eikon Basiliké*, which has been ranked among them, from the ambiguous claim of Gauden. A recent writer who would probably incline not to leave the monarch, were he living, not only his head but the little fame he might obtain by the *Verses* said to be written by him at Carisbrooke Castle, would deprive him also of these. Henderson's death-bed recantation is also reckoned among them; and we have a large collection of *Letters of Sir Henry Martin to his Lady of Delight*, which were the satirical effusions of a wit of that day, but by the price they have obtained, are probably considered as genuine ones, and exhibit an amusing picture of his loose rambling life.* There is

---

* Since this was published I have discovered that Harry Martin's *Letters* are not forgeries, but I cannot immediately recover my authority.

a ludicrous speech of the strange Earl of Pembroke, which was forged by the inimitable Butler; and Sir John Birkenhead, a great humourist and wit, had a busy pen in these spurious letters and speeches.

The Man of One Book

MR. MAURICE, in his animated memoirs, has recently acquainted us with a fact which may be deemed important in the life of a literary man. He tells us, "We have been just informed that Sir William Jones *invariably* read through every year the works of Cicero, whose life indeed was the great exemplar of his own." The same passion for the works of Cicero has been participated by others. When the best means of forming a good style were inquired of the learned Arnauld, he advised the daily study of Cicero; but it was observed that the object was not to form a Latin, but a French style: "In that case," replied Arnauld, "you must still read Cicero."

A predilection for some great author, among the vast number which must transiently occupy our attention, seems to be the happiest preservative for our taste: accustomed to that excellent author whom we have chosen for our favourite, we may in this intimacy possibly resemble him. It is to be feared, that if we do not form such a permanent attachment, we may be acquiring knowledge, while our enervated taste becomes less and less lively. Taste embalms the knowledge which otherwise cannot preserve itself. He who has long been intimate with one great author, will always be found to be a formidable antagonist; he has saturated his mind with the excellencies of genius; he has shaped his faculties insensibly to himself by his model, and he is like a man who ever sleeps in armour, ready at a moment! The old Latin proverb reminds us of this fact, *Cave ab homine unius libri*: Be cautious of the man of one book!

Pliny and Seneca give very safe advice on reading: that we should read much, but not many books—but they had no "monthly list of new publications"! Since their days others have favoured us with *Methods of Study*, and *Catalogues of Books to be read*. Vain attempts to circumscribe that invisible circle of human knowledge which is perpetually enlarging itself! The multiplicity of books is an evil for the many; for we now find an *helluo librorum* not only among the learned, but, with their pardon, among the unlearned; for those who, even to the prejudice of their health, persist only in reading the incessant booknovelties of our own time, will after many years acquire a sort of learned ignorance. We are now in want of an art to teach how books are to be read, rather than not to read them: such an art is practicable. But amidst this vast multitude still let us be "the man of one book," and preserve an uninterrupted intercourse with that great author with whose mode of thinking we sympathize, and whose charms of composition we can habitually retain.

It is remarkable that every great writer appears to have a predilection for some favourite author; and, with Alexander, had they possessed a golden casket, would have enshrined the works they so constantly turned over. Demosthenes felt such delight in the history of Thucydides, that, to obtain a familiar and perfect mastery of his style, he recopied his history eight times; while Brutus not only was constantly perusing Polybius even amidst the most busy periods of his life, but was abridging a copy of that author on the last awful night of his existence, when on the following day he was to try his fate against Antony and Octavius. Selim the Second had the *Commentaries* of Cæsar translated for his use; and it is recorded that his military ardour was heightened by the perusal. We are told that Scipio Africanus was made a hero by the writings of Xenophon. When Clarendon was employed in writing his history, he was in a constant study of Livy and Tacitus, to acquire the full and flowing style of the one, and the portrait-painting of the other: he records this circumstance in a letter. Voltaire had usually on his table the *Athalie* of Racine, and the *Petit Carême* of Massillon; the tragedies of the one were the finest model of French verse, the sermons of the other of French prose. "Were I obliged to sell my library," exclaimed Diderot, "I would keep back Moses, Homer, and Richardson"; and, by the *éloge* which this enthusiastic writer composed on our English novelist, it is doubtful, had the Frenchman been obliged to have lost two of them, whether Richardson had not been the elected favourite. Monsieur Thomas, a French writer, who at times displays high eloquence and profound thinking, Herault de Sechelles tells us, studied chiefly one author, but that author was Cicero; and never went into the country unaccompanied by some of his works. Fénelon was constantly employed on his Homer; he left a translation of the greater part of the *Odyssey,* without any design of publication, but merely as an exercise for style. Montesquieu was a constant student of Tacitus, of whom he must be considered a forcible imitator. He has, in the manner of Tacitus, characterized Tacitus. "That historian," he says, "who abridged every thing, because he saw every thing." The famous Bourdaloue re-perused every year Saint Paul, Saint Chrysostom, and Cicero. "These," says a French critic, "were the sources of his masculine and solid eloquence." Grotius had such a taste for Lucan, that he always carried a pocket edition about him, and has been seen to kiss his hand-book with the rapture of a true votary. If this anecdote be true, the elevated sentiments of the stern Roman were probably the attraction with the Batavian republican. The diversified reading of Liebnitz is well known; but he still attached himself to one or two favourites: Virgil was always in his hand when at leisure, and Leibnitz had read Virgil so often, that even in his old age he could repeat whole books by heart; Barclay's *Argenis* was his model for prose; when he was found dead in his chair, the *Argenis* had fallen from his hands. Rabelais and Marot were the perpetual favourites of La Fontaine; from one he borrowed his humour, and from the other his style. Quevedo was so passionately fond of the *Don Quixote* of Cervantes, that often in reading that unrivalled work he felt an impulse to burn his own inferior compositions: to be a sincere admirer and a hopeless rival is a case of authorship the hardest imaginable. Few writers can venture to anticipate the award of posterity; yet perhaps Quevedo had not even been what he was, without the perpetual excitement he received from his great master. Horace was the friend of his heart to Malherbe; he laid the Roman poet on his pillow, took him in the fields, and called his Horace his breviary. Plutarch, Montaigne, and Locke, were the three authors constantly in the hands of Rousseau, and he has drawn from them the groundwork of his ideas in his *Emile*. The favourite author of the great Earl of Chatham was Barrow; and on his style he had formed his eloquence, and had read his great master so constantly, as to be able to repeat his elaborate sermons from memory. The great Lord Burleigh always carried Tully's *Offices* in his pocket; Charles V. and Bonaparte had Machiavel frequently in their hands; and Davila was the perpetual study of Hampden: he seemed to have discovered in that historian of civil wars those which he anticipated in the land of his fathers.

These facts sufficiently illustrate the recorded circumstance of Sir William Jones's invariable habit of reading his Cicero through every year, and exemplify the happy result for him, who, amidst the multiplicity of his authors, still continues in this way to be "the man of one book."

Secret History of an Elective Monarchy
A Political Sketch

POLAND, once a potent and magnificent kingdom, when it sunk into an elective monarchy, became "venal thrice an age." That country must have exhibited many a diplomatic scene of intricate intrigue, which although they could not appear in its public, have no doubt been often consigned to its secret, history. With us the corruption of a rotten borough has sometimes exposed the guarded proffer of one party, and the dexterous chaffering of the other: but a master-piece of diplomatic finesse and political invention, electioneering viewed on the most magnificent scale, with a kingdom to be canvassed, and a crown to be won and lost, or lost and won in the course of a single day, exhibits a political drama, which, for the honour and happiness of mankind, is of rare and strange occurrence. There was one scene in this drama, which might appear somewhat too large for an ordinary theatre; the actors apparently were not less than fifty to a hundred thousand; twelve vast tents were raised on an extensive plain, a hundred thousand horses were in the environs —and palatines and castellans, the ecclesiastical orders, with the ambassadors of the royal competitors, all agitated by the ceaseless motion of different factions during the six weeks of the election, and of many preceding months of preconcerted measures and vacillating opinions, now were all solemnly assembled at the diet. —Once the poet, amidst his gigantic conception of a scene, resolved to leave it out:

> So vast a throng the stage can ne'er contain—
> Then build a new, or *act it in a plain!*

exclaimed "La Mancha's knight," kindling at a scene so novel and so vast!

Such an electioneering negotiation, the only one I am acquainted with, is opened in the *Discours* of Choisnin, the secretary of Montluc, bishop of Valence, the confidential agent of Catharine de' Medici, and who was sent to intrigue at the Polish diet, to obtain the crown of Poland for her son the Duke of Anjou, afterwards Henry the Third. This bold enterprise at first seemed hopeless, and in its progress encountered growing obstructions; but Montluc was one of the most finished diplomatists that the genius of the Gallic cabinet ever sent forth. He was nick-named in all the courts of Europe, from the circumstance of his limping, "le Boiteux": our political bishop was in cabinet intrigues the Talleyrand of his age, and sixteen embassies to Italy, Germany, England, Scotland, and Turkey, had made this *"connoisseur en hommes"* an extraordinary politician!

Catharine de' Medici was infatuated with the dreams of judicial astrology; her pensioned oracles had declared that she should live to see each of her sons crowned, by which prediction probably they had only purposed to flatter her pride and her love of dominion. They, however, ended in terrifying the credulous queen; and she dreading to witness a throne, in France, disputed perhaps by fratricides, anxiously sought a separate crown for each of her three sons. She had been trifled with in her earnest negotiations with our Elizabeth; twice had she seen herself baffled in her views in the Dukes of Alençon and of Anjou. Catharine then projected a new empire for Anjou, by incorporating into one kingdom Algiers, Corsica, and Sardinia; but the other despot, he of Constantinople, Selim the Second, dissipated the brilliant speculation of our female Machiavel. Charles the Ninth was sickly, jealous, and desirous of removing from the court the Duke of Anjou, whom two victories had made popular, though he afterwards sunk into a Sardanapalus. Montluc penetrated into the secret wishes of Catharine and Charles, and suggested to them the possibility of encircling the brows of Anjou with the diadem of Poland, the Polish monarch then being in a state of visible decline. The project was approved; and, like a profound politician, the bishop prepared for an event which might be remote and always problematical, by sending into Poland a natural son of his, Balagny, as a disguised agent; his youth, his humble rank, and his love of pleasure, would not create any alarm among the neighbouring powers, who were alike on the watch to snatch the expected spoil; but as it was necessary to have a more dexterous politician behind the curtain, he recommended his secretary, Choisnin, as a travelling tutor to a youth who appeared to want one.

Balagny proceeded to Poland, where, under the veil of dissipation, and in the midst of splendid festivities, with his trusty adjutant, this hair-brained boy of revelry began to weave those intrigues which were afterwards to be knotted, or untied, by Montluc himself. He had contrived to be so little suspected, that the agent of the emperor had often disclosed important secrets to his young and amiable friend. On the death of Sigismond Augustus, Balagny, leaving Choisnin behind to trumpet forth the virtues of Anjou, hastened to Paris to give an account of all which he had seen or heard. But poor Choisnin found himself in a dilemma among those who had so long listened to his panegyrics on the humanity and meek character of the Duke of Anjou; for the news of St. Bartholomew's massacre had travelled faster than the post; and Choisnin complains that he was now treated as an impudent liar, and the French prince as a monster. In vain he assured them that the whole was an exaggerated account, a mere insurrection of the people, or the effects of a few private enmities, praying the indignant Poles to suspend their decision till the bishop came: *"Attendez le Boiteux!"* cried he, in agony.

Meanwhile, at Paris, the choice of a proper person for this embassy had been difficult to settle. It was a business of intrigue more than of form, and required an orator to make speeches and addresses in a sort of popular assembly; for though the people, indeed, had no concern in the diet, yet the greater and the lesser nobles and gentlemen, all electors, were reckoned at one hundred thousand. It was supposed that a lawyer who could negotiate in good Latin, and one, as the French proverb runs, who could *aller et parler*, would more effectually puzzle their heads, and satisfy their consciences to vote for his client. Catharine at last fixed on Montluc himself, from the superstitious prejudice, which, however, in this case accorded with philosophical experience, that "Montluc had ever been *lucky* in his negotiations."

Montluc hastened his departure from Paris; and it appears that our political bishop had, by his skilful penetration into the French cabinet, foreseen the horrible catastrophe which occurred very shortly after he had left it; for he had warned the Count de Rochefoucault to absent himself; but this lord, like so many others, had no suspicions of the perfidious projects of Catharine and her cabinet. Montluc, however, had not long been on his journey, ere the news reached him, and it occasioned innumerable obstacles in his progress, which even his sagacity had not calculated on. At Strasburgh he had appointed to meet some able coadjutors, among whom was the famous Joseph Scaliger; but they were so terrified by *les Matinées Parisiennes*, that Scaliger flew to Geneva, and would not budge out of that safe corner: and the others ran home, not imagining that Montluc would venture to pass through Germany, where the Protestant indignation had made the roads too hot for a Catholic bishop. But Montluc had set his cast on the die. He had already passed through several hair-breadth escapes from the stratagems of the Guise faction, who more than once attempted to hang or drown the bishop, who, they cried out, was a Calvinist; the fears and jealousies of the Guises had been roused by this political mission. Among all these troubles and delays, Montluc was most affected by the rumour that the election was on the point of being made, and that the plague was universal throughout Poland, so that he must have felt that he might be too late for the one, and too early for the other.

At last Montluc arrived, and found that the whole weight of this negotiation was to fall on his single shoulders; and further, that he was to sleep every night on a pillow of thorns. Our bishop had not only to allay the ferment of the popular spirit of the Evangelicals, as the Protestants were then called, but even of the more rational Catholics of Poland. He had also to face those haughty and feudal lords, of whom each considered himself the equal of the sovereign whom he created, and whose avowed principle was, and many were incorrupt, that their choice of a sovereign should be regulated solely by the public interest; and it was hardly to be expected that the emperor, the czar, and the King of Sweden, would prove unsuccessful rivals to the cruel, and voluptuous, and bigoted Duke of Anjou, whose political interests were too remote and novel to have raised any faction among these independent Poles.

The crafty politician had the art of dressing himself up in all the winning charms of candour and loyalty; a sweet flow of honeyed words melted on his lips, while his heart, cold and immovable as a rock, stood unchanged amidst the most unforeseen difficulties.

The emperor had set to work the Abbé Cyre in a sort of ambiguous character, an envoy for the nonce, to be acknowledged or disavowed as was convenient; and by his activity he obtained considerable influence among the Lithuanians, the Wallachians, and nearly all Prussia, in favour of the Archduke Ernest. Two Bohemians, who had the advantage of speaking the Polish language, had arrived with a state and magnificence becoming kings rather than ambassadors. The Muscovite had written letters full of golden promises to the nobility, and was supported by a

palatine of high character; a perpetual peace between two such
great neighbours was too inviting a project not to find advocates;
and this party, Choisnin observes, appeared at first the most to
be feared. The King of Sweden was a close neighbour, who had
married the sister of their late sovereign, and his son urged his
family claims as superior to those of foreigners. Among these
parties was a patriotic one, who were desirous of a Pole for their
monarch; a king of their father-land, speaking their mother-
tongue, one who would not strike at the independence of his
country, but preserve its integrity from the stranger. This popular party was even agreeable to several of the foreign powers
themselves, who did not like to see a rival power strengthening
itself by so strict a union with Poland; but in this choice of a
sovereign from among themselves, there were at least thirty lords
who equally thought that they were the proper wood of which
kings should be carved out. The Poles therefore could not agree
on the Pole who deserved to be a *Piaste;* an endearing title for
a native monarch, which originated in the name of the family of
the *Piastis,* who had reigned happily over the Polish people for
the space of five centuries! The remembrance of their virtues
existed in the minds of the honest Poles in this affectionate title,
and their party were called the *Piastis.*

Montluc had been deprived of the assistance he had depended
on from many able persons, whom the massacre of St. Bartholomew had frightened away from every French political connection. He found that he had himself only to depend on. We are
told that he was not provided with the usual means which are
considered most efficient in elections, nor possessed the interest
nor the splendour of his powerful competitors: he was to derive
all his resources from diplomatic finesse. The various ambassadors
had fixed and distant residences, that they might not hold too
close an intercourse with the Polish nobles. Of all things, he was
desirous to obtain an easy access to these chiefs, that he might
observe, and that they might listen. He who would seduce by his
own ingenuity must come in contact with the object he would
corrupt. Yet Montluc persisted in not approaching them without
being sought after, which answered his purpose in the end. One
favourite argument which our Talleyrand had set afloat, was to
show that all the benefits which the different competitors had
promised to the Poles were accompanied by other circumstances
which could not fail to be ruinous to the country: while the offer
of his master, whose interests were remote, could not be adverse
to those of the Polish nation: so that much good might be ex-

pected from him, without any fear of accompanying evil. Montluc procured a clever Frenchman to be the bearer of his first
dispatch, in Latin, to the diet; which had hardly assembled, ere
suspicions and jealousies were already breaking out. The emperor's ambassadors had offended the pride of the Polish nobles
by travelling about the country without leave, and resorting to
the infanta; and besides, in some intercepted letters the Polish
nation was designated as *gens barbara et gens inepta*. "I do not
think that the said letter was really written by the said ambassadors, who were statesmen too politic to employ such unguarded
language," very ingenuously writes the secretary of Montluc.
However, it was a blow levelled at the imperial ambassadors;
while the letter of the French bishop, composed "in a humble
and modest style," began to melt their proud spirits, and two
thousand copies of the French bishop's letter were eagerly spread.

"But this good fortune did not last more than four-and-twenty
hours," mournfully writes our honest secretary; "for suddenly
the news of the fatal day of St. Bartholomew arrived, and every
Frenchman was detested."

Montluc, in this distress, published an apology for *les Matinées
Parisiennes*, which he reduced to some excesses of the people,
the result of a conspiracy plotted by the Protestants; and he
adroitly introduced as a personage his master Anjou, declaring
that "he scorned to oppress a party whom he had so often conquered with sword in hand." This pamphlet, which still exists,
must have cost the good bishop some invention; but in elections
the lie of the moment serves a purpose; and although Montluc
was in due time bitterly recriminated on, still the apology
served to divide public opinion.

Montluc was a whole cabinet to himself: he dispersed another
tract in the character of a Polish gentleman, in which the French
interests were urged by such arguments, that the leading chiefs
never met without disputing; and Montluc now found that he
had succeeded in creating a French party. The Austrian then employed a real Polish gentleman to write for his party; but this
was too genuine a production, for the writer wrote too much in
earnest; and in politics we must not be in a passion.

The mutual jealousies of each party assisted the views of our
negotiator; they would side with him against each other. The
archduke and the czar opposed the Turk; the Muscovite could
not endure that Sweden should be aggrandized by this new
crown; and Denmark was still more uneasy. Montluc had discovered how every party had its vulnerable point, by which it

could be managed. The cards had now got fairly shuffled, and he depended on his usual good play.

Our bishop got hold of a palatine to write for the French cause in the vernacular tongue; and appears to have held a more mysterious intercourse with another palatine, Albert Lasky. Mutual accusations were made in the open diet: the Poles accused some Lithuanian lords of having contracted certain engagements with the czar; these in return accused the Poles, and particularly this Lasky, with being corrupted by the gold of France. Another circumstance afterwards arose; the Spanish ambassador had forty thousand thalers sent to him, but which never passed the frontiers, as this fresh supply arrived too late for the election. "I believe," writes our secretary with great simplicity, "that this money was only designed to distribute among the trumpeters and the tabourines." The usual expedient in contested elections was now evidently introduced; our secretary acknowledging that Montluc daily acquired new supporters, because he did not attempt to gain them over *merely by promises* —resting his whole cause on this argument, that the interest of the nation was concerned in the French election.

Still would ill fortune cross our crafty politician when every thing was proceeding smoothly. The massacre was refreshed with more damning particulars; some letters were forged, and others were but too true; all parties, with rival intrepidity, were carrying on a complete scene of deception. A rumour spread that the French king disavowed his accredited agent, and apologized to the emperor for having yielded to the importunities of a political speculator, whom he was now resolved to recall. This somewhat paralyzed the exertions of those palatines who had involved themselves in the intrigues of Montluc, who was now forced patiently to wait for the arrival of a courier with renewed testimonials of his diplomatic character from the French court. A great odium was cast on the French in the course of this negotiation by a distribution of prints, which exposed the most inventive cruelties practised by the Catholics on the Reformed; such as women cleaved in half in the act of attempting to snatch their children from their butchers; while Charles the Ninth and the Duke of Anjou were hideously represented in their persons, and as spectators of such horrid tragedies, with words written in labels, complaining that the executioners were not zealous enough in this holy work. These prints, accompanied by libels and by horrid narratives, inflamed the popular indignation, and more particularly the women, who were affected to tears, as if these horrid scenes had been passing before their eyes.

Montluc replied to the libels as fast as they appeared, while he skilfully introduced the most elaborate panegyrics on the Duke of Anjou; and in return for the caricatures, he distributed two portraits of the king and the duke, to show the ladies, if not the diet, that neither of these princes had such ferocious and in-human faces. Such are the small means by which the politician condescends to work his great designs; and the very means by which his enemies thought they should ruin his cause, Montluc adroitly turned to his own advantage. Any thing of instant occurrence serves electioneering purposes, and Montluc eagerly seized this favourable occasion to exhaust his imagination on an ideal sovereign, and to hazard, with address, anecdotes, whose authenticity he could never have proved, till he perplexed even unwilling minds to be uncertain whether that intolerant and in-human duke was not the most heroic and most merciful of princes. It is probable that the Frenchman abused even the license of the French *éloge*, for a noble Pole told Montluc that he was always amplifying his duke with such ideal greatness, and attributing to him such immaculate purity of sentiment, that it was inferred there was no man in Poland who could possibly equal him; and that his declaration, that the duke was not desirous of reigning over Poland to possess the wealth and gran-deur of the kingdom, and that he was solely ambitious of the honour to be the head of such a great and virtuous nobility, had offended many lords, who did not believe that the duke sought the Polish crown *merely* to be the sovereign of a virtuous people.

These Polish statesmen appear, indeed, to have been more enlightened than the subtle politician perhaps calculated on; for when Montluc was over anxious to exculpate the Duke of Anjou from having been an actor in the Parisian massacre, a noble Pole observed, "That he need not lose his time at framing any apologies; for if he could prove that it was the interest of the country that the duke ought to be elected their king, it was all that was required. His cruelty, were it true, would be no reason to prevent his election, for we have nothing to dread from it: once in our kingdom, he will have more reason to fear us than we him, should he ever attempt our lives, our property, or our liberty."

Another Polish lord, whose scruples were as pious as his patriotism was suspicious, however observed that, in his con-ferences with the French bishop, the bishop had never once mentioned God, whom all parties ought to implore to touch the hearts of the electors, in their choice of God's "anointed." Montluc might have felt himself unexpectedly embarrassed at the religious scruples of this lord, but the politician was never at a fault. "Speaking to a man of letters, as his lordship was," replied the French bishop, "it was not for him to remind his lordship what he so well knew; but since he had touched on the subject, he would, however, say, that were a sick man desirous of having a physician, the friend who undertook to procure one would not do his duty should he say it was necessary to call in one whom God had chosen to restore his health; but another who should say that the most learned and skilful is he whom God has chosen, would be doing the best for the patient, and evince most judgment. By a parity of reason we must believe that God will not send an angel to point out the man whom he would have his anointed; sufficient for us that God has given us a knowledge of the requisites of a good king; and if the Polish gentleman choose such a sovereign, it will be him whom God has chosen." This shrewd argument delighted the Polish lord, who repeated the story in different companies, to the honour of the bishop. "And in this manner," adds the secretary with great *naïveté*, "did the *sieur*, strengthened by good arguments, divulge his opinions, which were received by many, and run from hand to hand."

Montluc had his inferior manœuvres. He had to equipoise the opposite interests of the Catholics and the Evangelists, or the Reformed: it was mingling fire and water without suffering them to hiss, or to extinguish one another. When the imperial ambassadors gave *fêtes* to the higher nobility only, they consequently offended the lesser. The Frenchman gave no banquets, but his house was open to all at all times, who were equally welcome. "You will see that the *fêtes* of the imperialists will do them more harm than good," observed Montluc to his secretary.

Having gained over by every possible contrivance a number of the Polish nobles, and showered his courtesies on those of the inferior orders, at length the critical moment approached, and the finishing hand was to be put to the work. Poland, with the appearance of a popular government, was a singular aristocracy of a hundred thousand electors, consisting of the higher and the lower nobility, and the gentry; the people had no concern with the government. Yet still it was to be treated by the politician as a popular government, where those who possessed the greatest influence over such large assemblies were orators, and he who delivered himself with the most fluency, and the most pertinent arguments, would infallibly bend every heart to the point he wished. The French bishop depended greatly on the effect which his oration was to produce when the ambassadors were respectively to be heard before the assembled diet; the great and concluding act of so many tedious and difficult negotiations—"which had cost my master," writes the ingenuous secretary, "six months' daily and nightly labours; he had never been assisted or comforted by any but his poor servants; and in the course of these six months had written ten reams of paper, a thing which for forty years he had not used himself to."

Every ambassador was now to deliver an oration before the assembled electors, and thirty-two copies were to be printed to present one to each palatine, who in his turn was to communicate it to his lords. But a fresh difficulty occurred to the French negotiator; as he trusted greatly to his address influencing the multitude, and creating a popular opinion in his favour, he regretted to find that the imperial ambassador would deliver his speech in the Bohemian language, so that he would be understood by the greater part of the assembly; a considerable advantage over Montluc, who could only address them in Latin. The inventive genius of the French bishop resolved on two things which had never before been practised: first, to have his Latin translated into the vernacular idiom; and, secondly, to print an edition of 1500 copies in both languages, and thus to obtain a vast advantage over the other ambassadors with their thirty-two manuscript copies, of which each copy was used to be read to 1200 persons. The great difficulty was to get it secretly translated and printed. This fell to the management of Choisnin, the secretary. He set off to the castle of the palatine, Solikotski, who was deep in the French interest; Solikotski dispatched the version in six days. Hastening with the precious MS. to Cracow, Choisnin flew to a trusty printer, with whom he was connected; the sheets were deposited every night at Choisnin's lodgings, and at the end of a fortnight the diligent secretary conducted the 1500 copies in secret triumph to Warsaw.

Yet this glorious labour was not ended; Montluc was in no haste to deliver his wonder-working oration, on which the fate of a crown seemed to depend. When his turn came to be heard, he suddenly fell sick; for the fact was, that he wished to speak last, which would give him the advantage of replying to any objection raised by his rivals, and admit also of an attack on their weak points.

He contrived to obtain copies of their harangues, and discovered five points which struck at the French interest. Our poor bishop had now to sit up through the night to rewrite five leaves of his printed oration, and cancel five which had been printed; and worse! he had to get them by heart, and to have them translated and inserted, by employing twenty scribes day and night. "It is scarcely credible what my master went through about this time," saith the historian of his *gestes*.

The council or diet was held in a vast plain. Twelve pavilions were raised to receive the Polish nobility and the ambassadors. One of a circular form was supported by a single mast, and was large enough to contain 6000 persons, without any one approaching the mast nearer than by twenty steps, leaving this space void to preserve silence; the different orders were placed around; the archbishop and the bishops, the palatines, the castellans, each according to their rank. During the six weeks of the sittings of the diet, 100,000 horses were in the environs, yet forage and every sort of provisions abounded. There were no disturbances, not a single quarrel occurred, although there wanted not in that meeting for enmities of long standing. It was strange, and even awful, to view such a mighty assembly preserving the greatest order, and every one seriously intent on this solemn occasion.

At length the elaborate oration was delivered: it lasted three hours, and Choisnin assures us not a single auditor felt weary. "A cry of joy broke out from the tent, and was reëchoed through the plain, when Montluc ceased: it was a public acclamation; and had the election been fixed for that moment, when all hearts were warm, surely the duke had been chosen without a dissenting voice." Thus writes, in rapture, the ingenuous secretary; and in the spirit of the times communicates a delightful augury attending this speech, by which evidently was foreseen its happy termination. "Those who disdain all things will take this to be a mere invention of mine," says honest Choisnin; "but true it is, that while the said *sieur* delivered his harangue, a lark was seen all the while upon the mast of the pavilion, singing and warbling, which was remarked by a great number of lords, because the lark is accustomed only to rest itself on the earth: the most impartial confessed this to be a good augury.* Also it was observed, that

---

* Our honest secretary reminds me of a passage in Geoffroy of Monmouth, who says, "at this place an *eagle spoke* while the wall of the town was building; and indeed I should not have failed *transmitting the speech to posterity* had I thought it *true* as the rest of the history."

when the other ambassadors were speaking, a hare, and at another time a hog, ran through the tent; and when the Swedish
ambassador spoke, the great tent fell half-way down. This lark
singing all the while did no little good to our cause; for many
of the nobles and gentry noted this curious particularity, because
when a thing which does not commonly happen occurs in a
public affair, such appearances give rise to hopes either of good
or of evil."

The singing of this lark in favour of the Duke of Anjou is not
so evident as the cunning trick of the other French agent, the
political Bishop of Valence, who now reaped the full advantage
of his 1500 copies over the thirty-two of his rivals. Every one had
the French one in hand or read it to his friends; while the others,
in manuscript, were confined to a very narrow circle.

The period from the 10th of April to the 6th of May, when
they proceeded to the election, proved to be an interval of infinite perplexities, troubles, and activity; it is probable that
the secret history of this period of the negotiations was never
written. The other ambassadors were for protracting the election,
perceiving the French interest prevalent: but delay would not
serve the purpose of Montluc, he not being so well provided
with friends and means on the spot as the others were. The public opinion which he had succeeded in creating, by some unforeseen circumstance might change.

During this interval, the bishop had to put several agents of
the other parties *hors de combat*. He got rid of a formidable
adversary in the Cardinal Commendon, an agent of the pope's,
whom he proved ought not to be present at the election, and the
cardinal was ordered to take his departure. A bullying colonel
was set upon the French negotiator, and went about from tent
to tent with a list of the debts of the Duke of Anjou, to show that
the nation could expect nothing profitable from a ruined spendthrift. The page of a Polish count flew to Montluc for protection,
entreating permission to accompany the bishop on his return to
Paris. The servants of the count pursued the page; but this
young gentleman had so insinuated himself into the favour of
the bishop, that he was suffered to remain. The next day the
page desired Montluc would grant him the full liberty of his
religion, being an Evangelical, that he might communicate this
to his friends, and thus fix them to the French party. Montluc
was too penetrating for this young political agent, whom he discovered to be a spy, and the pursuit of his fellows to have been a
farce; he sent the page back to his master, the Evangelical count,

observing that such tricks were too gross to be played on one who had managed affairs in all the courts of Europe before he came into Poland.

Another alarm was raised by a letter from the grand vizier of Selim the Second, addressed to the diet, in which he requested that they would either choose a king from among themselves, or elect the brother of the King of France. Some zealous Frenchman at the *Sublime Porte* had officiously procured this recommendation from the enemy of Christianity; but an alliance with Mahometanism did no service to Montluc, either with the Catholics or the Evangelicals. The bishop was in despair, and thought that his handy-work of six months' toil and trouble was to be shook into pieces in an hour. Montluc, being shown the letter, instantly insisted that it was a forgery, designed to injure his master the duke. The letter was attended by some suspicious circumstances; and the French bishop, quick at expedients, snatched at an advantage which the politician knows how to lay hold of in the chapter of accidents. "The letter was not sealed with the golden seal, nor inclosed in a silken purse or cloth of gold; and further, if they examined the translation," he said, "they would find that it was not written on Turkish paper." This was a piece of the *sieur's* good fortune, for the letter was not forged; but owing to the circumstance that the boyar of Wallachia had taken out the letter to send a translation with it, which the vizier had omitted, it arrived without its usual accompaniments; and the courier, when inquired after, was kept out of the way: so that, in a few days, nothing more was heard of the great vizier's letter. "Such was our fortunate escape," says the secretary, "from the friendly but fatal interference of the sultan, than which the *sieur* dreaded nothing so much."

Many secret agents of the different powers were spinning their dark intrigues; and often, when discovered or disconcerted, the creatures were again at their "dirty work." These agents were conveniently disavowed or acknowledged by their employers. The Abbé Cyre was an active agent of the emperor's, and though not publicly accredited was still hovering about. In Lithuania he had contrived matters so well as to have gained over that important province for the archduke; and was passing through Prussia to hasten to communicate with the emperor, but "some honest men," *quelques bons personnages*, says the French secretary, and no doubt some good friends of his master, "took him by surprise, and laid him up safely in the castle of Marienburgh, where truly he was a little uncivilly used by the soldiers, who rifled his portmanteau and sent us his papers, when we discovered all his foul practices." The emperor, it seems, was angry at the arrest of his secret agent; but as no one had the power of releasing the Abbé Cyre at that moment, what with receiving remonstrances and furnishing replies, the time passed away and a very troublesome adversary was in safe custody during the election. The dissensions between the Catholics and the Evangelicals were always on the point of breaking out; but Montluc succeeded in quieting these inveterate parties by terrifying their imaginations with sanguinary civil wars, and invasions of the Turks and the Tartars. He satisfied the Catholics with the hope that time would put an end to heresy, and the Evangelicals were glad to obtain a truce from persecution. The day before the election Montluc found himself so confident, that he dispatched a courier to the French court, and expressed himself in the true style of a speculative politician, that *"des douze tables du Damier nous en avons les Neufs assurés."*

There were preludes to the election; and the first was probably in acquiescence with a saturnalian humour prevalent in some countries, where the lower orders are only allowed to indulge their taste for the mockery of the great at stated times and on fixed occasions. A droll scene of a mock election, as well as combat, took place between the numerous Polish pages, who, saith the grave secretary, are still more mischievous than our own: these elected among themselves four competitors, made a senate to burlesque the diet, and went to loggerheads. Those who represented the archduke were well beaten, the Swede was hunted down, and for the *Piastis*, they seized on a cart belonging to a gentleman, laden with provisions, broke it to pieces, and burnt the axle-tree, which in that country is called a *piasti*, and cried out *The piasti is burnt!* nor could the senators at the diet that day command any order or silence. The French party wore white handkerchiefs in their hats, and they were so numerous as to defeat the others.

The next day however opened a different scene; "the nobles prepared to deliberate, and each palatine in his quarters was with his companions on their knees, and many with tears in their eyes, chanting a hymn to the Holy Ghost; it must be confessed, that this looked like a work of God," says our secretary, who probably understood the manœuvring of the mock combat, or the mock prayers, much better than we may. Every thing tells at an election, burlesque or solemnity!

The election took place, and the Duke of Anjou was proclaimed King of Poland—but the troubles of Montluc did not terminate. When they presented certain articles for his signature, the bishop discovered that these had undergone material alterations from the proposals submitted to him before the proclamation; these alterations referred to a disavowal of the Parisian massacre; the punishment of its authors, and toleration in religion. Montluc refused to sign, and cross-examined his Polish friends about the original proposals; one party agreed that some things had been changed, but that they were too trivial to lose a crown for; others declared that the alterations were necessary to allay the fears, or secure the safety, of the people. Our Gallic diplomatist was outwitted, and after all his intrigues and cunning, he found that the crown of Poland was only to be delivered on conditional terms.

In this dilemma, with a crown depending on a stroke of his pen,—remonstrating, entreating, arguing, and still delaying, like "Ancient Pistol" swallowing his leek, he witnessed with alarm some preparations for a new election, and his rivals on the watch with their protests. Montluc, in despair, signed the conditions— "assured, however," says the secretary, who groans over this *finale,* "that when the elected monarch should arrive, the states would easily be induced to correct them, and place things in *statu quo,* as before the proclamation. I was not a witness, being then dispatched to Paris with the joyful news, but I heard that the *sieur evesque* it was thought would have died in this agony, of being reduced to the hard necessity either to sign, or to lose the fruits of his labours. The conditions were afterwards for a long while disputed in France." De Thou informs us, in lib. lvii of his history, that Montluc after signing these conditions wrote to his master, that he was not bound by them, because they did not concern Poland in general, and that they had compelled him to sign, what at the same time he had informed them his instructions did not authorize. Such was the true Jesuitic conduct of a gray-haired politician, who at length found, that honest plain sense could embarrass and finally entrap the creature of the cabinet, the artificial genius of diplomatic finesse.

The secretary, however, views nothing but his master's glory in the issue of this most difficult negotiation; and the triumph of Anjou over the youthful archduke, whom the Poles might have moulded to their will, and over the King of Sweden, who claimed the crown by his queen's side, and had offered to unite his part of Livonia with that which the Poles possessed. He labours hard to prove that the palatines and the castellans were not *pratiqués,* i. e. had their votes bought up by Montluc, as was reported; from their number and their opposite interests, he confesses that the *sieur evesque* slept little, while in Poland, and that he only gained over the hearts of men by that natural gift of God, which acquired him the title of the *happy ambassador.* He rather seems to regret that France was not prodigal of her purchase-money, than to affirm that all palatines were alike scrupulous of their honour.

One more fact may close this political sketch; a lesson of the nature of court gratitude! The French court affected to receive Choisnin with favour, but their suppressed discontent was reserved for "the happy ambassador"! Affairs had changed; Charles the Ninth was dying, and Catharine de' Medici in despair for a son, to whom she had sacrificed all; while Anjou, already immersed in the wantonness of youth and pleasure, considered his elevation to the throne of Poland as an exile which separated him from his depraved enjoyments! Montluc was rewarded only by incurring disgrace; Catharine de' Medici and the Duke of Anjou now looked coldly on him, and expressed their dislike of his successful mission. "The mother of kings," as Choisnin designates Catharine de' Medici, to whom he addresses his *Memoirs,* with the hope of awakening her recollections of the zeal, the genius, and the success of his old master, had no longer any use for her favourite; and Montluc found, as the commentator of Choisnin expresses in a few words, an important truth in political morality, that "at court the interest of the moment is the measure of its affections and its hatreds."*

Whether Allowable to Ruin One's Self?

THE POLITICAL economist replies that it is!

One of our old dramatic writers, who witnessed the singular extravagance of dress among the modellers of fashion, our nobility, condemns their "superfluous bravery," echoing the popular cry,

---

* I have drawn up this article, for the curiosity of its subject and its details, from the *Discours au vray de tout ce qui s'est fait et passé pour l'entière Négociation de l'Election du Roi de Pologne, divisés en trois livres, par Jehan Choisnin du Chatelleraud, naguères Secrétaire de M. l'Evesque de Valence, 1574.*

There are a sort of men, whose coining heads
Are mints of all new fashions, that have done
More hurt to the kingdom, by superfluous bravery,
Which the foolish gentry imitate, than a war
Or a long famine. *All the treasure by*
This foul excess is got into the merchants',
Embroiderers', silk-men's, jewellers', tailors' hands,
And the third part of the land too! the nobility
Engrossing *titles only.*

Our poet might have been startled at the reply of our political
economist. If nobility, in follies such as these, only preserved
their "titles," while their "lands" were dispersed among the in-
dustrious classes, the people were not sufferers. The silly victims
ruining themselves by their excessive luxury, or their costly dress,
as it appears some did, was an evil which, left to its own course,
must check itself; if the rich did not spend, the poor would
starve. Luxury is the cure of that unavoidable evil in society—
great inequality of fortune! Political economists therefore tell
us, that any regulations would be ridiculous which, as Lord
Bacon expresses it, should serve for "the repressing of waste and
excess by *sumptuary laws.*" Adam Smith is not only indignant at
"sumptuary laws," but asserts, with a democratic insolence of
style, that "it is the highest impertinence and presumption in
kings and ministers to pretend to watch over the economy of
private people, and to restrain their expense by sumptuary laws.
They are themselves always the greatest spendthrifts in the
society; let them look well after their own expense, and they may
safely trust private people with theirs. If their own extravagance
does not ruin the state, that of their subjects never will." We
must therefore infer, that governments by extravagance may ruin
a state, but that individuals enjoy the remarkable privilege of
ruining themselves, without injuring society! Adam Smith afterwards distinguishes two sorts of luxury: the one exhausting itself
in "durable commodities, as in buildings, furniture, books,
statues, pictures," will increase "the opulence of a nation"; but
of the other, wasting itself in dress and equipages, in frivolous
ornaments, jewels, baubles, trinkets, &c. he acknowledges "no
trace or vestige would remain; and the effects of ten or twenty
years' profusion would be as completely annihilated as if they
had never existed." There is, therefore, a greater and a lesser evil
in this important subject of the opulent, unrestricted by any law,
ruining his whole generation.

Where "the wealth of nations" is made the solitary standard
of their prosperity, it becomes a fertile source of errors in the

science of morals; and the happiness of the individual is then too frequently sacrificed to what is called the prosperity of the state. If an individual, in the pride of luxury and selfism, annihilates the fortunes of his whole generation, untouched by the laws as a criminal, he leaves behind him a race of the discontented and the seditious, who, having sunk in the scale of society, have to reascend from their degradation by industry and by humiliation; but for the work of industry their habits have made them in-expert; and to humiliation, their very rank presents a perpetual obstacle.

Sumptuary laws, so often enacted, and so often repealed, and always eluded, were the perpetual, but ineffectual, attempts of all governments, to restrain what, perhaps, cannot be restrained —criminal folly! And to punish a man for having ruined himself would usually be to punish a most contrite penitent.

It is not surprising that before "private vices were considered as public benefits," the governors of nations instituted sumptuary laws—for the passion for pageantry, and an incredible prodigality in dress, were continually impoverishing great families; more equality of wealth has now rather subdued the form of private ruin than laid this evil domestic spirit. The incalculable ex-penditure and the blaze of splendour, of our ancestors, may startle the incredulity of our *élégantes.* We find men of rank exhausting their wealth and pawning their castles, and then desperately issuing from them, heroes for a crusade, or brigands for their neighbourhood!—and this frequently from the simple circumstance of having for a short time maintained some gor-geous chivalric festival on their own estates, or from having melted thousands of acres into cloth of gold; their sons were left to beg their bread on the estates which they were to have in-herited.

It was when chivalry still charmed the world by the remains of its seductive splendours, towards the close of the fifteenth cen-tury, that I find an instance of this kind occurring in the *Pas de Sandricourt,* which was held in the neighbourhood of the *sieur* of that name. It is a memorable affair, not only for us curious inquirers after manners and morals, but for the whole family of the Sandricourts; for though the said *sieur* is now receiving the immortality we bestow on him, and *la dame,* who presided in that magnificent piece of chivalry, was infinitely gratified, yet for ever after was the lord of Sandricourt ruined—and all for a short, romantic three months!

This story of the chivalric period may amuse. A *pas d'armes,* though consisting of military exercises and deeds of gallantry, was a sort of festival distinct from a tournament. It signified a *pas* or passage to be contested by one or more knights against all comers. It was necessary that the road should be such that it could not be passed without encountering some guardian knight. The *chevaliers* who disputed the *pas* hung their blazoned shields on trees, pales, or posts raised for this purpose. The aspirants after chivalric honours would strike with their lance one of these shields, and when it rung, it instantly summoned the owner to the challenge. A bridge or a road would sometimes serve for this military sport, for such it was intended to be, whenever the heat of the rivals proved not too earnest. The *sieur* of Sandricourt was a fine-dreamer of feats of chivalry, and in the neighbourhood of his castle he fancied that he saw a very spot adapted for every game; there was one admirably fitted for the barrier of a tilting-match; another embellished by a solitary pine-tree; another which was called the meadow of the Thorn; there was a *carrefour*, where, in four roads, four knights might meet; and, above all, there was a forest called *dévoyable*, having no path, so favourable for errant knights, who might there enter for strange adventures, and, as chance directed, encounter others as bewildered as themselves. Our chivalric Sandricourt found nine young *seigneurs* of the court of Charles the Eighth of France, who answered all his wishes. To sanction this glorious feat it was necessary to obtain leave from the king, and a herald of the Duke of Orleans to distribute the *cartel* or challenge all over France, announcing, that from such a day, ten young lords would stand ready to combat, in those different places, in the neighbourhood of Sandricourt's *château*. The names of this flower of chivalry have been faithfully registered, and they were such as instantly to throw a spark into the heart of every lover of arms! The world of fashion, that is, the chivalric world, was set in motion. Four bodies of assailants soon collected, each consisting of ten combatants. The herald of Orleans having examined the arms of these gentlemen, and satisfied himself of their ancient lineage, and their military renown, admitted their claims to the proffered honour. Sandricourt now saw with rapture the numerous shields of the assailants placed on the sides of his portals, and corresponding with those of the challengers which hung above them. Ancient lords were elected judges of the feats of the knights, accompanied by the ladies, for whose honour only the combatants declared they engaged.

The herald of Orleans tells the history in no very intelligible verse; but the burden of his stanza is still

> Du pas d'armes du chasteau Sandricourt.

He sings, or says,

> Oncques, depuis le tempts du roi Artus,
> Ne furent tant les armes exaulcées—
> Maint chevaliers et preux entreprenans—
> Princes plusieurs ont terres déplacées
> Pour y venir donner coups et poussées
> Qui ont été là tenus si de court
> Que par force n'ont prises et passées
> Les barriers, entrées, et passées
> Du pas d'armes du chasteau Sandricourt.

Doubtless there many a Roland met with his Oliver, and could not pass the barriers. Cased as they were in steel, *de pied en cap*, we presume that they could not materially injure themselves; yet, when on foot, the ancient judges discovered such symptoms of peril, that on the following day they advised our knights to satisfy themselves by fighting on horseback. Against this prudential counsel for some time they protested, as an inferior sort of glory. However, on the next day, the horse combat was appointed in the *carrefour*, by the pine-tree. On the following day they tried their lances in the meadow of the Thorn; but, though on horseback, the judges deemed their attacks were so fierce, that this assault was likewise not without peril; for some horses were killed, and some knights were thrown, and lay bruised by their own mail; but the barbed horses, wearing only *des chamfreins*, head-pieces magnificently caparisoned, found no protection in their ornaments. The last days were passed in combats of two to two, or in a single encounter a-foot, in the *forêt dévoyable*. These jousts passed without any accident, and the prizes were awarded in a manner equally gratifying to the claimants. The last day of the festival was concluded with a most sumptuous banquet. Two noble knights had undertaken the humble office of *maîtres-d'hôtel*; and while the knights were parading in the *forêt dévoyable* seeking adventures, a hundred servants were seen at all points, carrying white and red *hypocras*, and juleps, and *sirop de violars*, sweetmeats, and other spiceries, to comfort these wanderers, who, on returning to the *chasteau*, found a grand and plenteous banquet. The tables were crowded in the court apartment, where some held one hundred and twelve gentlemen, not including the *dames* and the *demoiselles*. In the

halls, and outside of the *chasteau,* were other tables. At that
festival more than two thousand persons were magnificently
entertained free of every expense; their attendants, their ar-
mourers, their *plumassiers,* and others, were also present. *La
Dame de Sandricourt, "fût moult aise d'avoir donné dans son
chasteau si belle, si magnifique, et gorgiasse fête."* Historians are
apt to describe their personages as they appear, not as they are: if
the lady of the *Sieur Sandricourt* really was *"moult aise"* during
these gorgeous days, one cannot but sympathize with the lady,
when her loyal knight and spouse confessed to her, after the
departure of the mob of two thousand visitors, neighbours,
soldiers, and courtiers,—the knights challengers, and the knights
assailants and the fine scenes at the pine-tree; the barrier in the
meadow of the Thorn; and the horse-combat at the *carrefour;*
and the jousts in the *forêt dévoyable;* the carousals in the castle-
halls; the jollity of the banquet tables; the *morescoes* danced till
they were reminded "how the waning night grew old!"—in a
word, when the costly dream had vanished,—that he was a ruined
man for ever, by immortalizing his name in one grand chivalric
festival! The *Sieur de Sandricourt,* like a great torch, had consumed himself in his own brightness; and the very land on
which the famous *Pas de Sandricourt* was held—had passed away
with it! Thus one man sinks generations by that wastefulness,
which a political economist would assure us was committing
no injury to society! The moral evil goes for nothing in financial
statements.

Similar instances of ruinous luxury we may find in the prodigal costliness of dress through the reigns of Elizabeth, James the
First, and Charles the First. Not only in their massy grandeur
they outweighed us, but the accumulation and variety of their
wardrobe displayed such a gaiety of fancy in their colours and
their ornaments, that the drawing-room in those days must have
blazed at their presence, and changed colours as the crowd
moved. But if we may trust to royal proclamations, the ruin was
general among some classes. Elizabeth issued more than one proclamation against "the excess of apparel"! and among other
evils which the government imagined this passion for dress occasioned, it notices "the wasting and undoing of a great number
of young gentlemen, otherwise serviceable; and that others,
seeking by show of apparel to be esteemed as gentlemen, and
allured by the vain show of these things, not only consume their
goods and lands, but also run into such debts and shifts, as they
cannot live out of danger of laws without attempting of unlaw-

ful acts." The queen bids her own household "to look unto it for good example to the realm; and all noblemen, archbishops, and bishops, all mayors, justices of peace, &c. should see them executed in their private households." The greatest difficulty which occurred to regulate the wear of apparel was ascertaining the incomes of persons, or in the words of the proclamation, "finding that it is very hard for any man's state of living and value to be truly understood by other persons." They were to be regulated, as they appear "sessed in the subsidy books." But if persons chose to be more magnificent in their dress, they were allowed to justify their means: in that case, if allowed, her majesty would not be the loser; for they were to be rated in the subsidy books according to such values as they themselves offered as a qualification for the splendour of their dress!

In my researches among manuscript letters of the times, I have had frequent occasion to discover how persons of considerable rank appear to have carried their acres on their backs, and with their ruinous and fantastical luxuries sadly pinched their hospitality. It was this which so frequently cast them into the nets of the "goldsmiths," and other trading usurers. At the coronation of James the First, I find a simple knight whose cloak cost him five hundred pounds; but this was not uncommon. At the marriage of Elizabeth, the daughter of James the First, "Lady Wotton had a gown of which the embroidery cost fifty pounds a yard. The Lady Arabella made four gowns, one of which cost £1500. The Lord Montacute (Montague) bestowed £1500 in apparel for his two daughters. One lady, under the rank of baroness, was furnished with jewels exceeding one hundred thousand pounds"; "and the Lady Arabella goes beyond her," says the letter-writer. "All this extreme costs and riches makes us all poor," as he imagined! I have been amused in observing grave writers of state dispatches jocular on any mischance or mortification to which persons are liable, whose happiness entirely depends on their dress. Sir Dudley Carleton, our minister at Venice, communicates, as an article worth transmitting, the great disappointment incurred by Sir Thomas Glover, "who was just come hither, and had appeared one day like a comet, all in crimson velvet and beaten gold, but had all his expectations marred on a sudden by the news of Prince Henry's death." A similar mischance, from a different cause, was the lot of Lord Hay, who made great preparations for his embassy to France, which, however, were chiefly confined to his dress. He was to remain there twenty days; and the letter-writer maliciously observes, that "He goes with twenty special suits of apparel for so many days' abode, besides his travelling robes; but news is very lately come that the French have lately altered their fashion, whereby he must needs be out of countenance, if he be not set out after the last edition!" To find himself out of fashion, with twenty suits for twenty days, was a mischance his lordship had no right to count on!

"The glass of fashion" was unquestionably held up by two very eminent characters, Raleigh and Buckingham; and the authentic facts recorded of their dress will sufficiently account for the frequent "Proclamations" to control that servile herd of imitators—the smaller gentry!

There is a remarkable picture of Sir Walter, which will at least serve to convey an idea of the gaiety and splendour of his dress. It is a white satin pinked vest, close sleeved to the wrist; over the body a brown doublet, finely flowered and embroidered with pearl. In the feather of his hat a large ruby and pearl drop at the bottom of the sprig, in place of a button; his trunk or breeches, with his stockings and riband garters, fringed at the end, all white, and buff shoes with white riband. Oldys, who saw this picture, has thus described the dress of Raleigh. But I have some important additions; for I find that Raleigh's shoes on great court days were so gorgeously covered with precious stones, as to have exceeded the value of six thousand six hundred pounds: and that he had a suit of armour of solid silver, with sword and belt blazing with diamonds, rubies and pearls, whose value was not so easily calculated. Raleigh had no patrimonial inheritance; at this moment he had on his back a good portion of a Spanish galleon, and the profits of a monopoly of trade he was carrying on with the newly discovered Virginia. Probably he placed all his hopes in his dress! The virgin queen, when she issued proclamations against "the excess of apparel," pardoned, by her looks, that promise of a mine which blazed in Raleigh's; and, parsimonious as she was, forgot the three thousand changes of dresses which she herself left in the royal wardrobe.

Buckingham could afford to have his diamonds tacked so loosely on, that when he chose to shake a few off on the ground, he obtained all the fame he desired from the pickers-up, who were generally *les dames de la cour;* for our duke never condescended to accept what he himself had dropped. His cloaks were trimmed with great diamond buttons, and diamond hatbands, cockades and ear-rings yoked with great ropes and knots of pearls. This was however but for ordinary dances. "He had twenty-seven suits of clothes made, the richest that embroidery, lace, silk, velvet, silver, gold, and gems, could contribute; one of which was a white uncut velvet, set all over, both suit and cloak, with diamonds valued at fourscore thousand pounds, besides a great feather stuck all over with diamonds, as were also his sword, girdle, hat, and spurs."* In the masques and banquets with which Buckingham entertained the court, he usually expended, for the evening, from one to five thousand pounds. To others I leave to calculate the value of money; the sums of this gorgeous wastefulness, it must be recollected, occurred before this million age of ours.

If, to provide the means for such enormous expenditure, Buckingham multiplied the grievances of monopolies; if he pillaged the treasury for his eighty thousand pounds' coat; if Raleigh was at length driven to his last desperate enterprise, to relieve himself of his creditors for a pair of six thousand pounds' shoes —in both these cases, as in that of the chivalric Sandricourt, the political economist may perhaps acknowledge that *there is a sort of luxury highly criminal.* All the arguments he may urge, all the statistical accounts he may calculate, and the healthful state of his circulating medium among "the merchants, embroiderers, silk-men, and jewellers"—will not alter such a moral evil, which leaves an eternal taint on "the wealth of nations"! It is the principle that "private vices are public benefits," and that men may be allowed to ruin their generations without committing any injury to society.

Recovery of Manuscripts

OUR ANCIENT classics had a very narrow escape from total annihilation. Many have perished: many are but fragments; and chance, blind arbiter of the works of genius, has left us some, not of the highest value; which, however, have proved very useful, as a test to show the pedantry of those who adore antiquity not from true feeling, but from traditional prejudice.

We lost a great number of ancient authors, by the conquest of Egypt by the Saracens, which deprived Europe of the use of the

---

* The Jesuit Drexelius, in one of his religious dialogues, notices the fact; but I am referring to an Harleian manuscript, which confirms the information of the Jesuit.

papyrus. They could find no substitute, and knew no other expedient but writing on parchment, which became every day
more scarce and costly. Ignorance and barbarism unfortunately
seized on Roman manuscripts, and industriously defaced pages
once imagined to have been immortal! The most elegant compositions of classic Rome were converted into the psalms of a
breviary, or the prayers of a missal. Livy and Tacitus "hide
their diminished heads" to preserve the legend of a saint, and
immortal truths were converted into clumsy fictions. It happened that the most voluminous authors were the greatest sufferers; these were preferred, because their volume being the
greatest, most profitably repaid their destroying industry, and
furnished ampler scope for future transcription. A Livy or a
Diodorus was preferred to the smaller works of Cicero or Horace;
and it is to this circumstance that Juvenal, Persius, and Martial
have come down to us entire, rather probably than to these
pious personages preferring their obscenities, as some have accused them. At Rome, a part of a book of Livy was found, between the lines of a parchment but half effaced, on which they
had substituted a book of the Bible; and a recent discovery of
Cicero *De Republicâ,* which lay concealed under some monkish
writing, shows the fate of ancient manuscripts.

That the Monks had not in high veneration the *profane*
authors, appears by a facetious anecdote. To read the classics
was considered as a very idle recreation, and some held them in
great horror. To distinguish them from other books, they invented a disgraceful sign: when a monk asked for a pagan
author, after making the general sign they used in their manual
and silent language when they wanted a book, he added a particular one, which consisted in scratching under his ear, as a dog,
which feels an itching, scratches himself in that place with his
paw—because, said they, an unbeliever is compared to a dog! In
this manner they expressed an *itching* for those *dogs* Virgil or
Horace!

There have been ages when, for the possession of a manuscript, some would transfer an estate, or leave in pawn for its
loan hundreds of golden crowns; and when even the sale or
loan of a manuscript was considered of such importance as to
have been solemnly registered by public acts. Absolute as was
Louis XI. he could not obtain the MS. of Rasis, an Arabian
writer, from the library of the Faculty of Paris, to have a copy
made, without pledging a hundred golden crowns; and the president of his treasury, charged with this commission, sold part

of his plate to make the deposit. For the loan of a volume of Avicenna, a Baron offered a pledge of ten marks of silver, which was refused: because it was not considered equal to the risk incurred of losing a volume of Avicenna! These events occurred in 1471. One cannot but smile, at an anterior period, when a Countess of Anjou bought a favourite book of homilies for two hundred sheep, some skins of martins, and bushels of wheat and rye.

In these times, manuscripts were important articles of commerce; they were excessively scarce, and preserved with the utmost care. Usurers themselves considered them as precious objects for pawn. A student of Pavia, who was reduced, raised a new fortune by leaving in pawn a manuscript of a body of law; and a grammarian, who was ruined by a fire, rebuilt his house with two small volumes of Cicero.

At the restoration of letters, the researches of literary men were chiefly directed to this point; every part of Europe and Greece was ransacked; and, the glorious end considered, there was something sublime in this humble industry, which often recovered a lost author of antiquity, and gave one more classic to the world. This occupation was carried on with enthusiasm, and a kind of mania possessed many, who exhausted their fortunes in distant voyages and profuse prices. In reading the correspondence of the learned Italians of these times, their adventures of manuscript-hunting are very amusing; and their raptures, their congratulations, or at times their condolence, and even their censures, are all immoderate. The acquisition of a province would not have given so much satisfaction as the discovery of an author little known, or not known at all. "Oh, great gain! Oh, unexpected felicity! I intreat you, my Poggio, send me the manuscript as soon as possible, that I may see it before I die!" exclaims Aretino, in a letter overflowing with enthusiasm, on Poggio's discovery of a copy of Quintilian. Some of the half-witted who joined in this great hunt were often thrown out, and some paid high for manuscripts not authentic; the knave played on the bungling amateur of manuscripts, whose credulity exceeded his purse. But even among the learned, much ill blood was inflamed; he who had been most successful in acquiring manuscripts was envied by the less fortunate, and the glory of possessing a manuscript of Cicero seemed to approximate to that of being its author. It is curious to observe that in these vast importations into Italy of manuscripts from Asia, John Aurispa, who brought many hundreds of Greek manuscripts, laments that he had chosen more profane than sacred writers; which circumstance he tells us was owing to the Greeks, who would not so easily part with theological works, but did not highly value profane writers!

These manuscripts were discovered in the obscurest recesses of monasteries; they were not always imprisoned in libraries, but rotting in dark unfrequented corners with rubbish. It required not less ingenuity to find out places where to grope in, than to understand the value of the acquisition. An universal ignorance then prevailed in the knowledge of ancient writers. A scholar of those times gave the first rank among the Latin writers to one Valerius, whether he meant Martial or Maximus is uncertain; he placed Plato and Tully among the poets, and imagined that Ennius and Statius were contemporaries. A library of six hundred volumes was then considered as an extraordinary collection.

Among those whose lives were devoted to this purpose, Poggio the Florentine stands distinguished; but he complains that his zeal was not assisted by the great. He found under a heap of rubbish in a decayed coffer, in a tower belonging to the monastery of St. Gallo, the work of Quintilian. He is indignant at its forlorn situation; at least, he cries, it should have been preserved in the library of the monks; but I found it *in teterrimo quodam et obscuro carcere*—and to his great joy drew it out of its grave! The monks have been complimented as the preservers of literature, but by facts, like the present, their real affection may be doubted.

The most valuable copy of Tacitus, of whom so much is wanting, was likewise discovered in a monastery of Westphalia. It is a curious circumstance in literary history, that we should owe Tacitus to this single copy; for the Roman emperor of that name had copies of the works of his illustrious ancestor placed in all the libraries of the empire, and every year had ten copies transcribed; but the Roman libraries seem to have been all destroyed, and the imperial protection availed nothing against the teeth of time.

The original manuscript of Justinian's *Pandects* was discovered by the Pisans, when they took a city in Calabria; that vast code of laws had been in a manner unknown from the time of that emperor. This curious book was brought to Pisa; and when Pisa was taken by the Florentines, was transferred to Florence, where it is still preserved.

It sometimes happened that manuscripts were discovered in the last agonies of existence. Papirius Masson found, in the house of a bookbinder of Lyons, the works of Agobart; the mechanic was on the point of using the manuscripts to line the covers of his books. A page of the second decade of Livy, it is said, was found by a man of letters in the parchment of his battledore, while he was amusing himself in the country. He hastened to the maker of the battledore—but arrived too late! The man had finished the last page of Livy—about a week before.

Many works have undoubtedly perished in this manuscript state. By a petition of Dr. Dee to Queen Mary, in the Cotton library, it appears that Cicero's treatise *De Republicâ* was once extant in this country. Huet observes that Petronius was probably entire in the days of John of Salisbury, who quotes fragments, not now to be found in the remains of the Roman bard. Raimond Soranzo, a lawyer in the papal court, possessed two books of Cicero on *Glory*, which he presented to Petrarch, who lent them to a poor aged man of letters, formerly his preceptor. Urged by extreme want, the old man pawned them, and returning home died suddenly without having revealed where he had left them. They have never been recovered. Petrarch speaks of them with ecstasy, and tells us that he had studied them perpetually. Two centuries afterwards, this treatise on *Glory* by Cicero was mentioned in a catalogue of books bequeathed to a monastery of nuns, but when inquired after was missing. It was supposed that Petrus Alcyonius, physician to that household, purloined it, and after transcribing as much of it as he could into his own writings, had destroyed the original. Alcyonius, in his book *De Exilio*, the critics observed, had many splendid passages which stood isolated in his work, and were quite above his genius. The beggar, or in this case the thief, was detected by mending his rags with patches of purple and gold.

In this age of manuscript, there is reason to believe, that when a man of letters accidentally obtained an unknown work, he did not make the fairest use of it, but cautiously concealed it from his contemporaries. Leonard Aretino, a distinguished scholar at the dawn of modern literature, having found a Greek manuscript of Procopius *De Bello Gothico,* translated it into Latin, and published the work; but concealing the author's name, it passed as his own, till another manuscript of the same work being dug out of its grave, the fraud of Aretino was apparent. Barbosa, a bishop of Ugento, in 1649, has printed among his works a treatise, obtained by one of his domestics bringing in a fish rolled in a leaf of written paper, which his curiosity led him to examine. He was sufficiently interested to run out and search the fish market, till he found the manuscript out of which it had been torn. He published it, under the title *De Officio Episcopi.* Machiavel acted more adroitly in a similar case; a manuscript of the *Apophthegms of the Ancients* by Plutarch having fallen into his hands, he selected those which pleased him, and put them into the mouth of his hero Castrucio Castricani.

In more recent times, we might collect many curious anecdotes concerning manuscripts. Sir Robert Cotton one day at his tailor's discovered that the man was holding in his hand, ready to cut up for measures—an original Magna Charta, with all its appendages of seals and signatures. This anecdote is told by Colomiés, who long resided in this country; and an original Magna Charta is preserved in the Cottonian library exhibiting marks of dilapidation.

Cardinal Granvelle left behind him several chests filled with a prodigious quantity of letters written in different languages, commented, noted, and underlined by his own hand. These curious manuscripts, after his death, were left in a garret to the mercy of the rain and the rats. Five or six of these chests the steward sold to the grocers. It was then that a discovery was made of this treasure. Several learned men occupied themselves in collecting sufficient of these literary relics to form eighty thick folios, consisting of original letters by all the crowned heads in Europe, with instructions for ambassadors, and other state-papers.

A valuable secret history by Sir George Mackenzie, the king's advocate in Scotland, was rescued from a mass of waste paper sold to a grocer, who had the good sense to discriminate it, and communicated this curious memorial to Dr. M'Crie. The original, in the handwriting of its author, has been deposited in the Advocate's library. There is an hiatus, which contained the history of six years. This work excited inquiry after the rest of the MSS., which were found to be nothing more than the sweepings of an attorney's office.

Montaigne's *Journal of his Travels into Italy* has been but recently published. A prebendary of Perigord, travelling through this province to make researches relative to its history, arrived at the ancient *château* of Montaigne, in possession of a descendant of this great man. He inquired for the archives, if there had been any. He was shown an old worm-eaten coffer, which had long held papers untouched by the incurious generations of Montaigne. Stifled in clouds of dust, he drew out the original manuscript of the travels of Montaigne. Two thirds of the work are in the handwriting of Montaigne, and the rest is written by a servant, who always speaks of his master in the third person. But he must have written what Montaigne dictated, as the expressions and the egotisms are all Montaigne's. The bad writing and orthography made it almost unintelligible. They confirmed Montaigne's own observations, that he was very negligent in the correction of his works.

Our ancestors were great hiders of manuscripts: Dr. Dee's singular MSS. were found in the secret drawer of a chest, which had passed through many hands undiscovered; and that vast collection of state-papers of Thurloe's, the secretary of Cromwell, which formed about seventy volumes in the original manuscripts, accidentally fell out of the false ceiling of some chambers in Lincoln's-Inn.

A considerable portion of Lady Mary Wortley Montagu's *Letters* I discovered in the hands of an attorney: family-papers are often consigned to offices of lawyers, where many valuable manuscripts are buried. Posthumous publications of this kind are too frequently made from sordid motives: discernment and taste would only be detrimental to the views of bulky publishers.

Imprisonment of the Learned

IMPRISONMENT HAS not always disturbed the man of letters in the progress of his studies, but has unquestionably greatly promoted them.

In prison Boethius composed his work on the *Consolations of Philosophy;* and Grotius wrote his *Commentary on Saint Matthew,* with other works; the detail of his allotment of time to different studies, during his confinement, is very instructive.

Buchanan, in the dungeon of a monastery in Portugal, composed his excellent *Paraphrases of the Psalms of David.*

Cervantes composed the most agreeable book in the Spanish language during his captivity in Barbary.

Fleta, a well-known law production, was written by a person confined in the Fleet for debt; the name of the *place,* though not that of the *author,* has thus been preserved; and another work, *Fleta Minor, or the Laws of Art and Nature in knowing the bodies of Metals, &c. by Sir John Pettus, 1683,* received its title from the circumstance of his having translated it from the German during his confinement in this prison.

Louis the Twelfth, when Duke of Orleans, was long imprisoned in the Tower of Bourges: applying himself to his studies, which he had hitherto neglected, he became, in consequence, an enlightened monarch.

Margaret, queen of Henry the Fourth, King of France, confined in the Louvre, pursued very warmly the studies of elegant literature, and composed a very skilful apology for the irregularities of her conduct.

Sir Walter Raleigh's unfinished *History of the World*, which leaves us to regret that later ages had not been celebrated by his eloquence, was the fruits of eleven years of imprisonment. It was written for the use of Prince Henry, as he and Dallington, who also wrote *Aphorisms* for the same prince, have told us; the prince looked over the manuscript. Of Raleigh it is observed, to employ the language of Hume, "They were struck with the extensive genius of the man, who, being educated amidst naval and military enterprises, had surpassed, in the pursuits of literature, even those of the most recluse and sedentary lives; and they admired his unbroken magnanimity, which, at his age, and under his circumstances, could engage him to undertake and execute so great a work, as his History of the World." He was assisted in this great work by the learning of several eminent persons, a circumstance which has not been usually noticed.

The plan of the *Henriade* was sketched, and the greater part composed, by Voltaire during his imprisonment in the Bastille; and the *Pilgrim's Progress* of Bunyan was performed in the circuit of a prison's walls.

Howell, the author of *Familiar Letters*, wrote the chief part of them, and almost all his other works, during his long confinement in the Fleet prison; he employed his fertile pen for subsistence; and in all his books we find much entertainment.

Lydiat, while confined in the King's Bench for debt, wrote his *Annotations on the Parian Chronicle*, which were first published by Prideaux. He was the learned scholar alluded to by Johnson; an allusion not known to Boswell and others.

The learned Selden, committed to prison for his attacks on the divine right of tithes and the king's prerogative, prepared during his confinement his *History of Eadmer*, enriched by his notes.

Cardinal Polignac formed the design of refuting the arguments of the skeptics which Bayle had been renewing in his dictionary; but his public occupations hindered him. Two exiles at length fortunately gave him the leisure; and the *Anti-Lucretius* is the fruit of the court disgraces of its author.

Freret, when imprisoned in the Bastille, was permitted only to have Bayle for his companion. His dictionary was always before him, and his principles were got by heart. To this circumstance we owe his works, animated by all the powers of skepticism.

Sir William Davenant finished his poem of Gondibert during his confinement by the rebels in Carisbrook Castle. George Wither dedicates his *Shepherd's Hunting*, "To his friends, my visitants in the Marshalsea": these "eclogues" having been printed in his imprisonment.

De Foe, confined in Newgate for a political pamphlet, began his *Review,* a periodical paper, which was extended to nine thick volumes in quarto, and it has been supposed served as the model of the celebrated papers of Steele.

Wicquefort's curious work on *Ambassadors* is dated from his prison, where he had been confined for state affairs. He softened the rigour of those heavy hours by several historical works.

One of the most interesting facts of this kind is the fate of an Italian scholar, of the name of Maggi. Early addicted to the study of the sciences, and particularly to the mathematics, and military architecture, he successfully defended Famagusta, besieged by the Turks, by inventing machines which destroyed their works. When that city was taken in 1571, they pillaged his library and carried him away in chains. Now a slave, after his daily labours he amused a great part of his nights by literary compositions; *De Tintinnabulis,* on Bells, a treatise still read by the curious, was actually composed by him when a slave in Turkey, without any other resource than the erudition of his own memory, and the genius of which adversity could not deprive him.

Amusements of the Learned

AMONG THE Jesuits it was a standing rule of the order, that after an application to study for two hours, the mind of the student should be unbent by some relaxation, however trifling. When Petavius was employed in his *Dogmata Theologica,* a work of the most profound and extensive erudition, the great recreation of the learned father was, at the end of every second hour, to twirl his chair for five minutes. After protracted studies Spinosa would mix with the family-party where he lodged, and join in the most trivial conversations, or unbend his mind by setting spiders to fight each other; he observed their combats with so much interest, that he was often seized with immoderate fits of laughter. A continuity of labour deadens the soul, observes Seneca, in closing his treatise on *The Tranquillity of the Soul,* and the mind must unbend itself by certain amusements. Socrates did not blush to play with children; Cato, over his bottle, found an alleviation from the fatigues of government; a circumstance, Seneca says in his manner, which rather gives honour to this defect, than the defect dishonours Cato. Some men of letters portioned out their day between repose and labour. Asinius Pollio would not suffer any business to occupy him beyond a stated hour; after that time he would not allow any letter to be opened, that his hours of recreation might not be interrupted by unforeseen labours. In the senate, after the tenth hour, it was not allowed to make any new motion.

Tycho Brahe diverted himself with polishing glasses for all kinds of spectacles, and making mathematical instruments; an employment too closely connected with his studies to be deemed an amusement.

D'Andilly, the translator of Josephus, after seven or eight hours of study every day, amused himself in cultivating trees; Barclay, the author of the *Argenis,* in his leisure hours was a florist; Balzac amused himself with a collection of crayon portraits; Peiresc found his amusement amongst his medals and antiquarian curiosities; the Abbé de Marolles with his prints; and Politian in singing airs to his lute. Descartes passed his afternoons in the conversation of a few friends, and in cultivating a little garden; in the morning, occupied by the system of the world, he relaxed his profound speculations by rearing delicate flowers.

Conrad ab Uffenbach, a learned German, recreated his mind, after severe studies, with a collection of prints of eminent persons, methodically arranged; he retained this ardour of the *Grangerite* to his last days.

Rohault wandered from shop to shop to observe the mechanics labour; Count Caylus passed his mornings in the *studios* of artists, and his evenings in writing his numerous works on art. This was the true life of an amateur.

Granville Sharpe, amidst the severity of his studies, found a social relaxation in the amusement of a barge on the Thames, which was well known to the circle of his friends; there, was festive hospitality with musical delight. It was resorted to by men of the most eminent talents and rank. His little voyages to Putney, to Kew, and to Richmond, and the literary intercourse they produced, were singularly happy ones. "The history of his amusements cannot be told without adding to the dignity of his character," observes Prince Hoare, in the life of this great philanthropist.

Some have found amusement in composing treatises on odd subjects. Seneca wrote a burlesque narrative of Claudius's death. Pierius Valerianus has written an eulogium on beards; and we have had a learned one recently, with due gravity and pleasantry, entitled *Eloge de Perruques*.

Holstein has written an eulogium on the North Wind; Heinsius, on *The Ass*; Menage, the *Transmigration of the Parasitical Pedant to a Parrot*; and also the *Petition of the Dictionaries*.

Erasmus composed, to amuse himself when travelling, his panegyric on *Moria*, or Folly; which, authorized by the pun, he dedicated to Sir Thomas More.

Sallengre, who would amuse himself like Erasmus, wrote, in imitation of his work, a panegyric on *Ebriety*. He says, that he is willing to be thought as drunken a man as Erasmus was a foolish one. Synesius composed a Greek panegyric on *Baldness*. These burlesques were brought into great vogue by Erasmus's *Moriæ Encomium*.

It seems, Johnson observes in his life of Sir Thomas Browne, to have been in all ages the pride of art to show how it could exalt the low and amplify the little. To this ambition perhaps we owe the *Frogs* of Homer; *The Gnat and the Bees* of Virgil; the *Butterfly* of Spenser; the *Shadow* of Wowerus; and the *Quincunx* of Browne.

Cardinal de Richelieu, amongst all his great occupations, found a recreation in violent exercises; and he was once discovered jumping with his servant, to try who could reach the highest side of a wall. De Grammont, observing the cardinal to be jealous of his powers, offered to jump with him; and, in the true spirit of a courtier, having made some efforts which nearly reached the cardinal's, confessed the cardinal surpassed him. This was jumping like a politician; and by this means he is said to have ingratiated himself with the minister.

The great Samuel Clarke was fond of robust exercise; and this profound logician has been found leaping over tables and chairs. Once perceiving a pedantic fellow, he said, "Now we must desist, for a fool is coming in!"

An eminent French lawyer, confined by his business to a Parisian life, amused himself with collecting from the classics all the passages which relate to a country life. The collection was published after his death.

Contemplative men seem to be fond of amusements which accord with their habits. The thoughtful game of chess, and the tranquil delight of angling, have been favourite recreations with the studious. Paley had himself painted with a rod and line in his hand; a strange characteristic for the author of *Natural Theology*. Sir Henry Wotton called angling "idle time not idly spent": we may suppose that his meditations and his amusements were carried on at the same moment.

The amusements of the great d'Aguesseau, chancellor of France, consisted in an interchange of studies; his relaxations were all the varieties of literature. "Le changement de l'étude est mon seul délassement," said this great man; and "in the age of the passions, his only passion was study."

Seneca has observed on amusements proper for literary men, that, in regard to robust exercises, it is not decent to see a man of letters exult in the strength of his arm, or the breadth of his back! Such amusements diminish the activity of the mind. Too much fatigue exhausts the animal spirits, as too much food blunts the finer faculties: but elsewhere he allows his philosopher an occasional slight inebriation; an amusement which was very prevalent among our poets formerly, when they exclaimed,

> Fetch me Ben Jonson's scull, and fill't with sack,
> Rich as the same he drank, when the whole pack
> Of jolly sisters pledged, and did agree
> It was no sin to be as drunk as he!

Seneca concludes admirably, "whatever be the amusements you choose, return not slowly from those of the body to the mind; exercise the latter night and day. The mind is nourished at a cheap rate; neither cold nor heat, nor age itself, can interrupt this exercise; give therefore all your cares to a possession which ameliorates even in its old age!"

An ingenious writer has observed, that "a garden just accommodates itself to the perambulations of a scholar, who would perhaps rather wish his walks abridged than extended." There is a good characteristic account of the mode in which the Literati may take exercise, in Pope's *Letters*. "I, like a poor squirrel, am continually in motion indeed, but it is but a cage of three foot! my little excursions are like those of a shopkeeper, who walks every day a mile or two before his own door, but minds his business all the while." A turn or two in a garden will often very happily close a fine period, mature an unripened thought, and raise up fresh associations, whenever the mind like the body becomes rigid by preserving the same posture. Buffon often quitted the old tower he studied in, which was placed in the midst of his garden, for a walk in it; Evelyn loved "books and a garden."

Destruction of Books

THE LITERARY treasures of antiquity have suffered from the malice of Men, as well as that of Time. It is remarkable that conquerors, in the moment of victory, or in the unsparing devastation of their rage, have not been satisfied with destroying *men*, but have even carried their vengeance to *books*.

The Persians, from hatred of the religion of the Phœnicians and the Egyptians, destroyed their books, of which Eusebius notices a great number. A Grecian library at Gnidus was burnt by the sect of Hippocrates, because the Gnidians refused to follow the doctrines of their master. If the followers of Hippocrates formed the majority, was it not very unorthodox in the Gnidians to prefer taking physic their own way? But Faction has often annihilated books.

The Romans burnt the books of the Jews, of the Christians, and the Philosophers; the Jews burnt the books of the Christians and the Pagans; and the Christians burnt the books of the Pagans and the Jews. The greater part of the books of Origen and other heretics were continually burnt by the orthodox party. Gibbon pathetically describes the empty library of Alexandria, after the Christians had destroyed it. "The valuable library of Alexandria was pillaged or destroyed; and near twenty years afterwards the appearance of the *empty shelves* excited the regret and indignation of every spectator, whose mind was not totally darkened by religious prejudice. The compositions of ancient genius, so many of which have irretrievably perished, might surely have been excepted from the wreck of idolatry, for the amusement and instruction of succeeding ages; and either the zeal or avarice of the archbishop might have been satiated with the richest spoils which were the rewards of his victory."

The pathetic narrative of Nicetas Choniates, of the ravages committed by the Christians of the thirteenth century in Constantinople, was fraudulently suppressed in the printed editions. It has been preserved by Dr. Clarke; who observes, that the Turks have committed fewer injuries to the works of art than the barbarous Christians of that age.

The reading of the Jewish Talmud has been forbidden by various edicts, of the Emperor Justinian, of many of the French and Spanish kings, and numbers of Popes. All the copies were ordered to be burnt: the intrepid perseverance of the Jews themselves preserved that work from annihilation. In 1569 twelve thousand copies were thrown into the flames at Cremona. John Reuchlin interfered to stop this universal destruction of Talmuds; for which he became hated by the monks, and condemned by the Elector of Mentz, but appealing to Rome, the prosecution was stopped; and the traditions of the Jews were considered as not necessary to be destroyed.

Conquerors at first destroy with the rashest zeal the national records of the conquered people; hence it is that the Irish people deplore the irreparable losses of their most ancient national memorials, which their invaders have been too successful in annihilating. The same event occurred in the conquest of Mexico; and the interesting history of the New World must ever remain imperfect, in consequence of the unfortunate success of the first missionaries. Clavigero, the most authentic historian of Mexico, continually laments this affecting loss. Every thing in that country had been painted, and painters abounded there as scribes in Europe. The first missionaries, suspicious that superstition was mixed with all their paintings, attacked the chief school of these artists, and collecting, in the market-place, a little mountain of these precious records, they set fire to it, and buried in the ashes the memory of many interesting events. Afterwards, sensible of their error, they tried to collect information from the mouths of the Indians; but the Indians were indignantly silent: when they attempted to collect the remains of these painted histories, the patriotic Mexican usually buried in concealment the fragmentary records of his country.

The story of the Caliph Omar proclaiming throughout the kingdom, at the taking of Alexandria, that the Koran contained every thing which was useful to believe and to know, and therefore commanding that all the books in the Alexandrian library should be distributed to the masters of the baths, amounting to

4000, to be used in heating their stoves during a period of six months, modern paradox would attempt to deny. But the tale would not be singular even were it true; it perfectly suits the character of a bigot, a barbarian, and a blockhead. A similar event happened in Persia. When Abdoolah, who in the third century of the Mohammedan æra governed Khorassan, was presented at Nishapoor with a MS. which was shown as a literary curiosity, he asked the title of it—it was the tale of Wamick and Oozra, composed by the great poet Noshirwan. On this Abdoolah observed, that those of his country and faith had nothing to do with any other book than the Koran; and all Persian MSS. found within the circle of his government, as the works of idolators, were to be burnt. Much of the most ancient poetry of the Persians perished by this fanatical edict.

When Buda was taken by the Turks, a Cardinal offered a vast sum to redeem the great library founded by Matthew Corvini, a literary monarch of Hungary; it was rich in Greek and Hebrew lore, and the classics of antiquity. Thirty amanuenses had been employed in copying MSS. and illuminating them by the finest art. The barbarians destroyed most of the books in tearing away their splendid covers and their silver bosses; an Hungarian soldier picked up a book as a prize: it proved to be the *Ethiopics* of Heliodorus, from which the first edition was printed in 1534.

Cardinal Ximenes seems to have retaliated a little on the Saracens; for at the taking of Granada, he condemned to the flames five thousand Korans.

The following anecdote respecting a Spanish missal, called St. Isidore's, is not incurious; hard fighting saved it from destruction. In the Moorish wars, all these missals had been destroyed, excepting those in the city of Toledo. There, in six churches, the Christians were allowed the free exercise of their religion. When the Moors were expelled several centuries afterwards from Toledo, Alphonsus the Sixth ordered the Roman missal to be used in those churches; but the people of Toledo insisted on having their own, as revised by St. Isidore. It seemed to them that Alphonsus was more tyrannical than the Turks. The contest between the Roman and the Toletan missals came to that height, that at length it was determined to decide their fate by single combat; the champion of the Toletan missal felled by one blow the knight of the Roman missal. Alphonsus still considered this battle as merely the effect of the heavy arm of the doughty Toletan, and ordered a fast to be proclaimed, and a great fire to be prepared, into which, after his majesty and the people had joined in prayer for heavenly assistance in this ordeal, both the rivals (not the men, but the missals), were thrown into the flames —again St. Isidore's missal triumphed, and this iron book was then allowed to be orthodox by Alphonsus, and the good people of Toledo were allowed to say their prayers as they had long been used to do. However, the copies of this missal at length became very scarce; for now, when no one opposed the reading of St. Isidore's missal, none cared to use it. Cardinal Ximenes found it so difficult to obtain a copy, that he printed a large impression, and built a chapel, consecrated to St. Isidore, that this service might be daily chaunted as it had been by the ancient Christians.

The works of the ancients were frequently destroyed at the instigation of the monks. They appear sometimes to have mutilated them, for passages have not come down to us, which once evidently existed; and occasionally their interpolations and other forgeries formed a destruction in a new shape, by additions to the originals. They were indefatigable in erasing the best works of the most eminent Greek and Latin authors, in order to transcribe their ridiculous lives of saints on the obliterated vellum. One of the books of Livy is in the Vatican most painfully defaced by some pious father for the purpose of writing on it some missal or psalter, and there have been recently others discovered in the same state. Inflamed with the blindest zeal against every thing pagan, Pope Gregory VII. ordered that the library of the Palatine Apollo, a treasury of literature formed by successive emperors, should be committed to the flames! He issued this order under the notion of confining the attention of the clergy to the holy scriptures! From that time all ancient learning which was not sanctioned by the authority of the church, has been emphatically distinguished as *profane* in opposition to *sacred*. This pope is said to have burnt the works of Varro, the learned Roman, that Saint Austin should escape from the charge of plagiarism, being deeply indebted to Varro for much of his great work *The City of God*.

The Jesuits, sent by the Emperor Ferdinand to proscribe Lutheranism from Bohemia, converted that flourishing kingdom comparatively into a desert. Convinced that an enlightened people could never be long subservient to a tyrant, they struck one fatal blow at the national literature; every book they condemned was destroyed, even those of antiquity; the annals of the nation were forbidden to be read, and writers were not permitted even to compose on subjects of Bohemian literature. The mother-tongue was held out as a mark of vulgar obscurity, and domiciliary visits were made for the purpose of inspecting the libraries of the Bohemians. With their books and their language they lost their national character and their independence.

The destruction of libraries in the reign of Henry VIII. at the dissolution of the monasteries, is wept over by John Bale. Those who purchased the religious houses took the libraries as part of the booty, with which they scoured their furniture, or sold the books as waste paper, or sent them abroad in ship-loads to foreign bookbinders.

The fear of destruction induced many to hide manuscripts under ground, and in old walls. At the Reformation popular rage exhausted itself on illuminated books, or MSS. that had red letters in the title-page; any work that was decorated was sure to be thrown into the flames as a superstitious one. Red letters and embellished figures were sure marks of being papistical and diabolical. We still find such volumes mutilated of their gilt letters and elegant initials. Many have been found under-ground, having been forgotten; what escaped the flames were obliterated by the damp: such is the deplorable fate of books during a persecution!

The puritans burned every thing they found which bore the vestige of popish origin. We have on record many curious accounts of their pious depredations, of their maiming images and erasing pictures. The heroic expeditions of one Dowsing are journalized by himself: a fanatical Quixote, to whose intrepid arm many of our noseless saints, sculptured on our Cathedrals, owe their misfortunes.

The following are some details from the diary of this redoubtable Goth, during his rage for reformation. His entries are expressed with a laconic conciseness, and it would seem with a little dry humour. "At *Sunbury*, we brake down ten mighty great angels in glass. At *Barham*, brake down the twelve apostles in the chancel, and six superstitious pictures more there; and eight in the church, one a lamb with a cross (+) on the back; and digged down the steps and took up four superstitious inscriptions in brass," &c. "*Lady Bruce's house,* the chapel, a picture of God the Father, of the Trinity, of Christ, the Holy Ghost, and the cloven tongues, which we gave orders to take down, and the lady promised to do it." At another place they "brake six hundred superstitious pictures, eight Holy Ghosts, and three of the Son." And in this manner he and his deputies scoured one hundred and fifty parishes! It has been humorously conjectured, that from this ruthless devastator originated the phrase to *give a*

Dowsing. Bishop Hall saved the windows of his chapel at Norwich from destruction, by taking out the heads of the figures; and this accounts for the many faces in church windows which we see supplied by white glass.

In the various civil wars in our country, numerous libraries have suffered both in MSS. and printed books. "I dare maintain," says Fuller, "that the wars betwixt York and Lancaster, which lasted sixty years, were not so destructive as our modern wars in six years." He alludes to the parliamentary feuds in the reign of Charles I. "For during the former their differences agreed in the *same religion,* impressing them with reverence to all allowed muniments! whilst our *civil wars,* founded in *faction* and *variety* of pretended *religions,* exposed all naked church records a prey to armed violence; a sad vacuum, which will be sensible in our *English historie.*"

When it was proposed to the great Gustavus of Sweden to destroy the palace of the Dukes of Bavaria, that hero nobly refused; observing, "Let us not copy the example of our unlettered ancestors, who, by waging war against every production of genius, have rendered the name of GOTH universally proverbial of the rudest state of barbarity."

Even the civilization of the eighteenth century could not preserve from the destructive fury of an infuriated mob, in the most polished city of Europe, the valuable MSS. of the great Earl of Mansfield, which were madly consigned to the flames during the riots of 1780; as those of Dr. Priestley were consumed by the mob at Birmingham.

In the year 1599, the Hall of the Stationers underwent as great a purgation as was carried on in Don Quixote's library. Warton gives a list of the best writers who were ordered for immediate conflagration by the prelates Whitgift and Bancroft, urged by the Puritanical and Calvinistic factions. Like thieves and outlaws, they were ordered *to be taken wheresoever they may be found.*—"It was also decreed that no satires or epigrams should be printed for the future. No plays were to be printed without the inspection and permission of the archbishop of Canterbury and the bishop of London; nor any *English historyes,* I suppose novels and romances, without the sanction of the privy council. Any pieces of this nature, unlicensed, or now at large and wandering abroad, were to be diligently sought, recalled, and delivered over to the ecclesiastical arm at London-house."

At a later period, and by an opposite party, among other extravagant motions made in Parliament, one was to destroy the

Records in the Tower, and to settle the nation on a new foundation! The very same principle was attempted to be acted on in the French Revolution by the "true sans-culottes." With us Sir Matthew Hale showed the weakness of the project, and while he drew on his side "all sober persons, stopped even the mouths of the frantic people themselves."

To descend to the losses incurred by individuals, whose names ought to have served as an amulet to charm away the demons of literary destruction. One of the most interesting is the fate of Aristotle's library; he who by a Greek term was first saluted as a collector of books! His works have come down to us accidentally, but not without irreparable injuries, and with no slight suspicion respecting their authenticity. The story is told by Strabo, in his thirteenth book. The books of Aristotle came from his scholar Theophrastus to Neleus, whose posterity, an illiterate race, kept them locked up without using them, buried in the earth! Apellion, a curious collector, purchased them, but finding the MSS. injured by age and moisture, conjecturally supplied their deficiencies. It is impossible to know how far Apellion has corrupted and obscured the text. But the mischief did not end here; when Sylla at the taking of Athens brought them to Rome, he consigned them to the care of Tyrannio, a grammarian, who employed scribes to copy them; he suffered them to pass through his hands without correction, and took great freedoms with them; the words of Strabo are strong: "Ibique Tyrannionem grammaticum iis usum atque (ut fama est) *intercidisse*, aut *invertisse*." He gives it indeed as a report; but the fact seems confirmed by the state in which we find these works: Averroes declared that he read Aristotle forty times over before he succeeded in perfectly understanding him; he pretends he did at the one-and-fortieth time! And to prove this, has published five folios of commentary!

We have lost much valuable literature by the illiberal or malignant descendants of learned and ingenious persons. Many of Lady Mary Wortley Montagu's letters have been destroyed, I am informed, by her daughter, who imagined that the family honours were lowered by the addition of those of literature: some of her best letters, recently published, were found buried in an old trunk. It would have mortified her ladyship's daughter to have heard, that her mother was the Sévigné of Britain.

At the death of the learned Peiresc, a chamber in his house filled with letters from the most eminent scholars of the age was discovered: the learned in Europe had addressed Peiresc in their difficulties, who was hence called "the attorney-general of the republic of letters." The niggardly niece, although repeatedly entreated to permit them to be published, preferred to use these learned epistles occasionally to light her fires!

The MSS. of Leonardo da Vinci have equally suffered from his relatives. When a curious collector discovered some, he generously brought them to a descendant of the great painter, who coldly observed, that "he had a great deal more in the garret, which had lain there for many years, if the rats had not destroyed them!" Nothing which this great artist wrote but showed an inventive genius.

Menage observes on a friend having had his library destroyed by fire, in which several valuable MSS. had perished, that such a loss is one of the greatest misfortunes that can happen to a man of letters. This gentleman afterwards consoled himself by composing a little treatise *De Bibliothecæ incendio*. It must have been sufficiently curious. Even in the present day men of letters are subject to similar misfortunes; for though the fire-offices will insure books, they will not allow *authors to value their own manuscripts*.

A fire in the Cottonian library shrivelled and destroyed many Anglo-Saxon MSS.—a loss now irreparable. The antiquary is doomed to spell hard and hardly at the baked fragments that crumble in his hand.

Meninsky's famous Persian dictionary met with a sad fate. Its excessive rarity is owing to the siege of Vienna by the Turks: a bomb fell on the author's house, and consumed the principal part of his indefatigable labours. There are few sets of this high-priced work which do not bear evident proofs of the bomb; while many parts are stained with the water sent to quench the flames.

The sufferings of an author for the loss of his manuscripts strongly appear in the case of Anthony Urceus, a great scholar of the fifteenth century. The loss of his papers seems immediately to have been followed by madness. At Forli, he had an apartment in the palace, and had prepared an important work for publication. His room was dark, and he generally wrote by lamp-light. Having gone out, he left the lamp burning; the papers soon kindled, and his library was reduced to ashes. As soon as he heard the news, he ran furiously to the palace, and knocking his head violently against the gate, uttered this blasphemous language: "Jesus Christ, what great crime have I done! who of those who believed in you have I ever treated so cruelly? Hear what I am saying, for I am in earnest, and am resolved. If by chance I should be so weak as to address myself to you at the point of death, don't hear me, for I will not be with you, but prefer hell and its eternity of torments." To which, by the by, he gave little credit. Those who heard these ravings, vainly tried to console him. He quitted the town, and lived franticly, wandering about the woods!

Ben Jonson's *Execration on Vulcan* was composed on a like occasion; the fruits of twenty years' study were consumed in one short hour; our literature suffered, for among some works of imagination there were many philosophical collections, a commentary on the poetics, a complete critical grammar, a life of Henry V., his journey into Scotland, with all his adventures in that poetical pilgrimage, and a poem on the ladies of Great Britain. What a catalogue of losses!

Castelvetro, the Italian commentator on Aristotle, having heard that his house was on fire, ran through the streets exclaiming to the people, *alla Poetica! alla Poetica! To the Poetic! To the Poetic!* He was then writing his commentary on the *Poetics* of Aristotle.

Several men of letters have been known to have risen from their death-bed, to destroy their MSS. So solicitous have they been not to venture their posthumous reputation in the hands of undiscerning friends. Colardeau, the elegant versifier of Pope's epistle of Eloisa to Abelard, had not yet destroyed what he had written of a translation of Tasso. At the approach of death, he recollected his unfinished labour; he knew that his friends would not have the courage to annihilate one of his works; this was reserved for him. Dying, he raised himself, and as if animated by an honourable action, he dragged himself along, and with trembling hands seized his papers, and consumed them in one sacrifice.—I recollect another instance of a man of letters, of our own country, who acted the same part. He had passed his life in constant study, and it was observed that he had written several folio volumes, which his modest fears would not permit him to expose to the eye even of his critical friends. He promised to leave his labours to posterity; and he seemed sometimes, with a glow on his countenance, to exult that they would not be unworthy of their acceptance. At his death his sensibility took the alarm; he had the folios brought to his bed: no one could open them, for they were closely locked. At the sight of his favourite and mysterious labours, he paused; he seemed disturbed in his mind, while he felt at every moment his strength decaying; suddenly he raised his feeble hands by an effort of firm resolve, burnt his papers, and smiled as the greedy Vulcan licked up every page. The task exhausted his remaining strength, and he soon afterwards expired. The late Mrs. Inchbald had written her life in several volumes; on her death-bed, from a motive perhaps of too much delicacy to admit of any argument, she requested a friend to cut them into pieces before her eyes—not having sufficient strength left herself to perform this funereal office. These are instances of what may be called the heroism of authors.

The republic of letters has suffered irreparable losses by shipwrecks. Guarino Veronese, one of those learned Italians who travelled through Greece for the recovery of MSS., had his perseverance repaid by the acquisition of many valuable works. On his return to Italy he was shipwrecked, and lost his treasures! So poignant was his grief on this occasion that, according to the relation of one of his countrymen, his hair turned suddenly white.

About the year 1700, Hudde, an opulent burgomaster of Middleburgh, animated solely by literary curiosity, went to China to instruct himself in the language, and in whatever was remarkable in this singular people. He acquired the skill of a mandarin in that difficult language; nor did the form of his Dutch face undeceive the physiognomists of China. He succeeded to the dignity of a mandarin; he travelled through the provinces under this character, and returned to Europe with a collection of observations, the cherished labour of thirty years, and all these were sunk in the bottomless sea.

The great Pinellian library, after the death of its illustrious possessor, filled three vessels to be conveyed to Naples. Pursued by corsairs, one of the vessels was taken; but the pirates finding nothing on board but books, they threw them all into the sea: such was the fate of a great portion of this famous library. National libraries have often perished at sea, from the circumstance of conquerors transporting them into their own kingdoms.

The Progress of Old Age in New Studies

OF THE pleasures derivable from the cultivation of the arts, sciences, and literature, time will not abate the growing passion; for old men still cherish an affection and feel a youthful enthusiasm in those pursuits, when all others have ceased to interest. Dr. Reid, to his last day, retained a most active curiosity in his various studies, and particularly in the revolutions of modern chemistry. In advanced life we may resume our former studies with a new pleasure, and in old age we may enjoy them with the same relish with which more youthful students commence. Adam Smith observed to Dugald Stewart, that "of all the amusements of old age, the most grateful and soothing is a renewal of acquaintance with the favourite studies and favourite authors of youth—a remark (adds Stewart) which, in his own case, seemed to be more particularly exemplified while he was re-perusing, with the enthusiasm of a student, the tragic poets of ancient Greece. I have heard him repeat the observation more than once, while Sophocles and Euripides lay open on his table."

Socrates learnt to play on musical instruments in his old age; Cato, at eighty, thought proper to learn Greek; and Plutarch, almost as late in his life, Latin.

Theophrastus began his admirable work on the *Characters of Men* at the extreme age of ninety. He only terminated his literary labours by his death.

Ronsard, one of the fathers of French poetry, applied himself late to study. His acute genius, and ardent application, rivalled those poetic models which he admired; and Boccaccio was thirty-five years of age when he commenced his studies in polite literature.

The great Arnauld retained the vigour of his genius, and the command of his pen, to the age of eighty-two, and was still the great Arnauld.

Sir Henry Spelman neglected the sciences in his youth, but cultivated them at fifty years of age. His early years were chiefly passed in farming, which greatly diverted him from his studies; but a remarkable disappointment respecting a contested estate disgusted him with these rustic occupations: resolved to attach himself to regular studies, and literary society, he sold his farms, and became the most learned antiquary and lawyer.

Colbert, the famous French minister, almost at sixty, returned to his Latin and law studies.

Dr. Johnson applied himself to the Dutch language but a few years before his death. The Marquis de Saint Aulaire, at the age of seventy, began to court the Muses, and they crowned him with their freshest flowers. The verses of this French Anacreon are full of fire, delicacy, and sweetness.

Chaucer's *Canterbury Tales* were the composition of his latest years: they were begun in his fifty-fourth year, and finished in his sixty-first.

Ludovico Monaldesco, at the extraordinary age of 115, wrote the memoirs of his times. A singular exertion, noticed by Voltaire; who himself is one of the most remarkable instances of the progress of age in new studies.

The most delightful of auto-biographies for artists is that of Benvenuto Cellini; a work of great originality, which was not begun till "the clock of his age had struck fifty-eight."

Koornhert began at forty to learn the Latin and Greek languages, of which he became a master; several students, who afterwards distinguished themselves, have commenced as late in life their literary pursuits. Ogilby, the translator of Homer and Virgil, knew little of Latin or Greek till he was past fifty; and Franklin's philosophical pursuits began when he had nearly reached his fiftieth year.

Accorso, a great lawyer, being asked why he began the study of the law so late, answered, beginning it late, he should master it the sooner.

Dryden's complete works form the largest body of poetry from the pen of a single writer in the English language; yet he gave no public testimony of poetic abilities till his twenty-seventh year. In his sixty-eighth year he proposed to translate the whole *Iliad*: and his most pleasing productions were written in his old age.

Michael Angelo preserved his creative genius even in extreme old age: there is a device said to be invented by him, of an old man represented in a *go-cart*, with an hour-glass upon it; the inscription *Ancora imparo!*—YET I AM LEARNING!

We have a literary curiosity in a favourite treatise with Erasmus and men of letters of that period, *De Ratione Studii*, by Joachim Sterck, otherwise Fortius de Ringelberg. The enthusiasm of the writer often carries him to the verge of ridicule; but something must be conceded to his peculiar situation and feelings; for Baillet tells us that this method of studying had been formed entirely from his own practical knowledge and hard experience: at a late period of life he had commenced his studies, and at length he imagined that he had discovered a more per-pendicular mode of ascending the hill of science than by its usual circuitous windings. His work has been compared to the sounding of a trumpet.

Menage, in his *Anti-Baillet,* has a very curious apology for writing verses in his old age, by showing how many poets amused themselves notwithstanding their grey hairs, and wrote sonnets or epigrams at ninety.

La Casa, in one of his letters, humorously said, *Io credo ch'io farò Sonnetti venti cinque anni, o trenta, poi che io sarò morto.* —"I think I may make sonnets twenty-five, or perhaps thirty years, after I shall be dead!" Petau tells us that he wrote verses to solace the evils of old age—

> Petavius æger
> Cantabat veteris quærens solatia morbi.

Malherbe declares the honours of genius were his, yet young—

> Je les posseday jeune, et les possède encore
> A la fin de mes jours!

Men of Genius Deficient in Conversation

THE STUDENT or the artist who may shine a luminary of learning and of genius, in his works, is found, not rarely, to lie obscured beneath a heavy cloud in colloquial discourse.

If you love the man of letters, seek him in the privacies of his study. It is in the hour of confidence and tranquillity that his genius shall elicit a ray of intelligence, more fervid than the labours of polished composition.

The great Peter Corneille, whose genius resembled that of our Shakspeare, and who has so forcibly expressed the sublime senti-ments of the hero, had nothing in his exterior that indicated his genius; his conversation was so insipid that it never failed of wearying. Nature, who had lavished on him the gifts of genius, had forgotten to blend with them her more ordinary ones. He did not even *speak* correctly that language of which he was such a master. When his friends represented to him how much more he might please by not disdaining to correct these trivial errors, he would smile, and say—"*I am not the less Peter Corneille!*"

Descartes, whose habits were formed in solitude and meditation, was silent in mixed company; it was said that he had received his intellectual wealth from nature in solid bars, but not in current coin; or as Addison expressed the same idea, by comparing himself to a banker who possessed the wealth of his friends at home, though he carried none of it in his pocket; or as that judicious moralist Nicolle, of the Port-Royal Society, said of a scintillant wit—"He conquers me in the drawing-room, but he surrenders to me at discretion on the staircase." Such may say with Themistocles, when asked to play on a lute,—"I cannot fiddle, but I can make a little village a great city."

The deficiencies of Addison in conversation are well known. He preserved a rigid silence amongst strangers; but if he was silent, it was the silence of meditation. How often, at that moment, he laboured at some future *Spectator*!

Mediocrity can *talk*; but it is for genius to *observe*.

The cynical Mandeville compared Addison, after having passed an evening in his company, to "a silent parson in a tie-wig."

Virgil was heavy in conversation, and resembled more an ordinary man than an enchanting poet.

La Fontaine, says La Bruyère, appeared coarse, heavy, and stupid; he could not speak or describe what he had just seen; but when he wrote he was the model of poetry.

It is very easy, said a humorous observer on La Fontaine, to be a man of wit, or a fool; but to be both, and that too in the extreme degree, is indeed admirable, and only to be found in him. This observation applies to that fine natural genius Goldsmith. Chaucer was more facetious in his tales than in his conversation, and the Countess of Pembroke used to rally him by saying, that his silence was more agreeable to her than his conversation.

Isocrates, celebrated for his beautiful oratorical compositions, was of so timid a disposition, that he never ventured to speak in public. He compared himself to the whetstone which will not cut, but enables other things to do so; for his productions served as models to other orators. Vaucanson was said to be as much a machine as any he had made.

Dryden says of himself,—"My conversation is slow and dull, my humour saturnine and reserved. In short, I am none of those who endeavour to break jests in company, or make repartees."

Dethroned Monarchs

FORTUNE NEVER appears in a more extravagant humour than when she reduces monarchs to become mendicants. Half a century ago it was not imagined that our own times should have to record many such instances. After having contemplated *kings* raised into *divinities*, we see them now depressed as *beggars*. Our own times, in two opposite senses, may emphatically be distinguished as *the age of kings*.

In *Candide, or the Optimist*, there is an admirable stroke of Voltaire's. Eight travellers meet in an obscure inn, and some of them with not sufficient money to pay for a scurvy dinner. In the course of conversation, they are discovered to be *eight monarchs* in Europe, who had been deprived of their crowns!

What added to this exquisite satire was, that there were eight living monarchs at that moment wanderers on the earth;—a circumstance which has since occurred!

Adelaide, the widow of Lothario King of Italy, one of the most beautiful women in her age, was besieged in Pavia by Berenger, who resolved to constrain her to marry his son after Pavia was taken; she escaped from her prison with her almoner. The archbishop of Reggio had offered her an asylum: to reach it, she and her almoner travelled on foot through the country by night, concealing herself in the day time among the corn, while the almoner begged for alms and food through the villages.

The Emperor Henry IV. after having been deposed and imprisoned by his son, Henry V., escaped from prison; poor, vagrant, and without aid, he entreated the bishop of Spires to grant him a lay prebend in his church. "I have studied," said he, "and have learned to sing, and may therefore be of some service to you." The request was denied, and he died miserably and obscurely at Liege, after having drawn the attention of Europe to his victories and his grandeur!

Mary of Medicis, the widow of Henry the Great, mother of Louis XIII., mother-in-law of three sovereigns, and regent of France, frequently wanted the necessaries of life, and died at Cologne in the utmost misery. The intrigues of Richelieu compelled her to exile herself, and live an unhappy fugitive. Her petition exists, with this supplicatory opening: "Supplie Marie, Reine de France et de Navarre, disant, que depuis le 23 Février elle aurait été arrêtée prisonnière au château de Compiègne, sans être ni accusée ni soupçonnée," &c. Lilly, the astrologer, in

his *Life and Death of King Charles the First,* presents us with
a melancholy picture of this unfortunate monarch. He has also
described the person of the old queen-mother of France:—

"In the month of August, 1641, I beheld the old queen-mother
of France departing from London, in company of Thomas Earl
of Arundel. A sad spectacle of mortality it was, and produced
tears from mine eyes and many other beholders, to see an aged,
lean, decrepit, poor queen, ready for her grave, necessitated to
depart hence, having no place of residence in this world left her,
but where the courtesy of her hard fortune assigned it. She had
been the only stately and magnificent woman of Europe: wife
to the greatest king that ever lived in France; mother unto one
king and unto two queens."

In the year 1595, died at Paris, Antonio King of Portugal. His
body is interred at the Cordeliers, and his heart deposited at the
Ave-Maria. Nothing on earth could compel this prince to renounce his crown. He passed over to England, and Elizabeth
assisted him with troops; but at length he died in France in great
poverty. This dethroned monarch was happy in one thing, which
is indeed rare: in all his miseries he had a servant, who proved
a tender and faithful friend, and who only desired to participate
in his misfortunes, and to soften his miseries; and for the rec-
ompense of his services he only wished to be buried at the feet of
his dear master. This hero in loyalty, to whom the ancient
Romans would have raised altars, was Don Diego Bothei, one of
the greatest lords of the court of Portugal, and who drew his
origin from the kings of Bohemia.

Hume supplies an anecdote of singular royal distress. The
Queen of England, with her son Charles, "had a moderate pension assigned her; but it was so ill paid, and her credit ran so
low, that one morning when the Cardinal de Retz waited on her,
she informed him that her daughter, the Princess Henrietta, was
obliged to lie a-bed for want of a fire to warm her. To such a
condition was reduced, in the midst of Paris, a queen of England, and a daughter of Henry IV. of France!" We find another
proof of her extreme poverty. Salmasius, after publishing his
celebrated political book, in favour of Charles I., the *Defensio
Regia,* was much blamed by a friend for not having sent a copy
to the widowed queen of Charles, who, he writes, "though poor,
would yet have paid the bearer."

The daughter of James the First, who married the Elector
Palatine, in her attempts to get her husband crowned, was reduced to the utmost distress, and wandered frequently in disguise.

A strange anecdote is related of Charles VII. of France. Our Henry V. had shrunk his kingdom into the town of Bourges. It is said that having told a shoemaker, after he had just tried a pair of his boots, that he had no money to pay for them, Crispin had such callous feelings that he refused his majesty the boots. "It is for this reason," says Comines, "I praise those princes who are on good terms with the lowest of their people; for they know not at what hour they may want them."

Many monarchs of this day have experienced more than once the truth of the reflection of Comines.

We may add here, that in all conquered countries the descendants of royal families have been found among the dregs of the populace. An Irish prince has been discovered in the person of a miserable peasant; and in Mexico, its faithful historian Clavigero notices, that he has known a locksmith, who was a descendant of its ancient kings, and a tailor, the representative of one of its noblest families.

Feudal Customs

BARBAROUS AS the feudal customs were, they were the first attempts at organizing European society. The northern nations, in their irruptions and settlements in Europe, were barbarians independent of each other, till a sense of public safety induced these hordes to confederate. But the private individual reaped no benefit from the public union; on the contrary, he seems to have lost his wild liberty in the subjugation; he in a short time was compelled to suffer from his chieftain; and the curiosity of the philosopher is excited by contemplating in the feudal customs a barbarous people carrying into their first social institutions their original ferocity. The institution of forming cities into communities at length gradually diminished this military and aristocratic tyranny; and the freedom of cities, originating in the pursuits of commerce, shook off the yoke of insolent lordships. A famous ecclesiastical writer of that day, who had imbibed the feudal prejudices, calls these communities, which were distinguished by the name of *libertates* (hence probably our municipal term the *liberties*), as "execrable inventions, by which, contrary to law and justice, slaves withdrew themselves from that obedience which they owed to their masters." Such was the expiring voice of aristocratic tyranny! This subject has been

ingeniously discussed by Robertson in his preliminary volume to
Charles V.; but the following facts constitute the picture which
the historian leaves to be gleaned by the minuter inquirer.

The feudal government introduced a species of servitude which
till that time was unknown, and which was called the servitude
of the land. The bondmen or serfs, and the villains or country
servants, did not reside in the house of the lord: but they entirely depended on his caprice; and he sold them, as he did the
animals, with the field where they lived, and which they cultivated.

It is difficult to conceive with what insolence the petty lords
of those times tyrannized over their villains: they not only
oppressed their slaves with unremitted labour, instigated by a
vile cupidity; but their whim and caprice led them to inflict
miseries without even any motive of interest.

In Scotland they had a shameful institution of maiden-rights;
and Malcolm the Third only abolished it, by ordering that they
might be redeemed by a quit-rent. The truth of this circumstance
Dalrymple has attempted, with excusable patriotism, to render
doubtful. There seems, however, to be no doubt of the existence
of this custom; since it also spread through Germany, and various parts of Europe; and the French barons extended their
domestic tyranny to three nights of involuntary prostitution.
Montesquieu is infinitely French, when he could turn this shameful species of tyranny into a *bon mot*; for he boldly observes on
this, "*C'étoit bien ces trois nuits-là qu'il falloit choisir; car pour
les autres on n'auroit pas donné beaucoup d'argent.*" The legislator in the wit forgot the feelings of his heart.

Others, to preserve this privilege when they could not enjoy
it in all its extent, thrust their leg booted into the bed of the
new-married couple. This was called the *droit de cuisse*. When
the bride was in bed, the esquire or lord performed this ceremony, and stood there, his thigh in the bed, with a lance in his
hand: in this ridiculous attitude he remained till he was tired;
and the bridegroom was not suffered to enter the chamber, till
his lordship had retired. Such indecent privileges must have
originated in the worst of intentions; and when afterwards they
advanced a step in more humane manners, the ceremonial was
preserved from avaricious motives. Others have compelled their
subjects to pass the first night at the top of a tree, and there to
consummate their marriage; to pass the bridal hours in a river;
or to be bound naked to a cart, and to trace some furrows as

they were dragged; or to leap with their feet tied over the horns of stags.

Sometimes their caprice commanded the bridegroom to appear in drawers at their castle, and plunge into a ditch of mud; and sometimes they were compelled to beat the waters of the ponds to hinder the frogs from disturbing the lord!

Wardship, or the privilege of guardianship enjoyed by some lords, was one of the barbarous inventions of the feudal ages; the guardian had both the care of the person, and for his own use the revenue of the estates. This feudal custom was so far abused in England, that the king sold these lordships to strangers; and when the guardian had fixed on a marriage for the infant, if the youth or maiden did not agree to this, they forfeited the value of the marriage; that is, the sum the guardian would have obtained by the other party had it taken place. This cruel custom was a source of domestic unhappiness, particularly in love-affairs, and has served as the groundwork of many a pathetic play by our elder dramatists.

There was a time when the German lords reckoned amongst their privileges that of robbing on the highways of their territory; which ended in raising up the famous Hanseatic Union, to protect their commerce against rapine and avaricious exactions of toll.

Geoffrey, lord of Coventry, compelled his wife to ride naked on a white pad through the streets of the town; that by this mode he might restore to the inhabitants those privileges of which his wantonness had deprived them. This anecdote some have suspected to be fictitious, from its extreme barbarity; but the character of the middle ages will admit of any kind of wanton barbarism.

When the abbot of Figeac made his entry into that town, the lord of Montbron, dressed in a harlequin's coat, and one of his legs naked, was compelled by an ancient custom to conduct him to the door of his abbey, leading his horse by the bridle. Blount's *Jocular Tenures* is a curious collection of such capricious clauses in the grants of their lands.

The feudal barons frequently combined to share among themselves those children of their villains who appeared to be the most healthy and serviceable, or remarkable for their talents; and not unfrequently sold them in their markets.

The feudal servitude is not, even in the present enlightened times, abolished in Poland, in Germany, and in Russia. In those countries, the bondmen are still entirely dependent on the caprice of their masters. The peasants of Hungary or Bohemia frequently revolt, and attempt to shake off the pressure of feudal tyranny.

An anecdote of comparatively recent date displays their unfeeling caprice. A lord or prince of the northern countries passing through one of his villages, observed a small assembly of peasants and their families amusing themselves with dancing. He commands his domestics to part the men from the women, and confine them in the houses. He orders the coats of the women to be drawn up above their heads, and tied with their garters. The men were then liberated, and those who did not recognize their wives in that state received a severe castigation.

Absolute dominion hardens the human heart; and nobles accustomed to command their bondmen will treat their domestics as slaves, as capricious or inhuman West Indians treated their domestic slaves. Those of Siberia punish theirs by a free use of the cudgel or rod. The Abbé Chappe saw two Russian slaves undress a chambermaid, who had by some trifling negligence given offence to her mistress; after having uncovered as far as her waist, one placed her head betwixt his knees; the other held her by the feet; while both, armed with two sharp rods, violently lashed her back till it pleased the domestic tyrant to decree *it was enough!*

After a perusal of these anecdotes of feudal tyranny, we may exclaim with Goldsmith—

> I fly from PETTY TYRANTS—to the THRONE.

Mr. Hallam's *State of Europe during the Middle Ages* renders this short article superfluous in a philosophical view.

Spanish Etiquette

THE ETIQUETTE, or rules to be observed in royal palaces, is necessary for keeping order at court. In Spain it was carried to such lengths as to make martyrs of their kings. Here is an instance, at which, in spite of the fatal consequences it produced, one cannot refrain from smiling.

Philip the Third was gravely seated by the fire-side: the fire-maker of the court had kindled so great a quantity of wood, that the monarch was nearly suffocated with heat, and his *grandeur* would not suffer him to rise from the chair; the domestics could not *presume* to enter the apartment, because it was against the *etiquette*. At length the Marquis de Potat appeared, and the king ordered him to damp the fire; but *he* excused himself; alleging that he was forbidden by the *etiquette* to perform such a function for which the Duke d'Usseda ought to be called upon, as it was his business. The duke was gone out: the *fire* burnt fiercer; and the *king* endured it, rather than derogate from his *dignity*. But his blood was heated to such a degree, that an erysipelas of the head appeared the next day, which, succeeded by a violent fever, carried him off in 1621, in the twenty-fourth year of his reign.

The palace was once on fire; a soldier, who knew the king's sister was in her apartment, and must inevitably have been consumed in a few moments by the flames, at the risk of his life rushed in, and brought her highness safe out in his arms! but the Spanish *etiquette* was here wofully broken into! The loyal soldier was brought to trial; and as it was impossible to deny that he had entered her apartment, the judges condemned him to die! The Spanish princess however condescended, in consideration of the circumstance, to *pardon* the soldier, and very benevolently saved his life.

When Isabella, mother of Philip II., was ready to be delivered of him, she commanded that all the lights should be extinguished: that if the violence of her pain should occasion her face to change colour, no one might perceive it. And when the midwife said, "Madam, cry out, that will give you ease," she answered in *good Spanish*, "How dare you give me such advice? I would rather die than cry out."

> Spain gives us *pride*—which Spain to all the earth
> May largely give, nor fear herself a dearth!
> CHURCHILL

Philip the Third was a weak bigot, who suffered himself to be governed by his ministers. A patriot wished to open his eyes, but he could not pierce through the crowds of his flatterers; besides that the voice of patriotism heard in a corrupted court would have become a crime never pardoned. He found, however, an ingenious manner of conveying to him his censure. He caused to be laid on his table, one day, a letter sealed, which bore this address—"To the King of Spain, Philip the Third, at present in the service of the Duke of Lerma."

In a similar manner, Don Carlos, son to Philip the Second, made a book with empty pages, to contain the voyages of his father, which bore this title—*The great and admirable Voyages of the King Mr. Philip*. All these voyages consisted in going to the Escurial from Madrid, and returning to Madrid from the Escurial. Jests of this kind at length cost him his life.

Anecdotes of Fashion

A VOLUME on this subject might be made very curious and entertaining, for our ancestors were not less vacillating, and perhaps more capriciously grotesque, though with infinitely less taste, than the present generation. Were a philosopher and an artist, as well as an antiquary, to compose such a work, much diversified entertainment, and some curious investigation of the progress of the arts and taste, would doubtless be the result; the subject otherwise appears of trifling value; the very farthing pieces of history.

The origin of many fashions was in the endeavour to conceal some deformity of the inventor: hence the cushions, ruffs, hoops, and other monstrous devices. If a reigning beauty chanced to have an unequal hip, those who had very handsome hips would load them with that false rump which the other was compelled by the unkindness of nature to substitute. Patches were invented in England in the reign of Edward VI. by a foreign lady, who in this manner ingeniously covered a wen on her neck. Full-bottomed wigs were invented by a French barber, one Duviller, whose name they perpetuated, for the purpose of concealing an elevation in the shoulder of the Dauphin. Charles VII. of France introduced long coats to hide his ill-made legs. Shoes with very long points, full two feet in length, were invented by Henry Plantagenet, Duke of Anjou, to conceal a large excrescence on one of his feet. When Francis I. was obliged to wear his hair short, owing to a wound he received in the head, it became a prevailing fashion at court. Others, on the contrary, adapted fashions to set off their peculiar beauties: as Isabella of Bavaria, remarkable for her gallantry, and the fairness of her complexion, introduced the fashion of leaving the shoulders and part of the neck uncovered.

Fashions have frequently originated from circumstances as silly as the following one. Isabella, daughter of Philip II. and wife of the Archduke Albert, vowed not to change her linen till Ostend was taken; this siege, unluckily for her comfort, lasted three years; and the supposed colour of the archduchess's

linen gave rise to a fashionable colour, hence called *l'Isabeau,*
or the Isabella; a kind of whitish-yellow-dingy. Sometimes they
originate in some temporary event; as after the battle of Steen-
kirk, where the allies wore large cravats, by which the French
frequently seized hold of them, a circumstance perpetuated on
the medals of Louis XIV., cravats were called Steenkirks; and
after the battle of Ramilies, wigs received that denomination.

The *court,* in all ages and in every country, are the modellers
of fashions; so that all the ridicule, of which these are so susceptible, must fall on them, and not upon their servile imitators
the *citizens.* This complaint is made even so far back as in 1586,
by Jean des Caures, an old French moralist, who, in declaiming
against the fashions of his day, notices one of the ladies carrying *mirrors fixed to their waists,* which seemed to employ their
eyes in perpetual activity. From this mode will result, according
to honest des Caures, their eternal damnation. "Alas! (he exclaims) in what an age do we live: to see such depravity which
we see, that induces them even to bring into church these
scandalous mirrors hanging about their waists! Let all histories,
divine, human, and profane, be consulted; never will it be found
that these objects of vanity were ever thus brought into public
by the most meretricious of the sex. It is true, at present none
but the ladies of the court venture to wear them; but long it will
not be before *every citizen's daughter* and every *female servant,*
will have them!" Such in all times has been the rise and decline
of fashion; and the absurd mimicry of the *citizens,* even of the
lowest classes, to their very ruin, in straining to rival the *newest
fashion,* has mortified and galled the courtier.

On this subject old Camden, in his *Remains,* relates a story of
a trick played off in a citizen, which I give in the plainness of his
own venerable style. "Sir Philip Calthrop purged John Drakes,
the *shoemaker of Norwich,* in the time of King Henry VIII. of
the *proud humour* which our *people have to be of the gentlemen's cut.* This knight bought on a time as much fine French
tawny cloth as should make him a gown, and sent it to the
taylor's to be made. John Drakes, a shoemaker of that town,
coming to this said taylor's, and seeing the knight's gown cloth
lying there, liking it well, caused the taylor to buy him as much
of the same cloth and price to the same intent, and further bade
him to *make it of the same fashion that the knight would have
his made of.* Not long after, the knight coming to the taylor's
to take measure of his gown, perceiving the like cloth lying
there, asked of the taylor whose it was? Quoth the taylor, it is

John Drakes's the *shoemaker*, who will have it *made of the self-same fashion that yours is made of!* 'Well!' said the knight, 'in good time be it! I will have mine made as *full of cuts as thy shears can make it.*' 'It shall be done!' said the taylor; whereupon, because the time drew near, he made haste to finish both their garments. John Drakes had no time to go to the taylor's till Christmas-day, for serving his customers, when he hoped to have worn his gown; perceiving the same to be *full of cuts* began to swear at the taylor, for the making his gown after that sort. 'I have done nothing,' quoth the taylor, 'but that you bid me; for as Sir Philip Calthrop's garment is, even so have I made yours!' 'By my latchet!' quoth John Drakes, '*I will never wear gentlemen's fashions again!*' "

Sometimes fashions are quite reversed in their use in one age from another. Bags, when first in fashion in France, were only worn *en déshabillé*; in visits of ceremony, the hair was tied by a riband and floated over the shoulders, which is exactly reversed in the present fashion. In the year 1735 the men had no hats but a little *chapeau de bras*; in 1745 they wore a very small hat; in 1755 they wore an enormous one, as may be seen in Jeffrey's curious *Collection of Habits in all Nations.* Old Puttenham, in *The Art of Poesie*, p. 239, on the present topic gives some curious information. "Henry VIII. caused his own head, and all his courtiers, to be *polled*, and his *beard* to be *cut short; before that time* it was thought *more decent*, both for old men and young, to be *all shaven*, and weare *long haire*, either rounded or square. Now *again at this time* (Elizabeth's reign), the young gentlemen of the court have *taken up the long haire* trayling on their shoulders, and think this more decent; for what respect I would be glad to know."

When the fair sex were accustomed to behold their lovers with beards, the sight of a shaved chin excited feelings of horror and aversion; as much indeed as, in this less heroic age, would a gallant whose luxuriant beard should

Stream like a meteor to the troubled air.

When Louis VII., to obey the injunctions of his bishops, cropped his hair, and shaved his beard, Eleanor, his consort, found him, with this unusual appearance, very ridiculous, and soon very contemptible. She revenged herself as she thought proper, and the poor shaved king obtained a divorce. She then married the Count of Anjou, afterwards our Henry II. She had for her marriage dower the rich provinces of Poitou and

Guienne; and this was the origin of those wars which for three hundred years ravaged France, and cost the French three millions of men. All which, probably, had never occurred had Louis VII. not been so rash as to crop his head and shave his beard, by which he became so disgustful in the eyes of our Queen Eleanor.

We cannot perhaps sympathize with the feelings of her Majesty, though at Constantinople she might not have been considered unreasonable. There must be something more powerful in *beards* and *mustachios* than we are quite aware of; for when these were in fashion—and long after this was written—the fashion has returned on us—with what enthusiasm were they not contemplated! When *mustachios* were in general use, an author, in his *Elements of Education*, published in 1640, thinks that "hairy excrement," as Armado in *Love's Labour's Lost* calls it, contributed to make men valorous. He says, "I have a favourable opinion of that young gentleman who is *curious in fine mustachios*. The time he employs in adjusting, dressing, and curling them, is no lost time; for the more he contemplates his mustachios, the more his mind will cherish and be animated by masculine and courageous notions." The best reason that could be given for wearing the *longest and largest beard* of any Englishman was that of a worthy clergyman in Elizabeth's reign, "that no act of his life might be unworthy of the gravity of his appearance."

The grandfather of Mrs. Thomas, the Corinna of Cromwell, the literary friend of Pope, by her account, "was very nice in the mode of that age, his valet being some hours every morning in *starching his beard* and *curling his whiskers;* during which time he was always read to." Taylor, the water poet, humorously describes the great variety of beards in his time, which extract may be found in Grey's *Hudibras*, Vol. I. p. 300. The *beard* dwindled gradually under the two Charleses, till it was reduced into *whiskers*, and became extinct in the reign of James II., as if its fatality had been connected with that of the house of Stuart.

The hair has in all ages been an endless topic for the declamation of the moralist, and the favourite object of fashion. If the *beau monde* wore their hair luxuriant, or their wig enormous, the preachers, in Charles the Second's reign, instantly were seen in the pulpit with their hair cut shorter, and their sermon longer, in consequence; respect was, however, paid by the world to the size of the *wig*, in spite of the *hair-cutter* in the pulpit. Our judges, and till lately our physicians, well knew its magical effect. In the reign of Charles II. the hair-dress of the ladies was very elaborate; it was not only curled and frizzled with the nicest art, but set off with certain artificial curls, then too emphatically known by the pathetic terms of *heart-breakers* and *love-locks*. So late as William and Mary, lads, and even children, wore wigs; and if they had not wigs, they curled their hair to resemble this fashionable ornament. Women then were the hairdressers.

There are flagrant follies in fashion which must be endured while they reign, and which never appear ridiculous till they are out of fashion. In the reign of Henry III. of France, they could not exist without an abundant use of comfits. All the world, the grave and the gay, carried in their pockets a *comfitbox*, as we do snuff-boxes. They used them even on the most solemn occasions; when the Duke of Guise was shot at Blois, he was found with his comfit-box in his hand.—Fashions indeed have been carried to so extravagant a length, as to have become a public offence, and to have required the interference of government. Short and tight breeches were so much the rage in France, that Charles V. was compelled to banish this disgusting mode by edicts, which may be found in Mezerai. An Italian author of the fifteenth century supposes an Italian traveller of nice modesty would not pass through France, that he might not be offended by seeing men whose clothes rather exposed their nakedness than hid it. The very same fashion was the complaint in the remoter period of our Chaucer, in his "Parson's Tale."

In the reign of our Elizabeth the reverse of all this took place; then the mode of enormous breeches was pushed to a most laughable excess. The beaux of that day stuffed out their breeches with rags, feathers, and other light matters, till they brought them out to an enormous size. They resembled wool-sacks, and in a public spectacle they were obliged to raise scaffolds for the seats of these ponderous beaux. To accord with this fantastical taste, the ladies invented large hoop farthingales; two lovers aside could surely never have taken one another by the hand. In a preceding reign the fashion ran on square toes; insomuch that a proclamation was issued that no person should wear shoes above six inches square at the toes! Then succeeded pickedpointed shoes! The nation was again, in the reign of Elizabeth, put under the royal authority. "In that time," says honest John Stowe, "he was held the greatest gallant that had the *deepest ruff* and *longest rapier*: the offence to the eye of the one, and hurt unto the life of the subject that came by the other—this caused her Majestie to *make proclamation against them both,* and to *place selected grave citizens at every gate, to cut the ruffes, and breake the rapiers' points* of all passengers that exceeded a yeard in length of their rapiers, and a nayle of a yeard in depth of their ruffes." These "grave citizens," at every gate cutting the ruffs and breaking the rapiers, must doubtless have encountered in their ludicrous employment some stubborn opposition; but this regulation was, in the spirit of that age, despotic and effectual. Paul, the Emperor of Russia, one day ordered the soldiers to stop every passenger who wore pantaloons, and with their hangers to cut off, upon the leg, the offending part of these superfluous breeches; so that a man's legs depended greatly on the adroitness and humanity of a Russ or a Cossack; however this war against *pantaloons* was very successful, and obtained a complete triumph in favour of the *breeches* in the course of the week.

A shameful extravagance in dress has been a most venerable folly. In the reign of Richard II. their dress was sumptuous beyond belief. Sir John Arundel had a change of no less than fifty-two new suits of cloth of gold tissue. The prelates indulged in all the ostentatious luxury of dress. Chaucer says, they had "chaunge of clothing everie daie." Brantome records of Elizabeth, Queen of Philip II. of Spain, that she never wore a gown twice; this was told him by her majesty's own *tailleur,* who from a poor man soon became as rich as any one he knew. Our own Elizabeth left no less than three thousand different habits in her wardrobe when she died. She was possessed of the dresses of all countries.

The Catholic religion has ever considered the pomp of the clerical habit as not the slightest part of its religious ceremonies; their devotion is addressed to the eye of the people. In the reign of our Catholic Queen Mary, the dress of a priest was costly indeed; and the sarcastic and good-humoured Fuller gives, in his *Worthies,* the will of a priest, to show the wardrobe of men of his order, and desires that the priest may not be jeered for the gallantry of his splendid apparel. He bequeaths to various parish churches and persons, "My vestment of crimson satin—my vestment of crimson velvet—my stole and fanon set with pearl—my black gown faced with taffeta," &c.

Chaucer has minutely detailed in "The Persone's Tale" the grotesque and the costly fashions of his day; and the simplicity of the venerable satirist will interest the antiquary and the philosopher. Much, and curiously, has his caustic severity or lenient humour descanted on the "moche superfluitee," and "wast of cloth in vanitee," as well as "the disordinate scantnesse." In the spirit of the good old times, he calculates "the coste of the embrouding or embroidering; endenting or barring; ounding or wavy; paling or imitating pales; and winding or bending; the costlewe furring in the gounes; so much pounsoning of chesel to maken holes (that is, punched with a bodkin); so moche dagging of sheres (cutting into slips); with the superfluitee in length of the gounes trailing in the dong and in the myre, on horse and eke on foot, as wel of man as of woman—that all thilke trailing," he verily believes, which wastes, consumes, wears threadbare, and is rotten with dung, is all to the damage of "the poor folk," who might be clothed only out of the flounces and draggle-tails of these children of vanity. But then his Parson is not less bitter against "the horrible disordinate scantnesse of clothing," and very copiously he describes, though perhaps in terms and with a humour too coarse for me to transcribe, the consequences of these very tight dresses. Of these persons, among other offensive matters, he sees "the buttokkes behind, as if they were the hinder part of a sheap, in the full of the mone." He notices one of the most grotesque modes, the wearing a particoloured dress; one stocking part white and part red, so that they looked as if they had been flayed. Or white and blue, or white and black, or black and red; this variety of colours gave an appearance to their members of St. Anthony's fire, or cancer, or other mischance!

The modes of dress during the thirteenth and fourteenth centuries were so various and ridiculous, that they afforded perpetual food for the eager satirist.

The conquests of Edward III. introduced the French fashions into England; and the Scotch adopted them by their alliance with the French court, and close intercourse with that nation.

Walsingham dates the introduction of French fashions among us from the taking of Calais in 1347; but we appear to have possessed such a rage for imitation in dress, that an English beau was actually a fantastical compound of all the fashions in Europe, and even Asia, in the reign of Elizabeth. In Chaucer's time, the prevalence of French fashions was a common topic with our satirist; and he notices the affectation of our female citizens in speaking the French language, a stroke of satire which, after four centuries, is not obsolete, if applied to their faulty pronunciation. In the prologue to the Prioresse, Chaucer has these humorous lines:—

Entewned in her voice full seemly,
And French she spake full feteously,
After the Scole of Stratford at Bowe;
The *French of Paris* was to her unknowe.

A beau of the reign of Henry IV. has been made out, by the labourious Henry. They wore then long-pointed shoes to such an immoderate length, that they could not walk till they were fastened to their knees with chains. Luxury improving on this ridiculous mode, these chains the English beau of the fourteenth century had made of gold and silver; but the grotesque fashion did not finish here, for the tops of their shoes were carved in the manner of a church window. The ladies of that period were not less fantastical.

The wild variety of dresses worn in the reign of Henry VIII. is alluded to in a print of a naked Englishman holding a piece of cloth hanging on his right arm, and a pair of shears in his left hand. It was invented by Andrew Borde, a learned wit of those days. The print bears the following inscription:—

I am an Englishman, and naked I stand here,
Musing in my mind, what rayment I shall were;
For now I will were this, and now I will were that,
And now I will were what I cannot tell what.

At a lower period, about the reign of Elizabeth, we are presented with a curious picture of a man of fashion by Puttenham, in his *Arte of Poetry*, p. 250. This author was a travelled courtier, and has interspersed his curious work with many lively anecdotes of the times. This is his fantastical beau in the reign of Elizabeth. "May it not seeme enough for a courtier to know how to *weare a feather* and *set his cappe* aflaunt; his *chain en echarpe*; a straight *buskin, al Inglese*; a loose *à la Turquesque*; the cape *alla Spaniola*; the breech *à la Françoise*, and, by twentie maner of new-fashioned garments, to disguise his body and his face with as many countenances, whereof it seems there be many that make a very arte and studie, who can shewe himselfe most fine, I will not say most foolish or ridiculous." So that a beau of those times wore in the same dress a grotesque mixture of all the fashions in the world. About the same period the *ton* ran in a different course in France. There, fashion consisted in an affected negligence of dress; for Montaigne honestly laments, in Book i. Cap. 25.—"I have never yet been apt to imitate the *negligent garb* which is yet observable among the *young men* of our time; to wear my *cloak on one shoulder*, my *bonnet on one side*, and *one stocking* in something *more disorder than the other*, meant to express a manly disdain of such exotic ornaments, and a contempt of art."

The fashions of the Elizabethan age have been chronicled by honest John Stowe. Stowe was originally a *tailor*, and when he laid down the shears, and took up the pen, the taste and curiosity for *dress* was still retained. He is the grave chronicler of matters not grave. The chronology of ruffs, and tufted taffetas; the revolution of steel poking-sticks, instead of bone or wood, used by the laundresses; the invasion of shoe-buckles, and the total rout of shoe-roses; that grand adventure of a certain Flemish lady, who introduced the art of starching the ruffs with a yellow tinge into Britain: while Mrs. Montague emulated her in the royal favour, by presenting her highness the queen with a pair of black silk stockings, instead of her cloth hose, which her majesty now for ever rejected; the heroic achievements of the Right Honourable Edward de Vere, Earl of Oxford, who first brought from Italy the whole mystery and craft of perfumery, and costly washes; and among other pleasant things besides, a perfumed jerkin, a pair of perfumed gloves trimmed with roses, in which the queen took such delight, that she was actually pictured with those gloves on her royal hands, and for many years after the scent was called the Earl of Oxford's Perfume. These, and occurrences as memorable, receive a pleasant kind of historical pomp in the important, and not incurious, narrative of the antiquary and the tailor. The toilet of Elizabeth was indeed an altar of devotion, of which she was the idol, and all her ministers were her votaries: it was the reign of coquetry, and the golden age of millinery! But of grace and elegance they had not the slightest feeling! There is a print by Vertue, of Queen Elizabeth going in a procession to Lord Hunsdon. This procession is led by Lady Hunsdon, who no doubt was the leader likewise of the fashion; but it is impossible, with our ideas of grace and comfort, not to commiserate this unfortunate lady, whose standing-up wire ruff, rising above her head; whose stays, or bodice, so long-waisted as to reach to her knees; and the circumference of her large hoop farthingale, which seems to enclose her in a capacious tub, mark her out as one of the most pitiable martyrs of ancient modes. The amorous Sir Walter Raleigh must have found some of the maids of honour the most impregnable fortification his gallant spirit ever assailed: a *coup de main* was impossible.

I shall transcribe from old Stowe a few extracts, which may amuse the reader:—

"In the second yeere of Queen Elizabeth 1560, her *silke woman*, Mistris Montague, presented her majestie for a new yeere's gift, a *paire of black knit silk stockings*, the which, after a few days' wearing, pleased her highness so well, that she sent for Mistris Montague, and asked her where she had them, and if she could help her to any more; who answered, saying. 'I made them very carefully of purpose only for your majestie, and seeing these please you so well, I will presently set more in hand.' 'Do so (quoth the queene), for *indeed I like silk stockings so well, because they are pleasant, fine, and delicate, that henceforth I will wear no more* CLOTH STOCKINGS'—and from that time unto her death the queene never wore any more *cloth hose*, but only silke stockings; for you shall understand that King Henry the Eight did weare onely cloath hose, or hose cut out of ell-broade taffety, or that by great chance there came a pair of *Spanish silk stockings* from Spain. King Edward the Sixt had a *payre of long Spanish silke stockings* sent him for a *great present.*—Dukes' daughters then wore gownes of satten of Bridges (Bruges) upon solemn dayes. Cushens, and window pillows of welvet and damaske, formerly only princely furniture, now be very plenteous in most citizens' houses."

"Milloners or haberdashers had not then any *gloves imbroydered*, or trimmed with gold, or silke; neither gold nor imbroydered girdles and hangers, neither could they *make any costly wash* or *perfume*, until about the fifteenth yeere of the queene, the Right Honourable Edward de Vere, Earl of Oxford, came from *Italy*, and brought with him gloves, sweete bagges, a perfumed leather jerkin, and other *pleasant things*; and that yeere the queene had a *pair of perfumed gloves* trimmed only with four tuffes, or *roses of coloured silk*. The queene took such pleasure in those gloves, that she was pictured with those gloves upon her handes, and for many years after it was called '*The Earl of Oxford's perfume.*'"

In such a chronology of fashions, an event not less important surely was the origin of *starching*; and here we find it treated with the utmost historical dignity.

"In the year 1564, Mistris Dinghen Van den Plasse, borne at Tænen in Flaunders, daughter to a worshipfull knight of that province, with her husband, came to London for their better safeties, and there professed herself a *starcher*, wherein she excelled, unto whom her owne nation presently repaired, and payed her very liberally for her worke. Some very few of the best and most curious wives of that time, observing the *neatness and*

delicacy of the Dutch for whitenesse and fine wearing of linen,
made them *cambricke ruffs,* and sent them to Mistris Dinghen to
starch, and after awhile they made them *ruffes of lawn,* which
was at that time a stuff most strange, and wonderfull, and there-
upon rose a *general scoffe* or *by-word,* that shortly they would
make *ruffs of a spider's web;* and then they began to send their
daughters and nearest kinswomen to Mistris Dinghen to *learn
how to starche;* her usuall price was at that time, foure or five
pound, to teach them how *to starch,* and twenty shillings how to
seeth starch."

Thus Italy, Holland, and France, supplied us with fashions
and refinements. But in those days they were, as I have shown
from Puttenham, as *extravagant dressers* as any of their present
supposed degenerate descendants. Stowe affords us another curious extract. "Divers noble personages made them *ruffes, a full
quarter of a yeard deepe,* and two lengthe in one ruffe. This
fashion in *London* was called the *French fashion;* but when
Englishmen came to *Paris,* the *French* knew it not, and in derision called it *the English monster."* An exact parallel this of
many of our own Parisian modes in the present day.

This was the golden period of cosmetics. The beaux of that
day, it is evident, used the abominable art of painting their faces
as well as the women. Our old comedies abound with perpetual
allusions to oils, tinctures, quintessences, pomatums, perfumes,
paint white and red, &c. One of their prime cosmetics was a
frequent use of the *bath,* and the application of *wine.* Strutt
quotes from an old MS. a recipe to make the face of a beautiful
red color. The person was to be in a bath that he might perspire,
and afterwards wash his face with wine, and "so should be both
faire and roddy." In Mr. Lodge's *Illustrations of British History,*
the Earl of Shrewsbury, who had the keeping of the unfortunate
Queen of Scots, complains of the expenses of the Queen for
bathing in wine, and requires a further allowance. A learned
Scotch professor informed me, that *white wine* was used for these
purposes. They also made a bath of *milk.* Elder beauties *bathed
in wine,* to get rid of their wrinkles; and perhaps not without
reason, wine being a great astringent. Unwrinkled beauties
bathed in milk, to preserve the softness and sleekness of the skin.
Our venerable beauties of the Elizabethan age were initiated
coquettes; and the mysteries of their toilet might be worth un-
veiling.

The reign of Charles II. was the dominion of French fashions.
In some respects the taste was a little lighter, but the moral effect

of dress, and which no doubt it has, was much worse. The dress was very inflammatory; and the nudity of the beauties of the portrait-painter, Sir Peter Lely, has been observed. The queen of Charles II. exposed her breast and shoulders without even the gloss of the lightest gauze; and the tucker, instead of standing up on her bosom, is with licentious boldness turned down, and lies upon her stays. This custom of baring the bosom was much exclaimed against by the authors of that age. That honest divine, Richard Baxter, wrote a preface to a book, entitled, "A just and seasonable reprehension of *naked breasts and shoulders.*" In 1672 a book was published, entitled, "New instructions unto youth for their behaviour, and also a discourse upon some innovations of habits and dressing; *against powdering of hair, naked breasts, black spots* (or patches), and other unseemly customs." A whimsical fashion now prevailed among the ladies, of strangely ornamenting their faces with abundance of black patches cut into grotesque forms, such as a coach and horses, owls, rings, suns, moons, crowns, cross and crosslets. The author has prefixed *two ladies' heads*; the one representing *Virtue*, and the other *Vice*. *Virtue* is a lady modestly habited, with a black velvet hood, and a plain white kerchief on her neck, with a border. *Vice* wears no handkerchief; her stays cut low, so that they display great part of the breasts; and a variety of fantastical patches on her face.

The innovations of fashions in the reign of Charles II. were watched with a jealous eye by the remains of those strict puritans, who now could only pour out their bile in such solemn admonitions. They affected all possible plainness and sanctity. When courtiers wore monstrous wigs, they cut their hair short; when they adopted hats with broad plumes, they clapped on round black caps, and screwed up their pale religious faces; and when shoe-buckles were revived, they wore strings. The sublime Milton, perhaps, exulted in his intrepidity of still wearing latchets! *The Tatler* ridicules Sir William Whitelocke for his singularity in still affecting them. "Thou dear *Will Shoestring*, how shall I draw thee? Thou dear outside, will you be *combing your wig*, playing with your *box*, or picking your *teeth*," &c. *Wigs* and *snuff-boxes* were then the rage. Steele's own wig, it is recorded, made at one time a considerable part of his annual expenditure. His large black periwig cost him, even at that day, no less than forty guineas!—We wear nothing at present in this degree of extravagance. But such a wig was the idol of fashion, and they were performing perpetually their worship with infinite self-complacency; combing their wigs in public was then the very spirit of gallantry and rank. The hero of Richardson, youthful and elegant as he wished him to be, is represented waiting at an assignation, and describing his sufferings in bad weather by lamenting that "his *wig* and his linen were dripping with the hoar frost dissolving on them." Even Betty, Clarissa's lady's maid, is described as "tapping on her *snuff-box*," and frequently taking *snuff*. At this time nothing was so monstrous as the head-dresses of the ladies in Queen Anne's reign: they formed a kind of edifice of three stories high; and a fashionable lady of that day much resembles the mythological figure of Cybele, the mother of the gods, with three towers on her head.

It is not worth noticing the changes in fashion, unless to ridicule them. However, there are some who find amusement in these records of luxurious idleness; these thousand and one follies! Modern fashions, till very lately a purer taste has obtained among our females, were generally mere copies of obsolete ones, and rarely originally fantastical. The dress of *some* of our *beaux* will only be known in a few years hence by their *caricatures*. In 1751 the dress of a *dandy* is described in the *Inspector*. A *black* velvet coat, a *green* and silver waistcoat, *yellow* velvet breeches, and *blue* stockings. This too was the æra of *black silk breeches*; an extraordinary novelty, against which "some frowsy people attempted to raise up *worsted* in emulation." A satirical writer has described a buck about forty years ago;* one could hardly have suspected such a gentleman to have been one of our contemporaries. "A coat of light green, with sleeves too small for the arms, and buttons too big for the sleeves; a pair of Manchester fine stuff breeches, without money in the pockets; clouded silk stockings, but no legs; a club of hair behind larger than the head that carries it; a hat of the size of sixpence on a block not worth a farthing."

As this article may probably arrest the volatile eyes of my fair readers, let me be permitted to felicitate them on their improvement in elegance in the forms of their dress; and the taste and knowledge of art which they frequently exhibit. But let me remind them that there are universal principles of beauty in dress independent of all fashions. Tacitus remarks of Poppea, the consort of Nero, that she concealed *a part of her face*; to the end that, the imagination having fuller play by irritating curiosity, they might think higher of her beauty than if the whole of her

---

* This was written in 1790.

face had been exposed. The sentiment is beautifully expressed by Tasso, and it will not be difficult to remember it:—

> Non copre sue bellezze, e non l'espone.

I conclude by a poem, written in my youth, not only because the late Sir Walter Scott once repeated some of the lines, from memory, to remind me of it, and has preserved it in *The English Minstrelsy*, but also as a memorial of some fashions which have become extinct in my own days.

STANZAS
ADDRESSED TO LAURA, ENTREATING HER NOT TO PAINT, TO POWDER, OR TO GAME, BUT TO RETREAT INTO THE COUNTRY

AH, LAURA! quit the noisy town,
　And FASHION's persecuting reign:
Health wanders on the breezy down,
　And Science on the silent plain.

How long from Art's reflected hues
　Shalt thou a mimic charm receive?
Believe, my fair! the faithful muse,
　They spoil the blush they cannot give.

Must ruthless art, with tortuous steel,
　Thy artless locks of gold deface,
In serpent folds their charms conceal,
　And spoil, at every touch, a grace.

Too sweet thy youth's enchanting bloom
　To waste on midnight's sordid crews:
Let wrinkled age the night consume,
　For age has but its hoards to lose.

Sacred to love and sweet repose,
　Behold that trellis'd bower is nigh!
That bower the verdant walls enclose,
　Safe from pursuing Scandal's eye.

There, as in every lock of gold
　Some flower of pleasing hue I weave,
A goddess shall the muse behold,
　And many a votive sigh shall heave.

So the rude Tartar's holy rite
　A feeble MORTAL once array'd;
Then trembled in that mortal's sight,
　And own'd DIVINE the power he MADE.*

---

* The *Lama*, or God of the Tartars, is composed of such frail materials as mere mortality; contrived, however, by the power of priestcraft, to appear immortal; the *succession of Lamas* never failing!

Literary Follies

THE GREEKS composed lipogrammatic works; works in which one letter of the alphabet is omitted. A lipogrammatist is a letter-dropper. In this manner Tryphiodorus wrote his *Odyssey*; he had not α in his first book, nor β in his second; and so on with the subsequent letters one after another. This *Odyssey* was an imitation of the lipogrammatic *Iliad* of Nestor. Among other works of this kind, Athenæus mentions an ode by Pindar, in which he had purposely omitted the letter S; so that this inept ingenuity appears to have been one of those literary fashions which are sometimes encouraged even by those who should first oppose such progresses into the realms of nonsense.

There is in Latin a little prose work of Fulgentius, which the author divides into twenty-three chapters, according to the order of the twenty-three letters of the Latin alphabet. From A to O are still remaining. The first chapter is without A; the second without B; the third without C; and so with the rest. There are five novels in prose of Lopes de Vega; the first without A, the second without E, the third without I, &c. Who will attempt to verify them?

The Orientalists are not without this literary folly. A Persian poet read to the celebrated Jami a gazel of his own composition, which Jami did not like: but the writer replied, it was notwithstanding a very curious sonnet, for the *letter Aliff* was not to be found in any one of the words! Jami sarcastically replied, "You can do a better thing yet; take away *all the letters* from every word you have written."

To these works may be added the *Ecloga de Calvis*, by Hugbald the monk. All the words of this silly work begin with a C. It is printed in Dornavius. *Pugna Porcorum*, all the words beginning with a P, in the *Nugæ Venales*. *Canum cum cattis certamen*; the words beginning with a C: a performance of the same kind in the same work. Gregorio Leti presented a discourse to the Academy of the Humorists at Rome, throughout which he had purposely omitted the letter R, and he entitled it the exiled R. A friend having requested a copy, as a literary curiosity, for so he considered this idle performance, Leti, to show that this affair was not so difficult, replied by a copious answer of seven pages, in which he had observed the same severe ostracism against the letter R! Lord North, in the court of James I., has written a set of Sonnets, each of which begins with a successive

letter of the alphabet. The Earl of Rivers, in the reign of Edward
IV., translated the "Moral Proverbs" of Christiana of Pisa, a
poem of about two hundred lines, the greatest part of which he
contrived to conclude with the letter E; an instance of his lordship's hard application, and the bad taste of an age which, Lord
Orford observes, had witticisms and whims to struggle with, as
well as ignorance.

It has been well observed of these minute triflers, that extreme
exactness is the sublime of fools, whose labours may be well
called, in the language of Dryden,

> Pangs without birth, and fruitless industry.

And Martial says,

> Turpe est difficiles habere nugas.
> Et stultus labor est ineptiarum.

Which we may translate,

> 'Tis a folly to sweat o'er a difficult trifle,
> And for silly devices invention to rifle.

I shall not dwell on the wits who composed verses in the forms
of hearts, wings, altars, and true-love knots; or as Ben Jonson
describes their grotesque shapes,

> A pair of scissors and a comb in verse.

Tom Nash, who loved to push the ludicrous to its extreme, in
his amusing invective against the classical Gabriel Harvey, tells
us that "he had writ verses in all kinds; in form of a pair of
gloves, a pair of spectacles, and a pair of pot-hooks," &c. They
are not less absurd, who expose to public ridicule the name of
their mistress by employing it to form their acrostics. I have seen
some of the latter where, *both sides* and *crossways*, the name of
the mistress or the patron has been sent down to posterity with
eternal torture. When *one name* is made out *four times* in the
same acrostic, the great difficulty must have been to have found
words by which the letters forming the name should be forced
to stand in their particular places. It might be incredible that so
great a genius as Boccaccio could have lent himself to these literary fashions; yet one of the most gigantic of acrostics may be seen
in his works; it is a poem of fifty cantos! Guinguené has preserved a specimen in his *Literary History of Italy*, vol. iii. p. 54.
Puttenham, in *The Art of Poesie*, p. 75, gives several odd specimens of poems in the forms of lozenges, rhomboids, pillars, &c.

Puttenham has contrived to form a defence for describing and making such trifling devices. He has done more: he has erected two pillars himself to the honour of Queen Elizabeth; every pillar consists of a base of eight syllables, the shaft or middle of four, and the capital is equal with the base. The only difference between the two pillars consists in this; in the one "ye must read upwards," and in the other the reverse. These pillars, notwithstanding this fortunate device and variation, may be fixed as two columns in the porch of the vast temple of literary folly.

It was at this period, when *words* or *verse* were tortured into such fantastic forms, that the trees in gardens were twisted and sheared into obelisks and giants, peacocks, or flower-pots. In a copy of verses, "To a hair of my mistress's eye-lash," the merit, next to the choice of the subject, must have been the arrangement, or the disarrangement, of the whole poem into the form of a heart. With a pair of wings many a sonnet fluttered, and a sacred hymn was expressed by the mystical triangle. *Acrostics* are formed from the initial letters of every verse; but a different conceit regulated *chronograms*, which were used to describe *dates*—the *numeral letters,* in whatever part of the word they stood, were distinguished from other letters by being written in capitals. In the following chronogram from Horace,

—feriam sidera vertice,

by a strange elevation of CAPITALS the *chronogrammatist* compels even Horace to give the year of our Lord thus,

—feriaM siDera VertIce. MDVI.

The Acrostic and the Chronogram are both ingeniously described in the mock epic of the *Scribleriad.* The *initial letters* of the acrostics are thus alluded to in the literary wars:—

> Firm and compact, in three fair columns wove,
> O'er the smooth plain, the bold *acrostics* move;
> *High* o'er the rest, the TOWERING LEADERS rise
> With *limbs gigantic*, and *superior size.*

But the looser character of the *chronograms*, and the disorder in which they are found, are ingeniously sung thus:—

> Not thus the *looser chronograms* prepare
> Careless their troops, undisciplined to war;
> With *rank irregular, confused* they stand,
> The CHIEFTAINS MINGLING with the vulgar band.

He afterwards adds others of the illegitimate race of wit:—

> To join these squadrons, o'er the champaign came
> A numerous race of no ignoble name;
> *Riddle* and *Rebus*, Riddle's dearest son,
> And *false Conundrum* and *insidious Pun.*
> *Fustian*, who scarcely deigns to tread the ground,
> And *Rondeau*, wheeling in repeated round.
> On their fair standards, by the wind display'd,
> *Eggs, altars, wings, pipes, axes*, were pourtray'd.

I find the origin of *Bouts-rimés*, or "Rhyming Ends," in Goujet's *Bib. Fr.* xvi. p. 181. One Dulot, a foolish poet, when sonnets were in demand, had a singular custom of preparing the rhymes of these poems to be filled up at his leisure. Having been robbed of his papers, he was regretting most the loss of three hundred sonnets: his friends were astonished that he had written so many which they had never heard. "They were *blank sonnets*," he replied; and explained the mystery by describing his *Bouts-rimés*. The idea appeared ridiculously amusing; and it soon became fashionable to collect the most difficult rhymes, and fill up the lines.

The *Charade* is of recent birth, and I cannot discover the origin of this species of logogriphes. It was not known in France so late as in 1771; in the great *Dictionnaire de Trévoux*, the term appears only as the name of an Indian sect of a military character. Its mystical conceits have occasionally displayed singular felicity.

Anagrams were another whimsical invention; with the *letters* of any *name* they contrived to make out some entire word descriptive of the character of the person who bore the name. These anagrams, therefore, were either satirical or complimentary. When in fashion, lovers made use of them continually: I have read of one, whose mistress's name was Magdalen, for whom he composed, not only an epic under that name, but as a proof of his passion, one day he sent her three dozen of anagrams all on her lovely name. Scioppius imagined himself fortunate that his adversary *Scaliger* was perfectly *Sacrilege* in all the oblique cases of the Latin language; on this principle Sir John *Wiat* was made out, to his own satisfaction—*a wit.* They were not always correct when a great compliment was required; the poet *John Cleveland* was strained hard to make *Heliconian dew.* This literary trifle has, however, in our own times, produced several, equally ingenious and caustic.

Verses of grotesque shapes have sometimes been contrived to convey ingenious thoughts. Pannard, a modern French poet, has tortured his agreeable vein of poetry into such forms. He has

made some of his Bacchanalian songs to take the figures of *bottles*
and others of *glasses*. These objects are perfectly drawn by the
various measures of the verses which form the songs. He has also
introduced an *echo* in his verses which he contrives so as not to
injure their sense. This was practised by the old French bards
in the age of Marot, and this poetical whim is ridiculed by Butler
in his *Hudibras*, Part I. Canto 3, Verse 190. I give an example
of these poetical echoes. The following ones are ingenious, lively,
and satirical:—

> Pour nous plaire, un pl*umet*
> *Met*
> Tout en usage:
>
> Mais on trouve sou*vent*
> *Vent*
> Dans son langage.
>
> On y voit des Com*mis*
> *Mis*
> Comme des Princes,
>
> Après être ve*nus*
> *Nuds*
> De leurs Provinces.

The poetical whim of Cretin, a French poet, brought into
fashion punning or equivocal rhymes. Marot thus addressed him
in his own way:—

> L'homme, sotart, et *non sçavant*
> Comme un rotisseur, *qui lave oye,*
> La faute d'autrui, *nonce avant,*
> Qu'il la cognoisse, ou *qu'il la voye,* &c.

In these lines of Du Bartas, this poet imagined that he imitated the harmonious notes of the lark: "the sound" is here,
however, *not* "an echo to the sense."

> La gentille aloüette, avec son tirelire,
> Tirelire, à lire, et tireliran, tire
> Vers la voûte du ciel, puis son vol vers ce lieu,
> Vire et désire dire adieu Dieu, adieu Dieu.

The French have an ingenious kind of Nonsense Verses called
Amphigouries. This word is composed of a Greek adverb signifying *about,* and of a substantive signifying *a circle.* The following
is a specimen, elegant in the selection of words, and what the
French called richly rhymed, but in fact they are fine verses without any meaning whatever. Pope's Stanzas, said to be written by

a *person of quality*, to ridicule the tuneful nonsense of certain bards, and which Gilbert Wakefield mistook for a serious composition, and wrote two pages of Commentary to prove this song was disjointed, obscure, and absurd, is an excellent specimen of these *Amphigouries*.

AMPHIGOURIE

Qu'il est heureux de se défendre
Quand le cœur ne s'est pas rendu!
Mais qu'il est fâcheux de se rendre
Quand le bonheur est suspendu!
Par un discours sans suite et tendre,
Égarez un cœur éperdu;
Souvent par un mal-entendu
L'amant adroit se fait entendre.

IMITATED

How happy to defend our heart,
When Love has never thrown a dart!
But ah! unhappy when it bends,
If pleasure her soft bliss suspends!
Sweet in a wild disordered strain,
A lost and wandering heart to gain!
Oft in mistaken language wooed,
The skilful lover's understood.

These verses have such a resemblance to meaning, that Fontenelle having listened to the song imagined that he had a glimpse of sense, and requested to have it repeated. "Don't you perceive," said Madame Tencin, "that they are *nonsense verses*?" The malicious wit retorted, "They are so much like the fine verses I have heard here, that it is not surprising I should be for once mistaken."

In the *Scribleriad* we find a good account of *the Cento*. A Cento primarily signifies a cloak made of patches. In poetry it denotes a work wholly composed of verses, or passages promiscuously taken from other authors, only disposed in a new form or order, so as to compose a new work, and a new meaning. Ausonius has laid down the rules to be observed in composing *Centos*. The pieces may be taken either from the same poet, or from several; and the verses may be either taken entire, or divided into two; one half to be connected with another half taken elsewhere; but two verses are never to be taken together. Agreeable to these rules he has made a pleasant nuptial *Cento* from Virgil.

The Empress Eudoxia wrote the life of Jesus Christ, in centos taken from Homer; Proba Falconia from Virgil. Among these grave triflers may be mentioned Alexander Ross, who published "Virgilius Evangelizans, sive Historia Domini et Salvatoris nostri Jesu Christi Virgilianis verbis et versibus descripta." It was republished in 1769.

A more difficult whim is that of *"Reciprocal Verses,"* which give the same words whether read backwards or forwards. The following lines by Sidonius Apollinaris were once infinitely admired:—

> Signa te signa temere me tangis et angis.
> Roma tibi subito motibus ibit amor.

The reader has only to take the pains of reading the lines backwards, and he will find himself just where he was after all his fatigue.

Capitaine Lasphrise, a French self-taught poet, boasts of his inventions; among other singularities, one has at least the merit of *la difficulté vaincue*. He asserts this novelty to be entirely his own; the last word of every verse forms the first word of the following verse:

> Falloit-il que le ciel me rendît amoureux,
> Amoureux, jouissant d'une beauté craintive,
> Craintive à recevoir la douceur excessive,
> Excessive au plaisir qui rend l'amant heureux;
> Heureux si nous avions quelques paisibles lieux,
> Lieux où plus sûrement l'ami fidèle arrive,
> Arrive sans soupçon de quelque amie attentive,
> Attentive à vouloir nous surprendre tous deux.

Francis Colonna, an Italian Monk, is the author of a singular book entitled *The Dream of Poliphilus,* in which he relates his amours with a lady of the name of Polia. It was considered improper to prefix his name to the work; but being desirous of marking it by some peculiarity, that he might claim it at any distant day, he contrived that the initial letters of every chapter should be formed of those of his name, and of the subject he treats. This strange invention was not discovered till many years afterwards: when the wits employed themselves in deciphering it, unfortunately it became a source of literary altercation, being susceptible of various readings. The correct appears thus:— POLIAM FRATER FRANCISCUS COLUMNA PERAMAVIT. "Brother Francis Colonna passionately loved Polia." This gallant monk, like another Petrarch, made the name of his mistress the subject of his amatorial meditations; and as the first called his Laura, his Laurel, this called his Polia, his Polita.

A few years afterwards, Marcellus Palingenius Stellatus em-

ployed a similar artifice in his *Zodiacus Vitæ*, "The Zodiac of
Life": the initial letters of the first twenty-nine verses of the
first book of this poem forming his name, which curious particular was probably unknown to Warton in his account of this
work.—The performance is divided into twelve books, but has
no reference to astronomy, which we might naturally expect. He
distinguished his twelve books by the twelve names of the celestial
signs, and probably extended or confined them purposely to that
number, to humour his fancy. Warton however observes, "this
strange pedantic title is not totally without a *conceit*, as the
author was born at *Stellada* or *Stellata*, a province of Ferrara,
and from whence he called himself Marcellus Palingenius Stellatus." The work itself is a curious satire on the pope and the
Church of Rome. It occasioned Bayle to commit a remarkable
literary blunder, which I shall record in its place. Of Italian
conceit in those times, of which Petrarch was the father, with
his perpetual play on words and on his *Laurel,* or his mistress
Laura, he has himself afforded a remarkable example. Our poet
lost his mother, who died in her thirty-eighth year: he has
commemorated her death by a sonnet composed of thirty-eight
lines. He seems to have conceived that the exactness of the number was equally natural and tender.

Are we not to class among *literary follies* the strange researches
which writers, even of the present day, have made in *Antedilu-
vian* times? Forgeries of the grossest nature have been alluded to,
or quoted as authorities. A *Book of Enoch* once attracted considerable attention; this curious forgery has been recently translated: the Sabeans pretend they possess a work written by *Adam*!
and this work has been *recently* appealed to in favour of a visionary theory! Astle gravely observes, that "with respect to *Writings*
attributed to the *Antediluvians*, it seems not only decent but
rational to say that we know nothing concerning them." Without
alluding to living writers, Dr. Parsons, in his erudite *Remains of
Japhet,* tracing the origin of the alphabetical character, supposes
that *letters* were known to *Adam*! Some too have noticed astro-
nomical libraries in the Ark of Noah! Such historical memorials
are the deliriums of learning, or are founded on forgeries.

Hugh Broughton, a writer of controversy in the reign of James
the First, shows us, in a tedious discussion on Scripture chronology, that Rahab was a harlot at *ten* years of age; and enters into
many grave discussions concerning the *colour* of Aaron's *ephod,*
and the language which *Eve* first spoke. This writer is ridiculed
in Ben Jonson's *Comedies*:—he is not without rivals even in the

present day! Covarruvias, after others of his school, discovers that when male children are born they cry out with an A, being the first vowel of the word *Adam*, while the female infants prefer the letter E, in allusion to *Eve*; and we may add that, by the pinch of a negligent nurse, they may probably learn all their vowels. Of the pedantic triflings of commentators, a controversy among the Portuguese on the works of Camoens is not the least. Some of these profound critics, who affected great delicacy in the laws of epic poetry, pretended to be doubtful whether the poet had fixed on the right time for a *king's dream*; whether, said they, a king should have a propitious dream on his *first going to bed* or at the *dawn of the following morning*? No one seemed to be quite certain; they puzzled each other till the controversy closed in this felicitous manner, and satisfied both the night and the dawn critics. Barreto discovered that an *accent* on one of the words alluded to in the controversy would answer the purpose, and by making king Manuel's dream to take place at the dawn would restore Camoens to their good opinion, and preserve the dignity of the poet.

Chevreau begins his *History of the World* in these words:— "Several learned men have examined in *what season* God created the world, though there could hardly be any season then, since there was no sun, no moon, nor stars. But as the world must have been created in one of the four seasons, this question has exercised the talents of the most curious, and opinions are various. Some say it was in the month of *Nisan*, that is, in the spring: others maintain that it was in the month of *Tisri*, which begins the civil year of the Jews, and that it was on the *sixth day* of this month, which answers to our *September*, that *Adam* and *Eve* were created, and that it was on a *Friday*, a little after four o'clock in the afternoon!" This is according to the Rabbinical notion of the eve of the sabbath.

The Irish antiquaries mention *public libraries* that were before the flood; and Paul Christian Ilsker, with profounder erudition, has given an exact catalogue of *Adam's*. Messieurs O'Flaherty, O'Connor, and O'Halloran, have most gravely recorded as authentic narrations the wildest legendary traditions; and more recently, to make confusion doubly confounded, others have built up what they call theoretical histories on these nursery tales. By which species of black art they contrive to prove that an Irishman is an Indian, and a Peruvian may be a Welshman, from certain emigrations which took place many centuries before Christ, and some about two centuries after the flood! Keating, in his *History of Ireland*, starts a favourite hero in the giant Partholanus, who was descended from Japhet, and landed on the coast of Munster 14th May, in the year of the world 1987. This giant succeeded in his enterprise, but a domestic misfortune attended him among his Irish friends:—his wife exposed him to their laughter by her loose behaviour, and provoked him to such a degree that he killed two favourite greyhounds; and this the learned historian assures us was the *first* instance of female infidelity ever known in Ireland!

The learned, not contented with Homer's poetical pre-eminence, make him the most authentic historian and most accurate geographer of antiquity, besides endowing him with all the arts and sciences to be found in our *Encyclopædia*. Even in surgery, a treatise has been written to show, by the variety of the *wounds* of his heroes, that he was a most scientific anatomist; and a military scholar has lately told us, that from him is derived all the science of the modern adjutant and quarter master-general; all the knowledge of *tactics* which we now possess; and that Xenophon, Epaminondas, Philip, and Alexander, owed all their warlike reputation to Homer!

To return to pleasanter follies. Des Fontaines, the journalist, who had wit and malice, inserted the fragment of a letter which the poet Rousseau wrote to the younger Racine whilst he was at the Hague. These were the words: "I enjoy the conversation within these few days of my associates in Parnassus. Mr. Piron is an excellent antidote against melancholy; *but*"—&c. Des Fontaines maliciously stopped at this *but*. In the letter of Rousseau it was, "but unfortunately he departs soon." Piron was very sensibly affected at this equivocal *but*, and resolved to revenge himself by composing one hundred epigrams against the malignant critic. He had written sixty before Des Fontaines died: but of these only two attracted any notice.

Towards the conclusion of the fifteenth century, Antonio Cornezano wrote a hundred different sonnets on one subject, "the eyes of his mistress"! to which possibly Shakspeare may allude, when Jaques describes a lover, with his

> Woeful ballad,
> Made to his mistress' eyebrow.

Not inferior to this ingenious trifler is Nicholas Franco, well known in Italian literature, who employed himself in writing two hundred and eighteen satiric sonnets, chiefly on the famous Peter Aretin. This lampooner had the honour of being hanged

at Rome for his defamatory publications. In the same class are
to be placed two other writers. Brebeuf, who wrote one hundred
and fifty epigrams against a painted lady. Another wit, desirous
of emulating him, and for a literary bravado, *continued* the
same subject, and pointed at this unfortunate fair three hundred
more, without once repeating the thoughts of Brebeuf! There is
a collection of poems called *La* PUCE *des grands jours de Poitiers,*
"The FLEA of the carnival of Poictiers." These poems were begun
by the learned Pasquier, who edited the collection, upon a FLEA
which was found one morning in the bosom of the famous
Catherine des Roches!

Not long ago, a Mr. and Mrs. Bilderdyk, in Flanders, published poems under the whimsical title of *White and Red.*—His
own poems were called white, from the colour of his hair; and
those of his lady red, in allusion to the colour of the rose. The
idea must be Flemish!

Gildon, in his *Laws of Poetry*, commenting on this line of the
Duke of Buckingham's *Essay on Poetry*,

Nature's chief master-piece is writing well:

very profoundly informs his readers "That what is here said has
not the least regard to the *penmanship*, that is, to the fairness
or badness of the handwriting," and proceeds throughout a
whole page, with a panegyric on a *fine handwriting*! The stupidity of dulness seems to have at times great claims to originality!

Littleton, the author of the *Latin and English Dictionary*,
seems to have indulged his favourite propensity to punning so
far as even to introduce a pun in the grave and elaborate work
of a Lexicon. A story has been raised to account for it, and it
has been ascribed to the impatient interjection of the lexicographer to his scribe, who, taking no offence at the peevishness
of his master, put it down in the *Dictionary*. The article alluded
to is, "CONCURRO, to run with others; to run together; to come
together; to fall foul of one another; to CON-*cur*, to CON-*dog*."

Mr. Todd, in his *Dictionary*, has laboured to show the "inac-
curacy of this pretended narrative." Yet a similar blunder appears to have happened to Ash. Johnson, while composing his
Dictionary, sent a note to the *Gentleman's Magazine* to inquire
the etymology of the word *curmudgeon*. Having obtained the
information, he records in his work the obligation to an anonymous letter-writer. "Curmudgeon, a vicious way of pronouncing
cœur méchant. An unknown correspondent." Ash copied the

word into his dictionary in this manner: "Curmudgeon: from the French *cœur*, unknown; and *méchant*, a correspondent." This singular negligence ought to be placed in the class of our *literary blunders*: these form a pair of lexicographical anecdotes.

Two singular literary follies have been practised on Milton. There is a *prose version* of his *Paradise Lost*, which was innocently *translated* from the French version of his epic! One Green published a specimen of a *new version* of the *Paradise Lost* into *blank verse*! For this purpose he has utterly ruined the harmony of Milton's cadences, by what he conceived to be "bringing that amazing work somewhat *nearer the summit of perfection.*"

A French author, when his book had been received by the French Academy, had the portrait of Cardinal Richelieu engraved on his title-page, encircled by a crown of *forty rays*, in each of which was written the name of the celebrated *forty academicians.*

The self-exultations of authors, frequently employed by injudicious writers, place them in ridiculous attitudes. A writer of a bad dictionary, which he intended for a Cyclopædia, formed such an opinion of its extensive sale, that he put on the title-page the words *"first edition,"* a hint to the gentle reader that it would not be the last. Desmarest was so delighted with his *Clovis*, an epic poem, that he solemnly concludes his preface with a thanksgiving to God, to whom he attributes all its glory! This is like that conceited member of a French Parliament, who was overheard, after his tedious harangue, muttering most devoutly to himself, *"Non nobis Domine."*

Several works have been produced from some odd coincidence with the *name of their authors.* Thus, De Saussay has written a folio volume, consisting of panegyrics of persons of eminence whose Christian names were *Andrew*; because *Andrew* was his own name. Two Jesuits made a similar collection of illustrious men whose Christian names were *Theophilus* and *Philip*, being their own. *Anthony Saunderus* has also composed a treatise of illustrious *Anthonies!* And we have one *Buchanan* who has written the lives of those persons who were so fortunate as to have been his namesakes.

Several forgotten writers have frequently been intruded on the public eye, merely through such trifling coincidences as being members of some particular society, or natives of some particular country. Cordeliers have stood forward to revive the writings of Duns Scotus, because he had been a cordelier; and a Jesuit compiled a folio on the antiquities of a province, merely from the circumstance that the founder of his order, Ignatius Loyola, had been born there. Several of the classics are violently extolled above others, merely from the accidental circumstance of their editors' having collected a vast number of notes, which they resolved to discharge on the public. County histories have been frequently compiled, and provincial writers have received a temporary existence, from the accident of some obscure individual being an inhabitant of some obscure town.

On such literary follies Malebranche has made this refined observation. The *critics*, standing in some way connected with *the author*, their *self-love* inspires them, and abundantly furnishes eulogiums which the author never merited, that they may thus obliquely reflect some praise on themselves. This is made so adroitly, so delicately, and so concealed, that it is not perceived.

The following are strange inventions, originating in the wilful bad taste of the authors. OTTO VENIUS, the master of Rubens, is the designer of *Le Théâtre moral de la Vie humaine*. In this emblematical history of human life, he has taken his subjects from Horace; but certainly his conceptions are not Horatian. He takes every image in a *literal* sense. If Horace says, *"Misce stultitiam* CONSILIIS BREVEM,*"* behold, Venius takes *brevis* personally, and represents Folly as *a little short child!* of not above three or four years old! In the emblem which answers Horace's *"Raro antecedentem scelestum deseruit* PEDE PŒNA CLAUDO,*"* we find Punishment with a *wooden leg.*—And for "PULVIS ET UMBRA SUMUS," we have a dark burying vault, with *dust* sprinkled about the floor, and a *shadow* walking upright between two ranges of urns. For *"Virtus est vitium fugere, et sapientia prima stultitiâ caruisse,"* most flatly he gives seven or eight Vices pursuing Virtue, and Folly just at the heels of Wisdom. I saw in an English Bible printed in Holland an instance of the same taste: the artist, to illustrate "Thou seest the *mote* in thy neighbor's eye, but not the *beam* in thine own," has actually placed an immense beam which projects from the eye of the caviller to the ground!

As a contrast to the too obvious taste of VENIUS, may be placed CESARE DI RIPA, who is the author of an Italian work, translated into most European languages, the *Iconologia*; the favourite book of the age, and the fertile parent of the most absurd offspring which Taste has known. Ripa is as darkly subtle as Venius is obvious; and as far-fetched in his conceits as the other is literal. Ripa represents Beauty by a naked lady, with her head in a cloud; because the true idea of beauty is hard to be conceived! Flattery, by a lady with a flute in her hand, and a stag at her feet, because stags are said to love music so much, that they suffer themselves to be taken, if you play to them on a flute. Fraud, with two hearts in one hand, and a mask in the other;—his collection is too numerous to point out more instances. Ripa also describes how the allegorical figures are to be coloured; Hope is to have a sky-blue robe, because she always looks towards heaven. Enough of these *capriccios*!

Literary Controversy

IN AN article on Milton, I had occasion to give some strictures on the asperity of literary controversy, drawn from his own and Salmasius's writings. If to some the subject has appeared exceptionable, to me, I confess, it seems useful, and I shall therefore add some other particulars; for this topic has many branches. Of the following specimens the grossness and malignity are extreme; yet they were employed by the first scholars in Europe.

Martin Luther was not destitute of genius, of learning, or of eloquence; but his violence disfigured his works with singularities of abuse. The great reformer of superstition had himself all the vulgar ones of his day; he believed that flies were devils; and that he had had a buffeting with Satan, when his left ear felt the prodigious beating. Hear him express himself on the Catholic divines. "The Papists are all asses, and will always remain asses; Put them in whatever sauce you choose, boiled, roasted, baked, fried, skinned, beat, hashed, they are always the same asses."

Gentle and moderate, compared with a salute to his Holiness: —"The Pope was born out of the Devil's posteriors. He is full of devils, lies, blasphemies, and idolatries; he is anti-Christ; the robber of churches; the ravisher of virgins; the greatest of pimps; the governor of Sodom, &c. If the Turks lay hold of us, then we shall be in the hands of the Devil; but if we remain with the Pope, we shall be in hell.—What a pleasing sight would it be to see the Pope and the Cardinals hanging on one gallows in exact order, like the seals which dangle from the bulls of the Pope! What an excellent council would they hold under the gallows!"

Sometimes, desirous of catching the attention of the vulgar, Luther attempts to enliven his style by the grossest buffooneries:

"Take care, my little Popa! my little ass! Go on slowly: the times are slippery: this year is dangerous: if thou fallest, they will exclaim, See! how our little Pope is spoilt!" It was fortunate for the cause of the Reformation that the violence of Luther was softened in a considerable degree by the meek Melanchthon, who often poured honey on the sting inflicted by the angry wasp. Luther was no respecter of kings; he was so fortunate, indeed, as to find among his antagonists a crowned head; a great good fortune for an obscure controversialist, and the very *punctum saliens* of controversy. Our Henry VIII. wrote his book against the new doctrine: then warm from scholastic studies, Henry presented Leo X. with a work highly creditable to his abilities, according to the genius of the age. Collier, in his *Ecclesiastical History*, has analyzed the book, and does not ill describe its spirit: "Henry seems superior to his adversary in the vigour and propriety of his style, in the force of his reasoning, and the learning of his citations. It is true he leans *too much* upon his character, argues in his *garter-robes,* and writes as 'twere with his *scepter."* But Luther in reply abandons his pen to all kinds of railing and abuse. He addresses Henry VIII. in the following style: "It is hard to say if folly can be more foolish, or stupidity more stupid, than is the head of Henry. He has not attacked me with the heart of a king, but with the impudence of a knave. This rotten worm of the earth having blasphemed the majesty of my king, I have a just right to bespatter his English majesty with his own dirt and ordure. This Henry has lied." Some of his original expressions to our Henry VIII. are these: "Stulta, ridicula, et verissimè *Henriciana* et *Thomastica* sunt hæc—Regem Angliæ Henricum istum planè mentiri, &c.—Hoc agit inquietus Satan, ut nos a Scripturis avocet per *sceleratos Henricos,"* &c.— He was repaid with capital and interest by an anonymous reply, said to have been written by Sir Thomas More, who concludes his arguments by leaving Luther in language not necessary to translate: "cum suis furiis et furoribus, cum suis merdis et stercoribus cacantem cacatumque." Such were the vigorous elegancies of a controversy on the Seven Sacraments! Long after, the court of Rome had not lost the taste of these "bitter herbs": for in the bull of the canonization of Ignatius Loyola in August, 1623, Luther is called *monstrum teterrimum et detestabilis pestis.*

Calvin was less tolerable, for he had no Melanchthon! His adversaries are never others than knaves, lunatics, drunkards, and assassins! Sometimes they are characterized by the familiar appellatives of bulls, asses, cats, and hogs! By him Catholic and

Lutheran are alike hated. Yet, after having given vent to this virulent humour, he frequently boasts of his mildness. When he reads over his writings he tells us, that he is astonished at his forbearance; but this, he adds, is the duty of every Christian! at the same time, he generally finishes a period with—"Do you hear, you dog?" "Do you hear, madman?"

Beza, the disciple of Calvin, sometimes imitates the luxuriant abuse of his master. When he writes against Tillemont, a Lutheran minister, he bestows on him the following titles of honour:—"Polyphemus; an ape; a great ass, who is distinguished from other asses by wearing a hat; an ass on two feet; a monster composed of part of an ape and wild ass; a villain who merits hanging on the first tree we find." And Beza was, no doubt, desirous of the office of executioner!

The Catholic party is by no means inferior in the felicities of their style. The Jesuit Raynaud calls Erasmus the "Batavian buffoon," and accuses him of nourishing the egg which Luther hatched. These men were alike supposed by their friends to be the inspired regulators of Religion!

Bishop Bedell, a great and good man, respected even by his adversaries, in an address to his clergy, observes, "Our calling is to deal with errors, not to disgrace the man with scolding words. It is said of Alexander, I think, when he overheard one of his soldiers railing lustily against Darius his enemy, that he reproved him, and added, 'Friend, I entertain thee to fight against Darius, not to revile him;' and my sentiments of treating the Catholics," concludes Bedell, "are not conformable to the practice of Luther and Calvin; but they were but men, and perhaps we must confess they suffered themselves to yield to the violence of passion."

The Fathers of the Church were proficients in the art of abuse, and very ingeniously defended it. St. Austin affirms that the most caustic personality may produce a wonderful effect, in opening a man's eyes to his own follies. He illustrates his position with a story, given with great simplicity, of his mother Saint Monica with her maid. Saint Monica certainly would have been a confirmed drunkard, had not her maid timelily and outrageously abused her. The story will amuse.—"My mother had by little and little accustomed herself to relish wine. They used to send her to the cellar, as being one of the soberest in the family: she first sipped from the jug and tasted a few drops, for she abhorred wine, and did not care to drink. However, she gradually accustomed herself, and from sipping it on her lips she swallowed a draught. As people from the smallest faults insensibly increase, she at length liked wine, and drank bumpers. But one day being alone with the maid who usually attended her to the cellar, they quarrelled, and the maid bitterly reproached her with being a *drunkard!* That *single word* struck her so poignantly that it opened her understanding; and reflecting on the deformity of the vice, she desisted forever from its use."

To jeer and play the droll, or, in his own words, *de bouffonner,* was a mode of controversy the great Arnauld defended, as permitted by the writings of the holy fathers. It is still more singular, when he not only brings forward as an example of this ribaldry, Elijah *mocking* at the false divinities, but *God* himself *bantering* the first man after his fall. He justifies the injurious epithets which he has so liberally bestowed on his adversaries by the example of Jesus Christ and the apostles! It was on these grounds also that the celebrated Pascal apologized for the invectives with which he has occasionally disfigured his *Provincial Letters.* A Jesuit has collected *An Alphabetical Catalogue of the Names of* Beasts *by which the Fathers characterized the Heretics!* It may be found in *Erotemata de malis ac bonis Libris,* p. 93, 4to. 1653, of Father Raynaud. This list of brutes and insects, among which are a vast variety of serpents, is accompanied by the names of the heretics designated!

Henry Fitzsermon, an Irish Jesuit, was imprisoned for his papistical designs and seditious preaching. During his confinement he proved himself to be a great amateur of controversy. He said, "he felt like a *bear* tied to a stake, and wanted somebody to *bait* him." A kind office, zealously undertaken by the learned *Usher,* then a young man. He *engaged* to *dispute* with him *once a week* on the subject of *antichrist!* They met several times. It appears that *our bear* was out-worried, and declined any further *dog-baiting.* This spread an universal joy through the Protestants in Dublin. At the early period of the Reformation, Dr. Smith of Oxford abjured papistry, with the hope of retaining his professorship, but it was given to Peter Martyr. On this our Doctor recants, and writes several controversial works against Peter Martyr; the most curious part of which is the singular mode adopted of attacking others, as well as Peter Martyr. In his margin he frequently breaks out thus: "Let Hooper read this!" —"Here, Ponet, open your eyes and see your errors!"—"Ergo, Cox, thou art damned!" In this manner, without expressly writing against these persons, the stirring polemic contrived to keep up a sharp bush-fighting in his margins. Such was the spirit of those times, very different from our own. When a modern bishop was just advanced to a mitre, his bookseller begged to re-publish a popular theological tract of his against another bishop, because he might now meet him on equal terms. My lord answered—"Mr. * * *, no more controversy now!" Our good bishop resembled Baldwin, who from a simple monk, arrived to the honour of the see of Canterbury. The successive honours successively changed his manners. Urban the Second inscribed his brief to him in this concise description—*Balduino Monastico ferventissimo, Abbati calido, Episcopo tepido, Archiepiscopo remisso!*

On the subject of literary controversies, we cannot pass over the various sects of the scholastics: a volume might be compiled of their ferocious wars, which in more than one instance were accompanied by stones and daggers. The most memorable, on account of the extent, the violence, and duration of their contests, are those of the NOMINALISTS and the REALISTS.

It was a most subtle question assuredly, and the world thought for a long while that their happiness depended on deciding, whether universals, that is *genera*, have a real essence, and exist independent of particulars, that is *species*:—whether, for instance, we could form an idea of asses, prior to individual asses? Roscelinus, in the eleventh century, adopted the opinion that universals have no real existence, either before or in individuals, but are mere names and words by which the kind of individuals is expressed; a tenet propagated by Abelard, which produced the sect of *Nominalists*. But the *Realists* asserted that universals existed independent of individuals,—though they were somewhat divided between the various opinions of Plato and Aristotle. Of the Realists the most famous were Thomas Aquinas and Duns Scotus. The cause of the Nominalists was almost desperate, till Occam in the fourteenth century revived the dying embers. Louis XI. adopted the Nominalists, and the Nominalists flourished at large in France and Germany; but unfortunately Pope John XXIII. patronized the Realists, and throughout Italy it was dangerous for a Nominalist to open his lips. The French king wavered, and the pope triumphed; his majesty published an edict in 1474, in which he silenced for ever the Nominalists, and ordered their books to be fastened up in their libraries with iron chains, that they might not be read by young students! The leaders of that sect fled into England and Germany, where they united their forces with Luther and the first Reformers.

Nothing could exceed the violence with which these disputes were conducted. Vives himself, who witnessed the contests, says that, "when the contending parties had exhausted their stock of verbal abuse, they often came to blows; and it was not uncommon in these quarrels about *universals*, to see the combatants engaging not only with their fists, but with clubs and swords, so that many have been wounded and some killed."

On this war of words and all this terrifying nonsense John of Salisbury observes, "that there had been more time consumed than the Cæsars had employed in making themselves masters of the world; that the riches of Crœsus were inferior to the treasures that had been exhausted in this controversy; and that the contending parties, after having spent their whole lives in this single point, had neither been so happy as to determine it to their satisfaction, nor to find in the labyrinths of science where they had been groping any discovery that was worth the pains they had taken." It may be added that Ramus having attacked Aristotle, for "teaching us chimeras," all his scholars revolted; the parliament put a stop to his lectures, and at length having brought the matter into a law court, he was declared "to be insolent and daring"—the king proscribed his works, he was ridiculed on the stage, and hissed at by his scholars. When at length, during the plague, he opened again his schools, he drew on himself a fresh storm by reforming the pronunciation of the letter Q, which they then pronounced like K—Kiskis for Quisquis, and Kamkam for Quamquam. This innovation was once more laid to his charge: a new rebellion! and a new ejection of the Anti-Aristotelian! The brother of that Gabriel Harvey who was the friend of Spenser, and with Gabriel had been the whetstone of the town-wits of his time, distinguished himself by his wrath against the Stagyrite. After having with Gabriel predicted an earthquake, and alarmed the kingdom, which never took place (that is the earthquake, not the alarm), the wits buffeted him. Nash says of him, that "Tarlton at the theatre made jests of him, and Elderton consumed his ale-crammed nose to nothing, in bear-baiting him with whole bundles of ballads." Marlow declared him to be "an ass fit only to preach of the iron age." Stung to madness by this lively nest of hornets, he avenged himself in a very cowardly manner—he attacked Aristotle himself! for he set *Aristotle* with his *heels upwards* on the school gates at Cambridge, and with *asses' ears* on his head!

But this controversy concerning Aristotle and the school divinity was even prolonged. A professor in the College at Naples published in 1688 four volumes of peripatetic philosophy, to establish the principles of Aristotle. The work was exploded, and he wrote an abusive treatise under the *nom de guerre* of Benedetto Aletino. A man of letters, Constantino Grimaldi, replied. Aletino rejoined; he wrote letters, an apology for the letters, and would have written more for Aristotle than Aristotle himself perhaps would have done. However, Grimaldi was no ordinary antagonist, and not to be outwearied. He had not only the best of the argument, but he was resolved to tell the world so, as long as the world would listen. Whether he killed off Father Benedictus, the first author, is not affirmed; but the latter died during the controversy. Grimaldi, however, afterwards pursued his ghost, and buffeted the father in his grave. This enraged the University of Naples; and the Jesuits, to a man, denounced Grimaldi to Pope Benedict XIII. and to the Viceroy of Naples. On this the pope issued a bull prohibiting the reading of Grimaldi's works, or keeping them, under pain of excommunication; and the viceroy, more active than the bull, caused all the copies which were found in the author's house to be thrown *into the sea*! The author with tears in his eyes beheld his expatriated volumes, hopeless that their voyage would have been successful. However, all the little family of the Grimaldi's were not drowned—for a storm arose, and happily drove ashore many of the floating copies, and these falling into charitable hands, the heretical opinions of poor Grimaldi against Aristotle and school divinity were still read by those who were not outterrified by the pope's bulls. The *salted* passages were still at hand, and quoted with a double zest against the Jesuits!

We now turn to writers whose controversy was kindled only by subjects of polite literature. The particulars form a curious picture of the taste of the age.

"There is," says Joseph Scaliger, that great critic and reviler, "an art of abuse or slandering, of which those that are ignorant may be said to defame others much less than they show a willingness to defame."

"Literary wars," says Bayle, "are sometimes as lasting as they are terrible." A disputation between two great scholars was so interminably violent, that it lasted thirty years! He humourously compares its duration to the German war which lasted as long.

Baillet, when he refuted the sentiments of a certain author, always did it without naming him; but when he found any observation which he deemed commendable, he quoted his name. Bayle observes, that "this is an excess of politeness, prejudicial to that freedom which should ever exist in the republic of letters; that it should be allowed always to name those whom we refute; and that it is sufficient for this purpose that we banish asperity, malice, and indecency."

After these preliminary observations, I shall bring forward various examples where this excellent advice is by no means regarded.

Erasmus produced a dialogue, in which he ridiculed those scholars who were servile imitators of Cicero; so servile, that they would employ no expression but what was found in the works of that writer; every thing with them was Ciceronianized. This dialogue is written with great humour. Julius Cæsar Scaliger, the father, who was then unknown to the world, had been long looking for some occasion to distinguish himself; he now wrote a defence of Cicero, but which in fact was one continued invective against Erasmus: he there treats the latter as illiterate, a drunkard, an impostor, an apostate, a hangman, a demon hot from hell! The same Scaliger, acting on the same principle of distinguishing himself at the cost of others, attacked Cardan's best work *De Subtilitate*: his criticism did not appear till seven years after the first edition of the work, and then he obstinately stuck to that edition, though Cardan had corrected it in subsequent ones; but this Scaliger chose, that he might have a wider field for his attack. After this, a rumour spread that Cardan had died of vexation from Julius Cæsar's invincible pen; then Scaliger pretended to feel all the regret possible for a man he had killed, and whom he now praised: however, his regret had as little foundation as his triumph; for Cardan outlived Scaliger many years, and valued his criticisms too cheaply to have suffered them to have disturbed his quiet. All this does not exceed the *Invectives* of Poggius, who has thus entitled several literary libels composed against some of his adversaries, Laurentius Valla, Philelphus, &c., who returned the poisoned chalice to his own lips; declamations of scurrility, obscenity, and calumny!

Scioppius was a worthy successor of the Scaligers: his favourite expression was, that he had trodden down his adversary.

Scioppius was a critic, as skilful as Salmasius or Scaliger, but still more learned in the language of abuse. This cynic was the Attila of authors. He boasted that he had occasioned the deaths of Casaubon and Scaliger. Detested and dreaded as the public scourge, Scioppius, at the close of his life, was fearful he should find no retreat in which he might be secure.

The great Casaubon employs the dialect of St. Giles's in his furious attacks on the learned Dalechamps, the Latin translator of Athenæus. To this great physician he stood more deeply indebted than he chose to confess; and to conceal the claims of this literary creditor, he called out *Vesanum! Insanum! Tiresiam!* &c. It was the fashion of that day with the ferocious heroes of the literary republic, to overwhelm each other with invectives, and to consider that their own grandeur consisted in the magnitude of their volumes; and their triumphs in reducing their brother giants into puny dwarfs. In science, Linnæus had a dread of controversy—conqueror or conquered we cannot escape without disgrace! Mathiolus would have been the great man of his day, had he not meddled with such matters. Who is gratified by "the mad Cornarus," or "the flayed Fox"? titles which Fuchsius and Cornarus, two eminent botanists, have bestowed on each other. Some who were too fond of controversy, as they grew wiser, have refused to take up the gauntlet.

The heat and acrimony of verbal critics have exceeded description. Their stigmas and anathemas have been long known to bear no proportion to the offences against which they have been directed. "God confound you," cried one grammarian to another, "for your theory of impersonal verbs!" There was a long and terrible controversy formerly, whether the Florentine dialect was to prevail over the others. The academy was put to great trouble, and the Anti-Cruscans were often on the point of annulling this supremacy; *una mordace scrittura* was applied to one of these literary canons; and in a letter of those times the following paragraph appears:—"Pescetti is preparing to give a second answer to Beni, which will not please him; I now believe the prophecy of Cavalier Tedeschi will be verified, and that this controversy, begun with pens, will end with poniards!"

Fabretti, an Italian, wrote furiously against Gronovius, whom he calls *Grunnovius*: he compared him to all those animals whose voice was expressed by the word *Grunnire, to grunt.* Gronovius was so malevolent a critic, that he was distinguished by the title of the "Grammatical Cur."

When critics venture to attack the person as well as the performance of an author, I recommend the salutary proceedings of Huberus, the writer of an esteemed *Universal History.* He had been so roughly handled by Perizonius, that he obliged him to make the *amende honorable* in a court of justice; where, however, I fear an English jury would give the smallest damages.

Certain authors may be distinguished by the title of Literary Bobadils, or fighting authors. One of our own celebrated writers drew his sword on a reviewer; and another, when his farce was condemned, offered to fight any one of the audience who hissed. Scudery, brother of the celebrated Mademoiselle Scudery, was a true Parnassian bully. The first publication which brought him into notice was his edition of the works of his friend Theophile. He concludes the preface with these singular expressions—"I do not hesitate to declare, that, amongst all the dead, and all the living, there is no person who has any thing to show that approaches the force of this vigorous genius; but if amongst the latter, any one were so extravagant as to consider that I detract from his imaginary glory, to show him that I fear as little as I esteem him, this is to inform him that my name is

"DE SCUDERY."

A similar rhodomontade is that of Claude Trellon, a poetical soldier, who begins his poems by challenging the critics; assuring them that if any one attempts to censure him, he will only condescend to answer sword in hand. Father Macedo, a Portuguese Jesuit, having written against Cardinal Noris, on the monkery of St. Austin, it was deemed necessary to silence both parties. Macedo, compelled to relinquish the pen, sent his adversary a challenge, and according to the laws of chivalry, appointed a place for meeting in the wood of Boulogne. Another edict to forbid the duel! Macedo then murmured at his hard fate, which would not suffer him, for the sake of St. Austin, for whom he had a particular regard, to spill either his *ink* or his *blood*.

ANTI, prefixed to the name of the person attacked, was once a favourite title to books of literary controversy. With a critical review of such books Baillet has filled a quarto volume; yet such was the abundant harvest, that he left considerable gleanings for posterior industry.

Anti-Gronovius was a book published against Gronovius, by Kuster. Perizonius, another pugilist of literature, entered into this dispute on the subject of the *Æs grave* of the ancients, to which Kuster had just adverted at the close of his volume. What was the consequence? Dreadful!—Answers and rejoinders from both, in which they bespattered each other with the foulest abuse. A journalist pleasantly blames this acrimonious controversy. He says, "To read the pamphlets of a Perizonius and a Kuster on the Æs grave of the ancients, who would not renounce all commerce with antiquity? It seems as if an Agamemnon and an Achilles were railing at each other. Who can refrain from laughter, when one of these commentators even points his attacks at the very name of his adversary? According to Kuster, the name of Perizonius signifies a *certain part* of the human body. How is it possible, that with such a name he could be right concerning the Æs grave? But does that of Kuster promise a better thing, since it signifies a beadle; a man who drives dogs out of churches?—What madness is this!"

Corneille, like our Dryden, felt the acrimony of literary irritation. To the critical strictures of D'Aubignac it is acknowledged he paid the greatest attention, for, after this critic's *Pratique du Théâtre* appeared, his tragedies were more artfully conducted. But instead of mentioning the critic with due praise, he preserved an ungrateful silence. This occasioned a quarrel between the poet and the critic, in which the former exhaled his bile in several abusive epigrams, which have, fortunately for his credit, not been preserved in his works.

The lively Voltaire could not resist the charm of abusing his adversaries. We may smile when he calls a blockhead, a blockhead; a dotard, a dotard; but when he attacks, for a difference of opinion, the *morals* of another man, our sensibility is alarmed. A higher tribunal than that of criticism is to decide on the *actions* of men.

There is a certain disguised malice, which some writers have most unfairly employed in characterizing a contemporary. Burnet called Prior, *one Prior*. In Bishop Parker's *History of his Own Times,* an innocent reader may start at seeing the celebrated Marvell described as an outcast of society; an infamous libeller; and one whose talents were even more despicable than his person. To such lengths did the hatred of party, united with personal rancour, carry this bishop, who was himself the worst of time-servers. He was, however, amply repaid by the keen wit of Marvell in "The Rehearsal Transposed," which may still be read with delight, as an admirable effusion of banter, wit, and satire. Le Clerc, a cool ponderous Greek critic, quarrelled with Boileau about a passage in Longinus, and several years afterwards, in revising Moreri's *Dictionary*, gave a short sarcastic notice of the poet's brother; in which he calls him the elder brother of *him who has written the book entitled "Satires of Mr. Boileau Despréaux"*!—the works of the modern Horace which were then delighting Europe, he calls, with simple impudence, "a book entitled Satires"!

The works of Homer produced a controversy, both long and virulent, amongst the wits of France; this literary quarrel is of some note in the annals of literature, since it has produced two valuable books; La Motte's *Réflexions sur la Critique*, and Madame Dacier's *Des Causes de la Corruption du Goût*. La Motte wrote with feminine delicacy, and Madame Dacier like a University pedant. "At length, by the efforts of Valincour, the friend of art, of artists, and of peace, the contest was terminated." Both parties were formidable in number, and to each he made remonstrances, and applied reproaches. La Motte and Madame Dacier, the opposite leaders, were convinced by his arguments, made reciprocal concessions, and concluded a peace. The treaty was formally ratified at a dinner, given on the occasion by a Madame De Staël, who represented "Neutrality." Libations were poured to the memory of old Homer, and the parties were reconciled.

Drinking-Customs in England

THE ANCIENT Bacchus, as represented in gems and statues, was a youthful and graceful divinity; he is so described by Ovid, and was so painted by Barry. He has the epithet of *Psilas*, to express the light spirits which give wings to the soul. His voluptuousness was joyous and tender; and he was never viewed reeling with intoxication. According to Virgil:

> Et quocunque deus circum *caput* egit *honestum*.
> *Georg.* II. 392.

which Dryden, contemplating on the red-faced boorish boy astride on a barrel on our sign-posts, tastelessly sinks into gross vulgarity:

> On whate'er side he turns his *honest* face.

This latinism of *honestum* even the literal inelegance of Davidson had spirit enough to translate, "Where'er the god hath moved around his *graceful head*." The hideous figure of that ebriety, in its most disgusting stage, the ancients exposed in the bestial Silenus and his crew; and with these rather than with the Ovidian and Virgilian deity, our own convivial customs have assimilated.

We shall, probably, outlive that custom of hard-drinking, which was so long one of our national vices. The Frenchman, the Italian, and the Spaniard, only taste the luxury of the grape, but seem never to have indulged in set convivial parties, or drinking-matches, as some of the northern people. Of this folly of ours, which was, however, a borrowed one, and which lasted for two centuries, the history is curious: the variety of its modes and customs; its freaks and extravagances; the technical language introduced to raise it into an art; and the inventions contrived to animate the progress of the thirsty souls of its votaries.

Nations, like individuals, in their intercourse are great imitators; and we have the authority of Camden, who lived at the time, for asserting that "the English in their long wars in the Netherlands first learnt to drown themselves with immoderate drinking, and by drinking others' healths to impair their own. Of all the northern nations, they had been before this most commended for their sobriety." And the historian adds, "that the vice had so diffused itself over the nation, that in our days it was first restrained by severe laws."*

Here we have the authority of a grave and judicious historian for ascertaining the first period and even origin of this custom; and that the nation had not, heretofore, disgraced itself by such prevalent ebriety is also confirmed by one of those curious contemporary pamphlets of a popular writer so invaluable to the philosophical antiquary. Tom Nash, a town-wit of the reign of Elizabeth, long before Camden wrote her history, in his *Pierce Pennilesse,* had detected the same origin.—"Superfluity in drink," says this spirited writer, "is a sin that ever since we have mixed ourselves with the Low-Countries is counted honourable; but before we knew their lingering wars, was held in that highest degree of hatred that might be. Then if we had seen a man go wallowing in the streets, or lain sleeping under the board, we should have spet at him, and warned all our friends out of his company."†

Such was the fit source of this vile custom, which is further

---

* Camden's *History of Queen Elizabeth*, Book III. Many statutes against drunkenness, by way of prevention, passed in the reign of James the First. Our law looks on this vice as an aggravation of any offence committed, not as an excuse for criminal misbehaviour. See *Blackstone*, Book IV. C. 2, Sect. 3. In Mr. Gifford's *Massinger*, vol. ii. 458, is a note to show that when we were young scholars, we soon equalled, if we did not surpass, our masters. Mr. Gilchrist there furnishes an extract from Sir Richard Baker's *Chronicle*, which traces the origin of this exotic custom to the source mentioned; but the whole passage from Baker is literally transcribed from Camden.

† Nash's *Pierce Pennilesse*, 1595, sig. F. 2.

confirmed by the barbarous dialect it introduced into our language; all the terms of drinking which once abounded with us are, without exception, of a base northern origin.*
But the best account I can find of all the refinements of this new science of potation, when it seems to have reached its height, is in our Tom Nash, who being himself one of these deep experimental philosophers, is likely to disclose all the mysteries of the craft.

He says, "Now, he is nobody that cannot drink *supernagulum*; *carouse* the hunter's *hoope*; quaff *vpse freeze crosse*; with *healths, gloves, mumpes, frolickes,* and a thousand such domineering inventions."†

---

* These barbarous phrases are Dutch, Danish, or German. The term *skinker*, a filler of wine, a butler or cup-bearer, according to Phillips; and in taverns, as appears by our dramatic poets, a *drawer*, is Dutch, or, according to Dr. Nott, purely Danish, from *skenker*.

Half-seas over, or nearly drunk, is likely to have been a proverbial phrase from the Dutch, applied to that state of ebriety by an idea familiar with those water-rats. Thus, *op-zee* Dutch, means literally *over-sea*. Mr. Gifford has recently told us in his *Jonson*, that it was a name given to a stupefying beer introduced into England from the Low-Countries; hence *op-zee* or over-sea; and *freezen* in German, signifies to *swallow greedily*; from this vile alliance they compounded a harsh term, often used in our old plays. Thus Jonson:

> I do not like the dullness of your eye,
> It hath a heavy cast, 'tis *upsee Dutch*.
> *Alchemist*, A. iv. S. 2.

And Fletcher has "upsee-freeze"; which Dr. Nott explains in his edition of Decker's *Gull's Hornbook*, as "a tipsy draught, or swallowing liquor till drunk." Mr. Gifford says it was the name of Friesland beer; the meaning, however, was "to drink swinishly like a Dutchman."

We are indebted to the Danes for many of our terms of jollity, such as a *rouse* and a *carouse*. Mr. Gifford has given not only a new but very distinct explanation of these classical terms in his *Massinger*. "A *rouse* was a large glass, in which a health was given, the drinking of which by the rest of the company formed a *carouse*. Barnaby Rich notices the *carouse* as an invention for which the first founder merited hanging. It is necessary to add, that there could be no *rouse* or *carouse*, unless the glasses were emptied." Although we have lost the terms, we have not lost the practice, as those who have the honour of dining in public parties are still gratified by the animating cry of "Gentlemen, charge your glasses."

According to Blount's *Glossographia*, carouse is a corruption of two old German words, *gar* signifying *all*, and *ausz*, *out*; so that to drink *garauz* is to drink *all out*: hence *carouse*.

† *Pierce Pennilesse*, 1595, sig. F. 2.

Drinking super-nagulum, that is *on the nail,* is a device, which Nash says is new come out of France: but it had probably a northern origin, for far northward it still exists. This new device consisted in this, that after a man, says Nash, hath turned up the bottom of the cup to drop it on his nail, and make a pearl with what is left, which if it shed, and cannot make it stand on, by reason there is too much, he must drink again for his penance.

The custom is also alluded to by Bishop Hall, in his satirical romance of *Mundus alter et idem,* "A Discovery of a New World," a work which probably Swift read, and did not forget. The Duke of Tenter-belly in his oration, when he drinks off his large goblet of twelve quarts, on his election, exclaims, should he be false to their laws, "Let never this goodly-formed goblet of wine go jovially through me; and then he set it to his mouth, stole it off every drop, save *a little remainder,* which he was by custom to *set upon his thumb's nail,* and lick it off as he did."

The phrase is in Fletcher:

> I am thine *ad unguem*——

that is he would drink with his friend to the last. In a manuscript letter of the times, I find an account of Columbo, the Spanish ambassador, being at Oxford, and drinking healths to the Infanta. The writer adds, "I shall not tell you how our doctors pledged healths to the Infanta and the archduchess; and if any left *too big a snuff,* Columbo would cry, *supernaculum! supernaculum!*"

This Bacchic freak seems still preserved: for a recent traveller, Sir George Mackenzie, has noticed the custom in his *Travels through Iceland.* "His host having filled a silver cup to the brim, and put on the cover, then held it towards the person who sat next to him, and desired him to take off the cover, and look into the cup, a ceremony intended to secure fair play in filling it. He drank our health, desiring to be excused from emptying the cup, on account of the indifferent state of his health; but we were informed at the same time that if any one of us should neglect any part of the ceremony, or *fail to invert the cup placing the edge on one of the thumbs* as a proof that we had swallowed every drop, the defaulter would be obliged by the laws of drinking to fill the cup again, and drink it off a second time. In spite of their utmost exertions, the penalty of a second draught was incurred by two of the company; we were dreading the consequences of having swallowed so much wine, and in terror lest the cup should be sent round again."

Carouse the hunter's hoop—"Carouse" has been already explained: *the hunter's hoop* alludes to the custom of hoops being marked on a drinking-pot, by which every man was to measure his draught. Shakspeare makes the Jacobin Jack Cade, among his furious reformations, promise his friends that "there shall be in England seven half-penny loaves sold for a penny: *the three hooped pot shall have ten hoops,* and I will make it a felony to drink small beer." I have elsewhere observed that our modern Bacchanalians, whose feats are recorded by the bottle, and who insist on an equality in their rival combats, may discover some ingenuity in that invention among our ancestors of their *peg-tankards,* of which a few may yet occasionally be found in Derbyshire;* the invention of an age less refined than the present, when we have heard of globular glasses and bottles, which by their shape cannot stand, but roll about the table; thus compelling the unfortunate Bacchanalian to drain the last drop, or expose his recreant sobriety.

We must have recourse again to our old friend Tom Nash, who acquaints us with some of "the general rules and inventions for drinking, as good as printed precepts or statutes by act of parliament, that go from drunkard to drunkard; as, still to *keep your first man*; not to leave any *flocks* in the bottom of the cup;

---

* These inventions for keeping every thirsty soul within bounds are alluded to by Tom Nash; I do not know that his authority will be great as an antiquary, but the things themselves he describes he had seen. He tells us, that "King Edgar, because his subjects should not offend in swilling and bibbing as they did, caused certain *iron cups* to be chained to every fountain and well-side, and at every vintner's door, with *iron pins in them,* to stint every man how much he should drink, and he who went *beyond one of those pins* forfeited a penny for every draught."

Pegge, in his *Anonymiana,* has minutely described these *peg-tankards,* which confirms this account of Nash, and nearly the antiquity of the custom. "They have in the inside a row of eight pins one above another, from top to bottom; the tankard holds two quarts, so that there is a gill of ale, i. e. half a pint of Winchester measure, between each pin. The first person that drank was to empty the tankard to the first peg or pin; the second was to empty to the next pin, &c. by which means the pins were so many measures to the compotators, *making them all drink alike,* or the same quantity: and as the distance of the pins was such as to contain a large draught of liquor, *the company would be very liable by this method to get drunk,* especially when, if they drank short of the pin or beyond it, they were obliged to drink again. In Archbishop Anselm's *Canons,* made in the council at London in 1102, priests are enjoined not to go to drinking-bouts, nor *to drink to pegs.* The words are *"Ut Presbyteri non eant ad potationes* nec AD PINNAS bibant." (Wilkins, vol. i. p. 388.) This shows the antiquity of this invention, which at least was as old as the Conquest.

to knock the glass on your thumb when you have done; to have some *shoeing-horn* to pull on your wine, as a rasher on the coals or a red-herring."

Shoeing-horns, sometimes called *gloves,* are also described by Bishop Hall in his *Mundus alter et idem.* "Then, sir, comes me up *a service of shoeing-horns* of all sorts; salt cakes, red-herrings, anchovies, and gammon of bacon, and abundance of such *pullers-on.*"

That famous surfeit of Rhenish and pickled herrings, which banquet proved so fatal to Robert Green, a congenial wit and associate of our Nash, was occasioned by these *shoeing-horns.*

Massinger has given a curious list of *"a service of shoeing-horns."*

> I usher
> Such an unexpected dainty bit for breakfast
> As never yet I cook'd; 'tis not Botargo,
> Fried frogs, potatoes marrow'd, cavear,
> Carps' tongues, the pith of an English chine of beef,
> *Nor our Italian delicate, oil'd mushrooms,*
> And yet *a drawer-on too;** and if you show not
> An appetite, and a strong one, I'll not say
> To eat it, but devour it, without grace too,
> (For it will not stay a preface) I am shamed,
> And all my past provocatives will be jeer'd at.
>
> MASSINGER, *The Guardian,* A. ii. S. 3.

---

* "And yet a *drawer-on too*"; *i. e.* an incitement to appetite: the phrase is yet in use. This drawer-on was also technically termed a *puller-on* and a *shoeing-horn* in drink.

On the "Italian delicate, oil'd mushrooms," still a favourite dish with the Italians, I have to communicate some curious knowledge. In an original manuscript letter dated Hereford, 15 Nov. 1659, the name of the writer wanting, but evidently the composition of a physician who had travelled, I find that the dressing of MUSHROOMS was then a novelty. The learned writer laments his error that he "disdained to learn the cookery that occurred in my travels, by a sullen principle of mistaken devotion, and thus declined the great helps I had to enlarge and improve human diet." This was an age of medicine, when it was imagined that the health of mankind essentially depended on diet; and Moffet had written his curious book on this principle. Our writer, in noticing the passion of the Romans for mushrooms, which was called "an Imperial dish," says, "he had eaten it often at Sir Henry Wotton's table (our resident ambassador at Venice), always dressed by the inspection of his Dutch-Venetian Johanna, or of Nic. Oudart, and truly it did deserve the old applause as I found it at his table; it was far beyond our English food. Neither did any of us find it of hard digestion, for we did not eat like Adamites, but as modest men would eat of musk-melons. If it were now lawful to hold any kind of intelligence with Nic. Oudart, I would only ask him *Sir Henry Wotton's art of dressing mushrooms,* and I hope that is not high treason."—Sloane MSS. 4292.

To *knock the glass on the thumb*, was to show they had performed their duty. Barnaby Rich describes this custom: after having drank, the president "turned the bottom of the cup upward, and in ostentation of his dexterity, gave it a fillip, to make it cry *ting*."

They had among these "domineering inventions" some which we may imagine never took place, till they were told by "the hollow cask"

How the waning night grew old.

Such were *flap-dragons*, which were small combustible bodies fired at one end and floated in a glass of liquor, which an experienced toper swallowed unharmed, while yet blazing. Such is Dr. Johnson's accurate description, who seems to have witnessed what he so well describes.* When Falstaff says of Poins's acts of dexterity to ingratiate himself with the prince, that "he drinks off *candle-ends* for flap-dragons," it seems that this was likewise one of these "frolics," for Nash notices that the liquor was "to be stirred about with a *candle's-end*, to make it taste better, and not to hold your peace while the pot is stirring," no doubt to mark the intrepidity of the miserable "skinker." The most illustrious feat of all is one, however, described by Bishop Hall. If the drinker "could put his finger into the flame of the candle without playing hit-I-miss-I! he is held a sober man, however otherwise drunk he might be." This was considered as a trial of victory among these "canary-birds," or bibbers of canary wine.†

We have a very common expression to describe a man in a state of ebriety, that "he is as drunk as a beast," or that "he is beastly drunk." This is a libel on the brutes, for the vice of ebriety is perfectly human. I think the phrase is peculiar to ourselves: and I imagine I have discovered its origin. When ebriety became first prevalent in our nation, during the reign of Elizabeth, it was a favourite notion among the writers of the time, and on which they have exhausted their fancy, that a man in the different stages of ebriety showed the most vicious quality of different animals, or that a company of drunkards exhibited a collection of brutes with their different characteristics.

---

* See Mr. Douce's curious *Illustrations of Shakspeare*, vol. i. 457; a gentleman more intimately conversant with our ancient and domestic manners than, perhaps, any single individual in the country.

† This term is used in *Bancroft's two books of Epigrams and Epitaphs*, 1639. I take it to have been an accepted one of that day.

"All dronkardes are beasts," says George Gascoigne, in a curious treatise on them,* and he proceeds in illustrating his proposition; but the satirist Nash has classified eight kinds of "drunkards"; a fanciful sketch from the hand of a master in humour, and which could only have been composed by a close spectator of their manners and habits.

"The first is *ape-drunk*, and he leaps and sings and hollows and danceth for the heavens; the second is *lyon-drunk*, and he flings the pots about the house, calls the hostess w—e, breaks the glass-windows with his dagger, and is apt to quarrel with any man that speaks to him; the third is *swine-drunk*, heavy, lumpish, and sleepy, and cries for a little more drink and a few more clothes; the fourth is *sheep-drunk,* wise in his own conceit when he cannot bring forth a right word; the fifth is *maudlen-drunk*, when a fellow will weep for kindness in the midst of his drink, and kiss you, saying, 'By God! captain, I love thee; go thy ways, thou dost not think so often of me as I do of thee: I would (if it pleased God) I could not love thee so well as I do,' and then he puts his finger in his eye and cries. The sixth is *martin-drunk*, when a man is drunk, and drinks himself sober ere he stir; the seventh is *goat-drunk*, when in his drunkenness he hath no mind but on lechery. The eighth is *fox-drunk*, when he is crafty-drunk, as many of the Dutchmen be, which will never bargain but when they are drunk. All these *species*, and more, I have seen practised in *one company at one sitting*; when I have been permitted to remain sober amongst them only to note their several humours." These beast-drunkards are characterized in a frontispiece to a curious tract on *Drunkenness* where the men are represented with the heads of apes, swine, &c. &c.

A new era in this history of our drinking-parties occurred about the time of the Restoration, when politics heated their wine, and drunkenness and loyalty became more closely connected. As the puritanic coldness wore off, the people were perpetually, in 1650, warmed in drinking the king's health on their knees; and, among various kinds of "ranting cavalierism," the cavaliers during Cromwell's usurpation usually put a crum of bread into their glass, and before they drank it off, with cautious ambiguity exclaimed, "God send this *crum well* down!"

---

* *A delicate Diet for daintie mouthed Droonkardes, wherin the fowle Abuse of common carowsing and quaffing with hartie Draughtes is honestlie admonished. By George Gascoigne, Esquier. 1576.*

which by the way preserves the orthöepy of that extraordinary man's name, and may be added to the instances adduced in our present volume "On the orthography of proper names."* We have a curious account of a drunken bout by some royalists, told by Whitelocke in his *Memorials*. It bore some resemblance to the drinking-party of Catiline; they mingled their own blood with their wine.† After the Restoration, Burnet complains of the excess of convivial loyalty. "Drinking the king's health was set up by too many as a distinguishing mark of loyalty, and drew many into great excess after his majesty's restoration."‡

Introduction of Tea, Coffee, and Chocolate

IT IS said that the frozen Norwegians, on the first sight of roses, dared not touch what they conceived were trees budding with fire: and the natives of Virginia, the first time they seized on a quantity of gunpowder, which belonged to the English colony, sowed it for grain, expecting to reap a plentiful crop of combustion by the next harvest, to blow away the whole colony.

In our own recollection, strange imaginations impeded the first period of vaccination; when some families, terrified by the warning of a physician, conceived their race would end in a species of Minotaurs:—

> Semibovemque virum, semivirumque bovem.

We smile at the simplicity of the men of nature, for their mistaken notions at the first introduction among them of exotic novelties; and yet, even in civilized Europe, how long a time those whose profession, or whose reputation, regulates public

---

* [Not reprinted here.—ED.]

† I shall preserve the story in the words of Whitelocke; it was something ludicrous, as well as terrific.

"From Berkshire (in May 1650) that five drunkards agreed to drink the king's health in their blood, and that each of them should cut off a piece of his buttock, and fry it upon the gridiron, which was done by four of them, of whom one did bleed so exceedingly, that they were fain to send for a chirurgeon, and so were discovered. The wife of one of them hearing that her husband was amongst them, came to the room, and taking up a pair of tongs laid about her, and so saved the cutting of her husband's flesh."—*Whitelock's Memorials,* p. 453, second edition.

‡ Burnet's *Life of Sir Matthew Hale.*

opinion, are influenced by vulgar prejudices, often disguised under the imposing form of science! and when their ludicrous absurdities and obstinate prejudices enter into the matters of history, it is then we discover that they were only imposing on themselves and on others.

It is hardly credible that on the first introduction of the Chinese leaf, which now affords our daily refreshment; or the American leaf, whose sedative fumes made it so long an universal favourite; or the Arabian berry, whose aroma exhilarates its European votaries; that the use of these harmless novelties should have spread consternation among the nations of Europe, and have been anathematized by the terrors and the fictions of some of the learned. Yet this seems to have happened. Patin, who wrote so furiously against the introduction of antimony, spread the same alarm at the use of tea, which he calls *"l'impertinente nouveauté du siècle."* In Germany, Hanneman considered tea-dealers as immoral members of society, lying in wait for men's purses and lives; and Dr. Duncan, in his treatise on hot liquors, suspected that the virtues attributed to tea were merely to encourage the importation.

Many virulent pamphlets were published against the use of this shrub, from various motives. In 1670 a Dutch writer says it was ridiculed in Holland under the name of hay-water. "The progress of this famous plant," says an ingenious writer, "has been something like the progress of truth; suspected at first, though very palatable to those who had courage to taste it; resisted as it encroached; abused as its popularity seemed to spread; and establishing its triumph at last, in cheering the whole land from the palace to the cottage, only by the slow and resistless efforts of time and its own virtues."*

The history of the Tea-shrub, by Dr. Lettsom, usually referred to on this subject, I consider little more than a plagiarism on Dr. Short's learned and curious dissertation on *Tea,* 1730, 4to. Lettsom has superadded the solemn trifling of his moral and medical advice.

These now common beverages are all of recent origin in Europe; neither the ancients nor those of the middle ages tasted of this luxury. The first accounts we find of the use of this shrub are the casual notices of travellers, who seem to have tasted it, and sometimes not to have liked it: a Russian ambassador, in

---

* *Edinburgh Review,* 1816, p. 117.

1639, who resided at the court of the Mogul, declined accepting a large present of tea for the Czar, "as it would only encumber him with a commodity for which he had no use." The appearance of "a black water" and an acid taste seems not to have recommended it to the German Olearius in 1633. Dr. Short has recorded an anecdote of a stratagem of the Dutch in their second voyage to China, by which they at first obtained their tea without disbursing money; they carried from home great store of dried sage, and bartered it with the Chinese for tea, and received three or four pounds of tea for one of sage: but at length the Dutch could not export sufficient quantities of sage to supply their demand. This fact, however, proves how deeply the imagination is concerned with our palate; for the Chinese, affected by the exotic novelty, considered our sage to be more precious than their tea.

The first introduction of tea into Europe is not ascertained; according to the common accounts it came into England from Holland, in 1666, when Lord Arlington and Lord Ossory brought over a small quantity: the custom of drinking tea became fashionable, and a pound weight sold then for sixty shillings. This account, however, is by no means satisfactory. I have heard of Oliver Cromwell's tea-pot in the possession of a collector, and this will derange the chronology of those writers who are perpetually copying the researches of others, without confirming or correcting them.

Amidst the rival contests of the Dutch and the English East India Companies, the honour of introducing its use into Europe may be claimed by both. Dr. Short conjectures that tea might have been known in England as far back as the reign of James the First, for the first fleet set out in 1600; but had the use of this shrub been known, the novelty had been chronicled among our dramatic writers, whose works are the annals of our prevalent tastes and humours. It is rather extraordinary that our East India Company should not have discovered the use of this shrub in their early adventures; yet it certainly was not known in England so late as in 1641, for in a scarce *Treatise of Warm Beer*, where the title indicates the author's design to recommend hot in preference to cold drinks, he refers to tea only by quoting the Jesuit Maffei's account, that "they of China do for the most part drink the strained liquor of an herb called *Chia*, hot." The word *Cha* is the Portuguese term for tea retained to this day, which they borrowed from the Japanese; while our intercourse with the Chinese made us no doubt adopt their term *Theh*, now prevalent throughout Europe, with the exception of the Portuguese. The Chinese origin is still preserved in the term *Bohea*, tea which comes from the country of *Vouhi*; and that of *Hyson* was the name of the most considerable Chinese then concerned in the trade.

The best account of the early use, and the prices of tea in England, appears in the hand-bill of one who may be called our first *Tea-maker*. This curious hand-bill bears no date, but as Hanway ascertained that the price was sixty shillings in 1660, his bill must have been dispersed about that period.

Thomas Garway, in Exchange-alley, tobacconist and coffee-man, was the first who sold and retailed tea, recommending it for the cure of all disorders. The following shop-bill is more curious than any historical account we have.

"Tea in England hath been sold in the leaf for six pounds, and sometimes for ten pounds the pound weight, and in respect of its former scarceness and dearness it hath been only used as a regalia in high treatments and entertainments, and presents made thereof to princes and grandees till the year 1657. The said Garway did purchase a quantity thereof, and first publicly sold the said tea in *leaf* or *drink*, made according to the directions of the most knowing merchants into those Eastern countries. On the knowledge of the said Garway's continued care and industry in obtaining the best tea, and making drink thereof, very many noblemen, physicians, merchants, &c., have ever since sent to him for the said leaf, and daily resort to his house to drink the drink thereof. He sells tea from 16*s.* to 50*s.* a pound."

Probably, tea was not in general use domestically so late as in 1687; for in the diary of Henry, Earl of Clarendon, he registers that "Père Couplet supped with me, and after supper we had tea, which he said was really as good as any he had drank in China." Had his lordship been in the general habit of drinking tea, he had not probably made it a subject for his diary.

While the honour of introducing tea may be disputed between the English and the Dutch, that of coffee remains between the English and the French. Yet an Italian intended to have occupied the place of honour; that admirable traveller Pietro della Valle, writing from Constantinople, 1615, to a Roman, his fellow-countryman, informing him that he should teach Europe in what manner the Turks took what he calls *"Cahué,"* or as the word is written in an Arabic and English pamphlet, printed at Oxford, in 1659, on "the nature of the drink *Kauhi* or Coffee." As this celebrated traveller lived to 1652, it may excite surprise that the first cup of coffee was not drank at Rome; this remains for the discovery of some member of the "Arcadian Society." Our own Sandys, at the time that Valle wrote, was also "a traveller," and well knew what was *"Coffa,"* which "they drank as hot as they can endure it; it is as black as soot, and tastes not much unlike it; good they say for digestion and mirth."

It appears by Le Grand's *Vie privée des François,* that the celebrated Thevenot, in 1658, gave coffee after dinner; but it was considered as the whim of a traveller; neither the thing itself, nor its appearance, was inviting: it was probably attributed by the gay to the humour of a vain philosophical traveller. But ten years afterwards a Turkish ambassador at Paris made the beverage highly fashionable. The elegance of the equipage recommended it to the eye, and charmed the women: the brilliant porcelain cups in which it was poured; the napkins fringed with gold, and the Turkish slaves on their knees presenting it to the ladies, seated on the ground on cushions, turned the heads of the Parisian dames. This elegant introduction made the exotic beverage a subject of conversation, and in 1672, an Armenian at Paris at the fair-time opened a coffee-house. But the custom still prevailed to sell beer and wine, and to smoke and mix with indifferent company in their first imperfect coffee-houses. A Florentine, one Procope, celebrated in his day as the arbiter of taste in this department, instructed by the error of the Armenian, invented a superior establishment, and introduced ices; he embellished his apartment, and those who had avoided the offensive coffee-houses repaired to Procope's; where literary men, artists, and wits resorted, to inhale the fresh and fragrant steam. Le Grand says that this establishment holds a distinguished place in the literary history of the times. It was at the coffee-house of Du Laurent that Saurin, La Motte, Danchet, Boindin, Rousseau, &c. met; but the mild streams of the aromatic berry could not mollify the acerbity of so many rivals, and the witty malignity of Rousseau gave birth to those famous couplets on all the coffee-drinkers, which occasioned his misfortune and his banishment.

Such is the history of the first use of coffee and its houses at Paris. We, however, had the use before even the time of Thevenot; for an English Turkish merchant brought a Greek servant in 1652, who, knowing how to roast and make it, opened a house to sell it publicly. I have also discovered his hand-bill, in which he sets forth, "The vertue of the coffee-drink, first publiquely made and sold in England, by Pasqua Rosee, in St. Michael's Alley, Cornhill, at the sign of his own head."

For about twenty years after the introduction of coffee in this kingdom, we find a continued series of invectives against its adoption, both for medicinal and domestic purposes. The use of coffee, indeed, seems to have excited more notice, and to have had a greater influence on the manners of the people, than that of tea. It seems at first to have been more universally used, as it still is on the Continent; and its use is connected with a resort for the idle and the curious: the history of coffee-houses, ere the invention of clubs, was that of the manners, the morals, and the politics of a people. Even in its native country, the government discovered that extraordinary fact, and the use of the Arabian berry was more than once forbidden where it grows; for Ellis, in his *History of Coffee*, 1774, refers to an Arabian MS., in the King of France's library, which shows that coffee-houses in Asia were sometimes suppressed. The same fate happened on its introduction into England.

Among a number of poetical satires against the use of coffee, I find a curious exhibition, according to the exaggerated notions of that day, in "A Cup of Coffee, or Coffee in its Colours," 1663. The writer, like others of his contemporaries, wonders at the odd taste which could make Coffee a substitute for Canary.

> For men and Christians to turn Turks and think
> To excuse the crime, because 'tis in their drink!
> Pure English apes! ye may, for aught I know,
> Would it but mode—learn to eat spiders too.*
> Should any of your grandsires' ghosts appear
> In your wax-candle circles, and but hear
> The name of coffee so much called upon,
> Then see it drank like scalding Phlegethon;
> Would they not startle, think ye, all agreed
> 'Twas conjuration both in word and deed?
> Or Catiline's conspirators, as they stood
> Sealing their oaths in draughts of blackest blood,
> The merriest ghost of all your sires would say,
> Your wine's much worse since his last yesterday.
> He'd wonder how the club had given a hop,
> O'er tavern-bars into a farrier's shop,
> Where he'd suppose, both by the smoke and stench,
> Each man a horse, and each horse at his drench.—

---

* This witty poet was not without a degree of prescience; the luxury of eating spiders has never indeed become "modish," but Mons. Lalande, the French astronomer, and one or two humble imitators of the modern philosopher, have shown this triumph over vulgar prejudices, and were Epicures of this stamp.

Sure you're no poets, nor their friends, for now,
Should Jonson's strenuous spirit, or the rare
Beaumont and Fletcher's, in your round appear,
They would not find the air perfumed with one
Castalian drop, nor dew of Helicon;
When they but men would speak as the Gods do,
They drank pure nectar as the Gods drink too,
Sublim'd with rich Canary—say, shall then
These less than coffee's self, these coffee-men;
These sons of nothing, that can hardly make
Their broth, for laughing how the jest does take,
Yet grin, and give ye for the vine's pure blood
A loathsome potion, not yet understood,
Syrop of soot, or essence of old shoes,
Dasht with diurnals and the books of news?

Other complaints arose from the mixture of the company in the first coffee-houses. In "A Broadside against Coffee, or the Marriage of the Turk," 1672, the writer indicates the growth of the fashion:—

Confusion huddles all into one scene,
Like Noah's ark, the clean and the unclean;
For now, alas! the drench has credit got,
And he's no gentleman who drinks it not.
That such a dwarf should rise to such a stature!
But custom is but a remove from nature.

In *The Women's Petition against Coffee*, 1674, they complained that "it made men as unfruitful as the deserts whence that unhappy berry is said to be brought; that the offspring of our mighty ancestors would dwindle into a succession of apes and pigmies; and on a domestic message, a husband would stop by the way to drink a couple of cups of coffee." It was now sold in convenient penny-worths; for in another poem in praise of a coffee-house, for the variety of information obtained there, it is called "a penny university."

Amidst these contests of popular prejudices, between the lovers of forsaken Canary, and the terrors of our females at the barrenness of an Arabian desert, which lasted for twenty years, at length the custom was universally established; nor were there wanting some reflecting minds desirous of introducing the use of this liquid among the labouring classes of society, to wean them from strong liquors. Howell, in noticing that curious philosophical traveller Sir Henry Blount's *Organon Salutis*, 1659, observed that "this coffa-drink hath caused a great sobriety among all nations: formerly apprentices, clerks, &c., used to take their morning draughts in ale, beer, or wine, which often made them unfit for business. Now they play the good-fellows in this wakeful and civil drink. The worthy gentleman Sir James Muddiford, who introduced the practice hereof first in London, deserves much respect of the whole nation." Here it appears, what is most probable, that the use of this berry was introduced by other Turkish merchants, besides Edwards and his servant Pasqua. But the custom of drinking coffee among the labouring classes does not appear to have lasted; and when it was recently even the cheapest beverage, the popular prejudices prevailed against it, and ran in favour of tea. The contrary practice prevails on the continent, where beggars are viewed making their coffee in the street. I remember seeing the large body of shipwrights at Helvoetsluys summoned by a bell, to take their regular refreshment of coffee; and the fleets of Holland were not then built by arms less robust than the fleets of Britain.

The frequenting of coffee-houses is a custom which has declined within our recollection, since institutions of a higher character, and society itself, have so much improved within late years. These were, however, the common assemblies of all classes of society. The mercantile man, the man of letters, and the man of fashion, had their appropriate coffee-houses. *The Tatler* dates from either to convey a character of his subject. In the reign of Charles the Second, 1675, a proclamation for some time shut them all up, having become the rendezvous of the politicians of that day. Roger North has given, in his *Examen*, a full account of this bold stroke: it was not done without some apparent respect to the British Constitution, the court affecting not to act against law, for the judges were summoned to a consultation, when, it seems, the five who met did not agree in opinion. But a decision was contrived that "the retailing of coffee and tea might be an innocent trade; but as it was said to nourish sedition, spread lies, and scandalize great men, it might also be a common nuisance." A general discontent, in consequence, as North acknowledges, took place, and emboldened the merchants and retailers of coffee and tea to petition; and permission was soon granted to open the houses to a certain period, under a severe admonition, that the masters should prevent all scandalous papers, books, and libels from being read in them; and hinder every person from spreading scandalous reports against the government. It must be confessed, all this must have frequently puzzled the coffee-house master to decide what was scandalous, what book was fit to be licensed to be read, and what political intelligence might be allowed to be communicated. The object of the government was, probably, to intimidate, rather than to persecute, at that moment.

Chocolate the Spaniards brought from Mexico, where it was denominated *Chocolatti*; it was a coarse mixture of ground cacao and Indian corn with rocou; but the Spaniards, liking its nourishment, improved it into a richer compound, with sugar, vanilla, and other aromatics. The immoderate use of chocolate, in the seventeenth century, was considered as so violent an inflamer of the passions, that Joan. Fran. Rauch published a treatise against it, and enforced the necessity of forbidding the *monks* to drink it; and adds, that if such an interdiction had existed, that scandal with which that holy order had been branded might have proved more groundless. This *Disputatio medico-diætetica de aëre et esculentis, necnon de potû*, Vienna, 1624, is a *rara avis* among collectors. This attack on the monks, as well as on chocolate, is said to be the cause of its scarcity; for we are told that they were so diligent in suppressing this treatise, that it is supposed not a dozen copies exist. We had chocolate-houses in London long after coffee-houses; they seemed to have associated something more elegant and refined in their new term when the other had become common. Roger North thus inveighs against them: "The use of coffee-houses seems much improved by a new invention, called chocolate-houses, for the benefit of rooks and cullies of quality, where gaming is added to all the rest, and the summons of W—— seldom fails; as if the devil had erected a new university, and those were the colleges of its professors, as well as his schools of discipline." Roger North, a high tory, and attorney-general to James the Second, observed, however, that these rendezvous were often not entirely composed of those "factious gentry he so much dreaded"; for he says "This way of passing time might have been stopped at first before people had possessed themselves of some convenience from them of meeting for short dispatches, and passing evenings with small expenses." And old Aubrey, the small Boswell of his day, attributes his general acquaintance to "the modern advantage of coffee-houses in this great city, before which men knew not how to be acquainted, but with their own relations, and societies"; a curious statement, which proves the moral connection with society of all sedentary recreations which induce the herding spirit.

On the Ridiculous Titles Assumed by
Italian Academies

THE ITALIANS are a fanciful people, who have often mixed a grain or two of pleasantry and even of folly with their wisdom. This fanciful character betrays itself in their architecture, in their poetry, in their extemporary comedy, and their *Improvvisatori*; but an instance not yet accounted for of this national levity, appears in those denominations of exquisite absurdity given by themselves to their Academies! I have in vain inquired for any assignable reason why the most ingenious men, and grave and illustrious personages, cardinals, and princes, as well as poets, scholars, and artists, in every literary city, should voluntarily choose to burlesque themselves and their serious occupations, by affecting mysterious or ludicrous titles, as if it were carnival-time, and they had to support masquerade characters, and accepting such titles as we find in the cant style of our own vulgar clubs, the Society of "Odd Fellows," and of "Eccentrics"! A principle, so whimsical but systematic, must surely have originated in some circumstance not hitherto detected.

A literary friend, recently in an Italian city exhausted by the *sirocco*, entered a house whose open door and circular seats appeared to offer to passengers a refreshing *sorbetto*; he discovered, however, that he had got into "the Academy of the Cameleons," where they met to delight their brothers, and any *spirito gentil* they could nail to a recitation. An invitation to join the academicians alarmed him, for with some impatient prejudice against these little creatures, vocal with *prose e rime*, and usually with odes and sonnets begged for, or purloined for the occasion, he waived all further curiosity and courtesy, and has returned home without any information how these "Cameleons" looked, when changing their colours in an *"accademia."*

Such literary institutions, prevalent in Italy, are the spurious remains of those numerous academies which simultaneously started up in that country about the sixteenth century. They assumed the most ridiculous denominations, and a great number is registered by Quadrio and Tiraboschi. Whatever was their design, one cannot fairly reproach them, as Mencken, in his *Charlatanaria Eruditorum*, seems to have thought, for pompous quackery; neither can we attribute to their modesty their choice of senseless titles, for to have degraded their own exalted pursuits was but folly! Literary history affords no parallel to this national absurdity of the refined Italians. Who could have suspected that the most eminent scholars, and men of genius, were associates of the *Oziosi*, the *Fantastici*, the *Insensati*? Why should Genoa boast of her "Sleepy," Viterbo of her "Obstinates," Sienna of her "Insipids," her "Blockheads," and her "Thunderstruck"; and Naples of her *Furiosi*; while Macerata exults in her "Madmen chained"? Both Quadrio and Tiraboschi cannot deny that these fantastical titles have occasioned these Italian academies to appear very ridiculous to the *oltramontani*; but these valuable historians are no philosophical thinkers. They apologize for this bad taste, by describing the ardour which was kindled throughout Italy at the restoration of letters and the fine arts, so that every one, and even every man of genius, were eager to enrol their names in these academies, and prided themselves in bearing their emblems, that is, the distinctive arms each academy had chosen. But why did they mystify themselves?

Folly, once become national, is a vigorous plant, which sheds abundant seed. The consequence of having adopted ridiculous titles for these academies, suggested to them many other characteristic fopperies. At Florence every brother of the *Umidi* assumed the name of something aquatic, or any quality pertaining to humidity. One was called "the Frozen," another "the Damp"; one was "the Pike," another "the Swan": and Grazzini, the celebrated novelist, is known better by the cognomen of *La Lasca*, "the Roach," by which he whimsically designates himself among the "Humids." I find among the *Insensati*, one man of learning taking the name of STORDIDO *Insensato*, another TENEBROSO *Insensato*. The famous Florentine academy of *La Crusca*, amidst their grave labours to sift and purify their language, threw themselves headlong into this vortex of folly. Their title, the academy of "Bran," was a conceit to indicate their art of sifting; bu it required an Italian prodigality of conceit to have induced these grave scholars to exhibit themselves in the burlesque scenery of a pantomimical academy, for their furniture consists of a mill and a bakehouse; a pulpit for the orator is a hopper, while the learned director sits on a mill-stone; the other seats have the forms of a miller's dossers, or great panniers, and the backs consist of the long shovels used in ovens. The table is a baker's kneading-trough, and the academician who reads has half his body thrust out of a great bolting sack, with I know not what else for their inkstands and portfolios. But the most celebrated of these academies is that *degli Arcadi*, at Rome, who are still carrying on their pretensions much higher. Whoever aspires to be aggregated to these Arcadian shepherds receives a pastoral name and a title, but not the deeds, of a farm, picked out of a map of the ancient Arcadia or its environs; for Arcadia itself soon became too small a possession for these partitioners of moonshine. Their laws, modelled by the twelve tables of the ancient Romans; their language in the venerable majesty of their renowned ancestors; and this erudite democracy dating by the Grecian Olympiads, which Crescimbeni, their first *custode*, or guardian, most painfully adjusted to the vulgar era, were designed that the sacred erudition of antiquity might for ever be present among these shepherds.* Goldoni, in his *Memoirs*, has given an amusing account of these honours. He says "He was presented with two diplomas; the one was my charter of aggregation to the *Arcadi* of Rome, under the name of *Polisseno*, the other gave me the investiture of the *Phlegræan* fields. I was on this saluted by the whole assembly in chorus, under the name of *Polisseno Phlegræio*, and embraced by them as a fellow shepherd and brother. The *Arcadians* are very rich, as you may perceive, my dear reader: we possess estates in Greece; we water them with our labours for the sake of reaping laurels, and the Turks sow them with grain, and plant them with vines, and laugh at both our titles and our songs." When Fontenelle became an Arcadian, they baptized the new *Pastor* by their graceful diminutive—*Fontanella*—allusive to the charm of his style; and further they magnificently presented him with the entire Isle of Delos! The late Joseph Walker, an enthusiast for Italian literature, dedicated his *Memoir on Italian Tragedy* to the Countess Spencer; not inscribing it with his Christian but his heathen name, and the title of his Arcadian estate, *Eubante Tirinzio*! Plain Joseph Walker, in his masquerade dress, with his Arcadian signet of Pan's reeds dangling in his title-page, was performing a character to which however well adapted, not being understood, he got stared at for his affectation! We have lately heard of some licentious revellings of these Arcadians, in receiving a man of genius from our own country, who, himself composing Italian *Rime*, had "conceit" enough to become a shepherd!† Yet let us inquire before we criticize.

---

* Crescimbeni, at the close of *La bellezza della Volgar Poesia*. Roma, 1700.
† *History of the Middle Ages*, ii. 584. See, also, Mr. Rose's *Letters from the North of Italy*, vol. i. 204. Mr. Hallam has observed, that "such an institution as the society *degli Arcadi* could at no time have endured public ridicule in England for a fortnight."

Even this ridiculous society of the Arcadians became a memorable literary institution; and Tiraboschi has shown how it successfully arrested the bad taste which was then prevailing throughout Italy, recalling its muses to purer sources; while the lives of many of its shepherds have furnished an interesting volume of literary history under the title of *The illustrious Arcadians.* Crescimbeni, and its founders, had formed the most elevated conceptions of the society at its origin; but poetical vaticinators are prophets only while we read their verses—we must not look for that dry matter of fact—the event predicted!

> Il vostro seme eterno
> Occuperà la terra, ed i confini
> D'Arcadia oltrapassando,
> Di non più visti gloriosi germi
> L'aureo feconderà lito del Gange
> E de' Cimmeri l'infeconde arene.

Mr. Mathias has recently with warmth defended the original *Arcadia*; and the assumed character of its members, which has been condemned as betraying their affectation, he attributes to their modesty. "Before the critics of the Arcadia (the *pastori*, as they modestly styled themselves), with Crescimbeni for their conductor, and with the *Adorato Albano* for their patron (Clement XI.), all that was depraved in language, and in sentiment, fled and disappeared."

The strange taste for giving fantastical denominations to literary institutions grew into a custom, though, probably, no one knew how. The founders were always persons of rank or learning, yet still accident or caprice created the mystifying title, and invented those appropriate emblems, which still added to the folly. The Arcadian society derived its title from a spontaneous conceit. This assembly first held its meetings, on summer evenings, in a meadow on the banks of the Tiber; for the fine climate of Italy promotes such assemblies in the open air. In the recital of an eclogue, an enthusiast, amidst all he was hearing and all he was seeing, exclaimed, "I seem at this moment to be in the Arcadia of ancient Greece, listening to the pure and simple strains of its shepherds." Enthusiasm is contagious amidst susceptible Italians, and this name, by inspiration and by acclamation, was conferred on the society! Even more recently, at Florence, the *accademia* called the *Colombaria*, or the "Pigeon-house," proves with what levity the Italians name a literary society. The founder was the Cavallero Pazzi, a gentleman, who, like Morose, abhorring noise, chose for his study a garret in his palazzo; it was, indeed, one of the old turrets which had not yet fallen in: there he fixed his library, and there he assembled the most ingenious Florentines to discuss obscure points, and to reveal their own contributions in this secret retreat of silence and philosophy. To get to this cabinet it was necessary to climb a very steep and very narrow staircase, which occasioned some facetious wit to observe, that these literati were so many pigeons who flew every evening to their dove-cot. The Cavallero Pazzi, to indulge this humour, invited them to a dinner entirely composed of their little brothers, in all the varieties of cookery; the members, after a hearty laugh, assumed the title of the *Colombaria*, invented a device consisting of the top of a turret, with several pigeons flying about it, bearing an epigraph from Dante, *"Quanto veder si può,"* by which they expressed their design not to apply themselves to any single object. Such facts sufficiently prove that some of the absurd or facetious denominations of these literary societies originated in accidental circumstances or in mere pleasantry; but this will not account for the origin of those mystifying titles we have noticed; for when grave men call themselves dolts or lunatics, unless they are really so, they must have some reason for laughing at themselves.

To attempt to develop this curious but obscure singularity in literary history, we must go further back among the first beginnings of these institutions. How were they looked on by the governments in which they first appeared? These academies, might, perhaps, form a chapter in the history of secret societies, one not yet written, but of which many curious materials lie scattered in history. It is certain that such literary societies, in their first origins, have always excited the jealousy of governments, but more particularly in ecclesiastical Rome, and the rival principalities of Italy. If two great nations, like those of England and France, had their suspicions and fears roused by a select assembly of philosophical men, and either put them down by force, or closely watched them, this will not seem extraordinary in little despotic states. We have accounts of some philosophical associations at home, which were joined by Sir Philip Sidney and Sir Walter Raleigh, but which soon got the odium of atheism attached to them; and the establishment of the French Academy occasioned some umbrage, for a year elapsed before the Parliament of Paris would register their patent, which was at length accorded by the political Richelieu observing to the president, that "he should like the members according as the members liked him." Thus we have ascertained one principle, that governments in those times looked on a new society with a political glance; nor is it improbable that some of them combined an ostensible with a latent motive.

There is no want of evidence to prove that the modern Romans, from the thirteenth to the fifteenth century, were too feelingly alive to their obscured glory, and that they too frequently made invidious comparisons of their ancient republic with the pontifical government; to revive Rome, with every thing Roman, inspired such enthusiasts as Rienzi, and charmed the visions of Petrarch. At a period when ancient literature, as if by a miracle, was raising itself from its grave, the learned were agitated by a correspondent energy; not only was an estate sold to purchase a manuscript, but the relic of genius was touched with a religious emotion. The classical purity of Cicero was contrasted with the barbarous idiom of the Missal; the glories of ancient Rome with the miserable subjugation of its modern pontiffs; and the metaphysical reveries of Plato, and what they termed the *"Enthusiasmus Alexandrinus"*—the dreams of the Platonists—seemed to the fanciful Italians more elevated than the humble and pure ethics of the Gospels. The vain and amorous Eloisa could even censure the gross manners, as it seemed to her, of the apostles, for picking the ears of corn in their walks, and at their meals eating with unwashed hands. Touched by this mania of antiquity, the learned affected to change their vulgar Christian name, by assuming the more classical ones of a Junius Brutus, a Pomponius, or a Julius, or any other rusty name unwashed by baptism. This frenzy for the ancient republic not only menaced the pontificate; but their Platonic, or their pagan ardours, seemed to be striking at the foundation of Christianity itself. Such were Marcellus Ficinus, and that learned society who assembled under the Medici. Pomponius Lætus, who lived at the close of the fifteenth century, not only celebrated by an annual festival the foundation of Rome, and raised altars to Romulus, but openly expressed his contempt for the Christian religion, which this visionary declared was only fit for barbarians; but this extravagance and irreligion, observes Niceron, were common with many of the learned of those times, and this very Pomponius was at length formally accused of the crime of changing the baptismal names of the young persons whom he taught, for pagan ones! "This was the taste of the times," says the author we have just quoted; but it was imagined that there was a mystery concealed in these changes of names.

At this period these literary societies first appear: one at Rome had the title of "Academy," and for its chief this very Pomponius; for he is distinguished as *"Romanæ Princeps Academiæ,"* by his friend Politian, in the *Miscellanea* of that elegant scholar. This was under the pontificate of Paul the Second. The regular meetings of "the Academy" soon excited the jealousy and suspicions of Paul, and gave rise to one of the most horrid persecutions and scenes of torture, even to death, in which these academicians were involved. This closed with a decree of Paul's, that for the future no one should pronounce, either seriously or in jest, the very name of *academy*, under the penalty of heresy! The story is told by Platina, one of the sufferers, in his *Life of Paul the Second*; and although this history may be said to bear the bruises of the wounded and dislocated body of the unhappy historian, the facts are unquestionable, and connected with our subject. Platina, Pomponius, and many of their friends, were suddenly dragged to prison; on the first and second day torture was applied, and many expired under the hands of their executioners. "You would have imagined," says Platina, "that the castle of St. Angelo was turned into the bull of Phalaris, so loud the hollow vault resounded with the cries of those miserable young men, who were an honour to their age for genius and learning. The torturers, not satisfied, though weary, having racked twenty men in these two days, of whom some died, at length sent for me to take my turn. The instruments of torture were ready; I was stripped, and the executioners put themselves to their work. Vianesius sat like another Minos on a seat of tapestry-work, gay as at a wedding; and while I hung on the rack in torment, he played with a jewel which Sanga had, asking him who was the mistress which had given him this love-token? Turning to me, he asked, 'why Pomponio, in a letter, should call me Holy Father? Did the conspirators agree to make you pope?' 'Pomponio,' I replied, 'can best tell why he gave me this title, for I know not.' At length, having pleased, but not satisfied himself with my tortures, he ordered me to be let down, that I might undergo tortures much greater in the evening. I was carried, half dead, into my chamber; but not long after, the inquisitor having dined, and being fresh in drink, I was fetched again, and the archbishop of Spalatro was there. They inquired of my conversations with Malatesta. I said, it only concerned ancient and modern learning, the military arts, and the characters of illustrious men, the ordinary subjects of conversation. I was bitterly threatened by Vianesius, unless I confessed the truth on the following day, and was carried back to my chamber, where I was seized with such extreme pain, that I had rather have died than endured the agony of my battered and dislocated limbs. But now those who were accused of heresy were charged with plotting treason. Pomponius being examined why he changed the names of his friends, he answered boldly, that this was no concern of his judges or the pope; it was, perhaps, out of respect for antiquity, to stimulate to a virtuous emulation. After we had now lain ten months in prison, Paul comes himself to the castle, where he charged us, among other things, that we had disputed concerning the immortality of the soul, and that we held the opinion of Plato; by disputing you call the being of a God in question. This, I said, might be objected to all divines and philosophers, who, to make the truth appear, frequently question the existence of souls and of God, and of all separate intelligences. St. Austin says, the opinion of Plato is like the faith of Christians. I followed none of the numerous heretical factions. Paul then accused us of being too great admirers of pagan antiquities; yet none were more fond of them than himself, for he collected all the statues and sarcophagi of the ancients to place in his palace, and even affected to imitate, on more than one occasion, the pomp and charm of their public ceremonies. While they were arguing, mention happened to be made of 'the Academy,' when the Cardinal of San Marco cried out, that we were not 'Academics,' but a scandal to the name; and Paul now declared that he would not have that term evermore mentioned under pain of heresy. He left us in a passion, and kept us two months longer in prison to complete the year, as it seems he had sworn."

Such is the interesting narrative of Platina, from which we may surely infer, that if these learned men assembled for the communication of their studies,—inquiries suggested by the monuments of antiquity, the two learned languages, ancient authors, and speculative points of philosophy,—these objects were associated with others, which terrified the jealousy of modern Rome.

Sometime after, at Naples, appeared the two brothers, John Baptiste and John Vincent Porta, those twin spirits, the Castor and Pollux of the natural philosophy of that age, and whose scenical museum delighted and awed, by its optical illusions, its treasure of curiosities, and its natural magic, all learned natives and foreigners. Their names are still famous, and their treatises *De Humana Physiognomia* and *Magia Naturalis*, are still opened by the curious, who discover these children of philosophy wandering in the arcana of nature, to them a world of perpetual beginnings! These learned brothers united with the Marquis of Manso, the friend of Tasso, in establishing an academy under the whimsical name *degli Oziosi* (the Lazy), which so ill described their intentions. This academy did not sufficiently embrace the views of the learned brothers; and then they formed another under their own roof, which they appropriately named *degli Secreti*. The ostensible motive was, that no one should be admitted into this interior society who had not signalized himself by some experiment or discovery. It is clear that, whatever they intended by the project, the election of the members was to pass through the most rigid scrutiny; and what was the consequence? The court of Rome again started up with all its fears, and, secretly obtaining information of some discussions which had passed in this academy *degli Secreti*, prohibited the Portas from holding such assemblies, or applying themselves to those illicit sciences, whose amusements are criminal, and turn us aside from the study of the Holy Scriptures.* It seems that one of the Portas had delivered himself in the style of an ancient oracle; but what was more alarming in this prophetical spirit, several of his predictions had been actually verified! The infallible court was in no want of a new school of prophecy. Baptista Porta went to Rome to justify himself; and, content to wear his head, placed his tongue in the custody of his Holiness, and no doubt preferred being a member of the *Accademia degli Oziosi* to that *degli Secreti*. To confirm this notion that these academies excited the jealousy of those despotic states of Italy, I find that several of them at Florence, as well as at Sienna, were considered as dangerous meetings, and in 1568, the Medici suddenly suppressed those of the "Insipids," the "Shy," the "Disheartened," and others, but more particularly the "Stunned," *gli Intronati*, which excited loud laments. We have also an account of an academy which called itself the "Lanternists," from the circumstance that their first meetings were held at night, the academicians not carrying torches, but only *Lanterns*. This academy, indeed, was at Toulouse, but evidently formed on the model of its neighbours. In fine, it cannot be denied, that these literary societies or academies were frequently objects of alarm to the little governments of Italy, and were often interrupted by political persecution.

From all these facts I am inclined to draw an inference. It is

---

* Niceron, vol. xliii. *Art. Porta.*

remarkable that the first Italian academies were only distinguished by the simple name of their founders. One was called
the Academy of Pomponius Lætus, another of Panormita, &c. It
was after the melancholy fate of the Roman academy of Lætus,
which could not, however, extinguish that growing desire of
creating literary societies in the Italian cities, from which the
members derived both honour and pleasure, that suddenly we
discover these academies bearing the most fantastical titles. I
have not found any writer who has attempted to solve this extraordinary appearance in literary history; and the difficulty seems
great, because, however frivolous or fantastical the titles they
assumed, their members were illustrious for rank and genius.
Tiraboschi, aware of this difficulty, can only express his astonish-
ment at the absurdity, and his vexation at the ridicule to which
the Italians have been exposed by the coarse jokes of Menkenius,
in his *Charlatanaria Eruditorum.** I conjecture, that the invention of these ridiculous titles for literary societies, was an attempt to throw a sportive veil over meetings which had alarmed
the papal and the other petty courts of Italy; and to quiet their
fears and turn aside their political wrath, they implied the innocence of their pursuits by the jocularity with which the
members treated themselves, and were willing that others should
treat them. This otherwise inexplicable national levity, of so
refined a people, has not occurred in any other country, because
the necessity did not exist anywhere but in Italy. In France, in
Spain, and in England, the title of the ancient *Academus* was
never profaned by an adjunct which systematically degraded and
ridiculed its venerable character and its illustrious members.

Long after this article was finished, I had an opportunity of
consulting an eminent Italian, whose name is already celebrated
in our country, Il Sigr. Ugo Foscolo; his decision ought necessarily to outweigh mine; but although it is incumbent on me to
put the reader in possession of the opinion of a native of his
high acquirements, it is not as easy for me, on this obscure and
curious subject, to relinquish my own conjecture.

Il Sigr. Foscolo is of opinion, that the origin of the fantastical
titles assumed by the Italian Academies entirely arose from a
desire of getting rid of the air of pedantry, and to insinuate that

---

* See Tiraboschi, vol. vii. cap. 4, *Accademie,* and Quadrio's *Della Storia
e della Ragione d'ogni Poesia.* In the immense receptacle of these seven
quarto volumes, printed with a small type, the curious may consult the
voluminous Index, art. *Accademia.*

their meetings and their works were to be considered merely as sportive relaxations, and an idle business.

This opinion may satisfy an Italian, and this he may deem a sufficient apology for such absurdity; but when scarlet robes and cowled heads, laureated bards and *Monsignores*, and *Cavalleros*, baptize themselves in a public assembly "Blockheads" or "Madmen," we *ultramontanes*, out of mere compliment to such great and learned men, would suppose that they had their good reasons; and that in this there must have been "something more than meets the ear." After all, I would almost flatter myself that our two opinions are not so wide of each other as they at first seem to be.

Secret History of Authors Who Have Ruined Their Booksellers

AULUS GELLIUS desired to live no longer than he was able to exercise the faculty of writing; he might have decently added,— and of finding readers! This would be a fatal wish for that writer who should spread the infection of weariness, without himself partaking of the epidemic. The mere act and habit of writing, without probably even a remote view of publication, has produced an agreeable delirium; and perhaps some have escaped from a gentle confinement by having cautiously concealed those voluminous reveries which remained to startle their heirs; while others again have left a whole library of manuscripts, out of the mere ardour of transcription, collecting and copying with peculiar rapture. I discovered that one of these inscribed this distich on his manuscript collection:

> Plura voluminibus jungenda volumina nostris,
> Nec mihi scribendi terminus ullus erit:

which, not to compose better verses than our original, may be translated,

> More volumes with our volumes still shall blend;
> And to our writing there shall be no end!

But even great authors have sometimes so much indulged in the seduction of the pen, that they appear to have found no substitute for the flow of their ink, and the delight of stamping blank paper with their hints, sketches, ideas, the shadows of their mind! Petrarch exhibits no solitary instance of this passion of the pen. "I read and I write night and day; it is my only consolation. My eyes are heavy with watching, my hand is weary with writing. On the table where I dine, and by the side of my bed, I have all the materials for writing; and when I awake in the dark, I write, although I am unable to read the next morning what I have written." Petrarch was not always in his perfect senses.

The copiousness and the multiplicity of the writings of many authors, have shown that too many find a pleasure in the act of composition, which they do not communicate to others. Great erudition and every-day application is the calamity of that voluminous author, who, without good sense, and, what is more rare, without that exquisite judgment which we call good taste, is always prepared to write on any subject, but at the same time on no one reasonably. At the early period of printing, two of the most eminent printers were ruined by the volumes of one author; we have their petition to the pope to be saved from bankruptcy. Nicholas de Lyra had inveigled them to print his interminable commentary on the Bible. Their luckless star prevailed, and their warehouse groaned with eleven hundred ponderous folios, as immovable as the shelves on which they for ever reposed! We are astonished at the fertility and the size of our own writers of the seventeenth century, when the theological war of words raged, spoiling so many pages and brains. They produced folio after folio, like almanacs; and Dr. Owen and Baxter wrote more than sixty to seventy volumes, most of them of the most formidable size. The truth is, however, that it was then easier to write up to a folio, than in our days to write down to an octavo; for correction, selection, and rejection, were arts as yet unpractised. They went on with their work, sharply or bluntly, like witless mowers, without stopping to whet their scythes. They were inspired by the scribbling demon of that rabbin, who, in his oriental style and mania of volume, exclaimed that were "the heavens formed of paper, and were the trees of the earth pens, and if the entire sea run ink, these only could suffice" for the monstrous genius he was about to discharge on the world. The Spanish Tostatus wrote three times as many leaves as the number of days he had lived; and of Lope de Vega it is said this calculation came rather short. We hear of another, who was unhappy that his lady had produced twins, from the circumstance that hitherto he had contrived to pair his labours with her own, but that now he was a book behind-hand.

I fix on four celebrated *Scribleri* to give their secret history; our Prynne, Gaspar Barthius, the Abbé de Marolles, and the Jesuit Theophilus Raynaud, who will all show that a book might be written on "authors whose works have ruined their book-sellers."

Prynne seldom dined: every three or four hours he munched a manchet, and refreshed his exhausted spirits with ale brought to him by his servant; and when "he was put into this road of writing," as crabbed Anthony telleth, he fixed on "a long quilted cap, which came an inch over his eyes, serving as an umbrella to defend them from too much light"; and then hunger nor thirst did he experience, save that of his voluminous pages. Prynne has written a library amounting, I think, to nearly two hundred books. Our unlucky author, whose life was involved in authorship, and his happiness, no doubt, in the habitual exuber-ance of his pen, seems to have considered the being debarred from pen, ink, and books, during his imprisonment, as an act more barbarous than the loss of his ears. The extraordinary perseverance of Prynne in this fever of the pen appears in the following title of one of his extraordinary volumes. *Comfortable Cordials against discomfortable Fears of Imprisonment; contain-ing some Latin Verses, Sentences, and Texts of Scripture,* written by Mr. Wm. Prynne, on his Chamber Walls, *in the Tower of London, during his imprisonment there; translated by him into English Verse, 1641.* Prynne literally verified Pope's description;

> Is there, who locked from ink and paper, scrawls
> With desperate charcoal round his darkened walls.

We have also a catalogue of printed books, written by Wm. Prynne, Esq., of Lincoln's Inn, in these classes,

BEFORE
DURING
and   } *his imprisonment,*
SINCE

with this motto, "*Jucundi acti labores,*" 1643. The secret history of this voluminous author concludes with a characteristic event: a contemporary who saw Prynne in the pillory at Cheapside, in-forms us that while he stood there they "burnt his huge volumes under his nose, which had almost suffocated him." Yet such was the spirit of party, that a puritanic sister bequeathed a legacy to

purchase all the works of Prynne for Sion College, where many
still repose; for, by an odd fatality, in the fire which happened
in that library these volumes were saved, from the idea that
folios were the most valuable!

The pleasure which authors of this stamp experience is of a
nature, which, whenever certain unlucky circumstances combine,
positively debarring them from publication, will not abate their
ardour one jot; and their pen will still luxuriate in the forbidden page which even booksellers refuse to publish. Many instances might be recorded, but a very striking one is the case of
Gaspar Barthius, whose *Adversaria*, in two volumes folio, are in
the collections of the curious.

Barthius was born to literature, for Baillet has placed him
among his *"Enfans célèbres."* At nine years of age he recited by
heart all the comedies of Terence, without missing a line. The
learned admired the puerile prodigy, while the prodigy was
writing books before he had a beard. He became, unquestionably, a student of very extensive literature, modern as well as
ancient. Such was his devotion to a literary life, that he retreated
from the busy world. It appears that his early productions were
composed more carefully and judiciously than his latter ones,
when the passion for voluminous writing broke out, which
showed itself by the usual prognostic of this dangerous disease—
extreme facility of composition, and a pride and exultation in
this unhappy faculty. He studied without using collections or
references, trusting to his memory, which was probably an extraordinary one, though it necessarily led him into many errors in
that delicate task of animadverting on other authors. Writing a
very neat hand, his first copy required no transcript; and he
boasts that he rarely made a correction: every thing was sent to
the press in its first state. He laughs at Statius, who congratulated
himself that he employed only two days in composing the
epithalamium upon Stella, containing two hundred and seventy-
eight hexameters. "This," says Barthius, "did not quite lay him
open to Horace's censure of the man who made two hundred
verses in an hour, 'stans pede in uno.' Not," adds Barthius, "but
that I think the censure of Horace too hyperbolical, for I am not
ignorant what it is to make a great number of verses in a short
time, and in three days I translated into Latin the three first
books of the Iliad, which amount to above two thousand verses."
Thus rapidity and volume were the great enjoyments of this
learned man's pen, and now we must look to the fruits.

Barthius, on the system he had adopted, seems to have written a whole library; a circumstance which we discover by the continual references he makes in his printed works to his manuscript productions. In the *Index Authorum* to his *Statius*, he inserts his own name, to which is appended a long list of unprinted works, which Bayle thinks, by their titles and extracts, conveys a very advantageous notion of them. All these, and many such as these, he generously offered the world, would any bookseller be intrepid or courteous enough to usher them from his press; but their cowardice or incivility was intractable. The truth is now to be revealed, and seems not to have been known to Bayle; the booksellers had been formerly so cajoled and complimented by our learned author, and had heard so much of the celebrated Barthius, that they had caught at the bait, and that the two folio volumes of the much referred-to *Adversaria* of Barthius had thus been published—but from that day no bookseller ever offered himself to publish again!

The *Adversaria* is a collection of critical notes and quotations from ancient authors, with illustrations of their manners, customs, laws, and ceremonies; all these were to be classed into one hundred and eighty books; sixty of which we possess in two volumes folio, with eleven indexes. The plan is vast, as the rapidity with which it was pursued: Bayle finely characterizes it by a single stroke—"Its immensity tires even the imagination." But the truth is, this mighty labour turned out to be a complete failure: there was neither order nor judgment in these masses of learning; crude, obscure, and contradictory; such as we might expect from a man who trusted to his memory, and would not throw away his time on any correction. His contradictions are flagrant; but one of his friends would apologize for these by telling us that "He wrote every thing which offered itself to his imagination; to-day one thing, to-morrow another, in order that when he should revise it again, this contrariety of opinion might induce him to examine the subject more accurately." The notions of the friends of authors are as extravagant as those of their enemies. Barthius evidently wrote so much, that often he forgot what he had written, as happened to another great book-man, one Didymus, of whom Quintilian records, that on hearing a certain history, he treated it as utterly unworthy of credit; on which the teller called for one of Didymus's own books, and showed where he might read it at full length! That the work failed, we have the evidence of Clement in his *Bibliothèque curieuse de Livres difficiles à trouver*, under the article *Barthius*, where we discover the winding up of the history of this book.

Clement mentions more than one edition of the *Adversaria*; but on a more careful inspection he detected that the old title-pages had been removed for others of a fresher date; the booksellers not being able to sell the book practised this deception. It availed little; they remained with their unsold edition of the first two volumes of the *Adversaria*, and the author with three thousand folio sheets in manuscript—while both parties complained together, and their heirs could acquire nothing from the works of an author, of whom Bayle says that "his writings rise to such a prodigious bulk, that one can scarce conceive a single man could be capable of executing so great a variety; perhaps no copying clerk, who lived to grow old amidst the dust of an office, ever transcribed as much as this author has written." This was the memorable fate of one of that race of writers who imagine that their capacity extends with their volume. Their land seems covered with fertility, but in shaking their wheat no ears fall.

Another memorable brother of this family of the *Scribleri* is the Abbé de Marolles, who with great ardour as a man of letters, and in the enjoyment of the leisure and opulence so necessary to carry on his pursuits, from an entire absence of judgment, closed his life with the bitter regrets of a voluminous author; and yet it cannot be denied that he has contributed one precious volume to the public stock of literature; a compliment which cannot be paid to some who have enjoyed a higher reputation than our author. He has left us his very curious *Memoirs*. A poor writer indeed, but the frankness and intrepidity of his character enable him, while he is painting himself, to paint man. Gibbon was struck me so forcibly as when I observed his delinquencies dulness of Michael de Marolles and Anthony Wood* acquires some value from the faithful representation of men and manners."

I have elsewhere shortly noticed the Abbé de Marolles in the character of "a literary sinner"; but the extent of his sins never struck me so forcibly as when I observed his delinquencies counted up in chronological order in Niceron's *Hommes Illus-*

---

* I cannot subscribe to the opinion that Anthony Wood was a dull man, although he had no particular liking for works of imagination; and used ordinary poets scurvily! An author's personal character is often confounded with the nature of his work. Anthony has sallies at times to which a dull man could not be subject; without the ardour of this hermit of literature where would be our literary history?

tres. It is extremely amusing to detect the swarming fecundity of
his pen; from year to year, with author after author, was this
translator wearying others, but remained himself unwearied.
Sometimes two or three classical victims in a season were dragged
into his slaughter-house. Of about seventy works, fifty were
versions of the classical writers of antiquity, accompanied with
notes. But some odd circumstances happened to our extraordinary translator in the course of his life. De l'Etang, a critic of
that day, in his *Règles de bien traduire*, drew all his examples
of bad translation from our abbé, who was more angry than
usual, and among his circle the cries of our Marsyas resounded.
De l'Etang, who had done this not out of malice, but from
urgent necessity to illustrate his principles, seemed very sorry,
and was desirous of appeasing the angried translator. One day
in Easter, finding the abbé in church at prayers, the critic fell
on his knees by the side of the translator: it was an extraordinary moment, and a singular situation to terminate a literary
quarrel. "You are angry with me," said De l'Etang, "and I think
you have reason; but this is a season of mercy, and I now ask
your pardon."—"In the manner," replied the abbé "which you
have chosen, I can no longer defend myself. Go, sir! I pardon
you." Some days after, the abbé, again meeting De l'Etang, reproached him with duping him out of a pardon, which he had
no desire to have bestowed on him. The last reply of the critic
was caustic: "Do not be so difficult; when one stands in need of
a general pardon, one ought surely to grant a particular one."
De Marolles was subject to encounter critics who were never so
kind as to kneel by him on an Easter Sunday. Besides these
fifty translations, of which the notes are often curious, and even
the sense may be useful to consult, his love of writing produced
many odd works. His volumes were richly bound, and freely distributed, for they found no readers! In a *Discours pour servir de
Préface sur les Poëtes traduits par Michel de Marolles*, he has
given an imposing list of "illustrious persons and contemporary
authors who were his friends," and has preserved many singular
facts concerning them. He was, indeed, for so long a time convinced that he had struck off the true spirit of his fine originals,
that I find he at several times printed some critical treatise to
back his last, or usher in his new version; giving the world
reasons why the versions which had been given of that particular author, "*soit en prose, soit en vers, ont été si peu approuvées
jusqu'ici*." Among these numerous translations he was the first

who ventured on the *Deipnosophists* of Athenæus, which still bears an excessive price. He entitles his work, *Les quinze Livres de Deipnosophistes d'Athénée, Ouvrage délicieux, agréablement diversifié et rempli de Narrations, sçavantes sur toutes Sortes de Matières et de Sujets.* He has prefixed various preliminary dissertations; yet, not satisfied with having performed this great labour, it was followed by a small quarto of forty pages, which might now be considered curious; *Analyse, en Description succincte des Choses contenues dans les quinzes Livres de Deipnosophistes.* He wrote, *Quatrains sur les Personnes de la Cour et les Gens de Lettres,* which the curious would now be glad to find. After having plundered the classical geniuses of antiquity by his barbarous style, when he had nothing more left to do, he committed sacrilege in translating the Bible; but, in the midst of printing, he was suddenly stopped by authority, for having inserted in his notes the reveries of the Pre-Adamite Isaac Peyrère. He had already revelled on the New Testament, to his version of which he had prefixed so sensible an introduction, that it was afterwards translated into Latin. Translation was the mania of the Abbé de Marolles. I doubt whether he ever fairly awoke out of the heavy dream of the felicity of his translations; for late in life I find him observing, "I have employed much time in study, and I have translated many books; considering this rather as an innocent amusement which I have chosen for my private life, than as things very necessary, although they are not entirely useless. Some have valued them, and others have cared little about them; but however it may be, I see nothing which *obliges me to believe that they contain not at least as much good as bad,* both for their own matter and the form which I have given to them." The notion he entertained of his translations was their closeness; he was not aware of his own spiritless style; and he imagined that poetry only consisted in the thoughts, not in grace and harmony of verse. He insisted that by giving the public his numerous translations, he was not vainly multiplying books, because he neither diminished nor increased their ideas in his faithful versions. He had a curious notion that some were more scrupulous than they ought to be respecting translations of authors who, living so many ages past, are rarely read from the difficulty of understanding them; and why should they imagine that a translation is injurious to them, or would occasion the utter neglect of the originals? "We do not think so highly of our own works," says the indefatigable and modest Abbé; "but neither do I despair that they may be useful even to these scrupulous persons. I will not suppress the truth, while I am noticing these ungrateful labours; if they have given me much pain by my assiduity, they have repaid me by the fine things they have taught me, and by the opinion which I have conceived that posterity, more just than the present times, will award a more favourable judgment." Thus a miserable translator terminates his long labours, by drawing his bill of fame on posterity, which his contemporaries will not pay; but in these cases, as the bill is certainly lost before it reaches acceptance, why should we deprive the drawers of pleasing themselves with the ideal capital?

Let us not, however, imagine that the Abbé de Marolles was nothing but the man he appears in the character of a voluminous translator; though occupied all his life on these miserable labours, he was evidently an ingenious and nobly-minded man, whose days were consecrated to literary pursuits, and who was among the primitive collectors in Europe of fine and curious prints. One of his works is a *Catalogue des Livres d'Estampes et de Figures en Taille-douce*, Paris, 1666, in 8vo. In the preface our author declares, that he had collected one hundred and twenty-three thousand four hundred prints, of six thousand masters, in four hundred large volumes, and one hundred and twenty small ones. This magnificent collection, formed by so much care and skill, he presented to the king; whether gratuitously given or otherwise, it was an acquisition which a monarch might have thankfully accepted. Such was the habitual ardour of our author, that afterwards he set about forming another collection, of which he has also given a catalogue in 1672, in 12mo. Both these catalogues of prints are of extreme rarity, and are yet so highly valued by the connoisseurs, that when in France I could never obtain a copy. A long life may be passed without even a sight of the *Catalogue des Livres d'Estampes* of the Abbé de Marolles.*

Such are the lessons drawn from this secret history of voluminous writers. We see one venting his mania in scrawling on his

---

* These two catalogues have always been of extreme rarity and price. Dr. Lister, when at Paris, 1668, notices this circumstance. I have since met with them in the very curious collections of my friend, Mr. Douce, who has uniques, as well as rarities. The monograms of our old masters in one of these catalogues are more correct than in some later publications; and the whole plan and arrangement of these catalogues of prints are peculiar and interesting.

prison walls; another persisting in writing folios, while the
booksellers, who were once caught, like Reynard who had lost
his tail, and whom no arts could any longer practise on, turn
away from the new trap; and a third, who can acquire no
readers but by giving his books away, growing grey in scourging
the sacred genius of antiquity by his meagre versions, and dying
without having made up his mind, whether he were as woeful a
translator as some of his contemporaries had assured him.

Among these worthies of the *Scribleri* we may rank the Jesuit
Theophilus Raynaud, once a celebrated name, eulogized by
Bayle and Patin. His collected works fill twenty folios; an edition, indeed, which finally sent the bookseller to the poor-house.
This enterprising bibliopolist had heard much of the prodigious
erudition of the writer; but he had not the sagacity to discover
that other literary qualities were also required to make twenty
folios at all salable. Of these *Opera omnia* perhaps not a single
copy can be found in England; but they may be a pennyworth on
the continent. Raynaud's works are theological; but a system of
grace maintained by one work and pulled down by another, has
ceased to interest mankind: the literature of the divine is of a
less perishable nature. Reading and writing through a life of
eighty years, and giving only a quarter of an hour to his dinner,
with a vigorous memory, and a whimsical taste for some singular
subjects, he could not fail to accumulate a mass of knowledge
which may still be useful for the curious; and besides, Raynaud
had the Ritsonian characteristic. He was one of those who,
exemplary in their own conduct, with a bitter zeal condemn
whatever does not agree with their own notions; and, however
gentle in their nature, yet will set no limits to the ferocity of
their pen. Raynaud was often in trouble with the censors of his
books, and much more with his adversaries; so that he frequently
had recourse to publishing under a fictitious name. A remarkable
evidence of this is the entire twentieth volume of his works. It
consists of the numerous writings published anonymously, or to
which were prefixed *noms de guerre*. This volume is described by
the whimsical title of *Apopompæus*; explained to us as the name
given by the Jews to the scape-goat, which, when loaded with all
their maledictions on its head, was driven away into the desert.
These contain all Raynaud's numerous *diatribes*; for whenever
he was refuted, he was always refuting; he did not spare his best
friends. The title of a work against Arnauld will show how he
treated his adversaries. *Arnauldus redivivus natus Brixiæ seculo
xii. renatus in Galliæ ætate nostra.* He dexterously applies the

name of Arnauld by comparing him with one of the same name in the twelfth century, a scholar of Abelard's, and a turbulent enthusiast, say the Romish writers, who was burnt alive for having written against the luxury and the power of the priesthood, and for having raised a rebellion against the pope. When the learned De Launoi had successfully attacked the legends of saints, and was called the *Dénicheur de Saints,*—the "Unnicher of Saints,"—every parish priest trembled for his favourite. Raynaud entitled a libel on this new iconoclast, *Hercules Commodianus Joannes Launoius repulsus, &c.*; he compares Launoi to the Emperor Commodus, who, though the most cowardly of men, conceived himself formidable when he dressed himself as Hercules. Another of these maledictions is a tract against Calvinism, described as a *religio bestiarum*, a religion of beasts, because the Calvinists deny free-will; but as he always fired with a double-barrelled gun, under the cloak of attacking Calvinism, he aimed a deadly shot at the Thomists, and particularly at a Dominican friar, whom he considered as bad as Calvin. Raynaud exults that he had driven one of his adversaries to take flight into Scotland, *ad pultes Scoticas transgressus*—to a Scotch pottage; an expression which Saint Jerome used in speaking of Pelagius. He always rendered an adversary odious by coupling him with some odious name. On one of these controversial books where Casalas refuted Raynaud, Monnoye wrote, "*Raynaudus et Casalas inepti; Raynaudo tamen Casalas ineptior.*" The usual termination of what then passed for sense, and now is the reverse.

I will not quit Raynaud without pointing out some of his more remarkable treatises, as so many curiosities of literature.

In a treatise on the attributes of Christ, he entitles a chapter, *Christus, bonus, bona, bonum*: in another on the seven-branched candlestick in the Jewish temple, by an allegorical interpretation, he explains the eucharist; and adds an alphabetical list of names and epithets which have been given to this mystery.

The seventh volume bears the title of *Mariolia*: all the treatises have for their theme the perfections and the worship of the Virgin. Many extraordinary things are here. One is a dictionary of names given to the Virgin, with observations on these names. Another on the devotion of the scapulary, and its wonderful effects, written against De Launoi, and for which the order of the Carmes, when he died, bestowed a solemn service and obsequies on him. Another of these *Mariolia* is mentioned by Gallois in the *Journal des Sçavans*, 1667, as a proof of his fertility; having to preach on the seven solemn anthems which the church sings before Christmas, and which begin by an O! he made this *letter only* the subject of his sermons, and barren as the letter appears, he has struck out "a multitude of beautiful particulars." This literary folly invites our curiosity.

In the eighth volume is a table of saints, classed by their station, condition, employment, and trades: a list of titles and prerogatives, which the councils and the fathers have attributed to the sovereign pontiff.

The thirteenth volume has a subject which seems much in the taste of the sermons on the letter O! it is entitled *Laus Brevitatis!* in praise of brevity. The maxims are brief, but the commentary long. One of the *natural* subjects treated on is that of *Noses*: he reviews a great number of noses, and, as usual, does not forget the Holy Virgin's. According to Raynaud, the nose of the Virgin Mary was long and aquiline, the mark of goodness and dignity; and as Jesus perfectly resembled his mother, he infers that he must have had such a nose.

A treatise entitled *Heteroclita spiritualia et anomala Pietatis Cœlestium, Terrestrium et Infernorum,* contains many singular practices introduced into devotion, which superstition, ignorance, and remissness, have made a part of religion.

A treatise directed against the new custom of hiring chairs in churches, and being seated during the sacrifice of the mass. Another on the Cæsarean operation, which he stigmatizes as an act against nature. Another on eunuchs. Another entitled *Hipparchus de Religioso Negotiatore,* is an attack on those of his own company, the monk turned merchant; the Jesuits were then accused of commercial traffic with the revenues of their establishment. The rector of a college at Avignon, who thought he was portrayed in this honest work, confined Raynaud in prison for five months.

The most curious work of Raynaud connected with literature, I possess; it is entitled *Erotemata de malis ac bonis Libris, deque justa aut injusta eorundem confixione. Lugduni,* 1653, 4to. with necessary indexes. One of his works having been condemned at Rome, he drew up these inquiries concerning good and bad books, addressed to the grand inquisitor. He divides his treatise into "bad and nocent books; bad books but not nocent; books not bad, but nocent; books neither bad nor nocent." His immense reading appears here to advantage, and his Ritsonian feature is prominent; for he asserts, that when writing against heretics all mordacity is innoxious; and an alphabetical list of abusive names, which the fathers have given to the heterodox, is entitled *Alphabetum bestialitatis Hæretici, ex Patrum Symbolis.*

After all, Raynaud was a man of vast acquirement, with a great flow of ideas, but tasteless, and void of all judgment. An anecdote may be recorded of him, which puts in a clear light the state of these literary men. Raynaud was one day pressing hard a reluctant bookseller to publish one of his works, who replied, "Write a book like Father Barri's, and I shall be glad to print it." It happened that the work of Barri was pillaged from Raynaud, and was much liked, while the original lay on the shelf. However, this only served to provoke a fresh attack from our redoubtable hero, who vindicated his rights, and emptied his quiver on him who had been ploughing with his heifer.

Such are the writers who, enjoying all the pleasures without the pains of composition, have often apologized for their repeated productions, by declaring that they write only for their own amusement; but such private theatricals should not be brought on the public stage. One Catherinot all his life was printing a countless number of *feuilles volantes* in history and on antiquities; each consisting of about three or four leaves in quarto: Lenglet du Fresnoy calls him *"grand auteur des petits livres."* This gentleman liked to live among antiquaries and historians; but with a crooked head-piece, stuck with whims, and hard with knotty combinations, all overloaded with prodigious erudition, he could not ease it at a less rate than by an occasional dissertation of three or four quarto pages. He appears to have published about two hundred pieces of this sort, much sought after by the curious for their rarity: Brunet complains he could never discover a complete collection. But Catherinot may escape "the pains and penalties" of our voluminous writers, for De Bure thinks he generously printed them to distribute among his friends. Such endless writers, provided they do not print themselves into an alms-house, may be allowed to print themselves out; and we would accept the apology which Monsieur Catherinot has framed for himself, which I find preserved in *Beyeri Memoriæ Librorum Rariorum.* "I must be allowed my freedom in my studies, for I substitute my writings for a game at the tennis-court, or a club at the tavern; I never counted among my honours these *opuscula* of mine, but merely as harmless amusements. It is my partridge, as with St. John the Evangelist; my cat, as with Pope St. Gregory; my little dog, as with St. Dominick; my lamb, as with St. Francis; my great black mastiff, as with Cornelius Agrippa; and my tame hare, as with Justus Lipsius." I have since discovered in Niceron that this Catherinot could never get a printer, and was rather compelled to study economy in his two hundred quartos of four or eight pages: his paper was of inferior quality; and when he could not get his dissertations into his prescribed number of pages, he used to promise the end at another time, which did not always happen. But his greatest anxiety was to publish and spread his works; in despair he adopted an odd expedient. Whenever Monsieur Catherinot came to Paris, he used to haunt the *quais* where books are sold, and while he appeared to be looking over them, he adroitly slided one of his own dissertations among these old books. He began this mode of publication early, and continued it to his last days. He died with a perfect conviction that he had secured his immortality; and in this manner had disposed of more than one edition of his unsalable works. Niceron has given the titles of 118 of his things, which he had looked over.

History of New Words

NEOLOGY, or the novelty of words and phrases, is an innovation, which, with the opulence of our present language, the English philologer is most jealous to allow; but we have puritans or precisians of English, superstitiously nice! The fantastic coinage of affectation or caprice will cease to circulate, from its own alloy; but shall we reject the ore of fine workmanship and solid weight? There is no government mint of words, and it is no statutable offence to invent a felicitous or daring expression unauthorized by Mr. Todd! When a man of genius, in the heat of his pursuits or his feelings, has thrown out a peculiar word, it probably conveyed more precision or energy than any other established word, otherwise he is but an ignorant pretender!

Julius Cæsar, who, unlike other great captains, is authority on words as well as about blows, wrote a large treatise on *Analogy*, in which that fine genius counselled to "avoid every unusual word as a rock!"* The cautious Quintilian, as might be expected, opposes all innovation in language. "If the new word is well received, small is the glory; if rejected, it raises laughter."†

---

* *Aulus Gellius*, lib. i. c. 10.
† *Instit.* lib. i. c. 5.

This only marks the penury of his feelings in this species of adventure! The great legislator of words, who lived when his own language was at its acme, seems undecided, yet pleaded for this liberty. "Shall that which the Romans allowed to Cæcilius and to Plautus be refused to Virgil and Varius?" The answer to the question might not be favourable to the inquirer. While a language is forming, writers are applauded for extending its limits; when established, for restricting themselves to them. But this is to imagine that a perfect language can exist! The good sense and observation of Horace perceived that there may be occasions where necessity must become the mother of invented words:—

> Si forte necesse est
> Indiciis monstrare recentibus abdita rerum.

> If you write of things abstruse or new,
> Some of your own inventing may be used,
> So it be seldom and discreetly done.
>
> ROSCOMMON

But Horace's canon for deciding on the legality of the new invention, or the standard by which it is to be tried, will not serve to assist the inventor of words:—

> licuit, semperque licebit,
> Signatum præsente nota procudere nummum.*

This *præsens nota*, or public stamp, can never be affixed to any new coinage of words; for many received at a season have perished with it. The privilege of stamping words is reserved for their greatest enemy—Time itself! and the inventor of a new word must never flatter himself that he has secured the public adoption, for he must lie in his grave before he can enter the dictionary.

In Willes's address to the reader, prefixed to the collection of voyages published in 1577, he finds fault with Eden's translation from Peter Martyr, for using words that "smelt too much of the Latine." We should scarcely have expected to find among them *ponderouse, portentouse, despicable, obsequious, homicide, imbibed, destructive, prodigious.* The only words he quotes, not thoroughly naturalized, are *dominators, ditionaries* (subjects), *solicitute* (careful).

The Tatler, No. 230, introduces several polysyllables intro-

---

* This verse was corrected by Bentley *procudere nummum*, instead of *producere nomen*, which the critics agree is one of his happy conjectures.

duced by military narrations, "which (he says), if they attack us too frequently, we shall certainly put them to flight, and cut off the rear"; every one of them still keep their ground.

Half the French words used affectedly by Melantha, in Dryden's *Marriage à-la-mode*, as innovations in our language, are now in common use, *naïveté, foible, chagrin, grimace, embarras, double entendre, equivoque, eclaircissement, ridicule,* all these words, which she learns by heart to use occasionally, are now in common use. A Dr. Russel called Psalm-singers *Ballad-singers,* having found the Song of Solomon in an old translation, the *Ballad of Ballads,* for which he is reproached by his antagonist for not knowing that the signification of words alters with time; should I call him *knave,* he ought not to be concerned at it, for the Apostle Paul is also called *a knave of Jesus Christ.*

Unquestionably, NEOLOGY opens a wide door to innovation; scarcely has a century passed since our language was patched up with Gallic idioms, as in the preceding century it was piebald with Spanish, and with Italian, and even with Dutch. The political intercourse of islanders with their neighbours has ever influenced their language. In Elizabeth's reign Italian phrases and Netherland words were imported; in James and Charles the Spanish framed the style of courtesy; in Charles the Second the nation and the language were equally Frenchified. Yet such are the sources whence we have often derived some of the wealth of our language!

There are three foul corruptors of a language: caprice, affectations, and ignorance! Such fashionable cant terms as "theatricals," and "musicals," invented by the flippant Topham, still survive among his confraternity of frivolity. A lady eminent for the elegance of her taste, and of whom one of the best judges, the celebrated Miss Edgeworth, observed to me, that she spoke the purest and most idiomatic English she had ever heard, threw out an observation which might be extended to a great deal of our present fashionable vocabulary. She is now old enough, she said, to have lived to hear the vulgarisms of her youth adopted in drawing-room circles. To *lunch,* now so familiar from the fairest lips, in her youth was only known in the servants' hall. An expression very rife of late among our young ladies, *a nice man,* whatever it may mean, whether that the man resemble a pudding or something more nice, conveys the offensive notion that they are ready to eat him up! When I was a boy, it was an age of *bon ton;* this *good tone* mysteriously conveyed a sublime idea of fashion; the term, imported late in the eighteenth century, closed with it. *Twaddle* for a while succeeded *bore*; but *bore* has recovered the supremacy. We want another Swift to give a new edition of his *Polite Conversation*. A dictionary of barbarisms too might be collected from some wretched neologists, whose pens are now at work! Lord Chesterfield, in his exhortations to conform to Johnson's *Dictionary*, was desirous, however, that the great lexicographer should add as an appendix, *"A neological dictionary*, containing those polite, though perhaps not strictly grammatical, words and phrases commonly used, and sometimes understood by the *beau-monde*." This last phrase was doubtless a contribution! Such a dictionary had already appeared in the French language, drawn up by two caustic critics, who, in the *Dictionnaire néologique à l'usage des beaux Esprits du Siècle*, collected together the numerous unlucky inventions of affectation, with their modern authorities! A collection of the fine words and phrases, culled from some very modern poetry, might show the real amount of the favours bestowed on us.

The attempts of neologists are, however, not necessarily to be condemned; and we may join with the commentators of Aulus Gellius, who have lamented the loss of a chapter of which the title only has descended to us. That chapter would have demonstrated what happens to all languages, that some neologisms, which at first are considered forced or inelegant, become sanctioned by use, and in time are quoted as authority in the very language which, in their early stage, they were imagined to have debased.

The true history of men's minds is found in their actions; their wants are indicated by their contrivances; and certain it is that in highly cultivated ages we discover the most refined intellects attempting NEOLOGISMS. It would be a subject of great curiosity to trace the origin of many happy expressions, when, and by whom created. Plato substituted the term *Providence* for *fate*; and a new system of human affairs arose from a single word. Cicero invented several; to this philosopher we owe the term of *moral* philosophy, which before his time was called the philosophy of *manners*. But on this subject we are perhaps more interested by the modern than by the ancient languages. Richardson, the painter of the human heart, has coined some expressions to indicate its little secret movements, which are admirable: that great genius merited a higher education and more literary leisure than the life of a printer could afford. Montaigne created some bold expressions, many of which have not survived him; his *incuriosité*, so opposite to curiosity, well describes that state of negligence where we will not learn that of which we are ignorant. With us the word *incurious* was described by Heylin, 1656, as an unusual word; it has been appropriately adopted by our best writers; although we still want *incuriosity*. Charron invented *étrangeté* unsuccessfully, but which, says a French critic, would be the true substantive of the word *étrange*; our Locke is the solitary instance produced for "foreignness" for "remoteness or want of relation to something." Malherbe borrowed from the Latin, *insidieux, sécurité,* which have been received; but a bolder word, *dévouloir,* by which he proposed to express *cesser de vouloir,* has not. A term, however, expressive and precise. Corneille happily introduced *invaincu* in a verse in *The Cid,*

> Vous êtes *invaincu,* mais non pas *invincible.*

Yet this created word by their great poet has not sanctioned this fine distinction among the French, for we are told that it is almost a solitary instance. Balzac was a great inventor of neologisms. *Urbanité* and *féliciter* were struck in his mint. "*Si le mot* féliciter *n'est pas française, il le sera l'année qui vient*"; so confidently proud was the neologist, and it prospered as well as *urbanité,* of which he says, "*Quand l'usage aura mûri parmi nous un mot de si mauvais goût, et corrigé* l'amertume de la nouveauté *qui s'y peut trouver, nous nous y accoutumerons comme aux autres que nous avons emprunté de la même langue.*" Balzac was, however, too sanguine in some other words; for his *délecter,* his *sériosité,* &c. still retain their "bitterness of novelty."

Menage invented a term of which an equivalent is wanting in our language; "*J'ai fait* prosateur *à l'imitation de l'italien* prosatore, *pour dire un homme qui écrit en prose.*" To distinguish a prose from a verse writer, we *once* had "a proser." Drayton uses it; but this useful distinction has unluckily degenerated, and the current sense is so daily urgent, that the purer sense is irrecoverable.

When D'Albancourt was translating Lucian, he invented in French the words *indolence* and *indolent,* to describe a momentary languor, rather than that habitual indolence, in which sense they are now accepted; and in translating Tacitus, he created the word *turbulemment;* but it did not prosper, any more than that of *temporisement.* Segrais invented the word *impardonnable,* which, after having been rejected, was revived, and is equivalent to our expressive *unpardonable.* Molière ridiculed some neologisms of the *Précieuses* of his day; but we are too apt to ridicule that which is new, and which we often adopt when it becomes old. Molière laughed at the term *s'encanailler*, to describe one who assumed the manners of a blackguard; the expressive word has remained in the language. The meaning is disputed as well as the origin is lost of some novel terms. This has happened to a word in daily use—*Fudge!* It is a cant term not in Grose, and only traced by Todd not higher than to Goldsmith. It is however no invention of his. In a pamphlet, entitled *Remarks upon the Navy, 1700*, the term is declared to have been the name of a certain nautical personage who had lived in the lifetime of the writer. "There was, sir, in our time, one *Captain Fudge*, commander of a merchant-man, who upon his return from a voyage, how ill-fraught soever his ship was, always brought home his owners a good cargo of lies; so much that now, aboard ship, the sailors, when they hear a great lie told, cry out, 'You *fudge* it!'" It is singular that such an obscure by-word among sailors, should have become one of the most popular in our familiar style; and not less, that recently at the bar, in a court of law, its precise meaning perplexed plaintiff and defendant and their counsel. I think it does not signify mere lies, but bouncing lies, or rhodomontades.

There are two remarkable French words created by the Abbé de Saint Pierre, who passed his meritorious life in the contemplation of political morality and universal benevolence—*bienfaisance* and *gloriole*. He invented *gloriole* as a contemptuous diminutive of *glorie*; to describe that vanity of some egotists, so proud of the small talents which they may have received from nature or from accident. *Bienfaisance* first appeared in this sentence: "*L'Esprit de la vraie religion et le principal but de l'évangile c'est la bienfaisance, c'est-à-dire la pratique de la charité envers le prochain.*" This word was so new, that in the moment of its creation this good man explained its necessity and origin. Complaining that "the word 'charity' is abused by all sorts of Christians in the persecution of their enemies, and even heretics affirm that they are practising Christian charity in persecuting other heretics, I have sought for a term which might convey to us a precise idea of doing good to our neighbours, and I can form none more proper to make myself understood than the term of *bienfaisance*, good-doing. Let those who like, use it; I would only be understood, and it is not equivocal." The happy word was at first criticized, but at length every kind heart found it responded to its own feeling. Some verses from Voltaire, alluding to the political reveries of the good abbé, notice the critical opposition; yet the new word answered to the great rule of Horace.

> Certain législateur, dont la plume féconde
> Fit tant de vains projets pour le bien du monde,
> Et qui depuis trente ans écrit pour des ingrats,
> Vient de créer un mot qui manque à Vaugelas:
> Ce mot est BIENFAISANCE; il me plaît, il rassemble
> Si le cœur en est cru, bien des vertus ensemble.
> Petits grammairiens, grands précepteurs de sots,
> Qui pesez la parole et mesurez les mots,
> Pareille expression vous semble hazardée,
> Mais l'univers entier doit en chérir l'idée!

The French revolutionists, in their rage for innovation, almost barbarized the pure French of the Augustan age of their literature, as they did many things which never before occurred; and sometimes experienced feelings as transitory as they were strange. Their nomenclature was copious; but the revolutionary jargon often shows the danger and the necessity of neologisms. They form an appendix to the Academy *Dictionary*. Our plain English has served to enrich this odd mixture of philology and politics: *Club, clubiste, comité, juré, juge de paix,* blend with their *terrorisme, lanterner,* a verb active, *levée en masse, noyades,* and the other verb active *septembriser,* &c. The barbarous term *démoralisation* is said to have been the invention of the horrid Capuchin Chabot; and the remarkable expression of *arrière pensée* belonged exclusively in its birth to the jesuitic astuteness of the Abbé Sieyes, that political actor, who, in changing sides, never required prompting in his new part!

A new word, the result of much consideration with its author, or a term which, though unknown to the language, conveys a collective assemblage of ideas by a fortunate designation, is a precious contribution of genius; new words should convey new ideas. Swift, living amidst a civil war of pamphlets, when certain writers were regularly employed by one party to draw up replies to the other, created a term not to be found in our dictionaries, but which, by a single stroke, characterizes these hirelings; he called them *answer-jobbers.* We have not dropped the fortunate expression from any want of its use, but of perception in our lexicographers. The celebrated Marquis of Lansdowne introduced a useful word, which has of late been warmly adopted in France as well as in England—*to liberalise;* the noun has been drawn out of the verb—for in the marquis's time, that was only an abstract conception which is now a sect; and *to liberalise* was theoretically introduced before the *liberals* arose.* It is curious to observe that as an adjective it had formerly in our language a very opposite meaning to its recent one. It was synonymous with "libertine or licentious"; we have "a *liberal* villain" and "a most profane and *liberal* counsellor"; we find one declaring "I have spoken *too liberally*." This is unlucky for the *liberals*, who will not—

> Give allowance to our *liberal* jests
> Upon their persons—
> BEAUMONT AND FLETCHER

Dr. Priestley employed a forcible, but not an elegant term, to mark the general information which had begun in his day; this he frequently calls "the *spread* of knowledge." Burke attempted to brand with a new name that set of pert, petulant, sophistical sciolists, whose philosophy the French, since their revolutionary period, have distinguished as *philosophism*, and the philosophers themselves as *philosophistes*. He would have designated them as *literators*, but few exotic words will circulate; new words must be the coinage of our own language to blend with the vernacular idiom. Many new words are still wanted. We have no word by which we could translate the *otium* of the Latins, the *dilettante* of the Italians, the *alembiqué* of the French, as an epithet to describe that sublimated ingenuity which exhausts the mind, till, like the fusion of the diamond, the intellect itself disappears. A philosopher, in an extensive view of a subject in all its bearings, may convey to us the result of his last considerations, by the coinage of a novel and significant expression as this of Professor Dugald Stewart—*political religionism*. Let me claim the honour of one pure neologism. I ventured to introduce the term of FATHER-LAND to describe our *natale solum*; I have lived to see it adopted by Lord Byron and by Mr. Southey, and the word is now common. A lady has even composed both the words and the air of a song on "Father-land." This energetic expression may therefore be considered as authenticated; and patriotism may stamp it with its glory and its affection. FATHER-LAND is congenial with the language in which we find that other fine expression MOTHER-TONGUE. The patriotic neologism originated with me in

---

* The *Quarterly Review* recently marked the word *liberalise* in Italics, as a strange word, undoubtedly not aware of its origin. It has been lately used by Mr. Dugald Stewart, "to *liberalise* the views." *Dissert.* 2d part, p. 138.

Holland, when, in early life, it was my daily pursuit to turn over the glorious history of its independence under the title of *Vaderlandsche Historie*—the history of FATHER-LAND!

If we acknowledge that the creation of some neologisms may sometimes produce the beautiful, the revival of the dead is the more authentic miracle; for a new word must long remain doubtful, but an ancient word happily recovered rests on a basis of permanent strength; it has both novelty and authority. A collection of *picturesque words*, found among our ancient writers, would constitute a precious supplement to the history of our language. Far more expressive than our term of *executioner* is their solemn one of the *deathsman*; than our *vagabond*, their *scatterling*; than our *idiot* or *lunatic*, their *moonling*,—a word which, Mr. Gifford observes, should not have been suffered to grow obsolete. Herrick finely describes by the term *pittering* the peculiar shrill and short cry of the grasshopper: the cry of the grasshopper, is pit! pit! pit! quickly repeated. Envy *"dusking the lustre"* of genius is a verb lost for us, but which gives a more precise expression to the feeling than any other words which we could use.

The late Dr. Boucher, in the prospectus of his proposed *Dictionary*, did me the honour, then a young writer, to quote an opinion I had formed early in life of the purest source of neology, which is in the *revival of old words*.

Words, that wise Bacon or brave Rawleigh spake!

We have lost many exquisite and picturesque expressions through the dulness of our lexicographers, or by their deficiency in that profounder study of our writers which their labours require far more than they themselves know. The natural graces of our language have been impoverished. The genius that throws its prophetic eye over the language, and the taste that must come from Heaven, no lexicographer imagines are required to accompany him amidst a library of old books!

The Philosophy of Proverbs

IN ANTIQUE furniture we sometimes discover a convenience which long disuse had made us unacquainted with, and are surprised by the aptness which we did not suspect was concealed in its solid forms. We have found the labour of the workmen to have been as admirable as the material itself, which is still resisting the mouldering touch of time among those modern inventions, elegant and unsubstantial, which, often put together with un-seasoned wood, are apt to warp and fly into pieces when brought into use. We have found how strength consists in the selection of materials, and that, whenever the substitute is not better than the original, we are losing something in that test of experience, which all things derive from duration.

Be this as it may! I shall not unreasonably await for the artists of our novelties to retrograde into massive greatness, al-though I cannot avoid reminding them how often they revive the forgotten things of past times! It is well known that many of our novelties were in use by our ancestors! In the history of the human mind there is, indeed, a sort of antique furniture which I collect, not merely for their antiquity, but for the sound con-dition in which I still find them, and the compactness which they still show. Centuries have not worm-eaten their solidity! and the utility and delightfulness which they still afford make them look as fresh and as ingenious as any of our patent inven-tions.

By the title of the present article the reader has anticipated the nature of the old furniture to which I allude. I propose to give what, in the style of our times, may be called the Philosophy of Proverbs—a topic which seems virgin. The act of reading proverbs has not, indeed, always been acquired even by some of their admirers; but my observations, like their subject, must be versatile and unconnected; and I must bespeak indulgence for an attempt to illustrate a very curious branch of literature, rather not understood than quite forgotten.

Proverbs have long been in disuse. "A man of fashion," observes Lord Chesterfield, "never has recourse to proverbs and vulgar aphorisms"; and, since the time his lordship so solemnly interdicted their use, they appear to have withered away under the ban of his anathema. His lordship was little conversant with the history of proverbs, and would unquestionably have smiled on those "men of fashion" of another stamp, who, in the days of Elizabeth, James, and Charles, were great collectors of them; would appeal to them in their conversations, and enforce them in their learned or their statesmanlike correspondence. Few, per-haps, even now suspect that these neglected fragments of wisdom, which exist among all nations, still offer many interesting ob-jects for the studies of the philosopher and the historian; and for men of the world still open an extensive school of human life and manners.

The homespun adages, and the rusty "sayed-saws," which remain in the mouths of the people, are adapted to their capacities and their humours. Easily remembered, and readily applied, these are the philosophy of the vulgar, and often more sound than that of their masters! whoever would learn what the people think, and how they feel, must not reject even these as insignificant. The proverbs of the street and of the market, true to nature, and lasting only because they are true, are records that the populace at Athens and at Rome were the same people as at Paris and at London, and as they had before been in the city of Jerusalem!

Proverbs existed before books. The Spaniards date the origin of their *refranes que dicen las viejas tras el fuego,* "sayings of old wives by their firesides," before the existence of any writings in their language, from the circumstance that these are in the old romance or rudest vulgar idiom. The most ancient poem in the *Edda,* "the sublime speech of Odin," abounds with ancient proverbs, strikingly descriptive of the ancient Scandinavians. Undoubtedly proverbs in the earliest ages long served as the unwritten language of morality, and even of the useful arts; like the oral traditions of the Jews, they floated down from age to age on the lips of successive generations. The name of the first sage who sanctioned the saying would in time be forgotten, while the opinion, the metaphor, or the expression, remained, consecrated into a proverb! Such was the origin of those memorable sentences by which men learnt to think and to speak appositely; they were precepts which no man could contradict, at a time when authority was valued more than opinion, and experience preferred to novelty. The proverbs of a father became the inheritance of a son; the mistress of a family perpetuated hers through her household; the workman condensed some traditional secret of his craft into a proverbial expression. When countries are not yet populous, and property has not yet produced great inequalities in its ranks, every day will show them how "the drunkard and the glutton come to poverty, and drowsiness clothes a man with rags." At such a period he who gave counsel gave wealth.

It might therefore have been decided, *à priori,* that the most homely proverbs would abound in the most ancient writers—and such we find in Hesiod; a poet whose learning was not drawn from books. It could only have been in the agricultural state

that this venerable bard could have indicated a state of repose by
this rustic proverb:—

Πηδάλιον μὲν ὑπὲρ καπνοῦ καταδεῖο,

Hang your plough-beam o'er the hearth!

The envy of rival workmen is as justly described by a reference
to the humble manufacturers of earthenware as by the elevated
jealousies of the literati and the artists of a more polished age.
The famous proverbial verse in Hesiod's *Works and Days*—

Καὶ κεραμεὺς κεραμεῖ κοτέει,

is literally, "The potter is hostile to the potter!"

The admonition of the poet to his brother, to prefer a
friendly accommodation to a litigious lawsuit, has fixed a para-
doxical proverb often applied,—

Πλέον ἥμισυ παντός,

The half is better than the whole!

In the progress of time, the stock of popular proverbs received
accessions from the highest sources of human intelligence; as the
philosophers of antiquity formed their collections, they increased
in "weight and number." Erasmus has pointed out some of these
sources, in the responses of oracles; the allegorical symbols of
Pythagoras; the verses of the poets; allusions to historical incidents; mythology and apologue; and other recondite origins.
Such dissimilar matters, coming from all quarters, were melted
down into this vast body of aphoristic knowledge. Those "WORDS
OF THE WISE and their DARK SAYINGS," as they are distinguished in
that large collection which bears the name of the great Hebrew
monarch, at length seem to have required commentaries; for
what else can we infer of the enigmatic wisdom of the sages,
when the royal parœmiographer classes among their studies, that
of "*understanding a proverb and the interpretation*"? This elevated notion of "the dark sayings of the wise" accords with the
bold conjecture of their origin which the Stagyrite has thrown
out, who considered them as the wrecks of an ancient philosophy
which had been lost to mankind by the fatal revolutions of all
human things, and that those had been saved from the general
ruin by their pithy elegance and their diminutive form; like
those marine shells found on the tops of mountains, the relics of
the Deluge! Even at a later period, the sage of Cheronea prized
them among the most solemn mysteries; and Plutarch has described them in a manner which proverbs may even still merit:

"Under the veil of these curious sentences are hid those germs of morals which the masters of philosophy have afterwards developed into so many volumes."

At the highest period of Grecian genius, the tragic and the comic poets introduced into their dramas the proverbial style. St. Paul quotes a line which still remains among the first exercises of our school-pens:—

> Evil communications corrupt good manners.

It is a verse found in a fragment of Menander the comic poet:

$$\Phi\vartheta\epsilon\acute{\iota}\rho o\upsilon\sigma\iota\upsilon\ \mathring{\eta}\vartheta\eta\ \chi\rho\acute{\eta}\sigma\vartheta'\ \acute{o}\mu\iota\lambda\acute{\iota}\alpha\iota\ \kappa\alpha\kappa\alpha\acute{\iota}.$$

As this verse is a proverb, and the apostle, and indeed the highest authority, Jesus himself, consecrates the use of proverbs by their occasional application, it is uncertain whether St. Paul quotes the Grecian poet, or only repeats some popular adage. Proverbs were bright shafts in the Greek and Latin quivers; and when Bentley, by a league of superficial wits, was accused of pedantry for his use of some ancient proverbs, the sturdy critic vindicated his taste by showing that Cicero constantly introduced Greek proverbs into his writings,—that Scaliger and Erasmus loved them, and had formed collections drawn from the stores of antiquity.

Some difficulty has occurred in the definition. Proverbs must be distinguished from proverbial phrases, and from sententious maxims; but as proverbs have many faces, from their miscellaneous nature, the class itself scarcely admits of any definition. When Johnson defined a proverb to be "a short sentence frequently repeated by the people," this definition would not include the most curious ones, which have not always circulated among the populace, nor even belong to them; nor does it designate the vital qualities of a proverb. The pithy quaintness of old Howell has admirably described the ingredients of an exquisite proverb to be *sense, shortness, and salt*. A proverb is distinguished from a maxim or an apophthegm, by that brevity which condenses a thought or a metaphor, where one thing is said and another is to be applied. This often produces wit, and that quick pungency which excites surprise, but strikes with conviction; this gives it an epigrammatic turn. George Herbert entitled the small collection which he formed *Jacula Prudentium*, Darts or Javelins! something hurled and striking deeply; a characteristic of a proverb which possibly Herbert may have borrowed from a remarkable passage in Plato's dialogue of *Protagoras or the Sophists.*

The influence of proverbs over the minds and conversations of a whole people is strikingly illustrated by this philosopher's explanation of the term *to laconize,*—the mode of speech peculiar to the Lacedæmonians. This people affected to appear *unlearned,* and seemed only emulous to excel the rest of the Greeks in fortitude and in military skill. According to Plato's notion, this was really a political artifice, with a view to conceal their preëminent wisdom. With the jealousy of a petty state, they attempted to confine their renowned sagacity within themselves, and under their military to hide their contemplative character! The philosopher assures those who in other cities imagined they *laconized,* merely by imitating the severe exercises and the other warlike manners of the Lacedæmonians, that they were grossly deceived; and thus curiously describes the sort of wisdom which this singular people practised.

"If any one wish to converse with the meanest of the Lacedæmonians, he will at first find him, for the most part, apparently despicable in conversation; but afterwards, when a proper opportunity presents itself, this same mean person, like a *skilful jaculator, will hurl a sentence,* worthy of attention, *short and contorted*; so that he who converses with him will appear to be in no respect superior to a boy! That *to laconize,* therefore, consists much more in philosophizing than in the love of exercise, is understood by some of the present age, and was known to the ancients, they being persuaded that the ability of *uttering such sentences* as these is the province of a man perfectly learned. The seven sages were emulators, lovers, and disciples of the *Lacedæmonian erudition.* Their wisdom was a thing of this kind, viz: *short sentences uttered by each, and worthy to be remembered.* These men, assembling together, consecrated to Apollo the first fruits of their wisdom; writing in the Temple of Apollo, at Delphi, those sentences which are celebrated by all men, viz: *Know thyself!* and *Nothing too much!* But on what account do I mention these things? To show that *the mode of philosophy among the ancients was a certain laconic diction.*"*

The "laconisms" of the Lacedæmonians evidently partook of the proverbial style: they were, no doubt, often proverbs themselves. The very instances which Plato supplies of this "laconizing" are two most venerable proverbs.

---

* Taylor's *Translation of Plato's works,* vol. v. p. 36.

All this elevates the science of PROVERBS, and indicates that these abridgments of knowledge convey great results, with a parsimony of words prodigal of sense. They have, therefore, preserved many "a short sentence, NOT repeated by the people."

It is evident, however, that the earliest writings of every people are marked by their most homely, or domestic proverbs; for these were more directly addressed to their wants. Franklin, who may be considered as the founder of a people, who were suddenly placed in a stage of civil society which as yet could afford no literature, discovered the philosophical cast of his genius, when he filled his almanacs with proverbs, by the ingenious contrivance of framing them into a connected discourse, delivered by an old man attending an auction. "These proverbs," he tells us, "which contained the wisdom of many ages and nations, when their scattered counsels were brought together, made a great impression. They were reprinted in Britain, in a large sheet of paper, and stuck up in houses: and were twice translated in France, and distributed among their poor parishioners." The same occurrence had happened with us ere we became a reading people. Sir Thomas Elyot, in the reign of Henry the Eighth, describing the ornaments of a nobleman's house, among his hangings, and plate, and pictures, notices the engraving of proverbs "on his plate and vessels, which served the guests with a most opportune counsel and comments." Later even than the reign of Elizabeth our ancestors had proverbs always before them, on every thing which had room for a piece of advice on it; they had them painted in their tapestries, stamped on the most ordinary utensils, on the blades of their knives, the borders of their plates,* and "conned them out of goldsmiths' rings." The usurer, in Robert Greene's *Groat's worth of Wit*, compressed all his philosophy into the circle of his ring, having learned sufficient Latin to understand the proverbial motto of *"Tu tibi cura!"* The husband was reminded of his lordly authority when he only looked into his trencher, one of its learned aphorisms having descended to us,—

The calmest husbands make the stormiest wives.

The English proverbs of the populace, most of which are still

---

* One of the *fruit trenchers*, for such these roundels are called in the *Gent. Mag.* for 1793, p. 398, is engraved there, and the inscriptions of an entire set given.—See also the *Supplement* to that volume, p. 1187.

in circulation, were collected by old John Heywood.* They are arranged by Tusser for "the parlour—the guest's chamber—the hall—table-lessons," &c. Not a small portion of our ancient proverbs were adapted to rural life, when our ancestors lived more than ourselves amidst the works of God, and less among those of men. At this time, one of our old statesmen, in commending the art of compressing a tedious discourse into a few significant phrases, suggested the use of proverbs in diplomatic intercourse, convinced of the great benefit which would result to the negotiators themselves, as well as to others! I give a literary curiosity of this kind. A member of the House of Commons, in the reign of Elizabeth, made a speech entirely composed of the most homely proverbs. The subject was a bill against double-payments of book-debts. Knavish tradesmen were then in the habit of swelling out their book-debts with those who took credit, particularly to their younger customers. One of the members who began to speak "for very fear shook," and stood silent. The nervous orator was followed by a blunt and true representative of the famed governor of Barataria, delivering himself thus—"It is now my chance to speak something, and that without humming or hawing. I think this law is a good law. Even reckoning makes long friends. As far goes the penny as the penny's master. *Vigilantibus non dormientibus jura subveniunt.* Pay the reckoning over-night, and you shall not be troubled in the morning. If ready money be *mensura publica,* let every one cut his coat according to his cloth. When his old suit is in the wane, let him stay till that his money bring a new suit in the increase."†

Another instance of the use of proverbs among our statesmen occurs in a manuscript letter of Sir Dudley Carlton, written in 1632, on the impeachment of Lord Middlesex, who, he says, is "this day to plead his own cause in the Exchequer-chamber, about an account of fourscore thousand pounds laid to his charge. How his lordship sped I know not, but do remember well the French proverb, *Qui mange de l'oye du Roy chiera une plume quarante ans après.* 'Who eats of the king's goose, will void a feather forty years after!' "

This was the era of proverbs with us; for then they were

---

* Heywood's *Dialogue, conteyninge the Number in Effecte of all the Proverbes in the English Tunge, 1561.* There are more editions of this little volume than Warton has noticed. There is some humour in his narrative, but his metre and his ribaldry are heavy taxes on our curiosity.

† Townshend's *Historical Collections,* p. 283.

spoken by all ranks of society. The free use of trivial proverbs got them into disrepute; and as the abuse of a thing raises a just opposition to its practice, a slender wit affecting "a cross humour," published a little volume of *Crossing of Proverbs, Cross-answers, and Cross-humours*. He pretends to contradict the most popular ones; but he has not always the genius to strike at amusing paradoxes.*

Proverbs were long the favourites of our neighbours; in the splendid and refined court of Louis the Fourteenth they gave rise to an odd invention. They plotted comedies and even fantastical ballets from their subjects. In these *Curiosities of Literature* I cannot pass by such eccentric inventions unnoticed.

A COMEDY *of proverbs* is described by the Duke de la Vallière, which was performed in 1634, with prodigious success. He considers that this comedy ought to be ranked among farces; but it is gay, well-written, and curious for containing the best proverbs, which are happily introduced in the dialogue.

A more extraordinary attempt was a BALLET *of proverbs*. Before the opera was established in France, the ancient ballets formed the chief amusement of the court, and Louis the Fourteenth himself joined with the performers. The singular attempt of forming a pantomimical dance out of proverbs is quite French; we have a *"ballet des proverbes, dansé par le Roi, en 1654."* At every proverb the scene changed, and adapted itself to the subject. I shall give two or three of the *entrées* that we may form some notion of these *capriccios*.

The proverb was,

> Tel menace qui a grand peur,
> He threatens who is afraid!

The scene was composed of swaggering scaramouches and some honest cits, who at length beat them off.

At another *entrée* the proverb was

---

* It was published in 1616: the writer only catches at some verbal expressions—as, for instance:—

The vulgar proverb runs, "The more the merrier."
The cross,—"Not so! one hand is enough in a purse."
The proverb, "It is a great way to the bottom of the sea."
The cross,—"Not so! it is but a stone's cast."
The proverb, "The pride of the rich makes the labours of the poor."
The cross,—"Not so! the labours of the poor make the pride of the rich."
The proverb, "He runs far who never turns."
The cross,—"Not so; he may break his neck in a short course."

L'occasion fait le larron,
Opportunity makes the thief.

Opportunity was acted by le Sieur Beaubrun, but it is difficult to
conceive how the real could personify the abstract personage.
The thieves were the Duke d'Amville and Monsieur de la Ches-
naye.

Another *entrée* was the proverb of

Ce qui vient de la flûte s'en va au tambour,
What comes by the pipe goes by the tabor.

A loose dissipated officer was performed by le Sieur l'Anglois;
the *Pipe* by St. Aignan, and the *Tabor* by le Sieur le Comte! In
this manner every proverb was *spoken in action*, the whole
connected by dialogue. More must have depended on the actors
than the poet.*

The French long retained this fondness for proverbs; for they
still have dramatic compositions entitled *proverbes*, on a more
refined plan. Their invention is so recent, that the term is not in
their great dictionary of Trevoux. These *proverbes* are dramas
of a single act, invented by Carmontel, who possessed a peculiar
vein of humour, but who designed them only for private theatricals. Each *proverb* furnished a subject for a few scenes, and
created a situation powerfully comic: it is a dramatic amusement
which does not appear to have reached us, but one which the
celebrated Catherine of Russia delighted to compose for her own
society.

Among the middle classes of society to this day, we may
observe that certain family proverbs are traditionally preserved:
the favourite saying of a father is repeated by the sons; and frequently the conduct of a whole generation has been influenced
by such domestic proverbs. This may be perceived in many of
the mottos of our old nobility, which seem to have originated in
some habitual proverb of the founder of the family. In ages
when proverbs were most prevalent, such pithy sentences would
admirably serve in the ordinary business of life, and lead on to
decision, even in its greater exigencies. Orators, by some lucky
proverb, without wearying their auditors, would bring conviction home to their bosoms; and great characters would appeal to
a proverb, or deliver that which in time by its aptitude became
one. When Nero was reproached for the ardour with which he

---

* It has been suggested that this whimsical amusement has been lately
revived, to a certain degree, in the *acting of charades* among juvenile parties.

gave himself up to the study of music, he replied to his censurers by the Greek proverb, "An artist lives everywhere." The emperor answered in the spirit of Rousseau's system, that every child should be taught some trade. When Cæsar, after anxious deliberation, decided on the passage of the Rubicon (which very event has given rise to a proverb), rousing himself with a start of courage, he committed himself to Fortune, with that proverbial expression on his lips, used by gamesters in desperate play: having passed the Rubicon, he exclaimed, "The die is cast!" The answer of Paulus Æmilius to the relations of his wife, who had remonstrated with him on his determination to separate himself from her against whom no fault could be alleged, has become one of our most familiar proverbs. This hero acknowledged the excellencies of his lady; but, requesting them to look on his shoe, which appeared to be well made, he observed, "None of you know where the shoe pinches!" He either used a proverbial phrase, or by its aptness it has become one of the most popular.

There are, indeed, proverbs connected with the characters of eminent men. They were either their favourite ones, or have originated with themselves. Such a collection would form an historical curiosity. To the celebrated Bayard are the French indebted for a military proverb, which some of them still repeat, "*Ce que le gantelet gagne le gorgerin le mange.*" "What the gauntlet gets, the gorget consumes." That reflecting soldier well calculated the profits of a military life, which consumes, in the pomp and waste which are necessary for its maintenance, the slender pay it receives, and even what its rapacity sometimes acquires. The favourite proverb of Erasmus was *Festina lente!* "Hasten slowly!"* He wished it to be inscribed wherever it could meet our eyes, on public buildings, and on our rings and seals. One of our own statesmen used a favourite sentence, which has enlarged our stock of national proverbs. Sir Amias Pawlet, when he perceived too much hurry in any business, was accustomed to say, "Stay awhile, to make an end the sooner." Oliver Cromwell's coarse but descriptive proverb conveys the contempt he felt for some of his mean and troublesome coadjutors: "Nits will be lice!" The Italians have a proverb, which has been occasionally applied to certain political personages:—

> Egli è quello che Dio vuole;
> E sarà quello che Dio vorrà!

---

* Now the punning motto of a noble family.

He is what God pleases;
He shall be what God wills!

Ere this was a proverb, it had served as an embroidered motto on the mystical mantle of Castruccio Castracani. That military genius, who sought to revolutionize Italy, and aspired to its sovereignty, lived long enough to repent the wild romantic ambition which provoked all Italy to confederate against him; the mysterious motto he assumed entered into the proverbs of his country! The Border proverb of the Douglases, "It were better to hear the lark sing than the mouse cheep," was adopted by every border chief, to express, as Sir Walter Scott observes, what the great Bruce had pointed out, that the woods and hills of their country were their safest bulwarks, instead of the fortified places which the English surpassed their neighbours in the arts of assaulting or defending. These illustrations indicate one of the sources of proverbs; they have often resulted from the spontaneous emotions or the profound reflections of some extraordinary individual, whose energetic expression was caught by a faithful ear, never to perish!

The poets have been very busy with proverbs in all the languages of Europe: some appear to have been the favourite lines of some ancient poem: even in more refined times, many of the pointed verses of Boileau and Pope have become proverbial. Many trivial and laconic proverbs bear the jingle of alliteration or rhyme, which assisted their circulation, and were probably struck off extempore; a manner which Swift practised, who was a ready coiner of such rhyming and ludicrous proverbs: delighting to startle a collector by his facetious or sarcastic humour, in the shape of an "old saying and true." Some of these rhyming proverbs are, however, terse and elegant: we have

Little strokes
Fell great oaks.

The Italian—

Chi due lepri caccia
Uno perde, e l'altro lascia.

Who hunts two hares, loses one and leaves the other.

The haughty Spaniard—

El dar es honor,
Y el pedir dolor.

To give is honour, to ask is grief.

And the French—

Ami de table
Est variable.

The friend of the table
Is very variable.

The composers of these short proverbs were a numerous race
of poets, who, probably, among the dreams of their immortality,
never suspected that they were to descend to posterity, themselves and their works unknown, while their extempore thoughts
would be repeated by their own nation.

Proverbs were at length consigned to the people, when books
were addressed to scholars; but the people did not find themselves so destitute of practical wisdom, by preserving their
national proverbs, as some of those closet students who had
ceased to repeat them. The various humours of mankind, in the
mutability of human affairs, had given birth to every species;
and men were wise, or merry, or satirical, and mourned or re-
joiced in proverbs. Nations held an universal intercourse of proverbs, from the eastern to the western world; for we discover
among those which appear strictly national, many which are
common to them all. Of our own familiar ones several may be
tracked among the snows of the Latins and the Greeks, and have
sometimes been drawn from 'The Mines of the East": like
decayed families which remain in obscurity, they may boast of a
high lineal descent whenever they recover their lost title-deeds.
The vulgar proverb, "To carry coals to Newcastle," local and
idiomatic as it appears, however, has been borrowed and applied
by ourselves; it may be found among the Persians: in the *Bustan*
of Sadi we have *Infers piper in Hindostan*; "To carry pepper to
Hindostan"; among the Hebrews, "To carry oil to the City of
Olives"; a similar proverb occurs in Greek; and in Galland's
Maxims of the East we may discover how many of the most
common proverbs among us, as well as some of Joe Miller's jests,
are of oriental origin.

The resemblance of certain proverbs in different nations,
must, however, be often ascribed to the identity of human nature; similar situations and similar objects have unquestionably
made men think and act and express themselves alike. All
nations are parallels of each other! Hence all parœmiographers,
or collectors of proverbs, complain of the difficulty of separating
their own national proverbs from those which had crept into
the language from others, particularly when nations have held
much intercourse together. We have a copious collection of

Scottish proverbs by Kelly, but this learned man was mortified at discovering that many which he had long believed to have been genuine Scottish, were not only English, but French, Italian, Spanish, Latin, and Greek ones; many of his Scottish proverbs are almost literally expressed among the fragments of remote antiquity. It would have surprised him further had he been aware that his Greek originals were themselves but copies, and might have been found in D'Herbelot, Erpenius, and Golius, and in many Asiatic works, which have been more recently introduced to the enlarged knowledge of the European student, who formerly found his most extended researches limited by Hellenistic lore.

Perhaps it was owing to an accidental circumstance that the proverbs of the European nations have been preserved in the permanent form of volumes. Erasmus is usually considered as the first modern collector, but he appears to have been preceded by Polydore Vergil, who bitterly reproaches Erasmus with envy and plagiarism, for passing by his collection without even a poor compliment for the inventor! Polydore was a vain, superficial writer, who prided himself in leading the way on more topics than the present. Erasmus, with his usual pleasantry, provokingly excuses himself, by acknowledging that he had forgotten his friend's book! Few sympathize with the quarrels of authors; and since Erasmus has written a far better book than Polydore Vergil's, the original *Adagia* is left only to be commemorated in literary history as one of its curiosities.*

The *Adagia* of Erasmus contains a collection of about five thousand proverbs, gradually gathered from a constant study of the ancients. Erasmus, blest with the genius which could enliven a folio, delighted himself and all Europe by the continued accessions he made to a volume which even now may be the companion of literary men for a winter day's fire-side. The successful example of Erasmus commanded the imitation of the learned in Europe, and drew their attention to their own national proverbs. Some of the most learned men, and some not sufficiently so, were now occupied in this new study.

In Spain, Fernandez Nunes, a Greek professor, and the Marquis of Santellana, a grandee, published collections of their

---

* At the ROYAL INSTITUTION there is a fine copy of Polydore Vergil's *Adagia*, with his other work curious in its day, *De Inventoribus Rerum*, printed by Frobenius, in 1521. The *wood-cuts* of this edition seem to me executed with inimitable delicacy, resembling a penciling which Raphael might have envied.

Refranes, or Proverbs, a term derived A REFERENDO, because it is often repeated. The *Refranes o Proverbios Castellanos, par Cæsar Oudin, 1624,* translated into French, is a valuable compilation. In Cervantes and Quevedo, the best practical illustrators, they are sown with no sparing hand. There is an ample collection of Italian proverbs, by Florio, who was an Englishman, of Italian origin, and who published *Il Giardino di Ricreatione* at London, so early as in 1591, exceeding six thousand proverbs; but they are unexplained, and are often obscure. Another Italian in England, Torriano, in 1649, published an interesting collection in the diminutive form of a twenty-fours. It was subsequent to these publications in England, that in Italy, Angelus Monosini, in 1604, published his collection; and Julius Varini, in 1642, produced his *Scuola del Vulgo.* In France, Oudin, after others had preceded him, published a collection of French proverbs, under the title of *Curiosités Françoises.* Fleury de Bellingen's *Explication de Proverbes François,* on comparing it with *Les Illustres Proverbes Historiques,* a subsequent publication, I discovered to be the same work. It is the first attempt to render the study of proverbs somewhat amusing. The plan consists of a dialogue between a philosopher and a Sancho Pança, who blurts out his proverbs with more delight than understanding. The philosopher takes that opportunity of explaining them by the events in which they originated, which, however, are not always to be depended on. A work of high merit on French proverbs is the unfinished one of the Abbé Tuet, sensible and learned. A collection of Danish proverbs, accompanied by a French translation, was printed at Copenhagen, in a quarto volume, 1761. England may boast of no inferior parœmiographers. The grave and judicious Camden, the religious Herbert, the entertaining Howell, the facetious Fuller, and the laborious Ray, with others, have preserved our national sayings. The Scottish have been largely collected and explained by the learned Kelly. An excellent anonymous collection, not uncommon, in various languages, 1707; the collector and translator was Dr. J. Mapletoft. It must be acknowledged, that although no nation exceeds our own in sterling sense, we rarely rival the delicacy, the wit, and the felicity of expression of the Spanish and the Italian, and the poignancy of some of the French proverbs.

The interest we may derive from the study of proverbs is not confined to their universal truths, nor to their poignant pleasantry; a philosophical mind will discover in proverbs a great variety of the most curious knowledge. The manners of a people are painted after life in their domestic proverbs; and it would not be advancing too much to assert, that the genius of the age might be often detected in its prevalent ones. The learned Selden tells us, that the proverbs of several nations were much studied by Bishop Andrews: the reason assigned was, because "by them he knew the minds of several nations, which," said he, "is a brave thing, as we count him wise who knows the minds and the insides of men, which is done by knowing what is habitual to them." Lord Bacon condensed a wide circuit of philosophical thought, when he observed that "the genius, wit, and spirit of a nation are discovered by their proverbs."

Proverbs peculiarly national, while they convey to us the modes of thinking, will consequently indicate the modes of acting among a people. The Romans had a proverbial expression for their last stake in play, *Rem ad triarios venisse,* "the reserve are engaged!" a proverbial expression, from which the military habits of the people might be inferred; the *triarii* being their reserve. A proverb has preserved a curious custom of ancient coxcombry, which originally came from the Greeks. To men of effeminate manners in their dress, they applied the proverb of *Unico digitulo scalpit caput.* Scratching the head with a single finger was, it seems, done by the critically nice youths in Rome, that they might not discompose the economy of their hair. The Arab, whose unsettled existence makes him miserable and interested, says, "Vinegar given is better than honey bought." Every thing of high esteem with him who is so often parched in the desert is described as *milk*—"How large his flow of milk!" is a proverbial expression with the Arab, to distinguish the most copious eloquence. To express a state of perfect repose, the Arabian proverb is, "I throw the rein over my back"; an allusion to the loosening of the cords of the camels, which are thrown over their backs when they are sent to pasture. We discover the rustic manners of our ancient Britons in the Cambrian proverbs; many relate to the *hedge.* "The cleanly Briton is seen in the *hedge*: the horse looks not on the *hedge* but the corn: the bad husband's *hedge* is full of gaps." The state of an agricultural people appears in such proverbs as "You must not count your yearlings till May-day": and their proverbial sentence for old age is, "An old man's end is to keep sheep!" Turn from the vagrant Arab and the agricultural Briton to a nation existing in a high state of artificial civilization: the Chinese proverbs frequently allude to magnificent buildings. Affecting a more solemn exterior than all other nations, a favourite proverb with them is,

"A grave and majestic outside is, as it were, the *palace* of the soul." Their notion of government is quite architectural. They say "A sovereign may be compared to a *hall*; his officers, to the steps that lead to it; the people to the ground on which they stand." What should we think of a people who had a proverb, that "He who gives blows is a master, he who gives none is a dog"? We should instantly decide on the mean and servile spirit of those who could repeat it; and such we find to have been that of the Bengalese, to whom the degrading proverb belongs, derived from the treatment they were used to receive from their Mogul rulers, who answered the claims of their creditors by a vigorous application of the whip! In some of the Hebrew proverbs, we are struck by the frequent allusions of that fugitive people to their own history. The cruel oppression exercised by the ruling power, and the confidence in their hope of change in the day of retribution, was delivered in this Hebrew proverb— "When the tale of bricks is doubled, Moses comes!" The fond idolatry of their devotion to their ceremonial law, and to every thing connected with their sublime Theocracy, in their magnificent Temple, is finely expressed by this proverb—"None ever took a stone out of the Temple, but the dust did fly into his eyes." The Hebrew proverb that "A fast for a dream, is as fire for stubble," which it kindles, could only have been invented by a people whose superstitions attached a holy mystery to fasts and dreams. They imagined that a religious fast was propitious to a religious dream; or to obtain the interpretation of one which had troubled their imagination. Peyssonel, who long resided among the Turks, observes, that their proverbs are full of sense, ingenuity, and elegance, the surest test of the intellectual abilities of any nation. He said this to correct the volatile opinion of De Tott, who, to convey an idea of their stupid pride, quotes one of their favourite adages, of which the truth and candour are admirable; "Riches in the Indies, wit in Europe, and pomp among the Ottomans."

The Spaniards may appeal to their proverbs to show that they were a high-minded and independent race. A Whiggish jealousy of the monarchical power stamped itself on this ancient one, *Va el rey hasta do puede, y no hasta do quiere*: "The king goes as far as he is able, not as far as he desires." It must have been at a later period, when the national genius became more subdued, and every Spaniard dreaded to find under his own roof a spy or an informer, that another proverb arose, *Con el rey y la inquisición, chitón!* "With the king and the Inquisition, hush!"

The gravity and taciturnity of the nation have been ascribed to the effects of this proverb. Their popular but suppressed feelings on taxation, and on a variety of dues exacted by their clergy, were murmured in proverbs—*Lo que no lleva Christo lleva el fisco!* "What Christ takes not, the exchequer carries away!" They have a number of sarcastic proverbs on the tenacious gripe of the "abad avariento," the avaricious priest, who, "having eaten the olio offered, claims the dish!" A striking mixture of chivalric habits, domestic decency, and epicurean comfort, appears in the Spanish proverb, *La muger y la salsa a la mano de la lança*: "The wife and the sauce by the hand of the lance"; to honour the dame, and to have the sauce near.

The Italian proverbs have taken a tinge from their deep and politic genius, and their wisdom seems wholly concentrated in their personal interests. I think every tenth proverb, in an Italian collection, is some cynical or some selfish maxim: a book of the world for worldlings! The Venetian proverb *Pria Veneziana, poi Christiana:* "First Venetian, and then Christian!" condenses the whole spirit of their ancient Republic into the smallest space possible. Their political proverbs, no doubt, arose from the extraordinary state of a people, sometimes distracted among republics, and sometimes servile in petty courts. The Italian says, *I popoli s'ammazzano ed i principi s'abbracciano*: "The people murder one another, and princes embrace one another." *Chi prattica co' grandi, l'ultimo a tavola, e'l primo a strapazzi*: "Who dangles after the great is the last at table, and the first at blows." *Chi non sa adulare, non sa regnare*: "Who knows not to flatter, knows not to reign." *Chi serve in corte muore sul pagliato*: "Who serves at court dies on straw." Wary cunning in domestic life is perpetually impressed. An Italian proverb, which is immortalized in our language, for it enters into the history of Milton, was that by which the elegant Wotton counselled the young poetic traveller to have—*Il viso sciolto, ed i pensieri stretti*, "An open countenance, but close thoughts." In the same spirit, *Chi parla semina, chi tace raccoglie*: "The talker sows, the silent reaps"; as well as *Fatti di miele, e ti mangieran le mosche*: "Make yourself all honey, and the flies will devour you." There are some which display a deep knowledge of human nature: *A Lucca ti vidi, a Pisa ti connobbi!* "I saw you at Lucca, I knew you at Pisa!" *Guardati d'aceto di vin dolce*: "Beware of vinegar made of sweet wine," provoke not the rage of a patient man!

Among a people who had often witnessed their fine country devastated by petty warfare, their notion of the military character was not usually heroic. *Il soldato per far male è ben pagato*: "The soldier is well paid for doing mischief." *Soldato, acqua, e fuoco, presto si fan luoco*: "A soldier, fire, and water, soon make room for themselves." But in a poetical people, endowed with great sensibility, their proverbs would sometimes be tender and fanciful. They paint the activity of friendship, *Chi ha l'amor nel petto, ha lo sprone ai fianchi*: "Who feels love in the breast, feels a spur in his limbs": or its generous passion, *Gli amici legano la borsa con un filo di ragnatelo*: "Friends tie their purse with a cobweb's thread." They characterized the universal lover by an elegant proverb—*Appiccare il Maio ad ogn' uscio*: "To hang every door with May"; alluding to the bough which in the nights of May the country people are accustomed to plant before the door of their mistress. If we turn to the French, we discover that the military genius of France dictated the proverb, *Maille à maille se fait le haubergeon*: "Link by link is made the coat of mail"; and, *Tel coup de langue est pire qu'un coup de lance*; "The tongue strikes deeper than the lance"; and *Ce qui vient du tambour s'en retourne à la flûte*; "What comes by the tabor goes back with the pipe." *Point d'argent point de Suisse* has become proverbial, observes an Edinburgh Reviewer; a striking expression, which, while French or Austrian gold predominated, was justly used to characterize the illiberal and selfish policy of the cantonal and federal governments of Switzerland, when it began to degenerate from its moral patriotism. The ancient, perhaps the extinct, spirit of Englishmen, was once expressed by our proverb, "Better be the head of a dog than the tail of a lion"; i. e. the first of the yeomanry rather than the last of the gentry. A foreign philosopher might have discovered our own ancient skill in archery among our proverbs; for none but true toxophilites could have had such a proverb as, "I will either make a shaft or a bolt of it!" signifying, says the author of *Ivanhoe*, a determination to make one use or other of the thing spoken of: the bolt was the arrow peculiarly fitted to the crossbow, as that of the long-bow was called a shaft. These instances sufficiently demonstrate that the characteristic circumstances and feelings of a people are discovered in their popular notions, and stamped on their familiar proverbs.

It is also evident that the peculiar, and often idiomatic, humour of a people is best preserved in their proverbs. There is a shrewdness, although deficient in delicacy, in the Scottish proverbs; they are idiomatic, facetious, and strike home. Kelly, who has collected three thousand, informs us, that, in 1725, the Scotch

were a great proverbial nation; for that few among the better
sort will converse any considerable time, but will confirm every
assertion and observation with a Scottish proverb. The speculative Scotch of our own times have probably degenerated in
prudential lore, and deem themselves much wiser than their
proverbs. They may reply by a Scotch proverb on proverbs, made
by a great man in Scotland, who, having given a splendid entertainment, was harshly told, that "Fools make feasts, and wise
men eat them"; but he readily answered, "Wise men make proverbs, and fools repeat them!"

National humour, frequently local and idiomatical, depends
on the artificial habits of mankind, so opposite to each other,
but there is a natural vein, which the populace, always true to
nature, preserve, even among the gravest people. The Arabian
proverb, "the barber learns his art on the orphan's face"; the
Chinese, "In a field of melons do not pull up your shoe; under a
plum-tree do not adjust your cap";—to impress caution in our
conduct under circumstance of suspicion;—and the Hebrew one,
"He that hath had one of his family hanged may not say to his
neighbour, *hang* up this fish!" are all instances of this sort of
humour. The Spaniards are a grave people, but no nation has
equalled them in their peculiar humour. The genius of Cervantes partook largely of that of his country; that mantle of
gravity, which almost conceals its latent facetiousness, and with
which he has imbued his style and manner with such untrans-
latable idiomatic raciness, may be traced to the proverbial erudition of his nation. "To steal a sheep, and give away the trotters
for God's sake!" is Cervantic nature! To one who is seeking an
opportunity to quarrel with another, their proverb runs, *Si
quieres dar palos a tu muger pidele al sol a beber,* "Hast thou
a mind to quarrel with thy wife, bid her bring water to thee in
the sunshine!"—a very fair quarrel may be picked up about the
motes in the clearest water! On the judges in Gallicia, who, like
our former justices of peace, "for half a dozen chickens would
dispense with a dozen of penal statutes," *A juezes Gallicianos,
con los pies en las manos:* "To the judges of Gallicia go with feet
in hand"; a droll allusion to a present of poultry, usually held
by the legs. To describe persons who live high without visible
means, *Los que cabritos venden, y cabras no tienen, de donde los
vienen?* "They that sell kids, and have no goats, how came they
by them?" *El vino no trae bragas,* "Wine wears no breeches";
for men in wine expose their most secret thoughts. *Vino di una
oreja,* "Wine of one ear!" is good wine; for at bad, shaking our

heads, both our ears are visible; but at good the Spaniard, by a natural gesticulation lowering on one side, shows a single ear.

Proverbs abounding in sarcastic humour, and found among every people, are those which are pointed at rival countries. Among ourselves, hardly has a country escaped from some popular quip; even neighbouring towns have their sarcasms, usually pickled in some unlucky rhyme. The egotism of man eagerly seizes on what ever serves to depreciate or to ridicule his neighbour; nations proverb each other; counties flout counties; obscure towns sharpen their wits on towns as obscure as themselves —the same evil principle lurking in poor human nature, if it cannot always assume predominance, will meanly gratify itself by insult or contempt. They expose some prevalent folly, or allude to some disgrace which the natives have incurred. In France, the Burgundians have a proverb, *Mieux vaut bon repas que bel habit*: "Better a good dinner than a fine coat." These good people are great gormandizers, but shabby dressers; they are commonly said to have "bowels of silk and velvet"; this is, all their silk and velvet goes for their bowels! Thus Picardy is famous for "hot heads"; and the Norman for *son dit et son dédit*, "his saying and his unsaying"! In Italy the numerous rival cities pelt one another with proverbs: *Chi ha a fare con Tosco non convien esser losco*, "He who deals with a Tuscan must not have his eyes shut." *A Venezia chi vi nasce, mal vi si pasce*, "Whom Venice breeds, she poorly feeds."

There is another source of national characteristics, frequently producing strange or whimsical combinations; a people, from a very natural circumstance, have drawn their proverbs from local objects, or from allusions to peculiar customs. The influence of manners and customs over the ideas and language of a people would form a subject of extensive and curious research. There is a Japanese proverb, that "A fog cannot be dispelled with a fan!" Had we not known the origin of this proverb, it would be evident that it could only have occurred to a people who had constantly before them fogs and fans; and the fact appears that fogs are frequent on the coast of Japan; and that from the age of five years both sexes of the Japanese carry fans. The Spaniards have an odd proverb to describe those who tease and vex a person before they do him the very benefit which they are about to confer—acting kindly, but speaking roughly; *Mostrar primero la horca que el lugar*, "To show the gallows before they show the town"; a circumstance alluding to their small towns, which have a gallows placed on an eminence, so that the gallows breaks on the eye of the traveller before he gets a view of the town itself.

The Cheshire proverb on marriage, "Better wed over the mixon than over the moor," that is, at home or in its vicinity; mixon alludes to the dung, &c. in the farm-yard, while the road from Chester to London is over the moorland in Staffordshire: this local proverb is a curious instance of provincial pride, perhaps of wisdom, to induce the gentry of that county to form intermarriages; to prolong their own ancient families, and perpetuate ancient friendships between them.

In the Isle of Man a proverbial expression forcibly indicates the object constantly occupying the minds of the inhabitants. The two Deemsters or judges, when appointed to the chair of judgment, declare they will render justice between man and man "as equally as the herring bone lies between the two sides": an image which could not have occurred to any people unaccustomed to the herring-fishery. There is a Cornish proverb, "Those who will not be ruled by the rudder must be ruled by the rock"—the strands of Cornwall, so often covered with wrecks, could not fail to impress on the imaginations of its inhabitants the two objects from whence they drew this salutary proverb, against obstinate wrong-heads.

When Scotland, in the last century, felt its allegiance to England doubtful, and when the French sent an expedition to the land of cakes, a local proverb was revived, to show the identity of interests which affected both nations:

> If Skiddaw hath a cap
> Scruffel wots full well of that.

These are two high hills, one in Scotland and one in England; so near, that what happens to the one will not be long ere it reach the other. If a fog lodges on the one, it is sure to rain on the other; the mutual sympathies of the two countries were hence deduced in a copious dissertation, by Oswald Dyke, on what was called "The Union-proverb," which *local proverbs* of our country, Fuller has interspersed in his *Worthies*, and Ray and Grose have collected separately.

I was amused lately by a curious financial revelation which I found in an opposition paper, where it appears that "Ministers pretend to make their load of taxes more portable, by shifting the burden, or altering the pressure, without, however, diminishing the weight; according to the Italian proverb, *Accomodare le bisaccie nella strada,* 'To fit the load on the journey' ": it is taken from a custom of the mule-drivers, who, placing their packages at first but awkwardly on the backs of their poor beasts, and seeing them ready to sink, cry out, "Never mind! we must fit them better on the road!" I was gratified to discover, by the present and some other modern instances, that the taste for proverbs was reviving, and that we were returning to those sober times, when the aptitude of a simple proverb would be preferred to the verbosity of politicians, Tories, Whigs, or Radicals!

There are domestic proverbs which originate in incidents known only to the natives of their province. Italian literature is particularly rich in these stores. The lively proverbial taste of that vivacious people was transferred to their own authors; and when these allusions were obscured by time, learned Italians, in their zeal for their national literature, and in their national love of story-telling, have written grave commentaries even on ludicrous, but popular tales, in which the proverbs are said to have originated. They resemble the old facetious *contes*, whose simplicity and humour still live in the pages of Boccaccio, and are not forgotten in those of the Queen of Navarre.

The Italians apply a proverb to a person who, while he is beaten, takes the blows quietly:—

> Per beato ch'elle non furon pesche!
> Luckily they were not peaches!

And to threaten to give a man—

> Una pesca in un occhio,
> A peach in the eye,

means to give him a thrashing. This proverb, it is said, originated in the close of a certain droll adventure. The community of the Castle Poggibonsi, probably from some jocular tenure observed on St. Bernard's day, pay a tribute of peaches to the court of Tuscany, which are usually shared among the ladies in waiting, and the pages of the court. It happened one season, in a great scarcity of peaches, that the good people of Poggibonsi, finding them rather dear, sent, instead of the customary tribute, a quantity of fine juicy figs, which was so much disapproved of by the pages, that as soon as they got hold of them, they began in rage to empty the baskets on the heads of the ambassadors of the Poggibonsi, who, in attempting to fly as well as they could from the pulpy shower, half-blinded, and recollecting that peaches would have had stones in them, cried out—

Per beato ch'elle non furon pesche!
Luckily they were not peaches!

Fare le scalee di Sant'Ambrogio; "To mount the stairs of Saint Ambrose," a proverb allusive to the business of the school of scandal. Varchi explains it by a circumstance so common in provincial cities. On summer evenings, for fresh air and gossip, the loungers met on the steps and landing-places of the church of St. Ambrose: whoever left the party, "they read in his book," as our commentator expresses it; and not a leaf was passed over! All liked to join a party so well informed of one another's concerns, and every one tried to be the very last to quit it,—not "to leave his character behind"! It became a proverbial phrase with those who left a company, and were too tender of their backs, to request they would not 'mount the stairs of St. Ambrose." Jonson has well described such a company:

> You are so truly fear'd, but not beloved
> One of another, as no one dares break
> Company from the rest, lest they should fall
> Upon him absent.

There are legends and histories which belong to proverbs; and some of the most ancient refer to incidents which have not always been commemorated. Two Greek proverbs have accidentally been explained by Pausanias: "He is a man of Tenedos!" to describe a person of unquestionable veracity; and "To cut with the Tenedian axe"; to express an absolute and irrevocable refusal. The first originated in a king of Tenedos, who decreed that there should always stand behind the judge a man holding an axe, ready to execute justice on any one convicted of falsehood. The other arose from the same king, whose father having reached his island, to supplicate the son's forgiveness for the injury inflicted on him by the arts of a step-mother, was preparing to land; already the ship was fastened by its cable to a rock; when the son came down, and sternly cutting the cable with an axe, sent the ship adrift to the mercy of the waves: hence, "to cut with the Tenedian axe," became proverbial to express an absolute refusal. "Business to-morrow!" is another Greek proverb, applied to a person ruined by his own neglect. The fate of an eminent person perpetuated the expression which he casually employed on the occasion. One of the Theban polemarchs, in the midst of a convivial party, received dispatches relating to a conspiracy: flushed with wine, although pressed by the courier to open them immediately, he smiled, and in gaiety laying the letter under the pillow of his couch, observed, "Business to-morrow!" Plutarch records that he fell a victim to the twenty-four hours he had lost, and became the author of a proverb which was still circulated among the Greeks.

The philosophical antiquary may often discover how many a proverb commemorates an event which has escaped from the more solemn monuments of history, and is often the solitary authority of its existence. A national event in Spanish history is preserved by a proverb. *Y vengar quiniento sueldos*; "And revenge five hundred pounds!" An odd expression to denote a person being a gentleman! but the proverb is historical. The Spaniards of Old Castile were compelled to pay an annual tribute of five hundred maidens to their masters, the Moors; after several battles, the Spaniards succeeded in compromising the shameful tribute, by as many pieces of coin: at length the day arrived when they entirely emancipated themselves from this odious imposition. The heroic action was performed by men of distinction, and the event perpetuated in the recollections of the Spaniards, by this singular expression, which alludes to the dishonourable tribute, was applied to characterize all men of high honour, and devoted lovers of their country.

Pasquier, in his *Recherches sur la France*, reviewing the periodical changes of ancient families in feudal times, observes, that a proverb among the common people conveys the result of all his inquiries; for those noble houses, which in a single age declined from nobility and wealth to poverty and meanness, gave rise to the proverb, *Cent ans bannières et cent ans civières!* "One hundred years a banner and one hundred years a barrow!" The Italian proverb, *Con l'Evangilio si diventa eretico*, "With the gospel we become heretics,"—reflects the policy of the court of Rome; and must be dated at the time of the Reformation, when a translation of the Scriptures into the vulgar tongue encountered such an invincible opposition. The Scotch proverb, *He that invented the maiden first hanselled it*; that is, got the first of it! The maiden is that well-known beheading engine, revived by the French surgeon Guillotine. This proverb may be applied to one who falls a victim to his own ingenuity; the artificer of his own destruction! The inventor was James, Earl of Morton, who for some years governed Scotland, and afterwards, it is said, very unjustly suffered by his own invention. It is a striking coincidence, that the same fate was shared by the French reviver; both alike sad examples of disturbed times! Among our own proverbs a remarkable incident has been com-

memorated; *Hand over head, as the men took the Covenant!*
This preserves the manner in which the Scotch covenant, so
famous in our history, was violently taken by above sixty thousand persons about Edinburgh, in 1638; a circumstance at that
time novel in our own revolutionary history, and afterwards
paralleled by the French in voting by "acclamation." An ancient
English proverb preserves a curious fact concerning our coinage.
Testers are gone to Oxford, to study at Brazennose. When Henry
the Eighth debased the silver coin, called *testers*, from their
having a head stamped on one side; the brass, breaking out in
red pimples of their silver faces, provoked the ill-humour of the
people to vent itself in this punning proverb, which has preserved for the historical antiquary the popular feeling which
lasted about fifty years, till Elizabeth reformed the state of the
coinage. A northern proverb among us has preserved the remarkable idea which seems to have once been prevalent, that the
metropolis of England was to be the city of York; *Lincoln was,
London is, York shall be!* Whether at the time of the union of
the crowns, under James the First, when England and Scotland
became Great Britain, this city, from its centrical situation, was
considered as the best adapted for the seat of government, or for
some other cause which I have not discovered, this notion must
have been prevalent to have entered into a proverb. The chief
magistrate of York is the only provincial one who is allowed the
title of Lord Mayor; a circumstance which seems connected with
this proverb.

The Italian history of its own small principalities, whose
well-being so much depended on their prudence and sagacity,
affords many instances of the timely use of a proverb. Many an
intricate negotiation has been contracted through a good-humoured proverb,—many a sarcastic one has silenced an adversary;
and sometimes they have been applied on more solemn, and even
tragical occasions. When Rinaldo degli Albizzi was banished by
the vigorous conduct of Cosmo de' Medici, Machiavel tells us,
the expelled man sent Cosmo a menace, in a proverb, *La gallina
covava!* "The hen is brooding!" said of one meditating vengeance. The undaunted Cosmo replied by another, that "There was
no brooding out of the nest!"

I give an example of peculiar interest; for it is perpetuated
by Dante, and is connected with the character of Milton.

When the families of the Amadei and the Uberti felt their
honour wounded in the affront the younger Buondelmonte had
put upon them, in breaking off his match with a young lady of

their family, by marrying another, a council was held, and the death of the young cavalier was proposed as the sole atonement for their injured honour. But the consequences which they anticipated, and which afterwards proved so fatal to the Florentines, long suspended their decision. At length Moscha Lamberti suddenly rising, exclaimed, in two proverbs, "That those who considered every thing would never conclude on any thing!" closing with an ancient proverbial saying—*cosa fatta capo ha!* "a deed done has an end!" The proverb sealed the fatal determination, and was long held in mournful remembrance by the Tuscans; for, according to Villani, it was the cause and beginning of the accursed factions of the Guelphs and the Ghibellines. Dante has thus immortalized the energetic expression in a scene of the *Inferno:*

> Ed un, ch'avea l'una e l'altra man mozza,
> Levando i moncherin per l'aura fosca,
> Si che'l sangue facea la faccia sozza,
> Gridò:—"Ricorderati anche del Mosca,
> Che dissi, lasso: *Capo ha cosa fatta,*
> Che fu'l mal seme della gente Tosca."

> ——————Then one
> Maim'd of each hand, uplifted in the gloom
> The bleeding stumps, that they with gory spots
> Sullied his face, and cried—"Remember thee
> Of Mosca too—I who, alas! exclaim'd,
> 'The deed once done, there is an end'—that proved
> A seed of sorrow to the Tuscan race."
>
> CARY'S DANTE

This Italian proverb was adopted by Milton; for when deeply engaged in writing *The Defence of the People,* and warned that it might terminate in his blindness, he resolvedly concluded his work, exclaiming with great magnanimity, although the fatal prognostication had been accomplished, *cosa fatta capo ha!* Did this proverb also influence his awful decision on that great national event, when the most honest-minded fluctuated between doubts and fears?

Of a person treacherously used, the Italian proverb says that he has eaten of

> Le frutta di fratre Alberigo.
> The fruit of brother Alberigo.

Landino, on the following passage of Dante, preserves the tragic story:—

————"Io son fratre Alberigo,
Io son quel dalle frutta del mal orto
Che qui reprendo," &c.
                    Canto xxxiii.

"The friar Alberigo," answered he,
"Am I, who from the evil garden pluck'd
Its fruitage, and am here repaid the date
More luscious for my fig."
                    CARY'S DANTE

This was Manfred, the Lord of Fuenza, who, after many cruelties, turned friar. Reconciling himself to those whom he had so often opposed, to celebrate the renewal of their friendship he invited them to a magnificent entertainment. At the end of the dinner the horn blew to announce the dessert—but it was the signal of this dissimulating conspirator!—and the fruits which that day were served to his guests were armed men, who, rushing in, immolated their victims.

Among these historical proverbs none are more entertaining than those which perpetuate national events, connected with those of another people. When a Frenchman would let us understand that he has settled with his creditors, the proverb is *J'ai payé tous mes Anglais*: "I have paid all my English." This proverb originated when John, the French king, was taken prisoner by our Black Prince. Levies of money were made for the king's ransom, and for many French lords; and the French people have thus perpetuated the military glory of our nation, and their own idea of it, by making the *English* and their *creditors* synonymous terms. Another relates to the same event—*Le Pape est devenu Français, et Jésus Christ Anglais*: "Now the Pope is become French and Jesus Christ English"; a proverb which arose when the Pope, exiled from Rome, held his court at Avignon in France; and the English prospered so well, that they possessed more than half the kingdom. The Spanish proverb concerning England is well known—

> Con todo el mondo guerra,
> Y paz con Inglaterra!

> War with the world,
> And peace with England!

Whether this proverb was one of the results of their memorable armada, and was only coined after their conviction of the splendid folly which they had committed, I cannot ascertain. England must always have been a desirable ally to Spain against her potent rival and neighbour. The Italians have a proverb, which formerly, at least, was strongly indicative of the travelled Englishman in their country, *Inglese Italianato è un diavolo incarnato;* "The Italianized Englishman is a devil incarnate." Formerly there existed a closer intercourse between our country and Italy than with France. Before and during the reigns of Elizabeth and James the First, that land of the elegant arts modelled our taste and manners; and more Italians travelled into England, and were more constant residents, from commercial concerns, than afterwards when France assumed a higher rank in Europe by her political superiority. This cause will sufficiently account for the number of Italian proverbs relating to England, which show an intimacy with our manners which could not else have occurred. It was probably some sarcastic Italian, and, perhaps, horologer, who, to describe the disagreement of persons, proverbed our nation— "They agree like the clocks of London!" We were once better famed for merry Christmases and their pies; and it must have been Italians who had been domiciliated with us who gave currency to the proverb—*Ha più da fare che i forni di natale in Inghilterra:* "He has more business than English ovens at Christmas." Our pie-loving gentry were notorious, and Shakspeare's folio was usually laid open in the great halls of our nobility to entertain their attendants, who devoured at once Shakspeare and their pasty. Some of those volumes have come down to us, not only with the stains, but inclosing even the identical pie-crusts of the Elizabethan age.

I have thus attempted to develop THE ART OF READING PROVERBS; but have done little more than indicate the theory, and must leave the skilful student to the delicacy of the practice. I am anxious to rescue from prevailing prejudices these neglected stores of curious amusement, and of deep insight into the ways of man, and to point out the bold and concealed truths which are scattered in these collections. There seems to be no occurrence in human affairs to which some proverb may not be applied. All knowledge was long aphoristical and traditional, pithily contracting the discoveries which were to be instantly comprehended, and easily retained. Whatever be the revolutionary state of man, similar principles and like occurrences are returning on us; and antiquity, whenever it is justly applicable to our times, loses its denomination, and becomes the truth of our own age. A proverb will often cut the knot which others in vain are attempting to untie. Jonson, palled with the redundant elegancies of modern composition, once said, "I fancy mankind may come in time to write all aphoristically, except in narrative; grow weary of preparation, and connection, and illustration, and all those arts by which a big book is made." Many a volume indeed has often been written to demonstrate, what a lover of proverbs could show had long been ascertained by a single one in his favourite collections.

An insurmountable difficulty, which every parœmiographer has encountered, is that of forming an apt, a ready, and a systematic classification: the moral Linnæus of such a *systema naturæ* has not yet appeared. Each discovered his predecessor's mode imperfect, but each was doomed to meet the same fate.* The arrangement of proverbs has baffled the ingenuity of every one of their collectors. Our Ray, after long premeditation, has chosen a system with the appearance of an alphabetical order; but, as it turns out, his system is no system, and his alphabet is no alphabet. After ten years' labour, the good man could only arrange his proverbs by common-places—by complete sentences—by phrases or forms of speech—by proverbial similes—and so on. All these are pursued in alphabetical order, "by the first letter of the most 'material word,' or if there be more words *'equally material,'* by that which usually stands foremost." The most patient examiner will usually find that he wants the sagacity of the collector to discover that word which is "the most material," or, "the words equally material." We have to search through all that multiplicity of divisions, or conjuring boxes, in which this juggler of proverbs pretends to hide the ball.

A still more formidable objection against a collection of proverbs, for the impatient reader, is their unreadableness. Taking in succession a multitude of insulated proverbs, their slippery nature resists all hope of retaining one in a hundred; the study of proverbs must be a frequent recurrence to a gradual collection of favourite ones, which we ourselves must form. The experience of life will throw a perpetual freshness over these short and simple texts; every day may furnish a new commentary; and we may grow old, and find novelty in proverbs by their perpetual application.

---

* Since the appearance of the present article, several collections of PROVERBS have been attempted. A little unpretending volume, entitled *Select Proverbs of all nations, with* Notes *and* Comments *by Thomas Fielding, 1824,* is not ill arranged; an excellent book for popular reading. The editor of a recent miscellaneous compilation, *The Treasury of Knowledge,* has whimsically bordered the four sides of the pages of a Dictionary with as many proverbs. The plan was ingenious but the proverbs are not. Triteness and triviality are fatal to a proverb.

There are, perhaps, about twenty thousand proverbs among the nations of Europe: many of these have spread in their common intercourse; many are borrowed from the ancients, chiefly the Greeks, who themselves largely took them from the eastern nations. Our own proverbs are too often deficient in that elegance and ingenuity which are often found in the Spanish and the Italian. Proverbs frequently enliven conversation, or enter into the business of life in those countries without any feeling of vulgarity being associated with them; they are too numerous, too witty, and too wise, to cease to please by their poignancy and their aptitude. I have heard them fall from the lips of men of letters and of statesmen. When recently the disorderly state of the manufacturers of Manchester menaced an insurrection, a profound Italian politician observed to me, that it was not of a nature to alarm a great nation; for that the remedy was at hand, in the proverb of the Lazzaroni of Naples, *Metà consiglio, metà esempio, metà denaro!* "Half advice, half example, half money!" The result confirmed the truth of the proverb, which, had it been known at the time, might have quieted the honest fears of a great part of the nation.

Proverbs have ceased to be studied, or employed in conversation, since the time we have derived our knowledge from books; but in a philosophical age they appear to offer infinite subjects for speculative curiosity. Originating in various eras, these memorials of manners, of events, and of modes of thinking, for historical as well as for moral purposes, still retain a strong hold on our attention. The collected knowledge of successive ages, and of different people, must always enter into some part of our own! Truth and nature can never be obsolete.

Proverbs embrace the wide sphere of human existence, they take all the colours of life, they are often exquisite strokes of genius, they delight by their airy sarcasm or their caustic satire, the luxuriance of their humour, the playfulness of their turn, and even by the elegance of their imagery, and the tenderness of their sentiment. They give a deep insight into domestic life, and open for us the heart of man, in all the various states which he may occupy—a frequent review of Proverbs should enter into our readings; and although they are no longer the ornaments of conversation, they have not ceased to be the treasuries of Thought!

CATALOG OF DOVER BOOKS

Literature, History of Literature

ARISTOTLE'S THEORY OF POETRY AND THE FINE ARTS, edited by S. H. Butcher. The celebrated Butcher translation of this great classic faced, page by page, with the complete Greek text. A 300 page introduction discussing Aristotle's ideas and their influence in the history of thought and literature, and covering art and nature, imitation as an aesthetic form, poetic truth, art and morality, tragedy, comedy, and similar topics. Modern Aristotelian criticism discussed by John Gassner. lxxvi + 421pp. 5⅜ x 8.   T42 Paperbound **$2.00**

INTRODUCTIONS TO ENGLISH LITERATURE, edited by B. Dobrée. Goes far beyond ordinary histories, ranging from the 7th century up to 1914 (to the 1940's in some cases.) The first half of each volume is a specific detailed study of historical and economic background of the period and a general survey of poetry and prose, including trends of thought, influences, etc. The second and larger half is devoted to a detailed study of more than 5000 poets, novelists, dramatists; also economists, historians, biographers, religious writers, philosophers, travellers, and scientists of literary stature, with dates, lists of major works and their dates, keypoint critical bibliography, and evaluating comments. The most compendious bibliographic and literary aid within its price range.

Vol. I. THE BEGINNINGS OF ENGLISH LITERATURE TO SKELTON, (1509), W. L. Renwick, H. Orton. 450pp. 5⅛ x 7⅞.   T75 Clothbound **$4.50**

Vol. II. THE ENGLISH RENAISSANCE, 1510-1688, V. de Sola Pinto. 381pp. 5⅛ x 7⅞.
T76 Clothbound **$4.50**

Vol. III. AUGUSTANS AND ROMANTICS, 1689-1830, H. Dyson, J. Butt. 320pp. 5⅛ x 7⅞.
T77 Clothbound **$4.50**

Vol. IV. THE VICTORIANS AND AFTER, 1830-1940's, E. Batho, B. Dobrée. 360pp. 5⅛ x 7⅞.
T78 Clothbound **$4.50**

EPIC AND ROMANCE, W. P. Ker. Written by one of the foremost authorities on medieval literature, this is the standard survey of medieval epic and romance. It covers Teutonic epics, Icelandic sagas, Beowulf, French chansons de geste, the Roman de Troie, and many other important works of literature. It is an excellent account for a body of literature whose beauty and value has only recently come to be recognized. Index. xxiv + 398pp. 5⅜ x 8.
T355 Paperbound **$2.00**

THE POPULAR BALLAD, F. B. Gummere. Most useful factual introduction; fund of descriptive material; quotes, cites over 260 ballads. Examines, from folkloristic view, structure; choral, ritual elements; meter, diction, fusion; effects of tradition, editors; almost every other aspect of border, riddle, kinship, sea, ribald, supernatural, etc., ballads. Bibliography. 2 indexes. 374pp. 5⅜ x 8.   T548 Paperbound **$1.65**

MASTERS OF THE DRAMA, John Gassner. The most comprehensive history of the drama in print, covering drama in every important tradition from the Greeks to the Near East, China, Japan, Medieval Europe, England, Russia, Italy, Spain, Germany, and dozens of other drama producing nations. This unsurpassed reading and reference work encompasses more than 800 dramatists and over 2000 plays, with biographical material, plot summaries, theatre history, etc. "Has no competitors in its field," THEATRE ARTS. "Best of its kind in English," NEW REPUBLIC. Exhaustive 35 page bibliography. 77 photographs and drawings. Deluxe edition with reinforced cloth binding, headbands, stained top. xxii + 890pp. 5⅜ x 8.   T100 Clothbound **$6.95**

THE DEVELOPMENT OF DRAMATIC ART, D. C. Stuart. The basic work on the growth of Western drama from primitive beginnings to Eugene O'Neill, covering over 2500 years. Not a mere listing or survey, but a thorough analysis of changes, origins of style, and influences in each period; dramatic conventions, social pressures, choice of material, plot devices, stock situations, etc.; secular and religious works of all nations and epochs. "Generous and thoroughly documented researches," Outlook. "Solid studies of influences and playwrights and periods," London Times. Index. Bibliography. xi + 679pp. 5⅜ x 8.
T693 Paperbound **$2.75**

A SOURCE BOOK IN THEATRICAL HISTORY (SOURCES OF THEATRICAL HISTORY), A. M. Nagler. Over 2000 years of actors, directors, designers, critics, and spectators speak for themselves in this potpourri of writings selected from the great and formative periods of western drama. On-the-spot descriptions of masks, costumes, makeup, rehearsals, special effects, acting methods, backstage squabbles, theatres, etc. Contemporary glimpses of Molière rehearsing his company, an exhortation to a Roman audience to buy refreshments and keep quiet, Goethe's rules for actors, Belasco telling of $6500 he spent building a river, Restoration actors being told to avoid "lewd, obscene, or indecent postures," and much more. Each selection has an introduction by Prof. Nagler. This extraordinary, lively collection is ideal as a source of otherwise difficult to obtain material, as well as a fine book for browsing. Over 80 illustrations. 10 diagrams. xxiii + 611pp. 5⅜ x 8.   T515 Paperbound **$2.75**

CATALOGUE OF DOVER BOOKS

WORLD DRAMA, B. H. Clark. The dramatic creativity of a score of ages and eras — all in two handy compact volumes. Over ⅓ of this material is unavailable in any other current edition! 46 plays from Ancient Greece, Rome, Medieval Europe, France, Germany, Italy, England, Russia, Scandinavia, India, China, Japan, etc. — including classic authors like Aeschylus, Sophocles, Euripides, Aristophanes, Plautus, Marlowe, Jonson, Farquhar, Goldsmith, Cervantes, Molière, Dumas, Goethe, Schiller, Ibsen, and many others. This creative collection avoids hackneyed material and includes only completely first-rate works which are relatively little known or difficult to obtain. "The most comprehensive collection of important plays from all literature available in English," SAT. REV. OF LITERATURE. Introduction. Reading lists. 2 volumes. 1364pp. 5⅜ x 8.　　　　　　　　　　　　　　Vol. 1, T57 Paperbound **$2.25**
　　　　　　　　　　　　　　　　　　　　　　　　　　　Vol. 2, T59 Paperbound **$2.25**

MASTERPIECES OF THE RUSSIAN DRAMA, edited with introduction by G. R. Noyes. This only comprehensive anthology of Russian drama ever published in English offers complete texts, in 1st-rate modern translations, of 12 plays covering 200 years. Vol. 1: "The Young Hopeful," Fonvisin; "Wit Works Woe," Griboyedov; "The Inspector General," Gogol; "A Month in the Country," Turgenev; "The Poor Bride," Ostrovsky; "A Bitter Fate," Pisemsky. Vol. 2: "The Death of Ivan the Terrible," Alexey Tolstoy "The Power of Darkness," Lev Tolstoy; "The Lower Depths," Gorky; "The Cherry Orchard," Chekhov; "Professor Storitsyn," Andreyev; "Mystery Bouffe," Mayakovsky. Bibliography. Total of 902pp. 5⅜ x 8.
　　　　　　　　　　　　　　　　　　　　　　　　　　　Vol. 1 T647 Paperbound **$2.00**
　　　　　　　　　　　　　　　　　　　　　　　　　　　Vol. 2 T648 Paperbound **$2.00**

EUGENE O'NEILL: THE MAN AND HIS PLAYS, B. H. Clark. Introduction to O'Neill's life and work. Clark analyzes each play from the early THE WEB to the recently produced MOON FOR THE MISBEGOTTEN and THE ICEMAN COMETH revealing the environmental and dramatic influences necessary for a complete understanding of these important works. Bibliography. Appendices. Index. ix + 182pp. 5⅜ x 8.　　　　　　　　T379 Paperbound **$1.25**

THE HEART OF THOREAU'S JOURNALS, edited by O. Shepard. The best general selection from Thoreau's voluminous (and rare) journals. This intimate record of thoughts and observations reveals the full Thoreau and his intellectual development more accurately than any of his published works: self-conflict between the scientific observer and the poet, reflections on transcendental philosophy, involvement in the tragedies of neighbors and national causes, etc. New preface, notes, introductions. xii + 228pp. 5⅜ x 8.　　　T741 Paperbound **$1.45**

H. D. THOREAU: A WRITER'S JOURNAL, edited by L. Stapleton. A unique new selection from the Journals concentrating on Thoreau's growth as a conscious literary artist, the ideals and purposes of his art. Most of the material has never before appeared outside of the complete 14-volume edition. Contains vital insights on Thoreau's projected book on Concord, thoughts on the nature of men and government, indignation with slavery, sources of inspiration, goals in life. Index. xxxiii + 234pp. 5⅜ x 8.　　　　　　　T678 Paperbound **$1.55**

THE HEART OF EMERSON'S JOURNALS, edited by Bliss Perry. Best of these revealing Journals, originally 10 volumes, presented in a one volume edition. Talks with Channing, Hawthorne, Thoreau, and Bronson Alcott; impressions of Webster, Everett, John Brown, and Lincoln; records of moments of sudden understanding, vision, and solitary ecstasy. "The essays do not reveal the power of Emerson's mind . . . as do these hasty and informal writings," N.Y. Times. Preface by Bliss Perry. Index. xiii + 357pp. 5⅜ x 8.　　T477 Paperbound **$1.85**

FOUNDERS OF THE MIDDLE AGES, E. K. Rand. This is the best non-technical discussion of the transformation of Latin pagan culture into medieval civilization. Covering such figures as Tertullian, Gregory, Jerome, Boethius, Augustine, the Neoplatonists, and many other literary men, educators, classicists, and humanists, this book is a storehouse of information presented clearly and simply for the intelligent non-specialist. "Thoughtful, beautifully written," AMERICAN HISTORICAL REVIEW. "Extraordinarily accurate," Richard McKeon, THE NATION. ix + 365pp. 5⅜ x 8.　　　　　　　　　　　　　　　T369 Paperbound **$1.85**

PLAY-MAKING: A MANUAL OF CRAFTSMANSHIP, William Archer. With an extensive, new introduction by John Gassner, Yale Univ. The permanently essential requirements of solid play construction are set down in clear, practical language: theme, exposition, foreshadowing, tension, obligatory scene, peripety, dialogue, character, psychology, other topics. This book has been one of the most influential elements in the modern theatre, and almost everything said on the subject since is contained explicitly or implicitly within its covers. Bibliography. Index. xlii + 277pp. 5⅜ x 8.　　　　　　　　　　　　　　　　　T651 Paperbound **$1.75**

HAMBURG DRAMATURGY, G. E. Lessing. One of the most brilliant of German playwrights of the eighteenth-century age of criticism analyzes the complex of theory and tradition that constitutes the world of theater. These 104 essays on aesthetic theory helped demolish the regime of French classicism, opening the door to psychological and social realism, romanticism. Subjects include the original functions of tragedy; drama as the rational world; the meaning of pity and fear, pity and fear as means for purgation and other Aristotelian concepts; genius and creative force; interdependence of poet's language and actor's interpretation; truth and authenticity; etc. A basic and enlightening study for anyone interested in aesthetics and ideas, from the philosopher to the theatergoer. Introduction by Prof. Victor Lange. xxii + 265pp. 4½ x 6⅜.　　　　　　　　　　　　　T32 Paperbound **$1.45**

Social Sciences

SOCIAL THOUGHT FROM LORE TO SCIENCE, H. E. Barnes and H. Becker. An immense survey of sociological thought and ways of viewing, studying, planning, and reforming society from earliest times to the present. Includes thought on society of preliterate peoples, ancient non-Western cultures, and every great movement in Europe, America, and modern Japan. Analyzes hundreds of great thinkers: Plato, Augustine, Bodin, Vico, Montesquieu, Herder, Comte, Marx, etc. Weighs the contributions of utopians, sophists, fascists and communists; economists, jurists, philosophers, ecclesiastics, and every 19th and 20th century school of scientific sociology, anthropology, and social psychology throughout the world. Combines topical, chronological, and regional approaches, treating the evolution of social thought as a process rather than as a series of mere topics. "Impressive accuracy, competence, and discrimination . . . easily the best single survey," Nation. Thoroughly revised, with new material up to 1960. 2 indexes. Over 2200 bibliographical notes. Three volume set. Total of 1586pp. 5⅜ x 8.

T901 Vol I	Paperbound	**$2.35**
T902 Vol II	Paperbound	**$2.35**
T903 Vol III	Paperbound	**$2.35**
	The set	**$7.05**

FOLKWAYS, William Graham Sumner. A classic of sociology, a searching and thorough examination of patterns of behaviour from primitive, ancient Greek and Judaic, Medieval Christian, African, Oriental, Melanesian, Australian, Islamic, to modern Western societies. Thousands of illustrations of social, sexual, and religious customs, mores, laws, and institutions. Hundreds of categories: Labor, Wealth, Abortion, Primitive Justice, Life Policy, Slavery, Cannibalism, Uncleanness and the Evil Eye, etc. Will extend the horizon of every reader by showing the relativism of his own culture. Prefatory note by A. G. Keller. Introduction by William Lyon Phelps. Bibliography. Index. xiii + 692pp. 5⅜ x 8.   T508 Paperbound **$2.49**

PRIMITIVE RELIGION, P. Radin. A thorough treatment by a noted anthropologist of the nature and origin of man's belief in the supernatural and the influences that have shaped religious expression in primitive societies. Ranging from the Arunta, Ashanti, Aztec, Bushman, Crow, Fijian, etc., of Africa, Australia, Pacific Islands, the Arctic, North and South America, Prof. Radin integrates modern psychology, comparative religion, and economic thought with first-hand accounts gathered by himself and other scholars of primitive initiations, training of the shaman, and other fascinating topics. "Excellent," NATURE (London). Unabridged reissue of 1st edition. New author's preface. Bibliographic notes. Index. x + 322pp. 5⅜ x 8.
T393 Paperbound **$1.85**

PRIMITIVE MAN AS PHILOSOPHER, P. Radin. A standard anthropological work covering primitive thought on such topics as the purpose of life, marital relations, freedom of thought, symbolism, death, resignation, the nature of reality, personality, gods, and many others. Drawn from factual material gathered from the Winnebago, Oglala Sioux, Maori, Baganda, Batak, Zuni, among others, it does not distort ideas by removing them from context but interprets strictly within the original framework. Extensive selections of original primitive documents. Bibliography. Index. xviii + 402pp. 5⅜ x 8.   T392 Paperbound **$2.25**

A TREATISE ON SOCIOLOGY, THE MIND AND SOCIETY, Vilfredo Pareto. This treatise on human society is one of the great classics of modern sociology. First published in 1916, its careful catalogue of the innumerable manifestations of non-logical human conduct (Book One); the theory of "residues," leading to the premise that sentiment not logic determines human behavior (Book Two), and of "derivations," beliefs derived from desires (Book Three); and the general description of society made up of non-elite and elite, consisting of "foxes" who live by cunning and "lions" who live by force, stirred great controversy. But Pareto's passion for isolation and classification of elements and factors, and his allegiance to scientific method as the key tool for scrutinizing the human situation made his a truly twentieth-century mind and his work a catalytic influence on certain later social commentators. These four volumes (bound as two) require no special training to be appreciated and any reader who wishes to gain a complete understanding of modern sociological theory, regardless of special field of interest, will find them a must. Reprint of revised (corrected) printing of original edition. Translated by Andrew Bongiorno and Arthur Livingston. Index. Bibliography. Appendix containing index-summary of theorems. 48 diagrams. Four volumes bound as two. Total of 2063pp. 5⅜ x 8½.   The set Clothbound **$15.00**

THE POLISH PEASANT IN EUROPE AND AMERICA, William I. Thomas, Florian Znaniecki. A seminal sociological study of peasant primary groups (family and community) and the disruptions produced by a new industrial system and immigration to America. The peasant's family, class system, religious and aesthetic attitudes, and economic life are minutely examined and analyzed in hundreds of pages of primary documentation, particularly letters between family members. The disorientation caused by new environments is scrutinized in detail (a 312-page autobiography of an immigrant is especially valuable and revealing) in an attempt to find common experiences and reactions. The famous "Methodological Note" sets forth the principles which guided the authors. When out of print this set has sold for as much as $50. 2nd revised edition. 2 vols. Vol. 1: xv + 1115pp. Vol. 2: 1135pp. Index. 6 x 9.
T478 Clothbound 2 vol. set **$12.50**

Philosophy, Religion

GUIDE TO PHILOSOPHY, C. E. M. Joad. A modern classic which examines many crucial problems which man has pondered through the ages: Does free will exist? Is there plan in the universe? How do we know and validate our knowledge? Such opposed solutions as subjective idealism and realism, chance and teleology, vitalism and logical positivism, are evaluated and the contributions of the great philosophers from the Greeks to moderns like Russell, Whitehead, and others, are considered in the context of each problem. "The finest introduction," BOSTON TRANSCRIPT. Index. Classified bibliography. 592pp. 5⅜ x 8.
T297 Paperbound $2.00

HISTORY OF ANCIENT PHILOSOPHY, W. Windelband. One of the clearest, most accurate comprehensive surveys of Greek and Roman philosophy. Discusses ancient philosophy in general, intellectual life in Greece in the 7th and 6th centuries B.C., Thales, Anaximander, Anaximenes, Heraclitus, the Eleatics, Empedocles, Anaxagoras, Leucippus, the Pythagoreans, the Sophists, Socrates, Democritus (20 pages), Plato (50 pages), Aristotle (70 pages), the Peripatetics, Stoics, Epicureans, Sceptics, Neo-platonists, Christian Apologists, etc. 2nd German edition translated by H. E. Cushman. xv + 393pp. 5⅜ x 8.
T357 Paperbound $1.85

ILLUSTRATIONS OF THE HISTORY OF MEDIEVAL THOUGHT AND LEARNING, R. L. Poole. Basic analysis of the thought and lives of the leading philosophers and ecclesiastics from the 8th to the 14th century—Abailard, Ockham, Wycliffe, Marsiglio of Padua, and many other great thinkers who carried the torch of Western culture and learning through the "Dark Ages": political, religious, and metaphysical views. Long a standard work for scholars and one of the best introductions to medieval thought for beginners. Index. 10 Appendices. xiii + 327pp. 5⅜ x 8.
T674 Paperbound $1.85

PHILOSOPHY AND CIVILIZATION IN THE MIDDLE AGES, M. de Wulf. This semi-popular survey covers aspects of medieval intellectual life such as religion, philosophy, science, the arts, etc. It also covers feudalism vs. Catholicism, rise of the universities, mendicant orders, monastic centers, and similar topics. Unabridged. Bibliography. Index. viii + 320pp. 5⅜ x 8.
T284 Paperbound $1.85

AN INTRODUCTION TO SCHOLASTIC PHILOSOPHY, Prof. M. de Wulf. Formerly entitled SCHOLASTICISM OLD AND NEW, this volume examines the central scholastic tradition from St. Anselm, Albertus Magnus, Thomas Aquinas, up to Suarez in the 17th century. The relation of scholasticism to ancient and medieval philosophy and science in general is clear and easily followed. The second part of the book considers the modern revival of scholasticism, the Louvain position, relations with Kantianism and Positivism. Unabridged. xvi + 271pp. 5⅜ x 8.
T296 Clothbound $3.50
T283 Paperbound $1.75

A HISTORY OF MODERN PHILOSOPHY, H. Höffding. An exceptionally clear and detailed coverage of western philosophy from the Renaissance to the end of the 19th century. Major and minor men such as Pomponazzi, Bodin, Boehme, Telesius, Bruno, Copernicus, da Vinci, Kepler, Galileo, Bacon, Descartes, Hobbes, Spinoza, Leibniz, Wolff, Locke, Newton, Berkeley, Hume, Erasmus, Montesquieu, Voltaire, Diderot, Rousseau, Lessing, Kant, Herder, Fichte, Schelling, Hegel, Schopenhauer, Comte, Mill, Darwin, Spencer, Hartmann, Lange, and many others, are discussed in terms of theory of knowledge, logic, cosmology, and psychology. Index. 2 volumes, total of 1159pp. 5⅜ x 8.
T117 Vol. 1, Paperbound $2.00
T118 Vol. 2, Paperbound $2.00

ARISTOTLE, A. E. Taylor. A brilliant, searching non-technical account of Aristotle and his thought written by a foremost Platonist. It covers the life and works of Aristotle; classification of the sciences; logic; first philosophy; matter and form; causes; motion and eternity; God; physics; metaphysics; and similar topics. Bibliography. New Index compiled for this edition. 128pp. 5⅜ x 8.
T280 Paperbound $1.00

THE SYSTEM OF THOMAS AQUINAS, M. de Wulf. Leading Neo-Thomist, one of founders of University of Louvain, gives concise exposition to central doctrines of Aquinas, as a means toward determining his value to modern philosophy, religion. Formerly "Medieval Philosophy Illustrated from the System of Thomas Aquinas." Trans. by E. Messenger. Introduction. 151pp. 5⅜ x 8.
T568 Paperbound $1.25

LEIBNIZ, H. W. Carr. Most stimulating middle-level coverage of basic philosophical thought of Leibniz. Easily understood discussion, analysis of major works: "Theodicy," "Principles of Nature and Grace," "Monadology"; Leibniz's influence; intellectual growth; correspondence; disputes with Bayle, Malebranche, Newton; importance of his thought today, with reinterpretation in modern terminology. "Power and mastery," London Times. Bibliography. Index. 226pp. 5⅜ x 8.
T624 Paperbound $1.35

CATALOGUE OF DOVER BOOKS

AN ESSAY CONCERNING HUMAN UNDERSTANDING, John Locke. Edited by A. C. Fraser. Unabridged reprinting of definitive edition; only complete edition of "Essay" in print. Marginal analyses of almost every paragraph; hundreds of footnotes; authoritative 140-page biographical, critical, historical prolegomena. Indexes. 1170pp. 5⅜ x 8.
T530 Vol. 1 (Books 1, 2) Paperbound **$2.25**
T531 Vol. 2 (Books 3, 4) Paperbound **$2.25**
2 volume set **$4.50**

THE PHILOSOPHY OF HISTORY, G. W. F. Hegel. One of the great classics of western thought which reveals Hegel's basic principle: that history is not chance but a rational process, the realization of the Spirit of Freedom. Ranges from the oriental cultures of subjective thought to the classical subjective cultures, to the modern absolute synthesis where spiritual and secular may be reconciled. Translation and introduction by J. Sibree. Introduction by C. Hegel. Special introduction for this edition by Prof. Carl Friedrich. xxxix + 447pp. 5⅜ x 8.
T112 Paperbound **$2.00**

THE PHILOSOPHY OF HEGEL, W. T. Stace. The first detailed analysis of Hegel's thought in English, this is especially valuable since so many of Hegel's works are out of print. Dr. Stace examines Hegel's debt to Greek idealists and the 18th century and then proceeds to a careful description and analysis of Hegel's first principles, categories, reason, dialectic method, his logic, philosophy of nature and spirit, etc. Index. Special 14 x 20 chart of Hegelian system. x + 526pp. 5⅜ x 8.
T254 Paperbound **$2.25**

THE WILL TO BELIEVE and HUMAN IMMORTALITY, W. James. Two complete books bound as one. THE WILL TO BELIEVE discusses the interrelations of belief, will, and intellect in man; chance vs. determinism, free will vs. determinism, free will vs. fate, pluralism vs. monism; the philosophies of Hegel and Spencer, and more. HUMAN IMMORTALITY examines the question of survival after death and develops an unusual and powerful argument for immortality. Two prefaces. Index. Total of 429pp. 5⅜ x 8.
T291 Paperbound **$2.45**

THE WORLD AND THE INDIVIDUAL, Josiah Royce. Only major effort by an American philosopher to interpret nature of things in systematic, comprehensive manner. Royce's formulation of an absolute voluntarism remains one of the original and profound solutions to the problems involved. Part One, Four Historical Conceptions of Being, inquires into first principles, true meaning and place of individuality. Part Two, Nature, Man, and the Moral Order, is application of first principles to problems concerning religion, evil, moral order. Introduction by J. E. Smith, Yale Univ. Index. 1070pp. 5⅜ x 8.
T561 Vol. 1 Paperbound **$2.75**
T562 Vol. 2 Paperbound **$2.75**
Two volume set **$5.50**

THE PHILOSOPHICAL WRITINGS OF PEIRCE, edited by J. Buchler. This book (formerly THE PHILOSOPHY OF PEIRCE) is a carefully integrated exposition of Peirce's complete system composed of selections from his own work. Symbolic logic, scientific method, theory of signs, pragmatism, epistemology, chance, cosmology, ethics, and many other topics are treated by one of the greatest philosophers of modern times. This is the only inexpensive compilation of his key ideas. xvi + 386pp. 5⅜ x 8.
T217 Paperbound **$2.00**

EXPERIENCE AND NATURE, John Dewey. An enlarged, revised edition of the Paul Carus lectures which Dewey delivered in 1925. It covers Dewey's basic formulation of the problem of knowledge, with a full discussion of other systems, and a detailing of his own concepts of the relationship of external world, mind, and knowledge. Starts with a thorough examination of the philosophical method; examines the interrelationship of experience and nature; analyzes experience on basis of empirical naturalism, the formulation of law, role of language and social factors in knowledge; etc. Dewey's treatment of central problems in philosophy is profound but extremely easy to follow. ix + 448pp. 5⅜ x 8.
T471 Paperbound **$2.00**

THE PHILOSOPHICAL WORKS OF DESCARTES. The definitive English edition of all the major philosophical works and letters of René Descartes. All of his revolutionary insights, from his famous "Cogito ergo sum" to his detailed account of contemporary science and his astonishingly fruitful concept that all phenomena of the universe (except mind) could be reduced to clear laws by the use of mathematics. An excellent source for the thought of men like Hobbes, Arnauld, Gassendi, etc., who were Descartes's contemporaries. Translated by E. S. Haldane and G. Ross. Introductory notes. Index. Total of 842pp. 5⅜ x 8.
T71 Vol. 1, Paperbound **$2.00**
T72 Vol. 2, Paperbound **$2.00**

THE CHIEF WORKS OF SPINOZA. An unabridged reprint of the famous Bohn edition containing all of Spinoza's most important works: Vol. I: The Theologico-Political Treatise and the Political Treatise. Vol. II: On The Improvement Of Understanding, The Ethics, Selected Letters. Profound and enduring ideas on God, the universe, pantheism, society, religion, the state, democracy, the mind, emotions, freedom and the nature of man, which influenced Goethe, Hegel, Schelling, Coleridge, Whitehead, and many others. Introduction. 2 volumes. 826pp. 5⅜ x 8.
T249 Vol. I, Paperbound **$1.50**
T250 Vol. II, Paperbound **$1.50**

CATALOGUE OF DOVER BOOKS

THE ANALYSIS OF MATTER, Bertrand Russell. A classic which has retained its importance in understanding the relation between modern physical theory and human perception. Logical analysis of physics, prerelativity physics, causality, scientific inference, Weyl's theory, tensors, invariants and physical interpretations, periodicity, and much more is treated with Russell's usual brilliance. "Masterly piece of clear thinking and clear writing," NATION AND ATHENAEUM. "Most thorough treatment of the subject," THE NATION. Introduction. Index. 8 figures. viii + 408pp. 5⅜ x 8.   S231 Paperbound **$1.95**

CONCEPTUAL THINKING (A LOGICAL INQUIRY), S. Körner. Discusses origin, use of general concepts on which language is based, and the light they shed on basic philosophical questions. Rigorously examines how different concepts are related; how they are linked to experience; problems in the field of contact between exact logical, mathematical, and scientific concepts, and the inexactness of everyday experience (studied at length). This work elaborates many new approaches to the traditional problems of philosophy—epistemology, value theories, metaphysics, aesthetics, morality. "Rare originality . . . brings a new rigour into philosophical argument," Philosophical Quarterly. New corrected second edition. Index. vii + 301pp. 5⅜ x 8.   T516 Paperbound **$1.75**

INTRODUCTION TO SYMBOLIC LOGIC, S. Langer. No special knowledge of math required — probably the clearest book ever written on symbolic logic, suitable for the layman, general scientist, and philosopher. You start with simple symbols and advance to a knowledge of the Boole-Schroeder and Russell-Whitehead systems. Forms, logical structure, classes, the calculus of propositions, logic of the syllogism, etc., are all covered. "One of the clearest and simplest introductions," MATHEMATICS GAZETTE. Second enlarged, revised edition. 368pp. 5⅜ x 8.   S164 Paperbound **$1.75**

LANGUAGE, TRUTH AND LOGIC, A. J. Ayer. A clear, careful analysis of the basic ideas of Logical Positivism. Building on the work of Schlick, Russell, Carnap, and the Viennese School, Mr. Ayer develops a detailed exposition of the nature of philosophy, science, and metaphysics; the Self and the World; logic and common sense, and other philosophic concepts. An aid to clarity of thought as well as the first full-length development of Logical Positivism in English. Introduction by Bertrand Russell. Index. 160pp. 5⅜ x 8.   T10 Paperbound **$1.25**

ESSAYS IN EXPERIMENTAL LOGIC, J. Dewey. Based upon the theory that knowledge implies a judgment which in turn implies an inquiry, these papers consider the inquiry stage in terms of: the relationship of thought and subject matter, antecedents of thought, data and meanings. 3 papers examine Bertrand Russell's thought, while 2 others discuss pragmatism and a final essay presents a new theory of the logic of values. Index. viii + 444pp. 5⅜ x 8.
T73 Paperbound **$1.95**

TRAGIC SENSE OF LIFE, M. de Unamuno. The acknowledged masterpiece of one of Spain's most influential thinkers. Between the despair at the inevitable death of man and all his works and the desire for something better, Unamuno finds that "saving incertitude" that alone can console us. This dynamic appraisal of man's faith in God and in himself has been called "a masterpiece" by the ENCYCLOPAEDIA BRITANNICA. xxx + 332pp. 5⅜ x 8.
T257 Paperbound **$2.00**

HISTORY OF DOGMA, A. Harnack. Adolph Harnack, who died in 1930, was perhaps the greatest Church historian of all time. In this epoch-making history, which has never been surpassed in comprehensiveness and wealth of learning, he traces the development of the authoritative Christian doctrinal system from its first crystallization in the 4th century down through the Reformation, including also a brief survey of the later developments through the Infallibility decree of 1870. He reveals the enormous influence of Greek thought on the early Fathers, and discusses such topics as the Apologists, the great councils, Manichaeism, the historical position of Augustine, the medieval opposition to indulgences, the rise of Protestantism, the relations of Luther's doctrines with modern tendencies of thought, and much more. "Monumental work; still the most valuable history of dogma . . . luminous analysis of the problems . . . abounds in suggestion and stimulus and can be neglected by no one who desires to understand the history of thought in this most important field," Dutcher's Guide to Historical Literature. Translated by Neil Buchanan. Index. Unabridged reprint in 4 volumes. Vol I: Beginnings to the Gnostics and Marcion. Vol II & III: 2nd century to the 4th century Fathers. Vol IV & V: 4th century Councils to the Carlovingian Renaissance. Vol VI & VII: Period of Clugny (c. 1000) to the Reformation, and after. Total of cii + 2407pp. 5⅜ x 8.

T904 Vol I	Paperbound **$2.50**
T905 Vol II & III	Paperbound **$2.50**
T906 Vol IV & V	Paperbound **$2.50**
T907 Vol VI & VII	Paperbound **$2.50**
	The set **$10.00**

THE GUIDE FOR THE PERPLEXED, Maimonides. One of the great philosophical works of all time and a necessity for everyone interested in the philosophy of the Middle Ages in the Jewish, Christian, and Moslem traditions. Maimonides develops a common meeting-point for the Old Testament and the Aristotelian thought which pervaded the medieval world. His ideas and methods predate such scholastics as Aquinas and Scotus and throw light on the entire problem of philosophy or science vs. religion. 2nd revised edition. Complete unabridged Friedländer translation. 55 page introduction to Maimonides's life, period, etc., with an important summary of the GUIDE. Index. lix + 414pp. 5⅜ x 8.   T351 Paperbound **$2.00**

Americana

THE EYES OF DISCOVERY, J. Bakeless. A vivid reconstruction of how unspoiled America appeared to the first white men. Authentic and enlightening accounts of Hudson's landing in New York, Coronado's trek through the Southwest; scores of explorers, settlers, trappers, soldiers. America's pristine flora, fauna, and Indians in every region and state in fresh and unusual new aspects. "A fascinating view of what the land was like before the first highway went through," Time. 68 contemporary illustrations, 39 newly added in this edition. Index. Bibliography. x + 500pp. 5⅜ x 8. **T761 Paperbound $2.00**

AUDUBON AND HIS JOURNALS, J. J. Audubon. A collection of fascinating accounts of Europe and America in the early 1800's through Audubon's own eyes. Includes the Missouri River Journals —an eventful trip through America's untouched heartland, the Labrador Journals, the European Journals, the famous "Episodes", and other rare Audubon material, including the descriptive chapters from the original letterpress edition of the "Ornithological Studies", omitted in all later editions. Indispensable for ornithologists, naturalists, and all lovers of Americana and adventure. 70-page biography by Audubon's granddaughter. 38 illustrations. Index. Total of 1106pp. 5⅜ x 8. **T675 Vol I Paperbound $2.25**
T676 Vol II Paperbound $2.25
The set $4.50

TRAVELS OF WILLIAM BARTRAM, edited by Mark Van Doren. The first inexpensive illustrated edition of one of the 18th century's most delightful books is an excellent source of first-hand material on American geography, anthropology, and natural history. Many descriptions of early Indian tribes are our only source of information on them prior to the infiltration of the white man. "The mind of a scientist with the soul of a poet," John Livingston Lowes. 13 original illustrations and maps. Edited with an introduction by Mark Van Doren. 448pp. 5⅜ x 8. **T13 Paperbound $2.00**

GARRETS AND PRETENDERS: A HISTORY OF BOHEMIANISM IN AMERICA, A. Parry. The colorful and fantastic history of American Bohemianism from Poe to Kerouac. This is the only complete record of hoboes, cranks, starving poets, and suicides. Here are Pfaff, Whitman, Crane, Bierce, Pound, and many others. New chapters by the author and by H. T. Moore bring this thorough and well-documented history down to the Beatniks. "An excellent account," N. Y. Times. Scores of cartoons, drawings, and caricatures. Bibliography. Index. xxviii + 421pp. 5⅝ x 8⅜. **T708 Paperbound $1.95**

THE EXPLORATION OF THE COLORADO RIVER AND ITS CANYONS, J. W. Powell. The thrilling first-hand account of the expedition that filled in the last white space on the map of the United States. Rapids, famine, hostile Indians, and mutiny are among the perils encountered as the unknown Colorado Valley reveals its secrets. This is the only uncut version of Major Powell's classic of exploration that has been printed in the last 60 years. Includes later reflections and subsequent expedition. 250 illustrations, new map. 400pp. 5⅝ x 8⅜. **T94 Paperbound $2.00**

THE JOURNAL OF HENRY D. THOREAU, Edited by Bradford Torrey and Francis H. Allen. Henry Thoreau is not only one of the most important figures in American literature and social thought; his voluminous journals (from which his books emerged as selections and crystallizations) constitute both the longest, most sensitive record of personal internal development and a most penetrating description of a historical moment in American culture. This present set, which was first issued in fourteen volumes, contains Thoreau's entire journals from 1837 to 1862, with the exception of the lost years which were found only recently. We are reissuing it, complete and unabridged, with a new introduction by Walter Harding, Secretary of the Thoreau Society. Fourteen volumes reissued in two volumes. Foreword by Henry Seidel Canby. Total of 1888pp. 8⅜ x 12¼. **T312-3 Two volume set, Clothbound $20.00**

GAMES AND SONGS OF AMERICAN CHILDREN, collected by William Wells Newell. A remarkable collection of 190 games with songs that accompany many of them; cross references to show similarities, differences among them; variations; musical notation for 38 songs. Textual discussions show relations with folk-drama and other aspects of folk tradition. Grouped into categories for ready comparative study: Love-games, histories, playing at work, human life, bird and beast, mythology, guessing-games, etc. New introduction covers relations of songs and dances to timeless heritage of folklore, biographical sketch of Newell, other pertinent data. A good source of inspiration for those in charge of groups of children and a valuable reference for anthropologists, sociologists, psychiatrists. Introduction by Carl Withers. New indexes of first lines, games. 5⅜ x 8½. xii + 242pp. **T354 Paperbound $1.65**

GARDNER'S PHOTOGRAPHIC SKETCH BOOK OF THE CIVIL WAR, Alexander Gardner. The first published collection of Civil War photographs, by one of the two or three most famous photographers of the era, outstandingly reproduced from the original positives. Scenes of crucial battles: Appomattox, Manassas, Mechanicsville, Bull Run, Yorktown, Fredericksburg, etc. Gettysburg immediately after retirement of forces. Battle ruins at Richmond, Petersburg, Gaines'Mill. Prisons, arsenals, a slave pen, fortifications, headquarters, pontoon bridges, soldiers, a field hospital. A unique glimpse into the realities of one of the bloodiest wars in history, with an introductory text to each picture by Gardner himself. Until this edition, there were only five known copies in libraries, and fewer in private hands, one of which sold at auction in 1952 for $425. Introduction by E. F. Bleiler. 100 full page 7 x 10 photographs (original size). 224pp. 8½ x 10¾. **T476 Clothbound $6.00**

A BIBLIOGRAPHY OF NORTH AMERICAN FOLKLORE AND FOLKSONG, Charles Haywood, Ph.D. The only book that brings together bibliographic information on so wide a range of folklore material. Lists practically everything published about American folksongs, ballads, dances, folk beliefs and practices, popular music, tales, similar material—more than 35,000 titles of books, articles, periodicals, monographs, music publications, phonograph records. Each entry complete with author, title, date and place of publication, arranger and performer of particular examples of folk music, many with Dr. Haywood's valuable criticism, evaluation. Volume I, "The American People," is complete listing of general and regional studies, titles of tales and songs of Negro and non-English speaking groups and where to find them, Occupational Bibliography including sections listing sources of information, folk material on cowboys, riverboat men, 49ers, American characters like Mike Fink, Frankie and Johnnie, John Henry, many more. Volume II, "The American Indian," tells where to find information on dances, myths, songs, ritual of more than 250 tribes in U.S., Canada. A monumental product of 10 years' labor, carefully classified for easy use. "All students of this subject . . . will find themselves in debt to Professor Haywood," Stith Thompson, in American Anthropologist. ". . . a most useful and excellent work," Duncan Emrich, Chief Folklore Section, Library of Congress, in "Notes." Corrected, enlarged republication of 1951 edition. New Preface. New index of composers, arrangers, performers. General index of more than 15,000 items. Two volumes. Total of 1301pp. 6⅛ x 9¼. **T797-798 Clothbound $12.50**

INCIDENTS OF TRAVEL IN YUCATAN, John L. Stephens. One of first white men to penetrate interior of Yucatan tells the thrilling story of his discoveries of 44 cities, remains of once-powerful Maya civilization. Compelling text combines narrative power with historical significance as it takes you through heat, dust, storms of Yucatan; native festivals with brutal bull fights; great ruined temples atop man-made mounds. Countless idols, sculptures, tombs, examples of Mayan taste for rich ornamentation, from gateways to personal trinkets, accurately illustrated, discussed in text. Will appeal to those interested in ancient civilizations, and those who like stories of exploration, discovery, adventure. Republication of last (1843) edition. 124 illustrations by English artist, F. Catherwood. Appendix on Mayan architecture, chronology. Two volume set. Total of xxviii + 927pp.

Vol I T926 Paperbound **$2.00**
Vol II T927 Paperbound **$2.00**
The set **$4.00**

A GENIUS IN THE FAMILY, Hiram Percy Maxim. Sir Hiram Stevens Maxim was known to the public as the inventive genius who created the Maxim gun, automatic sprinkler, and a heavier-than-air plane that got off the ground in 1894. Here, his son reminisces—this is by no means a formal biography—about the exciting and often downright scandalous private life of his brilliant, eccentric father. A warm and winning portrait of a prankish, mischievous, impious personality, a genuine character. The style is fresh and direct, the effect is unadulterated pleasure. "A book of charm and lasting humor . . . belongs on the 'must read' list of all fathers," New York Times. "A truly gorgeous affair," New Statesman and Nation. 17 illustrations, 16 specially for this edition. viii + 108pp. 5⅜ x 8½. **T948 Paperbound $1.00**

HORSELESS CARRIAGE DAYS, Hiram P. Maxim. The best account of an important technological revolution by one of its leading figures. The delightful and rewarding story of the author's experiments with the exact combustibility of gasoline, stopping and starting mechanisms, carriage design, and engines. Captures remarkably well the flavor of an age of scoffers and rival inventors not above sabotage; of noisy, uncontrollable gasoline vehicles and incredible mobile steam kettles. ". . . historic information and light humor are combined to furnish highly entertaining reading," New York Times. 56 photographs, 12 specially for this edition. xi + 175pp. 5⅜ x 8½. **T964 Paperbound $1.35**

BODY, BOOTS AND BRITCHES: FOLKTALES, BALLADS AND SPEECH FROM COUNTRY NEW YORK, Harold W. Thompson. A unique collection, discussion of songs, stories, anecdotes, proverbs handed down orally from Scotch-Irish grandfathers, German nurse-maids, Negro workmen, gathered from all over Upper New York State. Tall tales by and about lumbermen and pirates, canalers and injun-fighters, tragic and comic ballads, scores of sayings and proverbs all tied together by an informative, delightful narrative by former president of New York Historical Society. ". . . a sparkling homespun tapestry that every lover of Americana will want to have around the house," Carl Carmer, New York Times. Republication of 1939 edition. 20 line-drawings. Index. Appendix (Sources of material, bibliography). 530pp. 5⅜ x 8½. **T411 Paperbound $2.00**

Art, History of Art, Antiques, Graphic Arts, Handcrafts

ART STUDENTS' ANATOMY, E. J. Farris. Outstanding art anatomy that uses chiefly living objects for its illustrations. 71 photos of undraped men, women, children are accompanied by carefully labeled matching sketches to illustrate the skeletal system, articulations and movements, bony landmarks, the muscular system, skin, fasciae, fat, etc. 9 x-ray photos show movement of joints. Undraped models are shown in such actions as serving in tennis, drawing a bow in archery, playing football, dancing, preparing to spring and to dive. Also discussed and illustrated are proportions, age and sex differences, the anatomy of the smile, etc. 8 plates by the great early 18th century anatomic illustrator Siegfried Albinus are also included. Glossary. 158 figures, 7 in color. x + 159pp. 5⅝ x 8⅜. T744 Paperbound **$1.50**

AN ATLAS OF ANATOMY FOR ARTISTS, F Schider. A new 3rd edition of this standard text enlarged by 52 new illustrations of hands, anatomical studies by Cloquet, and expressive life studies of the body by Barcsay. 189 clear, detailed plates offer you precise information of impeccable accuracy. 29 plates show all aspects of the skeleton, with closeups of special areas, while 54 full-page plates, mostly in two colors, give human musculature as seen from four different points of view, with cutaways for important portions of the body. 14 full-page plates provide photographs of hand forms, eyelids, female breasts, and indicate the location of muscles upon models. 59 additional plates show how great artists of the past utilized human anatomy. They reproduce sketches and finished work by such artists as Michelangelo, Leonardo da Vinci, Goya, and 15 others. This is a lifetime reference work which will be one of the most important books in any artist's library. "The standard reference tool," AMERICAN LIBRARY ASSOCIATION. "Excellent," AMERICAN ARTIST. Third enlarged edition. 189 plates, 647 illustrations. xxvi + 192pp. 7⅞ x 10⅝. T241 Clothbound **$6.00**

AN ATLAS OF ANIMAL ANATOMY FOR ARTISTS, W. Ellenberger, H. Baum, H. Dittrich. The largest, richest animal anatomy for artists available in English. 99 detailed anatomical plates of such animals as the horse, dog, cat, lion, deer, seal, kangaroo, flying squirrel, cow, bull, goat, monkey, hare, and bat. Surface features are clearly indicated, while progressive beneath-the-skin pictures show musculature, tendons, and bone structure. Rest and action are exhibited in terms of musculature and skeletal structure and detailed cross-sections are given for heads and important features. The animals chosen are representative of specific families so that a study of these anatomies will provide knowledge of hundreds of related species. "Highly recommended as one of the very few books on the subject worthy of being used as an authoritative guide," DESIGN. "Gives a fundamental knowledge," AMERICAN ARTIST. Second revised, enlarged edition with new plates from Cuvier, Stubbs, etc. 288 illustrations. 153pp. 11⅜ x 9. T82 Clothbound **$6.00**

THE HUMAN FIGURE IN MOTION, Eadweard Muybridge. The largest selection in print of Muybridge's famous high-speed action photos of the human figure in motion. 4789 photographs illustrate 162 different actions: men, women, children—mostly undraped—are shown walking, running, carrying various objects, sitting, lying down, climbing, throwing, arising, and performing over 150 other actions. Some actions are shown in as many as 150 photographs each. All in all there are more than 500 action strips in this enormous volume, series shots taken at shutter speeds of as high as 1/6000th of a second! These are not posed shots, but true stopped motion. They show bone and muscle in situations that the human eye is not fast enough to capture. Earlier, smaller editions of these prints have brought $40 and more on the out-of-print market. "A must for artists," ART IN FOCUS. "An unparalleled dictionary of action for all artists," AMERICAN ARTIST. 390 full-page plates, with 4789 photographs. Printed on heavy glossy stock. Reinforced binding with headbands. xxi + 390pp. 7⅞ x 10⅝. T204 Clothbound **$10.00**

ANIMALS IN MOTION, Eadweard Muybridge. This is the largest collection of animal action photos in print. 34 different animals (horses, mules, oxen, goats, camels, pigs, cats, guanacos, lions, gnus, deer, monkeys, eagles—and 21 others) in 132 characteristic actions. The horse alone is shown in more than 40 different actions. All 3919 photographs are taken in series at speeds up to 1/6000th of a second. The secrets of leg motion, spinal patterns, head movements, strains and contortions shown nowhere else are captured. You will see exactly how a lion sets his foot down; how an elephant's knees are like a human's—and how they differ; the position of a kangaroo's legs in mid-leap; how an ostrich's head bobs; details of the flight of birds—and thousands of facets of motion only the fastest cameras can catch. Photographed from domestic animals and animals in the Philadelphia zoo, it contains neither semiposed artificial shots nor distorted telephoto shots taken under adverse conditions. Artists, biologists, decorators, cartoonists, will find this book indispensable for understanding animals in motion. "A really marvelous series of plates," NATURE (London). "The dry plate's most spectacular early use was by Eadweard Muybridge," LIFE. 3919 photographs; 380 full pages of plates. 440pp. Printed on heavy glossy paper. Deluxe binding with headbands. 7⅞ x 10⅝. T203 Clothbound **$10.00**

CATALOGUE OF DOVER BOOKS

ART ANATOMY, William Rimmer, M.D. Often called one of America's foremost contributions to art instruction, a work of art in its own right. More than 700 line drawings by the author, first-rate anatomist and dissector as well as artist, with a non-technical anatomical text. Impeccably accurate drawings of muscles, skeletal structure, surface features, other aspects of males and females, children, adults and aged persons show not only form, size, insertion and articulation but personality and emotion as reflected by physical features usually ignored in modern anatomical works. Complete unabridged reproduction of 1876 edition slightly rearranged. Introduction by Robert Hutchinson. 722 illustrations. xiii + 153pp. 7¾ x 10¾.
T908 Paperbound **$2.00**

ANIMAL DRAWING: ANATOMY AND ACTION FOR ARTISTS, C. R. Knight. The author and illustrator of this work was "the most distinguished painter of animal life." This extensive course in animal drawing discusses musculature, bone structure, animal psychology, movements, habits, habitats. Innumerable tips on proportions, light and shadow play, coloring, hair formation, feather arrangement, scales, how animals lie down, animal expressions, etc., from great apes to birds. Pointers on avoiding gracelessness in horses, deer; on introducing proper power and bulk to heavier animals; on giving proper grace and subtle expression to members of the cat family. Originally titled "Animal Anatomy and Psychology for the Artist and Layman." Over 123 illustrations. 149pp. 8¼ x 10½.
T426 Paperbound **$2.00**

DESIGN FOR ARTISTS AND CRAFTSMEN, L. Wolchonok. The most thorough course ever prepared on the creation of art motifs and designs. It teaches you to create your own designs out of things around you — from geometric patterns, plants, birds, animals, humans, landscapes, and man-made objects. It leads you step by step through the creation of more than 1300 designs, and shows you how to create design that is fresh, well-founded, and original. Mr. Wolchonok, whose text is used by scores of art schools, shows you how the same idea can be developed into many different forms, ranging from near representationalism to the most advanced forms of abstraction. The material in this book is entirely new, and combines full awareness of traditional design with the work of such men as Miro, Léger, Picasso, Moore, and others. 113 detailed exercises, with instruction hints, diagrams, and details to enable you to apply Wolchonok's methods to your own work. "A great contribution to the field of design and crafts," N. Y. SOCIETY OF CRAFTSMEN. More than 1300 illustrations. xv + 207pp. 7⅞ x 10¾.
T274 Clothbound **$4.95**

HAWTHORNE ON PAINTING. A vivid recreation, from students' notes, of instruction by Charles W. Hawthorne, given for over 31 years at his famous Cape Cod School of Art. Divided into sections on the outdoor model, still life, landscape, the indoor model, and water color, each section begins with a concise essay, followed by epigrammatic comments on color, form, seeing, etc. Not a formal course, but comments of a great teacher-painter on specific student works, which will solve problems in your own painting and understanding of art. "An excellent introduction for laymen and students alike," Time. Introduction. 100pp. 5⅜ x 8.
T653 Paperbound **$1.00**

THE ENJOYMENT AND USE OF COLOR, Walter Sargent. This book explains fascinating relations among colors, between colors in nature and art; describes experiments that you can perform to understand these relations more thoroughly; points out hundreds of little known facts about color values, intensities, effects of high and low illumination, complementary colors, color harmonies. Practical hints for painters, references to techniques of masters, questions at chapter ends for self-testing all make this a valuable book for artists, professional and amateur, and for general readers interested in world of color. Republication of 1923 edition. 35 illustrations, 6 full-page plates. New color frontispiece. Index. xii + 274pp. 5⅜ x 8.
T944 Paperbound **$2.25**

DECORATIVE ALPHABETS AND INITIALS, ed. by Alexander Nesbitt. No payment, no permission needed to reproduce any one of these 3924 different letters, covering 1000 years. Crisp, clear letters all in line, from Anglo-Saxon mss., Luebeck Cathedral, 15th century Augsburg; the work of Dürer, Holbein, Cresci, Beardsley, Rossing Wadsworth, John Moylin, etc. Every imaginable style. 91 complete alphabets. 123 full-page plates. 192pp. 7¾ x 10¾.
T544 Paperbound **$2.25**

THREE CLASSICS OF ITALIAN CALLIGRAPHY, edited by Oscar Ogg. Here, combined in a single volume, are complete reproductions of three famous calligraphic works written by the greatest writing masters of the Renaissance: Arrighi's OPERINA and IL MODO, Tagliente's LO PRESENTE LIBRO, and Palatino's LIBRO NUOVO. These books present more than 200 complete alphabets and thousands of lettered specimens. The basic hand is Papal Chancery, but scores of other alphabets are also given: European and Asiatic local alphabets, foliated and art alphabets, scrolls, cartouches, borders, etc. Text is in Italian. Introduction. 245 plates. x + 272pp. 6⅛ x 9¼.
T212 Paperbound **$2.25**

CALLIGRAPHY, J. G. Schwandner. One of the legendary books in the graphic arts, copies of which brought $500 each on the rare book market, now reprinted for the first time in over 200 years. A beautiful plate book of graceful calligraphy, and an inexhaustible source of first-rate material copyright-free, for artists, and directors, craftsmen, commercial artists, etc. More than 300 ornamental initials forming 12 complete alphabets, over 150 ornate frames and panels, over 200 flourishes, over 75 calligraphic pictures including a temple, cherubs, cocks, dodos, stags, chamois, foliated lions, greyhounds, etc. Thousand of calligraphic elements to be used for suggestions of quality, sophistication, antiquity, and sheer beauty. Historical introduction. 158 full-page plates. 368pp. 9 x 13.
T475 Clothbound **$10.00**

CATALOGUE OF DOVER BOOKS

METALWORK AND ENAMELLING, H. Maryon. This is probably the best book ever written on the subject. Prepared by Herbert Maryon, F.S.A., of the British Museum, it tells everything necessary for home manufacture of jewelry, rings, ear pendants, bowls, and dozens of other objects. Clearly written chapters provide precise information on such topics as materials, tools, soldering, filigree, setting stones, raising patterns, spinning metal, repoussé work, hinges and joints, metal inlaying, damascening, overlaying, niello, Japanese alloys, enamelling, cloisonné, painted enamels, casting, polishing, coloring, assaying, and dozens of other techniques. This is the next best thing to apprenticeship to a master metalworker. 363 photographs and figures. 374pp. 5½ x 8½. **T183 Clothbound $8.50**

SILK SCREEN TECHNIQUES, J. I. Biegeleisen, Max A. Cohn. A complete-to-the-last-detail copiously illustrated home course in this fast growing modern art form. Full directions for building silk screen out of inexpensive materials; explanations of five basic methods of stencil preparation—paper, blockout, tusche, film, photographic—and effects possible: light and shade, washes, dry brush, oil paint type impastos, gouaches, pastels. Detailed coverage of multicolor printing, illustrated by proofs showing the stages of a 4 color print. Special section on common difficulties. 149 illustrations, 8 in color. Sources of supply. xiv + 187pp. 6⅛ x 9¼. **T433 Paperbound $1.55**

A HANDBOOK OF WEAVES, G. H. Oelsner. Now back in print! Probably the most complete book of weaves ever printed, fully explained, differentiated, and illustrated. Includes plain weaves; irregular, double-stitched, and filling satins; derivative, basket, and rib weaves; steep, undulating, broken, offset, corkscrew, interlocking, herringbone, and fancy twills; honeycomb, lace, and crepe weaves; tricot, matelassé, and montagnac weaves; and much more. Translated and revised by S. S. Dale, with supplement on the analysis of weaves and fabrics. 1875 illustrations. vii + 402pp. 6 x 9¼. **T209 Clothbound $5.00**

BASIC BOOKBINDING, A. W. Lewis. Enables the beginner and the expert to apply the latest and most simplified techniques to rebinding old favorites and binding new paperback books. Complete lists of all necessary materials and guides to the selection of proper tools, paper, glue, boards, cloth, leather, or sheepskin covering fabrics, lettering inks and pigments, etc. You are shown how to collate a book, sew it, back it, trim it, make boards and attach them in easy step-by-step stages. Author's preface. 261 illustrations with appendix. Index. xi + 144pp. 5⅜ x 8. **T169 Paperbound $1.35**

BASKETRY, F. J. Christopher. Basic introductions cover selection of materials, use and care of tools, equipment. Easy-to-follow instructions for preparation of oval, oblong trays, lidded baskets, rush mats, tumbler holders, bicycle baskets, waste paper baskets, many other useful, beautiful articles made of coiled and woven reed, willow, rushes, raffia. Special sections present in clear, simple language and numerous illustrations all the how-to information you could need: linings, skein wire, varieties of stitching, simplified construction of handles, dying processes. For beginner and skilled craftsman alike. Edited by Majorie O'Shaugnessy. Bibliography. Sources of supply. Index. 112 illustrations. 108pp. 5 x 7¼. **T903 Paperbound 75¢**

THE ART OF ETCHING, E. S. Lumsden. Everything you need to know to do etching yourself. First two sections devoted to technique of etching and engraving, covering such essentials as relative merits of zinc and copper, cleaning and grounding plates, gravers, acids, arrangement of etching-room, methods of biting, types of inks and oils, mounting, stretching and framing, preserving and restoring plates, size and color of printing papers, much more. A review of the history of the art includes separate chapters on Dürer and Lucas van Leyden, Rembrandt and Van Dyck, Goya, Meryon, Haden and Whistler, British masters of nineteenth century, modern etchers. Final section is a collection of prints by contemporary etchers with comments by the artists. Professional etchers and engravers will find this a highly useful source of examples. Beginners and teachers, students of art and printing will find it a valuable tool. Index. 208 illustrations. 384pp. 5⅜ x 8. **T49 Paperbound $2.50**

WHITTLING AND WOODCARVING, E. J. Tangerman. What to make and how to make it for even a moderately handy beginner. One of the few works that bridge gap between whittling and serious carving. History of the art, background information on selection and use of woods, grips, types of strokes and cuts, handling of tools and chapters on rustic work, flat toys and windmills, puzzles, chains, ships in bottle, nested spheres, fans, more than 100 useful, entertaining objects. Second half covers carving proper: woodcuts, low relief, sculpture in the round, lettering, inlay and marquetry, indoor and outdoor decorations, pierced designs, much more. Final chapter describes finishing, care of tools. Sixth edition. Index. 464 illustrations. x + 239pp. 5½ x 8⅛. **T965 Paperbound $1.75**

THE PRACTICE OF TEMPERA PAINTING, Daniel V. Thompson, Jr. A careful exposition of all aspects of tempera painting, including sections on many possible modern uses, propensities of various woods, choice of material for panel, making and applying the gesso, pigments and brushes, technique of the actual painting, gilding and so on—everything one need know to try a hand at this proven but neglected art. The author is unquestionably the world's leading authority on tempera methods and processes and his treatment is based on exhaustive study of manuscript material. Drawings and diagrams increase clarity of text. No one interested in tempera painting can afford to be without this book. Appendix, "Tempera Practice in Yale Art School," by Lewis E. York. 85 illustrations by York; 4 full-page plates. ix x 149pp. 5⅜ x 8½. **T343 Paperbound $1.50**

Dover Classical Records

Now available directly to the public exclusively from Dover: top-quality recordings of fine classical music for only $2 per record! Originally released by a major company (except for the previously unreleased Gimpel recording of Bach) to sell for $5 and $6, these records were issued under our imprint only after they had passed a severe critical test. We insisted upon:

First-rate music that is enjoyable, musically important and culturally significant.

First-rate performances, where the artists have carried out the composer's intentions, in which the music is alive, vigorous, played with understanding and sympathy.

First-rate sound—clear, sonorous, fully balanced, crackle-free, whir-free.

Have in your home music by major composers, performed by such gifted musicians as Elsner, Gitlis, Wührer, the Barchet Quartet, Gimpel. Enthusiastically received when first released, many of these performances are definitive. The records are not seconds or remainders, but brand new pressings made on pure vinyl from carefully chosen master tapes. "All purpose" 12" monaural 33⅓ rpm records, they play equally well on hi-fi and stereo equipment. Fine music for discriminating music lovers, superlatively played, flawlessly recorded: there is no better way to build your library of recorded classical music at remarkable savings. There are no strings; this is not a come-on, not a club, forcing you to buy records you may not want in order to get a few at a lower price. Buy whatever records you want in any quantity, and never pay more than $2 each. Your obligation ends with your first purchase. And that's when ours begins. Dover's money-back guarantee allows you to return any record for any reason, even if you don't like the music, for a full, immediate refund, no questions asked.

MOZART: STRING QUARTET IN A MAJOR (K.464); STRING QUARTET IN C MAJOR ("DISSONANT", K.465), Barchet Quartet. The final two of the famed Haydn Quartets, high-points in the history of music. The A Major was accepted with delight by Mozart's contemporaries, but the C Major, with its dissonant opening, aroused strong protest. Today, of course, the remarkable resolutions of the dissonances are recognized as major musical achievements. "Beautiful warm playing," MUSICAL AMERICA. "Two of Mozart's loveliest quartets in a distinguished performance," REV. OF RECORDED MUSIC. (Playing time 58 mins.)   HCR 5200 **$2.00**

MOZART: QUARTETS IN G MAJOR (K.80); D MAJOR (K.155); G MAJOR (K.156); C MAJOR (K157), Barchet Quartet. The early chamber music of Mozart receives unfortunately little attention. First-rate music of the Italian school, it contains all the lightness and charm that belongs only to the youthful Mozart. This is currently the only separate source for the composer's work of this time period. "Excellent," HIGH FIDELITY. "Filled with sunshine and youthful joy; played with verve, recorded sound live and brilliant," CHRISTIAN SCI. MONITOR. (Playing time 51 mins.)   HCR 5201 **$2.00**

MOZART: SERENADE #9 IN D MAJOR ("POSTHORN", K.320); SERENADE #6 IN D MAJOR ("SERENATA NOTTURNA", K.239), Pro Musica Orch. of Stuttgart, under Edouard van Remoortel. For Mozart, the serenade was a highly effective form, since he could bring to it the immediacy and intimacy of chamber music as well as the free fantasy of larger group music. Both these serenades are distinguished by a playful, mischievous quality, a spirit perfectly captured in this fine performance. "A triumph, polished playing from the orchestra," HI FI MUSIC AT HOME. "Sound is rich and resonant, fidelity is wonderful," REV. OF RECORDED MUSIC. (Playing time 51 mins.)   HCR 5202 **$2.00**

MOZART: DIVERTIMENTO IN E FLAT MAJOR FOR STRING TRIO (K.563); ADAGIO AND FUGUE IN F MINOR FOR STRING TRIO (K.404a), Kehr Trio. The Divertimento is one of Mozart's most beloved pieces, called by Einstein "the finest, most perfect trio ever heard." It is difficult to imagine a music lover who will not be delighted by it. This is the only recording of the lesser known Adagio and Fugue, written in 1782 and influenced by Bach's Well-Tempered Clavichord. "Extremely beautiful recording, strongly recommended," THE OBSERVER. "Superior to rival editions," HIGH FIDELITY. (Playing time 51 mins.)   HCR 5203 **$2.00**

SCHUMANN: KREISLERIANA (OP.16); FANTASY IN C MAJOR ("FANTASIE," OP.17), Vlado Perlemuter, Piano. The vigorous Romantic imagination and the remarkable emotional qualities of Schumann's piano music raise it to special eminence in 19th century creativity. Both these pieces are rooted to the composer's tortuous romance with his future wife, Clara, and both receive brilliant treatment at the hands of Vlado Perlemuter, Paris Conservatory, proclaimed by Alfred Cortot "not only a great virtuoso but also a great musician." "The best Kreisleriana to date," BILLBOARD. (Playing time 55 mins.)   HCR 5204 **$2.00**

SCHUMANN: TRIO #1, D MINOR; TRIO #3, G MINOR, Trio di Bolzano. The fiery, romantic, melodic Trio #1, and the dramatic, seldom heard Trio #3 are both movingly played by a fine chamber ensemble. No one personified Romanticism to the general public of the 1840's more than did Robert Schumann, and among his most romantic works are these trios for cello, violin and piano. "Ensemble and overall interpretation leave little to be desired," HIGH FIDELITY. "An especially understanding performance," REV. OF RECORDED MUSIC. (Playing time 54 mins.)   HCR 5205 **$2.00**

CATALOGUE OF DOVER BOOKS

SCHUBERT: SONATA IN C MINOR; SONATA IN B MAJOR (OP.177), Wührer, piano. Schubert's sonatas retain the structure of the classical form, but delight listeners with romantic freedom and a special melodic richness. The C Minor, one of the Three Grand Sonatas, is a product of the composer's maturity. The B Major was not published until 15 years after his death. "Remarkable interpretation, reproduction of the first rank," DISQUES. "A superb pianist for music like this, musicianship, sweep, power, and an ability to integrate Schubert's measures such as few pianists have had since Schnabel," Harold Schonberg. (Playing time 49 mins.)
HCR 5207 **$2.00**

STRAVINSKY: VIOLIN CONCERTO IN D MAJOR, Gitlis, Concerts Colonne Orch. under Byrns; DUO CONCERTANT, Gitlis, Zelka; JEU DE CARTES, Bamberg Symphony under Hollreiser. Igor Stravinsky is probably the most important composer of this century, and these three works are among the most significant of his works during his neoclassical period of the 1930's. The Violin Concerto is one of the few modern classics. Jeu de Cartes, a ballet score, bubbles with gaiety, color and melodiousness. "Imaginatively played and beautifully recorded," E. T. Canby, HARPERS MAGAZINE. "Gitlis is excellent, Hollreiser beautifully worked out," HIGH FIDELITY. (Playing time 55 mins.)
HCR 5208 **$2.00**

GEMINIANI: SIX CONCERTI GROSSI (OP.3), Barchet, Quartet, Helma Elsner, Harpsichord, Pro Musica String Orch. of Stuttgart under Reinhardt. Francesco Geminiani (1687-1762) has been rediscovered in the same musical exploration that revealed Scarlatti, Vivaldi and Corelli. In form he is more sophisticated than the earlier Italians, but his music delights modern listeners with its combination of contrapuntal techniques and the full harmonies and rich melodies characteristic of Italian music. This is the only recording of the six 1733 concerti: D Major, B Flat Minor, E Minor, G Minor, E Minor (bis), and D Minor. "I warmly recommend it, spacious, magnificent, I enjoyed every bar," C. Cudworth, RECORD NEWS. "Works of real charm, recorded with understanding and style," ETUDE. (Playing time 52 mins.)
HCR 5209 **$2.00**

TELEMANN: 12 FANTASIES FOR HARPSICHORD, Helma Elsner, Harpsichord. Until recently, Georg Philip Telemann (1681-1767) was one of the mysteriously neglected great men of music. Recently he has received the attention he deserves. Intent upon grafting Italian melodic richness and French delicacy onto German solidity, he created music that delights modern listeners with its freshness and originality. "This is another blessing of the contemporary LP output. Miss Elsner plays with considerable sensitivity and a great deal of understanding," REV. OF RECORDED MUSIC. "Fine recorded sound," Harold Schonberg. "Recommended warmly, very high quality," DISQUES. (Playing time 50 mins.)
HCR 5210 **$2.00**

BARTOK: VIOLIN CONCERTO; SONATA FOR UNACCOMPANIED VIOLIN, Gitlis, Pro Musica Orch. of Vienna under Hornstein. Both these works are outstanding examples of Bartok's final period, and they show his powers at their fullest. The Violin Concerto is, in the opinion of many authorities, Bartok's finest work, and the Sonata, his last work, is "a masterpiece" (F. Sackville West). "Wonderful, finest performances of both Bartok works I have ever heard," GRAMOPHONE. "Gitlis makes such potent and musical sense out of these works that I suspect many general music lovers [not otherwise in sympathy with modern music] will discover to their amazement that they like it. Exceptionally good sound," AUDITOR. (Playing time 54 mins.)
HCR 5211 **$2.00**

J. S. BACH: PARTITAS #3 IN E MAJOR & #2 IN D MINOR FOR UNACCOMPANIED VIOLIN, Gimpel, violin. Bach's works for unaccompanied violin fall within the same era as produced the Brandenburg Concerti, the Orchestral Suites, and the first part of the Well-Tempered Clavichord. The D Minor is considered one of Bach's masterpieces; the E Major is a buoyant work with exceptionally interesting bariolage effects. This is the first release of a truly memorable recording by Bronisiaw Gimpel, "as a violinist, the equal of the greatest" (P. Leron, in OPERA, Paris). (Playing time 53 mins.)
HCR 5212 **$2.00**

SCHUBERT: QUINTET IN A MAJOR ("TROUT", OP.114), Wührer, Barchet, Reimann, Hirschfelder, Kruger; NOCTURNE IN E FLAT MAJOR (OP.148), Wührer, Barchet, Reimann. If there is a single piece of chamber music that is a universal favorite, it is probably Schubert's "Trout" Quintet. Delightful melody, harmonic resources, musical exuberance are its characteristics. The Nocturne is an exquisite piece with a deceptively simple theme and harmony. "The best Trout on the market—Wührer is a fine Vienese-style Schubertian, and his spirit infects the Barchets," ATLANTIC MONTHLY. "Exquisitely recorded," ETUDE. (Playing time 44 mins.)
HCR 5206 **$2.00**

This is only a partial listing of Dover's classical music records. Write to us for complete listings.

Entertainments, Humor

ODDITIES AND CURIOSITIES OF WORDS AND LITERATURE, C. Bombaugh, edited by M. Gardner. The largest collection of idiosyncratic prose and poetry techniques in English, a legendary work in the curious and amusing bypaths of literary recreations and the play technique in literature—so important in modern works. Contains alphabetic poetry, acrostics, palindromes, scissors verse, centos, emblematic poetry, famous literary puns, hoaxes, notorious slips of the press, hilarious mistranslations, and much more. Revised and enlarged with modern material by Martin Gardner. 368pp. 5⅜ x 8. T759 Paperbound **$1.50**

A NONSENSE ANTHOLOGY, collected by Carolyn Wells. 245 of the best nonsense verses ever written, including nonsense puns, absurd arguments, mock epics and sagas, nonsense ballads, odes, "sick" verses, dog-Latin verses, French nonsense verses, songs. By Edward Lear, Lewis Carroll, Gelett Burgess, W. S. Gilbert, Hilaire Belloc, Peter Newell, Oliver Herford, etc., 83 writers in all plus over four score anonymous nonsense verses. A special section of limericks, plus famous nonsense such as Carroll's "Jabberwocky" and Lear's "The Jumblies" and much excellent verse virtually impossible to locate elsewhere. For 50 years considered the best anthology available. Index of first lines specially prepared for this edition. Introduction by Carolyn Wells. 3 indexes: Title, Author, First lines. xxxiii + 279pp. T499 Paperbound **$1.35**

THE BAD CHILD'S BOOK OF BEASTS, MORE BEASTS FOR WORSE CHILDREN, and A MORAL ALPHA-BET, H. Belloc. Hardly an anthology of humorous verse has appeared in the last 50 years without at least a couple of these famous nonsense verses. But one must see the entire volumes—with all the delightful original illustrations by Sir Basil Blackwood—to appreciate fully Belloc's charming and witty verses that play so subacidly on the platitudes of life and morals that beset his day—and ours. A great humor classic. Three books in one. Total of 157pp. 5⅜ x 8. T749 Paperbound **$1.00**

THE DEVIL'S DICTIONARY, Ambrose Bierce. Sardonic and irreverent barbs puncturing the pomposities and absurdities of American politics, business, religion, literature, and arts, by the country's greatest satirist in the classic tradition. Epigrammatic as Shaw, piercing as Swift, American as Mark Twain, Will Rogers, and Fred Allen, Bierce will always remain the favorite of a small coterie of enthusiasts, and of writers and speakers whom he supplies with "some of the most gorgeous witticisms of the English language" (H. L. Mencken). Over 1000 entries in alphabetical order. 144pp. 5⅜ x 8. T487 Paperbound **$1.00**

THE PURPLE COW AND OTHER NONSENSE, Gelett Burgess. The best of Burgess's early nonsense, selected from the first edition of the "Burgess Nonsense Book." Contains many of his most unusual and truly awe-inspiring pieces: 36 nonsense quatrains, the Poems of Patagonia, Alphabet of Famous Goops, and the other hilarious (and rare) adult nonsense that place him in the forefront of American humorists. All pieces are accompanied by the original Burgess illustrations. 123 illustrations. xiii + 113pp. 5⅜ x 8. T772 Paperbound **$1.00**

MY PIOUS FRIENDS AND DRUNKEN COMPANIONS and MORE PIOUS FRIENDS AND DRUNKEN COMPANIONS, Frank Shay. Folksingers, amateur and professional, and everyone who loves singing: here, available for the first time in 30 years, is this valued collection of 132 ballads, blues, vaudeville numbers, drinking songs, sea chanties, comedy songs. Songs of pre-Beatnik Bohemia; songs from all over America, England, France, Australia; the great songs of the Naughty Nineties and early twentieth-century America. Over a third with music. Woodcuts by John Held, Jr. convey perfectly the brash insouciance of an era of rollicking unabashed song. 12 illustrations by John Held, Jr. Two indexes (Titles and First lines and Choruses). Introductions by the author. Two volumes bound as one. Total of xvi + 235pp. 5⅜ x 8½. T946 Paperbound **$1.00**

HOW TO TELL THE BIRDS FROM THE FLOWERS, R. W. Wood. How not to confuse a carrot with a parrot, a grape with an ape, a puffin with nuffin. Delightful drawings, clever puns, absurd little poems point out far-fetched resemblances in nature. The author was a leading physicist. Introduction by Margaret Wood White. 106 illus. 60pp. 5⅜ x 8. T523 Paperbound **75¢**

PECK'S BAD BOY AND HIS PA, George W. Peck. The complete edition, containing both volumes, of one of the most widely read American humor books. The endless ingenious pranks played by bad boy "Hennery" on his pa and the grocery man, the outraged pomposity of Pa, the perpetual ridiculing of middle class institutions, are as entertaining today as they were in 1883. No pale sophistications or subtleties, but rather humor vigorous, raw, earthy, imaginative, and, as folk humor often is, sadistic. This peculiarly fascinating book is also valuable to historians and students of American culture as a portrait of an age. 100 original illustrations by True Williams. Introduction by E. F. Bleiler. 347pp. 5⅜ x 8. T497 Paperbound **$1.35**

CATALOGUE OF DOVER BOOKS

THE HUMOROUS VERSE OF LEWIS CARROLL. Almost every poem Carroll ever wrote, the largest collection ever published, including much never published elsewhere: 150 parodies, burlesques, riddles, ballads, acrostics, etc., with 130 original illustrations by Tenniel, Carroll, and others. "Addicts will be grateful . . . there is nothing for the faithful to do but sit down and fall to the banquet," N. Y. Times. Index to first lines. xiv + 446pp. 5⅜ x 8.
T654 Paperbound **$1.85**

DIVERSIONS AND DIGRESSIONS OF LEWIS CARROLL. A major new treasure for Carroll fans! Rare privately published humor, fantasy, puzzles, and games by Carroll at his whimsical best, with a new vein of frank satire. Includes many new mathematical amusements and recreations, among them the fragmentary Part III of "Curiosa Mathematica." Contains "The Rectory Umbrella," "The New Belfry," "The Vision of the Three T's," and much more. New 32-page supplement of rare photographs taken by Carroll. x + 375pp. 5⅜ x 8.
T732 Paperbound **$1.65**

THE COMPLETE NONSENSE OF EDWARD LEAR. This is the only complete edition of this master of gentle madness available at a popular price. A BOOK OF NONSENSE, NONSENSE SONGS, MORE NONSENSE SONGS AND STORIES in their entirety with all the old favorites that have delighted children and adults for years. The Dong With A Luminous Nose, The Jumblies, The Owl and the Pussycat, and hundreds of other bits of wonderful nonsense. 214 limericks, 3 sets of Nonsense Botany, 5 Nonsense Alphabets, 546 drawings by Lear himself, and much more. 320pp. 5⅜ x 8.
T167 Paperbound **$1.00**

THE MELANCHOLY LUTE, The Humorous Verse of Franklin P. Adams ("FPA"). The author's own selection of light verse, drawn from thirty years of FPA's column, "The Conning Tower," syndicated all over the English-speaking world. Witty, perceptive, literate, these ninety-six poems range from parodies of other poets, Millay, Longfellow, Edgar Guest, Kipling, Masefield, etc., and free and hilarious translations of Horace and other Latin poets, to satiric comments on fabled American institutions—the New York Subways, preposterous ads, suburbanites, sensational journalism, etc. They reveal with vigor and clarity the humor, integrity and restraint of a wise and gentle American satirist. Introduction by Robert Hutchinson. vi + 122pp. 5⅜ x 8½.
T108 Paperbound **$1.00**

SINGULAR TRAVELS, CAMPAIGNS, AND ADVENTURES OF BARON MUNCHAUSEN, R. E. Raspe, with 90 illustrations by Gustave Doré. The first edition in over 150 years to reestablish the deeds of the Prince of Liars exactly as Raspe first recorded them in 1785—the genuine Baron Munchausen, one of the most popular personalities in English literature. Included also are the best of the many sequels, written by other hands. Introduction on Raspe by J. Carswell. Bibliography of early editions. xliv + 192pp. 5⅜ x 8.
T698 Paperbound **$1.00**

THE WIT AND HUMOR OF OSCAR WILDE, ed. by Alvin Redman. Wilde at his most brilliant, in 1000 epigrams exposing weaknesses and hypocrisies of "civilized" society. Divided into 49 categories—sin, wealth, women, America, etc.—to aid writers, speakers. Includes excerpts from his trials, books, plays, criticism. Formerly "The Epigrams of Oscar Wilde." Introduction by Vyvyan Holland, Wilde's only living son. Introductory essay by editor. 260pp. 5⅜ x 8.
T602 Paperbound **$1.00**

MAX AND MORITZ, Wilhelm Busch. Busch is one of the great humorists of all time, as well as the father of the modern comic strip. This volume, translated by H. A. Klein and other hands, contains the perennial favorite "Max and Moritz" (translated by C. T. Brooks), Plisch and Plum, Das Rabennest, Eispeter, and seven other whimsical, sardonic, jovial, diabolical cartoon and verse stories. Lively English translations parallel the original German. This work has delighted millions, since it first appeared in the 19th century, and is guaranteed to please almost anyone. Edited by H. A. Klein, with an afterword. x + 205pp. 5⅝ x 8½.
T181 Paperbound **$1.00**

HYPOCRITICAL HELENA, Wilhelm Busch. A companion volume to "Max and Moritz," with the title piece (Die Fromme Helena) and 10 other highly amusing cartoon and verse stories, all newly translated by H. A. Klein and M. C. Klein: Adventure on New Year's Eve (Abenteuer in der Neujahrsnacht), Hangover on the Morning after New Year's Eve (Der Katzenjammer am Neujahrsmorgen), etc. English and German in parallel columns. Hours of pleasure, also a fine language aid. x + 205pp. 5⅝ x 8½.
T184 Paperbound **$1.00**

THE BEAR THAT WASN'T, Frank Tashlin. What does it mean? Is it simply delightful wry humor, or a charming story of a bear who wakes up in the midst of a factory, or a satire on Big Business, or an existential cartoon-story of the human condition, or a symbolization of the struggle between conformity and the individual? New York Herald Tribune said of the first edition: ". . . a fable for grownups that will be fun for children. Sit down with the book and get your own bearings." Long an underground favorite with readers of all ages and opinions. v + 51pp. Illustrated. 5⅜ x 8½.
T939 Paperbound **75¢**

RUTHLESS RHYMES FOR HEARTLESS HOMES and MORE RUTHLESS RHYMES FOR HEARTLESS HOMES, Harry Graham ("Col. D. Streamer"). Two volumes of Little Willy and 48 other poetic disasters. A bright, new reprint of oft-quoted, never forgotten, devastating humor by a precursor of today's "sick" joke school. For connoisseurs of wicked, wacky humor and all who delight in the comedy of manners. Original drawings are a perfect complement. 61 illustrations. Index. vi + 69pp. Two vols. bound as one. 5⅜ x 8½.
T930 Paperbound **75¢**

Music

A GENERAL HISTORY OF MUSIC, Charles Burney. A detailed coverage of music from the Greeks up to 1789, with full information on all types of music: sacred and secular, vocal and instrumental, operatic and symphonic. Theory, notation, forms, instruments, innovators, composers, performers, typical and important works, and much more in an easy, entertaining style. Burney covered much of Europe and spoke with hundreds of authorities and composers so that this work is more than a compilation of records . . . it is a living work of careful and first-hand scholarship. Its account of thoroughbass (18th century) Italian music is probably still the best introduction on the subject. A recent NEW YORK TIMES review said, "Surprisingly few of Burney's statements have been invalidated by modern research . . . still of great value." Edited and corrected by Frank Mercer. 35 figures. Indices. 1915pp. 5⅜ x 8. 2 volumes. **T36 The Set, Clothbound $12.50**

A DICTIONARY OF HYMNOLOGY, John Julian. This exhaustive and scholarly work has become known as an invaluable source of hundreds of thousands of important and often difficult to obtain facts on the history and use of hymns in the western world. Everyone interested in hymns will be fascinated by the accounts of famous hymns and hymn writers and amazed by the amount of practical information he will find. More than 30,000 entries on individual hymns, giving authorship, date and circumstances of composition, publication, textual variations, translations, denominational and ritual usage, etc. Biographies of more than 9,000 hymn writers, and essays on important topics such as Christmas carols and children's hymns, and much other unusual and valuable information. A 200 page double-columned index of first lines — the largest in print. Total of 1786 pages in two reinforced clothbound volumes. 6¼ x 9¼. The set, **T333 Clothbound $15.00**

MUSIC IN MEDIEVAL BRITAIN, F. Ll. Harrison. The most thorough, up-to-date, and accurate treatment of the subject ever published, beautifully illustrated. Complete account of institutions and choirs; carols, masses, and motets; liturgy and plainsong; and polyphonic music from the Norman Conquest to the Reformation. Discusses the various schools of music and their reciprocal influences; the origin and development of new ritual forms; development and use of instruments; and new evidence on many problems of the period. Reproductions of scores, over 200 excerpts from medieval melodies. Rules of harmony and dissonance; influence of Continental styles; great composers (Dunstable, Cornysh, Fairfax, etc.), and much more. Register and index of more than 400 musicians. Index of titles. General Index. 225-item bibliography. 6 Appendices. xix + 491pp. 5⅝ x 8¾. **T705 Clothbound $10.00**

THE MUSIC OF SPAIN, Gilbert Chase. Only book in English to give concise, comprehensive account of Iberian music; new Chapter covers music since 1941. Victoria, Albéniz, Cabezón, Pedrell, Turina, hundreds of other composers; popular and folk music; the Gypsies; the guitar; dance, theatre, opera, with only extensive discussion in English of the Zarzuela; virtuosi such as Casals; much more. "Distinguished . . . readable," Saturday Review. 400-item bibliography. Index. 27 photos. 383pp. 5⅜ x 8. **T549 Paperbound $2.00**

ON STUDYING SINGING, Sergius Kagen. An intelligent method of voice-training, which leads you around pitfalls that waste your time, money, and effort. Exposes rigid, mechanical systems, baseless theories, deleterious exercises. "Logical, clear, convincing . . . dead right," Virgil Thomson, N.Y. Herald Tribune. "I recommend this volume highly," Maggie Teyte, Saturday Review. 119pp. 5⅜ x 8. **T622 Paperbound $1.25**

WILLIAM LAWES, M. Lefkowitz. This is the definitive work on Lawes, the versatile, prolific, and highly original "King's musician" of 17th century England. His life is reconstructed from original documents, and nearly every piece he ever wrote is examined and evaluated: his fantasias, pavans, violin "sonatas," lyra viol and bass viol suites, and music for harp and theorbo; and his songs, masques, and theater music to words by Herrick ("Gather Ye Rosebuds"), Jonson, Suckling, Shirley, and others. The author shows the innovations of dissonance, augmented triad, and other Italian influences Lawes helped introduce to England. List of Lawes' complete works and several complete scores by this major precursor of Purcell and the 18th century developments. Index. 5 Appendices. 52 musical excerpts, many never before in print. Bibliography. x + 320pp. 5⅜ x 8. **T706 Clothbound $10.00**

THE FUGUE IN BEETHOVEN'S PIANO MUSIC, J. V. Cockshoot. The first study of a neglected aspect of Beethoven's genius: his ability as a writer of fugues. Analyses of early studies and published works demonstrate his original and powerful contributions to composition. 34 works are examined, with 143 musical excerpts. For all pianists, teachers, students, and music-minded readers with a serious interest in Beethoven. Index. 93-item bibliography. Illustration of original score for "Fugue in C." xv + 212pp. 5⅝ x 8⅜. **T704 Clothbound $6.00**

JOHANN SEBASTIAN BACH, Philipp Spitta. The complete and unabridged text of the definitive study of Bach. Written some 70 years ago, it is still unsurpassed for its coverage of nearly all aspects of Bach's life and work. There could hardly be a finer non-technical introduction to Bach's music than the detailed, lucid analyses which Spitta provides for hundreds of individual pieces. 26 solid pages are devoted to the B minor mass, for example, and 30 pages to the glorious St. Matthew Passion. This monumental set also includes a major analysis of the music of the 18th century: Buxtehude, Pachelbel, etc. "Unchallenged as the last word on one of the supreme geniuses of music," John Barkham, SATURDAY REVIEW SYNDICATE. Total of 1819pp. 2 volumes. Heavy cloth binding. 5⅜ x 8. T252 The set, Clothbound **$12.50**

THE LIFE OF MOZART, O. Jahn. Probably the largest amount of material on Mozart's life and works ever gathered together in one book! Its 1350 authoritative and readable pages cover every event in his life, and contain a full critique of almost every piece he ever wrote, including sketches and intimate works. There is a full historical-cultural background, and vast research into musical and literary history, sources of librettos, prior treatments of Don Juan legend, etc. This is the complete and unaltered text of the definitive Townsend translation, with foreword by Grove. 5 engraved portraits from Salzburg archives. 4 facsimiles in Mozart's hand. 226 musical examples. 4 Appendixes, including complete list of Mozart's compositions, with Köchel numbers (fragmentary works included). Total of xxviii + 1352pp. Three volume set. 5⅜ x 8.
T85 Vol. I Clothbound **$5.00**
T86 Vol. II Clothbound **$5.00**
The set **$10.00**

BEETHOVEN'S QUARTETS, J. de Marliave. The most complete and authoritative study ever written, enjoyable for scholar and layman alike. The 16 quartets and Grand Fugue all analyzed bar by bar and theme by theme, not over-technically, but concentrating on mood and effects. Complete background material for each composition: influences, first reviews, etc. Preface by Gabriel Fauré. Introduction and notes by J. Escarra. Translated by Hilda Andrews. 321 musical examples. xxiii + 379pp. 5⅜ x 8. T694 Paperbound **$1.85**

STRUCTURAL HEARING: TONAL COHERENCE IN MUSIC, Felix Salzer. Written by a pupil of the late Heinrich Schenker, this is not only the most thorough exposition in English of the Schenker method but also extends the Schenker approach to include modern music, the middle ages, and renaissance music. It explores the phenomenon of tonal organization by means of a detailed analysis and discussion of more than 500 musical pieces. It casts new light for the reader acquainted with harmony upon the understanding of musical compositions, problems of musical coherence, and connection between theory and composition. "Has been the foundation on which all teaching in music theory has been based at this college," Leopold Mannes, President of The Mannes College of Music. 2 volumes. Total of 658pp. 6½ x 9¼. The set, T418 Clothbound **$8.00**

ANTONIO STRADIVARI: HIS LIFE AND WORK (1644-1737), W. Henry Hill, Arthur F. Hill, and Alfred E. Hill. Still the only book that really delves into life and art of the incomparable Italian craftsman, maker of the finest musical instruments in the world today. The authors, expert violin-makers themselves, discuss Stradivari's ancestry, his construction and finishing techniques, distinguished characteristics of many of his instruments and their locations. Included, too, is story of introduction of his instruments into France, England, first revelation of their supreme merit, and information on his labels, number of instruments made, prices, mystery of ingredients of his varnish, tone of pre-1684 Stradivari violin and changes between 1684 and 1690. An extremely interesting, informative account for all music lovers, from craftsman to concert-goer. Republication of original (1902) edition. New introduction by Sydney Beck, Head of Rare Book and Manuscript Collections, Music Division, New York Public Library. Analytical index by Rembert Wurlitzer. Appendixes. 68 illustrations. 30 full-page plates. 4 in color. xxvi + 315pp. 5⅜ x 8½. T425 Paperbound **$2.25**

THREE CLASSICS IN THE AESTHETIC OF MUSIC, Claude Debussy, Ferrucio Busoni, and Charles Ives. Three very different points of view by three top-ranking modern composers. "M. Croche, the Dilettante-Hater" consists of twenty-five brief articles written by Debussy between the years 1901 and 1905, a sparkling collection of personal commentary on a wide range of topics. Busoni's "Toward a New Aesthetic of Music" considers the nature of absolute music in an attempt to suggest answers to the question, What are the aims of music?, and discusses modern systems of tonality and harmony, the concept of unity of keys, etc. Ives's "Essays Before a Sonata," a literary complement to the movements of the author's "Concord, 1845" piano sonata, contains his most mature analysis of his art. Stimulating reading for musicians, music lovers, and philosophers of the arts. iv + 188pp. 5⅜ x 8½. T320 Paperbound **$1.45**

CATALOGUE OF DOVER BOOKS

ROMAIN ROLLAND'S ESSAYS ON MUSIC, ed. by David Ewen. 16 best essays by great critic of our time, Nobel Laureate, discuss Mozart, Beethoven, Gluck, Handel, Berlioz, Wagner, Wolf, Saint-Saëns, Metastasio, Lully, Telemann, Grétry, "Origins of 18th Century 'Classic' Style," and musical life of 18th century Germany and Italy. "Shows the key to the high place that Rolland still holds in the world of music," Library Journal. 371pp. 5⅜ x 8.
T550 Paperbound **$1.50**

A GENERAL HISTORY OF THE SCIENCE AND PRACTICE OF MUSIC, Sir John Hawkins. Originally published in 1776, long regarded a genuine classic of musicology. Traces the origin and development of music theory, harmonic and contrapuntal processes, polyphony, musical notation, orchestration, instrumentation, etc. from earliest recorded evidence of music experiment to the author's own time, taking into account a score of musical forms—plainsong, motet, ballad, oratorio, opera, madrigal, canon, cantata, many more—and the particular contributions of various peoples. Still extremely valuable for its consideration of musical theorists and their work and detailed summaries and exact quotes from historically important works unavailable except in largest libraries. Biographical and critical information about hundreds of musicians undeservedly forgotten and now being rediscovered. A unique and significant work of music scholarship, prized by musicologists, composers, performers, historians of culture, and musical amateurs. Reproduction of 1853 edition. New introduction by Charles Cudworth, Curator, Pendlebury Library of Music, Cambridge, England. 315 illustrations; 60 full-page plates. 153 musical excerpts. 20 facsimiles of ancient manuscripts. Memoir of author. Index. Two volumes. Total of 1020pp. of text. 7⅞ x 10¾.
T1048-49 The set, Clothbound **$15.00**

THE GIFT TO BE SIMPLE, Edward Deming Andrews. Students of American history and culture, hymnologists, musicians, historians of religion, and anyone interested in reading about unusual peoples and customs will welcome this unique and authoritative account of Shaker music. Examines the origin of verses and of numerous Shaker dances; the rituals and gestures that accompanied singing; the unusual music theory developed by Shaker musicians and the melodies that were produced. Captures the spirit of an humble and devout people as expressed in many actual texts of hymns, dance songs, ritualistic songs, songs of humility, etc. Includes musical notations of about eighty melodies. A short introduction shows the development of the Shaker movement from its origins (about 1750), through the period of its greatest influence in the 1840's, to its post-Civil War decline. Index of first lines and melodies. Bibliography. 17 illustrations. ix + 170pp. 5⅜ x 8.   T22 Paperbound **$1.50**

BEETHOVEN AND HIS NINE SYMPHONIES, George Grove, editor of Grove's Dictionary of Music and Musicians. In this modern middle-level classic of musicology Grove not only analyzes all nine of Beethoven's symphonies very thoroughly in terms of their musical structure, but also discusses the circumstances under which they were written, Beethoven's stylistic development, and much other background material. This is an extremely rich book, yet very easily followed; it is highly recommended to anyone seriously interested in music. Over 250 musical passages. Index. viii + 407pp. 5⅜ x 8.   T334 Paperbound **$2.00**

AIDA BY GIUSEPPI VERDI, translated and introduced by Ellen H. Bleiler. Full handbook to the most popular opera of all; everything the operagoer (or listener) needs except the music itself. Complete Italian libretto, with all repeats, with new, modern English translation in parallel columns; biography of Verdi and librettists; background to composition of Aida; musical history; plot summary; musical excerpts; pictorial section of 76 illustrations showing Verdi, famous singers, famous performances, etc. Large clear type for easy reading. 147pp. 5⅜ x 8½.   T405 Paperbound **$1.00**

LA BOHEME BY GIACOMO PUCCINI, translated and introduced by Ellen H. Bleiler. Complete handbook for the operagoer, with everything needed for full enjoyment except the musical score itself. Complete Italian libretto, with new modern English line-by-line translation—the only libretto printing all repeats; biography of Puccini; the librettists; background to the opera, Murger's La Boheme, etc.; circumstances of composition and performances; plot summary; and pictorial section of 73 illustrations showing Puccini, famous singers and performances, etc. Large clear type for easy reading. 124pp. 5⅜ x 8½. T404 Paperbound **$1.00**

Prices subject to change without notice.

Dover publishes books on art, music, philosophy, literature, languages, history, social sciences, psychology, handcrafts, orientalia, puzzles and entertainments, chess, pets and gardens, books explaining science, intermediate and higher mathematics, mathematical physics, engineering, biological sciences, earth sciences, classics of science, etc. Write to:

Dept. catrr.
Dover Publications, Inc.
180 Varick Street, N. Y. 14, N. Y.